SYNTHETIC CH

D0629446

THE LEUKOTRIENES

Chemistry and Biology

THE LEUKOTRIENES

Chemistry and Biology

Edited by

LAWRENCE W. CHAKRIN
DENIS M. BAILEY
Sterling–Winthrop Research Institute
Division of Sterling Drug Inc.
Rensselaer, New York

1984

ACADEMIC PRESS, INC.
(Harcourt Brace Jovanovich, Publishers)
Orlando   San Diego   San Francisco   New York   London
Toronto   Montreal   Sydney   Tokyo   São Paulo

ACADEMIC PRESS, INC.
Orlando, Florida 32887

United Kingdom Edition published by
ACADEMIC PRESS, INC. (LONDON) LTD.
24/28 Oval Road, London NW1 7DX

Library of Congress Cataloging in Publication Data

Main entry under title:

The Leukotrienes : chemistry and biology.

  Includes bibliographies and index.
  1. Leukotrienes. I. Chakrin, Lawrence W.
II. Bailey, Denis M.
QP801.L47L47 1984   599'.02   84-6407
ISBN 0-12-166750-2 (alk. paper)

PRINTED IN THE UNITED STATES OF AMERICA

84 85 86 87   9 8 7 6 5 4 3 2 1

CONTENTS

3. Platelet Arachidonate Lipoxygenase

David Aharony, J. Bryan Smith, and Melvin J. Silver

4. The Lipoxygenases in Leukocytes and Other Mammalian Cells

Charles W. Parker

5. Characterization of Leukotriene Formation

Barbara A. Jakschik and Christine G. Kuo

6. Inhibitors of Leukotriene Synthesis and Action

Michael K. Bach

7. Lipoxygenase Products: Mediation of Inflammatory Responses and Inhibition of Their Formation

P. Bhattacherjee and K. E. Eakins

8. Biological Actions of the Leukotrienes

Priscilla J. Piper

9. Biochemical and Cellular Characteristics of the Regulation of Human Leukocyte Function by Lipoxygenase Products of Arachidonic Acid

Donald G. Payan, Daniel W. Goldman, and Edward J. Goetzl

10. Pulmonary Pharmacology of the Leukotrienes

A. G. Leitch and J. M. Drazen

Contents

11.   Pharmacologic Antagonism of the Leukotrienes

Robert D. Krell, Frederick J. Brown, Alvin K. Willard, and Ralph E. Giles

CONTRIBUTORS

Numbers in parentheses indicate the pages on which the authors' contributions begin.

David Aharony (103), Stuart Pharmaceuticals, Division of ICI America, Pulmonary Pharmacology Section, Wilmington, Delaware 19897

K. Frank Austen (1), Department of Medicine, Harvard Medical School, and Department of Rheumatology and Immunology, Brigham and Women's Hospital, Boston, Massachusetts 02115

Michael K. Bach (163), The Upjohn Company, Kalamazoo, Michigan 49001

P. Bhattacherjee (195), Department of Pharmacology, The Wellcome Research Laboratories, Langley Court, Beckenham, Kent, United Kingdom

Frederick J. Brown (271), ICI Americas, Inc., Wilmington, Delaware 19897

David A. Clark (13), Pfizer Central Research, Groton, Connecticut 06340

E. J. Corey (13), Department of Chemistry, Harvard University, Cambridge, Massachusetts 02138

J. M. Drazen (247), Department of Physiology, Harvard Medical School, Boston, Massachusetts 02115

K. E. Eakins (195), Department of Pharmacology, Therapeutic Research Division, The Wellcome Research Laboratories, Langley Court, Beckenham, Kent BR3 3BS, United Kingdom

Ralph E. Giles (271), ICI Americas, Inc., Wilmington, Delaware 19897

Edward J. Goetzl (231), Howard Hughes Medical Institute, and University of California Medical Center, San Francisco, California 94143

Daniel W. Goldman (231), University of California, San Francisco, California 94143

Barbara A. Jakschik (139), Department of Pharmacology, Washington University, St. Louis, Missiouri 63110

Robert D. Krell (271), Stuart Pharmaceuticals, Division of ICI Americas, Inc., Wilmington, Delaware 19897

Christine G. Kuo (139), Department of Pharmacology, Washington University, St. Louis, Missouri 63110

A. G. Leitch (247), Department of Physiology, Harvard Medical School, Boston, Massachusetts 02115

ix

Robert A. Lewis (1), Department of Medicine, Harvard Medical School, and Department of Rheumatology and Immunology, Brigham and Women's Hospital, Boston, Massachusetts 02115

Anthony Marfat (13), Pfizer Central Research, Groton, Connecticut 06340

Charles W. Parker (125), Howard Hughes Medical Institute Laboratory, and Department of Internal Medicine, Division of Allergy and Immunology, Washington University School of Medicine, St. Louis, Missouri 63110

Donald G. Payan (231), Howard Hughes Medical Institute, Department of Medicine, University of California San Francisco, San Francisco, California 94143

Priscilla J. Piper (215), Department of Pharmacology, Royal College of Surgeons of England, London WC2A 3PN, England

Melvin J. Silver (103), Cardeza Foundation, and Department of Pharmacology, Thomas Jefferson University, Philadelphia, Pennsylvania 19107

J. Bryan Smith (103), Center for Thrombosis Research, Temple University Medical School, Philadelphia, Pennsylvania 19140

Alvin K. Willard (271), ICI Americas, Inc., Wilmington, Delaware 19897

PREFACE

Leukotrienes are formed from the unsaturated fatty acid, arachidonic acid, through an unstable epoxide intermediate, leukotriene A_4. Enzymatic conversion yields leukotriene B_4 by hydration and leukotriene C_4 by addition of glutathione. Subsequently, leukotriene C_4 is metabolized to leukotriene D_4 and leukotriene E_4 respectively through elimination of a γ-glutamyl, and later a glycine, residue.

The extraordinary tale of the more than 40 years of scientific progress from the discovery of one of the mediators of anaphylaxis, slow-reacting substance (SRS), through the chemical identification of SRS-A as a mixture of leukotrienes C_4, D_4, and E_4 to a comprehensive understanding of these fascinating molecules is told in *The Leukotrienes*. In particular, the last decade has witnessed an enormous increase in research on the chemistry and biology of these and related substances, especially as they relate to the etiology of allergic and inflammatory diseases. This research interest has been fueled by the identification of lipoxygenase products from human platelets in 1974 and the recognition in 1977 of the relationship of the SRSs to the arachidonate lipoxygenase enzyme system. These and other evolutionary events have been put into perspective in the various chapters of *The Leukotrienes*, all of which are authored by major contributors to the field.

Readers interested in the role that the leukotrienes may play as mediators of immediate hypersensitivity reactions and inflammation will find this volume thoughtful and provocative, as will scientists specifically interested in exploiting arachidonic acid metabolism for the development of therapeutic agents specifically designed to either inhibit the synthesis or antagonize the effects of the leukotrienes.

Lawrence W. Chakrin
Denis M. Bailey

1

Historical and Continuing Perspectives on the Biology of the Leukotrienes

K. FRANK AUSTEN AND ROBERT A. LEWIS*

Department of Medicine, Harvard Medical School
Department of Rheumatology and Immunology, Brigham and Women's Hospital
Boston, Massachusetts

I. INTRODUCTION

At a time when the biology, chemistry, and pharmacology of the leukotriene constituents of slow-reacting substance of anaphylaxis (LTC_4, LTD_4, and LTE_4) and of the chemotactic leukotriene (LTB_4) have come of age, there may be some merit in reevaluating some of the contributions to this field over a period of several years, during which the technologies available did

* Dr. Lewis is the recipient of an Allergic Diseases Award (AI-00399) from the National Institutes of Health.

not permit the structural definition of the sulfidopeptide leukotrienes. The concept of a membrane-derived mediator that was generated via the oxidative metabolism of arachidonic acid and was composed of a lipid backbone and a sulfidopeptide adduct was not conceivable at a time when the recognized chemical mediators were basic amines or polypeptides. The lack of chemical definition of the moiety prompted the suffix "anaphylaxis," to emphasize that the product was derived from an immediate-type hypersensitivity reaction and to require that this mechanism of generation be part of the final definition (Brocklehurst, 1953). Thus, a substantial portion of the history of the field relates to the isolation and characterization of structurally unique moieties, the sulfidopeptide leukotrienes, as immunologic reaction products with profiles of pharmacologic activity distinct from those of other known chemical mediators. Indeed, the cumbersome definition of slow-reacting substance of anaphylaxis (SRS-A) may account for the fact that some of the critical observations were made in parallel by several investigators without a full appreciation of the relationship of their reports.

II. ISOLATION AND CHARACTERIZATION OF SRS-A

A. Discovery and Initial Characterization

It is generally held that SRS-A was initially described by Kellaway and Trethewie (1940) as a product of an immediate-type hypersensitivity reaction, recovered from the isolated perfused guinea pig lung, which constricted smooth muscle tissue more slowly than did histamine. In considering the literature, however, it is quite possible that Harkavy (1930) recognized a similar substance in the sputum of asthmatic humans, that is, a contractile material that he believed to be distinct in nature from histamine. It was not possible to address seriously the isolation of SRS-A until Brocklehurst (1953) utilized an antihistamine (now known to be of the H_1 class) to block the *in vitro* contractile response of smooth muscle to histamine in the perfusate or diffusate of an immediate-type hypersensitivity tissue reaction and fully uncover that to SRS-A. Utilizing this bioassay, both Brocklehurst, and Strandberg and Üvnas addressed the problem of isolation. Both laboratories were able to demonstrate that SRS-A was a unique "polar lipid," on the basis of its physical properties (Brocklehurst, 1962; Strandberg and Üvnas, 1971). Strandberg and Üvnas (1971) were also able to conclude that SRS-A was distinct from the family of lipid moieties identified as prostaglandins. The capacity of SRS-A to bind to various support media as well as to proteins and phospholipids represented an additional complication. Thus, those interested in the isolation and characterization of SRS-A were limited to systems that generated relatively small amounts of material—that is, the immunologic release of SRS-A from guinea pig lung tissue or the release by 48/80 from the cat's paw (Änggård et al., 1963)—and were further handicapped by very substantial losses during isolation attempts.

In the late 1960s, Austen and his colleagues recognized that SRS-A was released into the peritoneal fluid by an intraperitoneal antigen–antibody reaction utilizing either hyperimmune rabbit or rat serum (Orange et al., 1967, 1968a, 1969). These observations not only provided a system for generating larger amounts of SRS-A than had previously been available, but also revealed for the first time that the generation of SRS-A did not require a conventional immediate-type hypersensitivity reaction. Indeed, it was demonstrated that the generation of SRS-A in the peritoneal cavity of the rat was dependent on the presence of rat neutrophilic polymorphonuclear leukocytes and of an intact complement system, and did not require the presence of histamine-containing mast cells within that cavity and its adjacent tissues (Orange et al., 1968a). That SRS-A could be generated in the peritoneal cavity by a mast cell-dependent reaction involving rat IgE-type immunoglobulin (Orange et al., 1970) indicated for the first time that in a single species the chemical mediator could be provided by cellular interactions involving different antibody classes and apparently different cells of origin. As had been done by earlier workers, Orange and co-workers separated SRS-A from proteins by precipitation of the latter with ethanol, and SRS-A was then isolated by conventional chromatographic methods depending on hydrophobicity, charge, and molecular size. Base hydrolysis was also utilized to eliminate the phospholipids, and the apparent molecular weight of this moiety was indicated to be approximately 500 (Orange et al., 1973). Various methods were employed for volatilizing this material, but all were unsuccessful as preparations for mass spectral analysis, suggesting that SRS-A might be highly involatile (Orange et al., 1973). Accordingly, an elemental analysis by spark source spectroscopy revealed that the SRS-A, derived from the rat peritoneal cavity by the interaction of antigen with hyperimmune serum and then partially purified, was enriched for sulfur (Orange et al., 1973). This finding was compatible with the apparent involatility of the material. Nonetheless, because it was difficult to define a "control substance" that would prove that the SRS-A was truly enriched for sulfur, it was necessary to confirm this conclusion by an independent approach.

B. Methods for Inactivation

That confirmation, based on the inactivation of SRS-A by arylsulfatases (AS) of many species, was, in retrospect, fortuitous but not correct. Three lines of evidence were used to substantiate the capacity of arylsulfatases to inactivate SRS-A: the inactivation was achieved by partially purified aryl-sulfatases from a variety of different sources including limpet, snail, and human eosinophils (ASB), human lung tissue (ASA and ASB), and rat baso-phil leukemia cells (ASA and ASB) (Orange *et al.*, 1974; Wasserman *et al.*, 1975a; Wasserman and Austen, 1976, 1977); human esinophils from hypereo-sinophilic donors, which are enriched for ASB, preferentially inactivated SRS-A, as compared to human neutrophils, which are essentially devoid of the enzyme (Wasserman *et al.*, 1975b); and partially purified SRS-A pre-vented arylsulfatase from cleaving the synthetic substrate, *p*-nitrocatechol sulfate (Wasserman *et al.*, 1975a; Wasserman and Austen, 1976, 1977).

It is now evident that the loss of biologic activity in SRS-A on treatment with the various arylsulfatases must have been due to their contamination by dipeptidases, which converted LTD_4 to the less spasmogenic LTE_4, as mea-sured on the guinea pig ileum. The capacity of eosinophils from hypereo-sinophilic donors to inactivate SRS-A is now attributed to the fact that such cells generate hypochlorous acid through the interaction of a peroxidase, hydrogen peroxide, and chlorine, because they are in an "activated state," as compared to neutrophils from normal donors (Lee *et al.*, 1982, 1983; Hen-derson *et al.*, 1982; Weller *et al.*, 1983). Neutrophils have the same capacity for sulfidopeptide inactivation, but only when they have been activated, as would occur with phorbol myristate acetate (Lee *et al.*, 1982, 1983). Interest-ingly, it has been confirmed that the synthetic sulfidopeptide leukotriene constituents of SRS-A are remarkably active inhibitors of purified human eosinophil ASB on its synthetic substrate (Weller *et al.*, 1981). Presumably, the enzyme interacts with the sulfidopeptide leukotrienes as if they possess sulfur-bearing aromatic rings, and molar concentrations 3–4 logs less than that of *p*-nitrocatechol sulfate are sufficient to interfere significantly with cleavage of that substrate (Weller *et al.*, 1981).

III. RECOGNITION OF THE COMPONENTS OF SRS-A, THE LEUKOTRIENES

A. Calcium Ionophore Activation

In the early 1970s it was possible to demonstrate that an almost pure population of basophil leukemia cells of human origin would respond to activation with the calcium ionophore, so as to release a material indistin-guishable by chromatographic and pharmacologic characteristics from the immunologically generated SRS-A of rat origin (Lewis *et al.*, 1975). This observation made it possible for others in the field to utilize the ionophore as an activating principle for generating SRS-A from cell types without depending on the complex requirements for an immunologic reaction. None-theless, because the total amounts of SRS-A generated were very small relative to other materials having similar characteristics by the chromato-graphic methods employed, two of the initial reports indicating that radiola-beled SRS-A could be obtained from cells or tissues preincubated with ^{35}S-labeled amino acid or [^{14}C]arachidonic acid were later modified to indi-cate resolution of biologic activity from radiolabel, and the correct conclu-sions were retracted (Dawson et al., 1975; Bach et al., 1977, 1979).

Subsequently, Parker and colleagues did incorporate radiolabeled arachi-donic acid into SRS-A, which was released by ionophore activation of the rat basophil leukemia cell line (Jakschik et al., 1977). Murphy, who had worked with Austen and Orange in the isolation of SRS-A and its resolution as a 500-MW chemical mediator (Orange et al., 1973, 1974), then joined with Samuelsson in demonstrating the incorporation of both [^{35}S]cysteine and [^{14}C]arachidonic acid into the material released from mouse mastocytoma cells activated with calcium ionophore A23187 (Murphy et al., 1979).

Just before that observation, Borgeat and Samuelsson had reported a new class of lipid products, dihydroxyeicosatetraenoic acids including LTB$_4$, derived from human neutrophils activated with the calcium ionophore (Borgeat and Samuelsson, 1979). Samuelsson and colleagues immediately appreciated that the unique triene structure of LTB$_4$, as characterized by its ultraviolet absorption spectrum, was also present as a shoulder in the re-ported spectrum of the partially purified SRS-A of rat origin (Orange et al., 1973) and in the ultraviolet absorption spectrum of highly purified material obtained some years later from guinea pig lung tissue by Morris and co-workers (1978). By cleaving the carbon–sulfur bond between the sulfidopep-tide moiety and the lipid backbone, Samuelsson and colleagues identified the essential components of SRS-A by amino acid analysis of the peptide portion and by mass spectroscopic analysis of the lipid portion (Murphy et al., 1979). Even at that point there were approximately 128 possible stereo-chemical structures, and thus it was essential for Corey and colleagues to complete a stereospecific synthesis and to demonstrate functional identity on a weight basis between the synthetic and the natural LTC$_4$ (Hammar-ström et al., 1979). It was subsequently recognized by Samuelsson and col-leagues, by Morris, Piper, and colleagues, and by Lewis, Austen, and col-leagues that biologically generated SRS-A was composed not only of LTC$_4$ but also of the biologically active peptide conversion products LTD$_4$ and LTE$_4$ (Örning et al., 1980; Morris et al., 1980; Lewis et al., 1980a,b).

Working from a knowledge of the reaction products, Samuelsson and his colleagues definitively established the reaction sequence from arachidonic acid in biochemical terms as involving the formation of hydroperoxyeicosa-tetraenoic acid (5-HPETE) followed by LTA$_4$, which was then converted either to LTB$_4$ or LTC$_4$ (Rådmark et al., 1980a,b). Equally important was the fact that Corey and colleagues completed a stereochemically specific synthesis of each postulated intermediate as well as each end product (Rådmark *et al.*, 1980c; Corey *et al.*, 1980a,b), thereby definitively establishing the structures.

B. Inhibition by Diethylcarbamazine

In retrospect, the first selective inhibitor of SRS-A generation, reported in the late 1960s, was diethylcarbamazine. In earlier studies it had been demonstrated that certain pharmacologic interventions that prevented immunologic mast cell activation suppressed not only histamine release, but also SRS-A generation (Austen and Brocklehurst, 1961). However, when administered intraperitoneally to the rat, diethylcarbamazine prevented SRS-A generation without influencing the release of histamine in a system that utilized the hyperimmune antibody and was not dependent on the participation of the mast cell (Orange *et al.*, 1968b; Orange and Austen, 1968).

Following the structural elucidation of the constituents of SRS-A, Murphy and colleagues demonstrated that diethylcarbamazine appeared to have a unique site of action in preventing the conversion of 5-HPETE to LTA_4 in the ionophore-activated mouse mastocytoma cell (Mathews and Murphy, 1982). This was subsequently confirmed by Austen and colleagues, utilizing a homogeneous population of murine bone marrow-derived mast cells sensitized with monoclonal antibody and activated with hapten-specific antigen (Razin *et al.*, in press). Diethylcarbamazine prevented the generation of LTC_4 and LTB_4 in this cell system in association with an accumulation of the reduced product of 5-HPETE, 5-hydroxyeicosatetraenoic acid (5-HETE). The specificity of the site of action was further supported by the finding that inhibition of leukotriene generation was not accompanied by the prevention of granule release as assessed by the granule marker β-hexosaminidase (Razin *et al.*, in press). These observations are of particular interest because preliminary studies (Mallén, 1965) had indicated that treatment of asthmatic humans with diethylcarbamazine could partially attenuate the problem of clinical asthma.

IV. STUDIES OF TARGET TISSUE RESPONSES

A. Spasmogenic Activity

1. Bioconversion of Leukotriene Moieties

As previously noted, the spasmogenic activity of SRS-A was distinguished by its unique tissue profile. The most reactive smooth muscle preparations were guinea pig ileum, guinea pig airway, and human airway (Brocklehurst, 1962). Studies with the chemically synthesized sulfidopeptide leukotrienes C_4, D_4, and E_4 indicated that, even among responsive tissues, there was not a fixed ratio of activities for the SRS-A components (Lewis *et al.*, 1980b; Dahlén *et al.*, 1980; Drazen *et al.*, 1980; Hanna *et al.*, 1981). The selectivity and heterogeneity of the smooth muscle response suggested that there could be a level of complexity beyond the usual agonist–target tissue interaction.

Piper and colleagues, observing that the contraction of the guinea pig ileum to LTC_4 was delayed as compared to the response to LTD_4, suggested that LTC_4 would not be biologically active unless the target tissue converted this moiety to LTD_4 (Piper *et al.*, 1982). This reasonable assumption was subsequently corrected by the studies of Lewis, Austen, and colleagues, in which they utilized radiolabeled leukotrienes and analyzed the bioconversion of the agonist during the spasmogenic response of the guinea pig ileum (Krilis *et al.*, 1983a). These studies demonstrated that LTC_4 had inherent contractile activity after a 60-sec latent period and with only minimal conversion to LTD_4. This was confirmed by adding serine borate complex to the organ bath to prevent any conversion of LTC_4 to LTD_4, a circumstance in which the biologic activity of LTC_4 was maintained with the same 60-sec latent period. In contrast, LTD_4 elicited an immediate contraction, which, unlike that of LTC_4, was not sustained because of bioconversion of LTD_4 to the less active LTE_4 by the responding guinea pig ileum (Krilis *et al.*, 1983a). Thus, despite the inherent activity of each sulfidopeptide leukotriene, one variable in target tissue response clearly related to the rate and nature of the peptide cleavage of the initial sulfidopeptide leukotriene moieties.

2. Secondary Generation of Cyclooxygenase Products

A second variable related to the secondary generation of oxidative products of arachidonic acid by the cyclooxygenase pathway during the response of a tissue to the leukotrienes. Depending on the manner in which the in vitro experiment was designed, the contribution of the cyclooxygenase products — as assessed by attenuation of the spasmogenic response with indomethacin — was substantial, modest, or negligible (Piper and Samhoun, 1981; Weichman *et al.*, 1982; Hedqvist and Dahlén, 1983). Indeed, in detailed studies in which both indomethacin and the three synthetic sulfidopeptide leukotrienes were examined in a dose–response fashion, Austen and colleagues demonstrated that the smooth muscle contribution could either augment or attenuate the response (Austen *et al.*, 1983), presumably depending on whether the major product was the bronchoconstrictor, thromboxane, or a bronchodilator, prostaglandin. The most important variable, however, is likely neither bioconversion nor the secondary generation of cyclooxygenase products, but the distribution of specific receptors for the sulfidopeptide leukotrienes.

3. Role of Specific Receptors

It has been demonstrated that a smooth muscle cell line derived from the hamster vas deferens, as well as smooth muscle segments from the guinea pig ileum, bear receptors for LTC_4 (Krilis *et al.*, 1983b, and in press). In these studies the presence of cell membrane receptors was demonstrated by three criteria: saturation of $[^3H]LTC_4$ binding at 4°C in a time-dependent fashion, reversibility of binding at equilibrium by the introduction of excess unlabeled LTC_4, and stereospecific competition for binding by LTC_4 and its biologically active analogs, but not by a biologically inactive LTC_4 analog or an unrelated structure such as LTB_4. As these studies were carried out with intact cells and intact muscle segments at 4°C, it is appropriate to conclude that the receptor recognized was on the plasma membrane. What is particularly noteworthy is that the other biologically active natural sulfidopeptide leukotrienes, LTD_4 and LTE_4, did not compete effectively with the radiolabeled LTC_4 for these plasma membrane binding sites. This of course suggested that there must be an independent and second receptor for LTD_4 distinct from that for LTC_4. Such a possibility had already been raised by the physiologic studies of Drazen, Lewis, Austen, and colleagues, in which there were two significant observations utilizing guinea pig lung pulmonary parenchymal strips. The response of these tissue strips to LTD_4 was biphasic. A low-dose response to LTD_4 occurred in a range 2–3 logs below the response threshhold to LTC_4 and was competitively inhibited by the putative receptor antagonist FPL55712. In contrast, the response of the pulmonary parenchymal strips to high-dose LTD_4 or to any dose of LTC_4 was not inhibited by FPL55712. These pharmacologic observations prompted the investigators to suggest the existence of receptor heterogeneity (Drazen *et al.*, 1980).

Drazen and Fanta have repeated these studies in the presence of a calcium channel blocker, diltiazem, and have demonstrated that, under these conditions, FPL55712 inhibits the response to LTD_4 throughout the agonist dose-response range (Drazen and Fanta, in press). Accordingly, the physiologic studies of Drazen and colleagues and the radioligand-binding studies of Lewis, Austen, and colleagues have led to the suggestion that there are two separate receptors designated as sulfidopeptide leukotriene receptor 1 (that for LTD_4) and sulfidopeptide leukotriene receptor 2 (that for LTC_4). In view of the existence of at least two specific receptors for the sulfidopeptide leukotrienes and the bioconversion of these agonists during smooth muscle tissue responses, there is a complexity of controls for the integrated tissue response that is relatively unique to this system. Clearly, this is an important consideration in attempting to develop specific inhibitors for these agonists, using tissue bioassay.

B. Vasoactivity

Although the spasmogenic activity of SRS-A was recognized on its discovery, the vasoactivity of this material was not appreciated until the studies of Orange and Austen (1969) utilizing the partially purified SRS-A prepared from inflammatory rat peritoneal exudates. More than 10 years later, Lewis, Austen, and colleagues made the observation that LTC_4 did not mimic the effect of rat SRS-A when injected into guinea pig skin, since it did not augment local venular permeability as appreciated by the leakage of blue dye, except at the periphery of the injection site. In contrast, LTD_4 and LTE_4 increased venular permeability at concentrations estimated to be comparable to those in the partially purified SRS-A (Lewis *et al.*, 1980b; Drazen *et al.*, 1980). This led to the observation that the failure of LTC_4 to augment the bluing reaction was due to its marked arteriolar constrictor properties.

Thus, SRS-A, depending on the distribution of its sulfidopeptide leukotriene constituents, constricts arterioles and, at the same time, augments venular permeability. This point was made independently in studies with the hamster cheek pouch mucosal surface on which the leukotrienes were directly applied (Dahlén *et al.*, 1981). When sulfidopeptide leukotrienes were administered systemically to sheep (Michelassi *et al.*, 1982) and to rats (Pfeffer *et al.*, 1983), their powerful vasoconstrictor activity was fully appreciated in terms of an increase in peripheral resistance and a fall in cardiac output due to coronary constriction with impaired cardiac blood supply. Thus, although the major interest in SRS-A had been based on the possibility that it might play a role in reversible bronchoconstrictive airway disease, there is an additional dimension to the biology of this class of substances provided by their action on the vascular system.

V. CLINICAL PHARMACOLOGY

It was the postdoctoral relationship that Austen had with Brocklehurst that introduced him to the possibility that these materials might play a role in human bronchial asthma. Thus, when the leukotrienes were available in synthetic form almost 25 years later, he and his colleagues, together with Corey and colleagues, immediately addressed their clinical pharmacology. When inhaled by normal subjects, LTC_4 was 4000, and LTD_4 was 6000 times as potent, on a molar basis, as histamine (Weiss *et al.*, 1982, 1983). In addition, in the human, their action was predominantly on peripheral rather than central airways, an observation that Drazen and Austen (1974) had made some 10 years previously in studying the effects of highly purified natural SRS-A on the pulmonary mechanics of the anesthetized and unanesthetized normal guinea pig. When LTD_4 was administered to asymptomatic asthmatic subjects, it was still 100 times as potent as histamine on a molar basis, but the potency of LTD_4 on a molar basis was similar in normal subjects and asthmatics (Weiss *et al.*, 1983; Griffin *et al.*, 1983).

Bronchial asthma, by definition, is a condition of airway hyperirritability, and the population studied responded to histamine at a concentration 2–3 logs less than that required to elicit impaired pulmonary function in normal subjects. Indeed, asthmatics exhibit airway hyperresponsiveness, not only to a variety of agonists such as histamine, methylcholine, and bradykinin, but to a number of irritants such as sulfur dioxide, citric acid, and cold air (Townley *et al.*, 1965; Boushey *et al.*, 1980). Thus, LTD_4 represents the first nonvascular smooth muscle constrictor that, when introduced into the airway of asthmatics, as compared to normal subjects, does not evoke hyperresponsiveness of several orders of magnitude. In view of this finding and of the remarkable potency of LTD_4 relative to histamine, two interpretations can be set forth: (1) that leukotrienes are important mediators of reversible airway disease in bronchial asthma, especially in the periphery, and, more importantly, (2) that leukotrienes may be responsible for airway hyperirritability to other agonists and irritants. The recognition that there are separate receptors for at least two of the sulfidopeptide leukotriene constituents raises the further possibility that one might be involved in airway hyperirritability and the other in the bronchospastic response.

REFERENCES

Änggård, E., Berqvist, U., Högberg, B., Johansson, K., Thon, J. L., and Üvnas, B. (1963). *Acta Physiol. Scand.* **59**, 97–110.

Austen, K. F., and Brocklehurst, W. E. (1961). *J. Exp. Med.* **113**, 521–539.

Austen, K. F., Corey, E. J., Drazen, J. M., and Leitch, A. G. (1983). *Br. J. Pharmacol.* **80**, 47–53.

Bach, M. K., Brashler, J. R., and Gorman, R. R. (1977). *Prostaglandins* **14**, 21–38.

Bach, M. K., Brashler, J. R., Brooks, C. D., and Neerken, A. J. (1979). *J. Immunol.* **122**, 160–165.

Borgeat, P., and Samuelsson, B. (1979). *J. Biol. Chem.* **254**, 2643–2646.

Boushey, H. A., Holtzman, M. J., Sheller, J. R., and Nadel, J. A. (1980). *Am. Rev. Respir. Dis.* **121**, 389–413.

Brocklehurst, W. E. (1953). *J. Physiol. (Lond.)* **129**, 16P–17P.

Brocklehurst, W. E. (1962). *Progr. Allergy* **6**, 539–558.

Corey, E. J., Clark, D. A., Goto, G., Marfat, A., Mioskowski, C., Samuelsson, B., and Hammarström, S. (1980a). *J. Am. Chem. Soc.* **108**, 1436–1439, and 3663.

Corey, E. J., Marfat, A., Goto, G., and Brion, F. (1980b). *J. Am. Chem. Soc.* **102**, 7984–7985.

Dahlén, D.-E., Hedqvist, P., Hammarström, S., and Samuelsson, B. (1980). *Nature (London)* **288**, 484–486.

Dahlén, D.-E., Bjork, J., Hedqvist, P., Arfors, K.-E., Hammarström, S., Lindgren, J.-Å., and Samuelsson, B. (1981). *Proc. Natl. Acad. Sci. U.S.A.* **78**, 3887–3891.

Dawson, W., Lewis, R. L., and Tomlinson, R. (1975). *J. Physiol. (Lond.)* **247**, 37P–38P.

Drazen, J. M., and Austen, K. F. (1974). *J. Clin. Invest.* **53**, 1679–1685.

Drazen, J. M., and Fanta, C. *Fed. Proc.,* in press.

Drazen, J. M., Austen, K. F., Lewis, R. A., Clark, D. A., Goto, G., Marfat, A., and Corey, E. J. (1980). *Proc. Natl. Acad. Sci. U.S.A.* **77**, 4354–4358.

Griffin, M., Weiss, J. W., Leitch, A. G., McFadden, E. R., Jr., Corey, E. J., Austen, K. F., and Drazen, J. M. (1983). *N. Engl. J. Med.* **308**, 436–439.

Hammarström, S., Murphy, R. C., Samuelsson, B., Clark, D. A., Mioskowski, C., and Corey, E. J. (1979). *Biochem. Biophys. Res. Commun.* **91**, 1266–1272.

Hanna, C. J., Bach, M. K., Pare, P. D., and Schellenberg, R. R. (1981). *Nature (London)* **290**, 343–344.

Harkavy, J. (1930). *Arch. Int. Med.* **45**, 641–646.

Hedqvist, P., and Dahlén, S.-E. (1983). *Adv. Prostaglandins, Thromboxane, Leukotriene Res.* **11**, 27–32.

Henderson, W. R., Jorg, A., and Klebanoff, S. J. (1982). *J. Immunol.* **128**, 2609–2613.

Jakschik, B. A., Falkenhein, S., and Parker, C. W. (1977). *Proc. Natl. Acad. Sci. U.S.A.* **74**, 4577–4581.

Kellaway, C. H., and Trethewie, W. R. (1940). *Quart. J. Exp. Physiol.* **30**, 121–145.

Krilis, S., Lewis, R. A., Corey, E. J., and Austen, K. F. (1983a). *J. Clin. Invest.* **71**, 909–915.

Krilis, S., Lewis, R. A., Corey, E. J., and Austen, K. F. (1983b). *J. Clin. Invest.* **72**, 1516–1519.

Krilis, S., Lewis, R. A., and Austen, K. F. *In* "Icosanoids and Ion Transport" (P. Braquet, ed.) Raven Press, New York, in press.

Lee, C. W., Lewis, R. A., Corey, E. J., Barton, A., Oh, H., Tauber, A. I., and Austen, K. F. (1982). *Proc. Natl. Acad. Sci. U.S.A.* **79**, 4166–4170.

Lee, C. W., Lewis, R. A., Tauber, A. I., Mehrotra, M. M., Corey, E. J., and Austen, K. F. (1983). *J. Biol. Chem.,* **258**, 15004–15010.

Lewis, R. A., Goetzl, E. J., Wasserman, S. I., Valone, F. H., Rubin, R. H., and Austen, K. F. (1975). *J. Immunol.* **114**, 87–92.

Lewis, R. A., Austen, K. F., Drazen, J. M., Clark, D. A., and Corey, E. J. (1980a). *Proc. Natl. Acad. Sci. U.S.A.* **78**, 3195–3198.

Lewis, R. A., Drazen, J. M., Austen, K. F., Clark, D. A., and Corey, E. J. (1980b). *Biochem. Biophys. Res. Commun.* **96**, 271–277.

Mallén, M. S. (1965). *Ann. Allergy* **23**, 534–537.

Mathews, W. R. and Murphy, R. C. (1982). *Biochem. Pharmacol.* **31**, 2129–2132.

Michelassi, F., Landa, L., Hill, R. D., Lowenstein, E., Watkins, W. D., Petkau, A. J., and Zapol, W. M. (1982). *Science* **217**, 841–843.

Morris, H. R., Taylor, G. W., Piper, P. J., Sirois, P., and Tippins, J. R. (1978). *FEBS Lett.* **87**, 203–206.

Morris, H. R., Taylor, G. W. Piper, P. J., and Tippins, J. R. (1980). *Nature (London)* **285**, 204–205.

Murphy, R. C., Hammarström, S., and Samuelsson, B. (1979). *Proc. Natl. Acad. Sci. U.S.A.* **76**, 4275–4279.

Orange, R. P., and Austen, K. F. (1968). *Proc. Soc. Exp. Biol. Med.* **129**, 834–841.

Orange, R. P., and Austen, K. F. (1969). *In* "Cellular and Humoral Mechanisms in Anaphylaxis and Allergy" (H. Z. Movat, ed.), pp. 196–206. S. Karger, Basel.

Orange, R. P., Valentine, M. D., and Austen, K. F. (1967). *Science* **157**, 318–319.

Orange, R. P., Valentine, M. D., and Austen, K. F. (1968a). *J. Exp. Med.* **127**, 767–782.

Orange, R. P., Valentine, M. D., and Austen, K. F. (1968b). *Proc. Soc. Exp. Biol. Med.* **127**, 127–132.
Orange, R. P., Stechschulte, D. J., and Austen, K. F. (1969). *Fed. Proc.* **28**, 1710–1715.
Orange, R. P., Stechschulte, D. J., and Austen, K. F. (1970). *J. Immunol.* **105**, 1087–1095.
Orange, R. P., Murphy, R. C., Karnovsky, M. L., and Austen, K. F. (1973). *J. Immunol.* **110**, 760–770.
Orange, R. P., Murphy, R. C., and Austen, K. F. (1974). *J. Immunol.* **113**, 316–322.
Örning, L., Hammarström, S., and Samuelsson, B. (1980). *Proc. Natl. Acad. Sci. U.S.A.* **77**, 2014–2017.
Pfeffer, M. A., Pfeffer, J. M., Lewis, R. A., Braunwald, E., Corey, E. J., and Austen, K. F. (1983). *Am. J. Physiol.* **244**, H628–H633.
Piper, P. J., and Samhoun, M. N. (1981). *Prostaglandins* **21**, 793–803.
Piper, P. J., Letts, L. G., Samhoun, M. N., Tippins, J. R., and Palmer, M. A. (1982). *Adv. Prostaglandin, Thromboxane, and Leukotriene Res.* **9**, 169–181.
Rådmark, O., Malmsten, C., Samuelsson, B., Clark, D. A., Goto, G., Marfat, A., and Corey, E. J. (1980a). *Biochem. Biophys. Res. Commun.* **96**, 271–277.
Rådmark, O., Malmsten, C., and Samuelsson, B. (1980b). *FEBS Lett.* **110**, 213–215.
Rådmark, O., Malmsten, C., Samuelsson, B., Goto, G., Marfat, A., and Corey, E. J. (1980c). *J. Biol. Chem.* **255**, 11828–11831.
Razin, E. R., Lewis, R. A., Corey, E. J., and Austen, K. F. *Fed. Proc.,* in press.
Strandberg, K. and Üvnas, B. (1971). *Acta Physiol. Scand.* **82**, 358–374.
Townley, R. G., Dennis, M., and Itkin, I. H. (1965). *J. Allergy* **36**, 121–137.
Wasserman, S. I., and Austen, K. F. (1976). *J. Clin. Invest.* **57**, 738–744.
Wasserman, S. I., and Austen, K. F. (1977). *J. Biol. Chem.* **252**, 7074–7080.
Wasserman, S. I., Goetzl, E. J., and Austen, K. F. (1975a). *J. Immunol.* **114**, 645–649.
Wasserman, S. I., Goetzl, E. J., and Austen, K. F. (1975b). *J. Allergy Clin. Immunol.* **55**, 72a.
Weichman, B. M., Muccitelli, R. M., Osborn, R. R., Holden, D. A., Gleason, J. G., and Wasserman, M. A. (1982). *J. Pharmacol. Exp. Ther.* **222**, 202–208.
Weiss, J. W., Drazen, J. M., Coles, N., McFadden, E. R. Jr., Weller, P. F., Corey, E. J., Lewis, R. A., and Austen, K. F. (1982). *Science* **216**, 196–198.
Weiss, J. W., Drazen, J. M., McFadden, E. R. Jr., Weller, P. F., Corey, E. J., Lewis, R.A., and Austen, K. F. (1983). *J. Am. Med. Assoc.* **249**, 2814–2817.
Weller, P. F., Lewis, R. A., Corey, E. J., and Austen, K. F. (1981). *Fed. Proc.* **40**, 1023a.
Weller, P. F., Lee, C. W., Foster, D. W., Corey, E. J., Austen, K. F., and Lewis, R. A. (1983). *Proc. Natl. Acad. Sci. U.S.A.* **80**, 7626–7630.

2

Structure Elucidation and Total Synthesis ·of the Leukotrienes

E. J. COREY

Department of Chemistry
Harvard University
Cambridge, Massachusetts

DAVID A. CLARK AND ANTHONY MARFAT

Pfizer Central Research
Groton, Connecticut

THE LEUKOTRIENES

Copyright 1984 by Academic Press, Inc.
All rights of reproduction in any form reserved.
ISBN 0-12-166750-2

I. INTRODUCTION

The leukotrienes are a group of newly discovered derivatives of arachidonic acid that were originally isolated from leukocytes. The assignment of stereochemistry and structure of these trace, biologically active mammalian metabolites resulted from a combination of chemical synthetic, enzymic, and spectroscopic studies. The elucidation of structure and the biological properties of the leukotrienes have been reviewed (7,18,19,23,27,29,64,68,86, 116–119,129–132,136–139,142). The purpose of this chapter is to outline the role of the synthetic chemist in these developments and to describe more recent synthetic approaches to these substances and various structural analogs (Scheme 1).

II. DISCOVERY OF THE LEUKOTRIENES

The pioneering work of Bergström (12) on the structures of the prostaglandins (PGs) set the stage for the recognition during the 1960s of arachidonic acid as a key biosynthetic progenitor of primary PGs by the cyclooxygenase pathway. The discovery in the mid-1970s of thromboxane A$_2$ (73) and prostacyclin (26,81,93) expanded the family of bioactive substances and broadened the physiological role of the cyclooxygenase pathway (Scheme 2). The initial step of the cyclooxygenase pathway is a lipoxygenase-type reaction of arachidonic acid at C-11. The importance of the lipoxygenase reaction at other positions of arachidonic acid has subsequently become clear as the arachidonic cascade has been extended (8). Although the presence of lipoxygenase enzymes in plants was known for many years, it was not until 1974 that

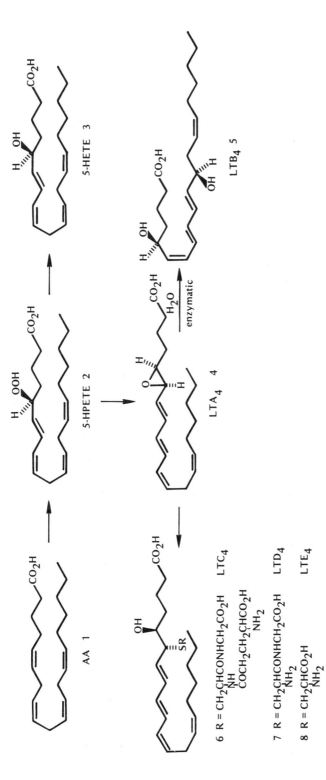

Scheme 1

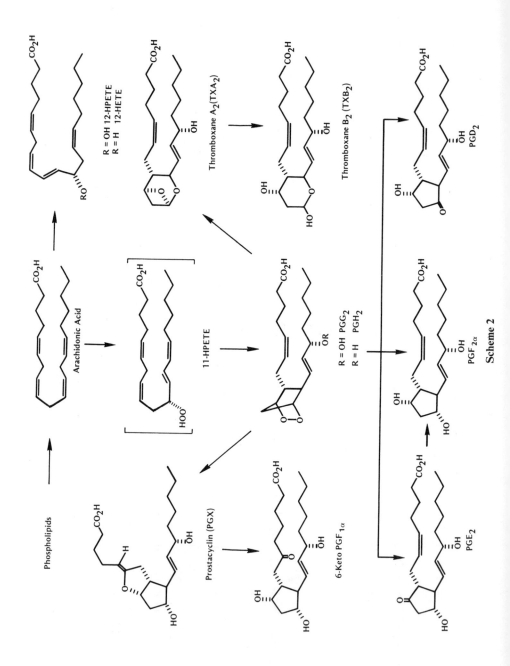

R = OH 12-HPETE
R = H 12-HETE

Thromboxane A$_2$(TXA$_2$)

Thromboxane B$_2$ (TXB$_2$)

PGD$_2$

Arachidonic Acid

11-HPETE

R = OH PGG$_2$
R = H PGH$_2$

PGF$_{2\alpha}$

Phospholipids

Prostacyclin (PGX)

6-Keto PGF$_{1\alpha}$

PGE$_2$

Scheme 2

lipoxygenase enzymes were identified in mammalian tissue. Samuelsson (72) and Nugteren (103) first demonstrated a lipoxygenase in blood platelets that oxidizes arachidonic acid to (12S)-HPETE and (12S)-HETE.

Encouraged by the discovery of the 12-lipoxygenase pathway in platelets, Samuelsson undertook a study of the metabolism of arachidonic acid in rabbit polymorphonuclear leukocytes (PMNs) (14–17,20). In 1976 Borgeat and Samuelsson demonstrated that leukocytes convert arachidonic acid to (5S)-hydroxy-6,8,11,14-eicosatetraenoic acid (5-HETE) and 8,11,14-eicosa-trienoic acid to (8S)-hydroxy-9,11,14-eicosatrienoic acid. A third metabolite was later identified as (5S,12R)-dihydroxy-6,8,10,14-eicosatetraenoic acid (133) (Scheme 3). The term *leukotriene* B_4 (LTB$_4$) was later suggested for this last metabolite (134,135), which was found not to have contractile activity in measurements on a conventional smooth muscle preparation, guinea pig ileum. Isotopic oxygen incorporation experiments demonstrated that the oxygen of the C-5 alcohol originated from molecular oxygen, whereas the oxygen of the alcohol group at C-12 was derived from water. Samuelsson reasoned that this substance was perhaps a transformation product of a less stable, but biologically active and more interesting molecule.

This reasonable hypothesis found a parallel in his earlier studies on the metabolites of arachidonic acid in platelets, in which the inactive thrombox-

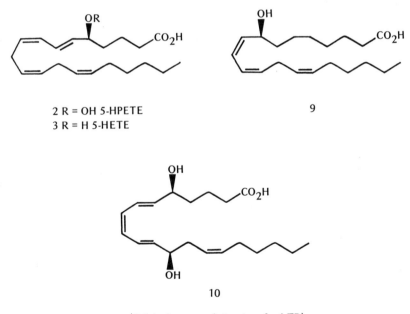

2 R = OH 5-HPETE
3 R = H 5-HETE

9

10

(Original proposed structure for LTB)

Scheme 3

ane B_2 was found to be a metabolite of the potent inducer of platelet aggregation, thromboxane A_2 (71). In this study the unstable intermediate thromboxane A_2 was converted to thromboxane B_2 methyl ether in a quenching experiment using methanol. A similar methanol-trapping experiment in the polymorphonuclear leukocyte system led to a new product that was obviously formed by interception of a metastable intermediate. By microchemical degradation and mass spectroscopy it was demonstrated that the free hydroxy was attached at C-5 and the methoxy group at C-12. Thin-layer chromatographic (TLC) analysis indicated that the methanol-trapping product was homogeneous, and it seemed to have the R configuration at C-12 from degradation studies.

On the basis of these data Samuelsson postulated as a possible structure for the unstable intermediate LTA_4 the nine-membered oxacyclononatriene (12) (Scheme 4). During an informal discussion of these results in March 1978 an alternative structure for the unstable intermediate was proposed by Corey, in part because a highly strained oxacyclononatriene should undergo attack by methanol at both C-5 and C-12 by an S_N1 process to form a mixture of isomeric methoxy compounds. Previous experience on the synthesis of costunolides (37) via an unstable structure having one more ring member, a cyclodeca-1,3,5-triene (Scheme 5), and the examination of molecular models of the oxacyclononatriene structure cast further doubt on the formulation 12. A biosynthetically attractive alternative for the polymorphonuclear leukocyte-derived predecessor of LTB_4 and the proposed pathway for biosynthesis are shown in Scheme 6. This scheme readily explained enzymic 5,12-diol formation but also required that the methanol-quenching reaction should produce epimeric C-12 methoxy compounds and probably C-6 methoxy compounds as well. The proposed allylic hydroperoxide-to-epoxide conversion found precedence in earlier synthetic studies in the triterpene series (1) (Scheme 7). The transoiddiene, transoidoxirane 4 stereochemistry for the intermedite seemed more likely on chemical grounds, but other stereoisomeric forms of 4 could not be excluded.

Reexamination by Samuelsson (99) of the metastable intermediate from neutrophils using HPLC analysis indeed showed that mixtures of methoxy-hydroxy or dihydroxy compounds were formed in quenching experiments using, respectively, methanol or aqueous acid. Four diols were formed by quenching of the reactive intermediate with aqueous acid, two of which were diastereomeric 5,12-diols with all-*trans*-triene geometry and two of which were diastereomeric 5,6-diols (Scheme 8). In each case the hydroxy group at C-5 was of the S configuration and was shown to be derived from molecular oxygen. The second hydroxy moiety at C-6 or C-12 was derived from water. These results lent strong support to the hypothesis of the trienic epoxide structure for the unstable intermediate. By this time a sample of racemic

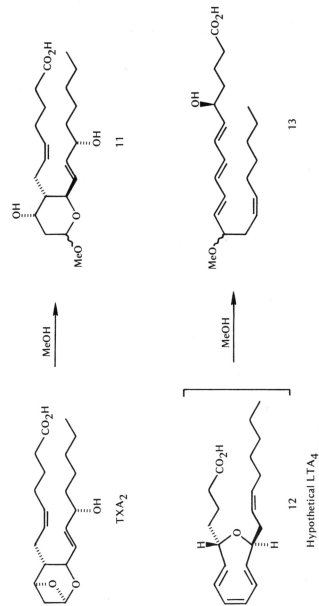

TXA₂

Hypothetical LTA₄

12

Scheme 4

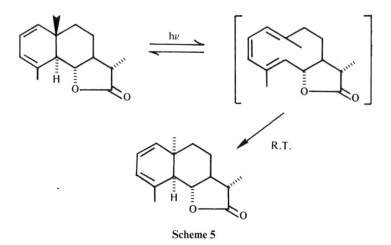

Scheme 5

epoxide had been obtained as a mixture of *cis*- and *trans*-oxiranes by chemical synthesis (39). The key intermediate trienic alcohol (**18a**) was prepared by Wittig condensation between dienal (**16**) and ylide (**17**) followed by desilylation (Scheme 9). The sensitive epoxy methyl ester (**19a,b**) was prepared from the allylic alcohol (**18a**) in a one-pot sequence involving several unisolated intermediates. Conversion of alcohol **18a** via the mesylate to sulfonium salt **18b** followed by ylide formation and reaction with methyl 4-formylbutyrate

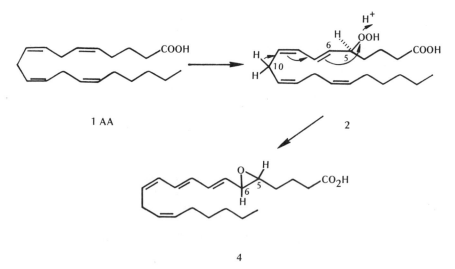

Scheme 6

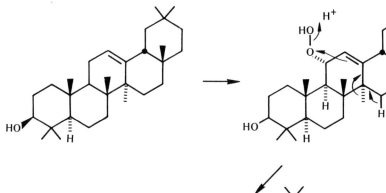

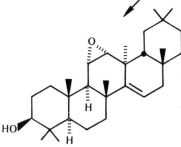

Scheme 7

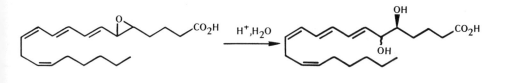

LTA   14

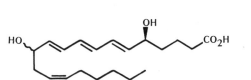

15

Scheme 8

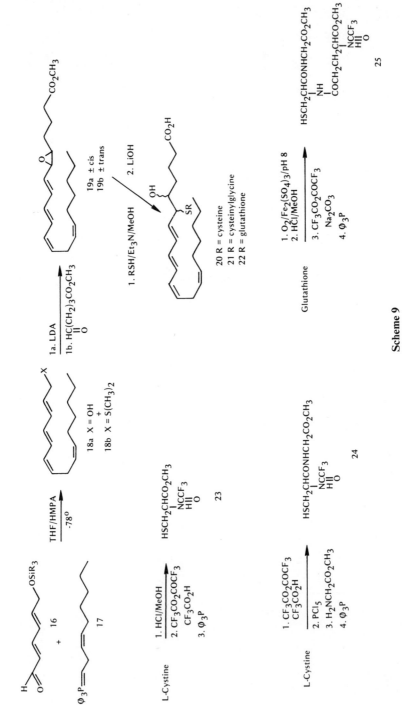

Scheme 9

afforded the acid-sensitive tetraenic epoxy methyl ester **19a,b** in 35% yield after purification on triethylamine-deactivated silica gel as a 1:1 cis–trans mixture. Comparative quenching experiments with the biosynthesized intermediate and the synthetic epoxide gave identical results as first revealed at the Fourth International Meeting on Prostaglandins in Washington, D.C., in May 1979.

III. STRUCTURE ELUCIDATION AND SYNTHESIS OF SRS-A

The final structural elucidation of the naturally occurring slow-reacting substances of anaphylaxis (LTC_4, LTD_4, and LTE_4) was intimately linked to the discovery and characterization of the leukotrienes just mentioned. The term "slow-reacting substance" (SRS) was introduced by Feldberg and Kellaway (62) in 1938 for a substance isolated from a perfusion of guinea pig lung with cobra venom as well as more conventional antigens (84). Brocklehurst (24,25) later used the term "slow-reacting substance of anaphylaxis" (SRS-A) to describe material produced by lungs on immunological challenge by antigens, since it was unknown whether this substance and the previously described SRS were identical. The acronyms SRS and SRS-A can now be used interchangeably, because the chemical substance in question has been shown to be the same whether produced by nonimmunological challenge, immunological challenge, or chemical synthesis.

Because the SRS-As are formed in only trace amounts and are intrinsically unstable, the chemical structure of these substances eluded researchers for over 40 years. Brocklehurst (25) developed extractive techniques for isolation of crude SRS and published a substantial review of the pharmacological and chemical properties of SRS. Orange and Austen (106) updated these results with a second major review in 1969. Early structural work had demonstrated that SRS was a polar lipid (25,109) with a strong ultraviolet absorbance and possibly contained sulfur. The presence of sulfur was suggested by spark source mass spectroscopy (110), and the presence of a sulfate ester was suggested by inactivation of SRS by arylsulfatase (110,114,115). More recent findings have attributed this result to the presence of proteases in the crude arylsulfatase, in that purified arylsulfatase has been shown not to inactivate SRS-A. Additional evidence for the presence of sulfur was the finding that cysteine (107) and various thiols (4,108,138a) stimulated SRS production. A precursor role of arachidonic acid for SRS was again suggested by several lines of evidence. The cyclooxygenase inhibitor indomethacin was found to augment SRS-A release (149), but conflicting reports appeared for the cyclooxygenase and lipoxygenase inhibitor eicosatetraynoic acid (13). Parker (80) and others (8,60,99) demonstrated that arachidonic acid stimulated the release of SRS-A and that radiolabeled arachidonic acid could be incorporated into SRS. Sirois (61,141,143) demonstrated that SRS was inactivated by lipoxygenase in a true enzyme–substrate reaction and proposed that SRS contained a *cis,cis*-1,4-pentadiene unit. A relationship between SRS and the leukotrienes was suggested by the observation that ionophore A23187 stimulated production of SRS as well as 5-HETE and LTB_4 (15,80). Morris *et al.* (94,95,96) pioneered the use of HPLC purification of SRS and showed that pure material had an absorbance λ_{max} of 280 nm, thus providing the key link between SRS and the leukotrienes.

A direct insight into the structure of SRS arose when Samuelsson conceived that the oxirane LTA_4 might be an intermediate in SRS synthesis and that epoxide opening by a thiol nucleophile would lead to a unique conjugate of an amino acid with a fatty acid. Incubation of tritiated arachidonic acid with mastocytoma cells in the presence of [^{14}C]cysteine and ionophore A23187 generated SRS (LTC_4) that was radiolabeled with ^{14}C and ^{3}H. These results and further chemical work led him to propose that LTC_4 was a 5-hydroxy-7,9,11,14-eicosatetraenoic acid that was substituted at C-6 by cysteine or some cysteine-containing peptide (99). The geometry of the triene was undetermined, although the C-11 olefinic unit was presumably cis. At this point the synthetic group (78) accomplished the conversion of synthetic (±)-leukotriene A_4 methyl ester to the cysteine conjugate as a first step in a comparison of synthetic and native compounds. Conditions were established using simple model dienic epoxides (Scheme 10) for effecting the desired S_N2 displacement at the oxirane moiety ($RSH-Et_3N-MeOH$). In addition, alternative conditions were found for directing epoxide opening via an S_N1 pathway leading to the isomeric structures ($RSH-LiClO_4-$ether). The products of S_N1 and S_N2 opening were readily distinguished by the PMR chemical shift of the C-5 hydrogen in the proton NMR. Hydrolysis conditions to remove the protecting groups were developed ($LiOH-DME-H_2O$), and reconversion of the cysteine adduct to the protected derivative demonstrated that no other transformations occurred during hydrolysis. Using the S_N2 reaction conditions, the synthetic racemic mixture of 5,6-*cis*- and 5,6-*trans*-epoxides of methyleicosa-7,9-*trans*-11,14-*cis*-tetraenoate (**19a,b**) was transformed into a mixture of the four diastereomeric 6-L-cysteinyl conjugates **20** (Scheme 9). Analysis of the mixture by reverse-phase HPLC (RP-HPLC) showed, as expected, equal amounts of the four diastereomers. The mixture of synthetic cysteine adducts was sent to Samuelsson's group for HPLC comparison with the mastocytoma SRS (LTC_4). *None* of the isomers was identical to LTC_4. In fact, the large difference in HPLC retention time between these adducts and LTC_4 suggested that a more polar cysteine-containing peptide was attached to the C_{20} chain.

The next derivatives prepared were the cysteinylglycine analogs **21**. Reac-

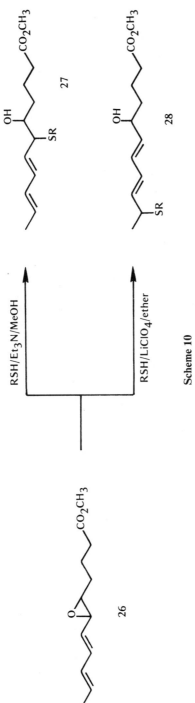

Scheme 10

tion of the cis–trans–epoxide mixture with methyl N-trifluoroacetylcys-
teinylglycine (24) followed by hydrolysis generated the four diastereomeric
cysteinylglycine conjugates, which were again compared to LTC_4 by reverse-
phase HPLC. Again, none of these isomers were identical to LTC_4. Interestingly, one of the diastereomers was found to have 10 times the activity of
LTC_4 on guinea pig ileum, but the HPLC retention time was quite distinct
from that of LTC_4 and a more polar peptide still seemed necessary.

The third sulfur side chain examined was glutathione (γ-glutamylcystein-
ylglycine). The four diastereomers were prepared, and one glutathione conjugate was found to be identical to LTC_4 as shown by ultraviolet absorption,
reverse-phase HPLC retention time, bioassay using guinea pig ileum, and
reaction with soybean lipoxygenase (78). The peptide moiety and the triene
geometry were thus established, and the only remaining question was the
absolute configuration at C-5 and C-6.

Simultaneously with the completion of the first synthesis of LTA_4 as the
racemate, another route designed specifically to yield (5S)-trans-5,6-oxido-
7,9-trans-11,14-cis-eicosatetraenoic acid was undertaken that utilized D-($-$)-
ribose for construction of the C-1 to C-7 unit (46). Wittig reaction of the
2,3,5-tribenzoyl derivative of D-($-$)-ribose followed by acetylation afforded
ester 29 as a mixture of E and Z isomers (Scheme 11). Reductive debenzoyla-
tion and subsequent hydrogenation produced acetate 30a, which was converted to the crystalline tosylate 30b. Treatment of 30b with potassium
carbonate in methanol cleanly afforded the trans-epoxyalcohol 32, presumably through the intermediacy of epoxyalcohol 31. Collins oxidation provided the key intermediate (5S,6R)-epoxyaldehyde 33. The trans stereochemistry of the C-5, C-6 epoxide was clearly indicated by the 2.0-Hz coupling
constant for $J_{5,6}$. Four-carbon chain extension by reaction with 1-lithio-4-
ethoxybutadiene, mesylation of the resultant secondary alcohol, and vinyl
ether hydrolysis and elimination afforded crystalline dienal 34. Wittig condensation of dienal 34 and ylide 17 afforded LTA_4 methyl ester 35 in 35%
yield after purification on triethylamine-deactivated silica gel. The epoxy-
tetraene 35 was found to be extremely acid-sensitive but could be safely
stored frozen in a benzene matrix in the presence of triethylamine. Reaction of the epoxy methyl ester 35 with N-trifluoroacetylglutathione dimethyl ester and triethylamine in concentrated methanol solution afforded
a single adduct 36 in 80% yield. The conjugate 36 exhibited the characteristic λ_{max}^{MeOH} 280 nm ($\epsilon = 40,000$) and ^{1}H-NMR peaks characteristic of
$C=C-CH_2-C=C$ at δ 2.9–3.1, but no peak for an allylic carbinol proton
$[C=C-CH(OH)]$ in the 4.1–4.2 ppm region. Hydrolysis of the protecting
groups with lithium hydroxide or potassium carbonate generated a single
diastereomer that proved to be identical with LTC_4 isolated from mouse

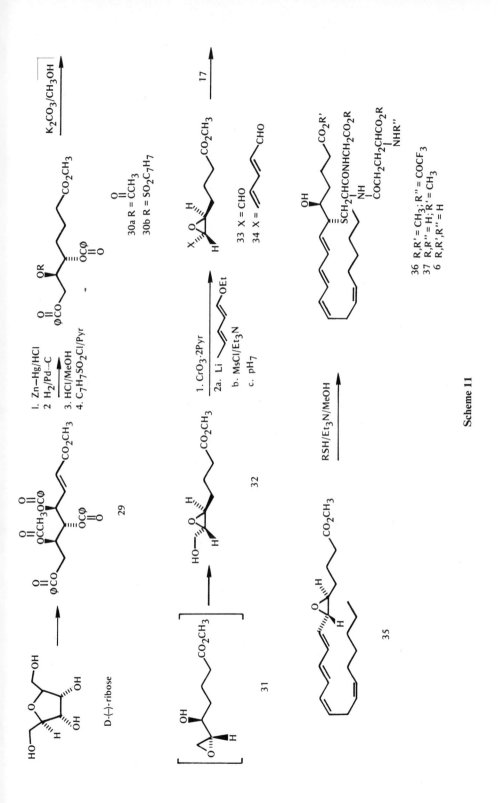

Scheme 11

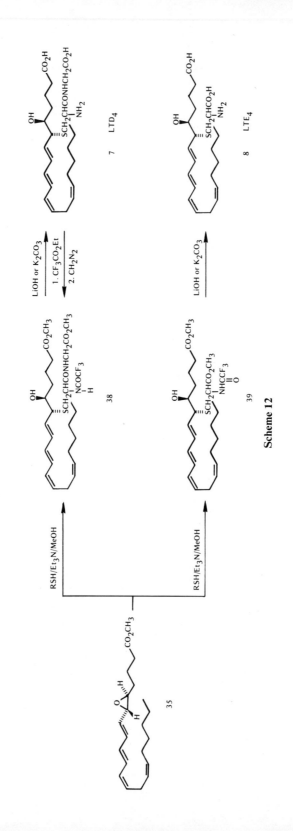

Scheme 12

mastocytoma cells (79). Alternatively, LTA_4 methyl ester could be converted to LTC_4 by reaction with unprotected glutathione followed by base hydrolysis of the resultant monomethyl ester **37**. This total synthesis thus afforded the first unambiguous structure determination of a naturally occurring slow-reacting substance of anaphylaxis. In addition, the synthetic acid LTA_4 (prepared by lithium hydroxide hydrolysis of ester **35**) was shown to be enzymatically converted to LTB_4, thus confirming the stereochemical structure of this key biosynthetic intermediate (120). The generation of the $5S,6R$-diastereomer by S_N2 epoxide opening mimics the biosynthetic step that probably also occurs by simple S_N2 reaction.

The identification of LTD_4 as a natural SRS followed shortly thereafter, when three groups reported cysteinylglycine to be the peptide on an SRS isolated from rat basophilic leukemia cells (97,111) and rat peritoneum (6). Leukotriene D_4 was also shown to be derived from LTC_4 by the action of γ-glutamyl transpeptidase (111). The SRS-A released on immunological challenge of sensitized guinea pig lung was shown to be identical to the SRS from nonimmunological challenge with the aid of electron impact mass spectrometry (98). Reaction of LTA_4 methyl ester with N-trifluoroacetylcysteinylglycine methyl ester (**24**) produced a single conjugate, as expected, whose structure was again supported by UV, ^{1}H-NMR, and mass spectral data (Scheme 12). Hydrolysis with lithium hydroxide or potassium carbonate afforded a single diastereomer that was shown to be identical to SRS-A isolated from rat peritoneal cavity and human lung (50,87). Synthetic LTD_4 was also cleanly reconverted to the N-trifluoroacetyl dimethyl ester derivative **38** to demonstrate again that no other changes occurred during protecting-group hydrolysis. Interestingly, this $5S,6R$-isomer was shown to be the same diastereomer that was found to be 10 times more active than LTC_4 on guinea pig ileum during the initial identification of the peptide moiety on LTC_4. This early result was perhaps the first evidence that a family of naturally occurring SRS-As existed. Finally, the cysteine $5S,6R$-diastereomer was prepared using the same synthetic methodology, and this adduct was shown to be identical to a third SRS-A component from rat peritoneum (88).

IV. TRIENIC ISOMERS OF LTA₄ AND LTC₄

A second slow-reacting substance was also isolated from mouse mastocytoma cells, which was originally termed leukotriene C-2 (17). Samuelsson demonstrated that this substance had a slightly longer retention time on reverse-phase HPLC, was less active on guinea pig ileum (one-tenth that of

LTC$_4$), had a UV λ_{max} of 278 nm, and did not react with lipoxygenase. These data were suggestive of an all-*trans*-7,9,11-triene system. It was also observed during early synthetic work that basic hydrolysis of homogeneous *N*-trifluoroacetyl trimethyl ester **36** produced a mixture of LTC$_4$ and LTC-2, and that the ratio of LTC-2 increased if air was present during hydrolysis. This result would require isomerization of the cis C-11 double bond to the thermodynamically more stable trans unit by a radical chain mechanism initiated by oxygen. Model studies demonstrated that epimerization of the peptide moiety under the hydrolysis conditions was unlikely, thus ruling out this possibility.

To verify this hypothesis, 11-*trans*-LTA$_4$ methyl ester was synthesized (30,50,87) by modification of the Wittig condensation between dienal **34** and ylide **17** (Scheme 13). Reaction between **34** and **17** at 0°C in ether–tetrahydrofuran (THF) in the presence of lithium iodide produced a mixture (3:1) of LTA$_4$ methyl ester **35** and 11-*trans*-LTA$_4$ methyl ester **40**. The mixture was not separated but was converted to the separable glutathione adducts **37** and **41**. The purified monomethyl ester **41** (λ_{max}^{MeOH} 278 nm) was hydrolyzed with potassium carbonate to afford 11-*trans*-LTC$_4$, which was identical to the native material by HPLC retention time, UV spectroscopy, and bioassay on guinea pig ileum. Similar isomerizations for synthetic LTD$_4$ and LTE$_4$ have been observed to produce the corresponding 11-*trans*-isomers. To date these substances have not been isolated from natural sources and characterized. The question whether 11-*trans*-LTC$_4$ is naturally biosynthesized under enzymic control cannot be settled at present. Experimental observations on the stability of pure leukotriene C$_4$ under conditions used for the isolation of 11-*trans*-LTC$_4$ from mastocytoma cells argue against the possibility that 11-*trans*-LTC$_4$ is an artifact produced during isolation.

In their original report of the synthesis of (−)-LTA$_4$ methyl ester Corey *et al.* (46) reported the reaction of (Z,Z)-dienic phosphonium ylid **43** and enal **44** (prepared from aldehyde **33** and the *tert*-butylimine of trimethylsilylacetaldehyde). The reaction produced an inseparable (TLC) mixture of LTA$_4$ methyl ester **35** and the (7E,9Z,11E)-trienic epoxide **45** (originally misassigned as the 7E,9Z,11Z-isomer), which was converted to the (7E,9Z,11E)-LTC$_4$ isomer (Scheme 14). This reaction sequence was later reported by two other groups (9,67), and Baker (9) reported the isolation of three trienic isomers whose ratios were solvent-dependent. Separation of the isomers by HPLC and detailed 270-MHz ^{1}H-NMR analysis showed these trienes to be isomeric at the C-9 and C-11 double bonds. This group also found that the 7E,9Z,11Z-isomer **46** readily underwent a rearrangement at room temperature to the conjugated tetraene **47**. A similar rearrangement presumed to proceed by a 1,7-hydrogen shift had been reported earlier by Rokach (122).

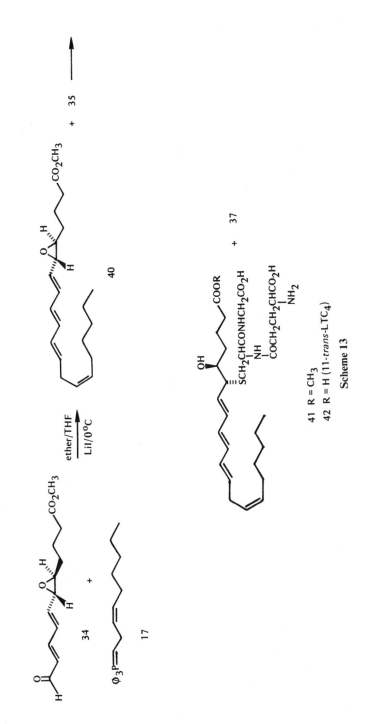

34 + 17 → 40 + 35

$\Phi_3P=$ (17)

ether/THF
LiI/0°C

40

41 R = CH$_3$
42 R = H (11-*trans*-LTC$_4$)

Scheme 13

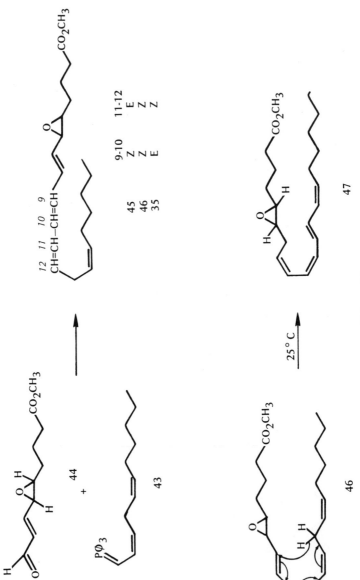

Scheme 14

V. ADDITIONAL SYNTHESES OF LTA$_4$ AND DIASTEREOMERS

Since the original report of the preparation of LTA$_4$ from D-(−)-ribose, several groups have reported syntheses of this material or the key intermediate epoxyaldehyde **33** in racemic or optically active form. One of the earliest syntheses of racemic LTA$_4$ methyl ester was reported by Rosenberg at Hoffmann La Roche (127). The oxirane moiety was constructed by condensation of sulfonium salt **50d** and methyl 4-formylbutyrate in a similar manner to the original synthesis of racemic **19b** (Scheme 15). The sulfonium salt **50d** was prepared in several steps by copper-catalyzed coupling of 1-bromo-2-octyne (**48**) with the ethyl vinyl ether adduct of (E)-1-hydroxy-2-pentene-4-yne (**49**), followed by hydrolysis to afford alcohol **50a**. This alcohol was converted to the *trans,trans*-bromide, which on treatment with tetrahydrothiophene yielded the unstable sulfonium salt **50d**. The salt **50d** and methyl 4-formylbutyrate were treated with the phase-transfer catalyst benzyltriethylammonium chloride to afford a 3:1 mixture of *trans–cis*-epoxides, which were separable by preparative HPLC. Hydrogenation of the *trans*-epoxide produced racemic LTA$_4$ methyl ester **19b**. Reaction of this oxirane with L-cysteine methyl ester and triethylamine in water–methanol at pH 8.5 generated two separable diastereomeric cysteine adducts, and subsequent hydrolysis produced LTE$_4$.

A second report from the Hoffmann La Roche group (31) utilized D-araboascorbic acid and L-diethyl tartrate as starting materials to prepare epoxyaldehyde **33** (Scheme 16). 2,3-O-Isopropylidene-D-erythrose was prepared by modification of known methods and was converted to lactone **53** by straightforward procedures. Mesylation followed by lactone opening and epoxide formation generated alcohol **32**, which was oxidized to aldehyde **33**. The (5S,6R)-*cis*-epoxide **55** was prepared from the *trans*-diol **54** by a similar reaction sequence.

Rokach at Merck has published several different routes to LTA$_4$ methyl

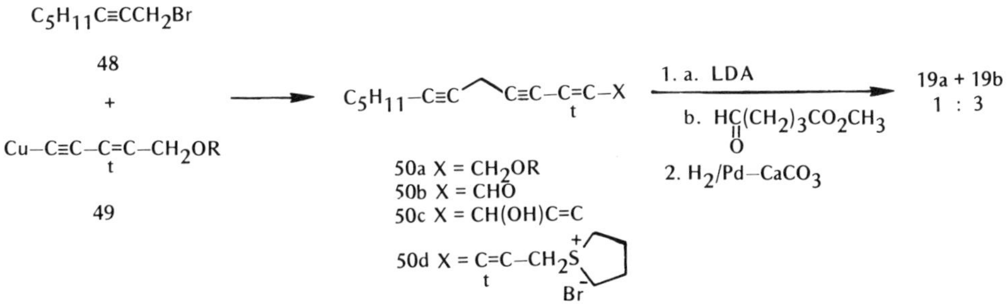

Scheme 15

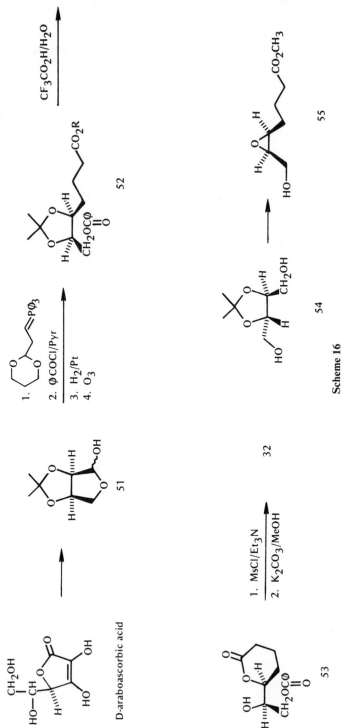

Scheme 16

ester. In the first synthesis by this group (122), Wittig condensation between dienal **56** and phosphonium ylide **17** produced the ester **57**, which was reduced to tetraenic alcohol **18a**, the intermediate in the first Harvard synthesis (Scheme 17). The alcohol was converted by analogous chemistry to a mixture of *cis–trans*-epoxides, which were separated by HPLC. The introduction of the C-6 thio substituent was accomplished from *trans*-epoxide **19b** using the *S*-trimethylsilyl derivatives of methyl *N*-trifluoroacetylcysteine or dimethyl *N*-trifluoroacetylglutathione in dichloromethane to afford the corresponding 5*S*,6*R* and 5*R*,6*S* diastereomeric sulfides in each case. In this same article the synthesis of trienic alcohol **59b** from dienal **58** and ylide **17** was reported. Attempts to convert alcohol **59b** to the (7*E*,9*Z*,11*Z*)-trienic epoxide **46** were frustrated, however, by the instability of alcohol **59b**. On standing at room temperature for 1 to 2 days this alcohol underwent rearrangement to the tetraene **60** presumably by a 1,7-hydrogen shift. This observation cast serious doubt on the possibility of this trienic geometry for LTA_4 or SRS, a result that was subsequently verified by Baker (9).

Rokach (123) later reported the synthesis of the four enantiomerically pure stereoisomers of **33** from D- and L-glyceraldehyde (Scheme 18). Wittig reaction of the acetonide of D-glyceraldehyde generated *cis*-olefin **62**, which was isomerized to the *trans*-olefin **63**. Reaction of **63** with m-CPBA afforded a mixture of separable diastereomeric epoxides, which unfortunately favored the isomer with the unnatural configuration at C-5 and C-6. The same reaction sequence starting from the acetonide of L-glyceraldehyde (synthesized from arabinose) afforded the natural LTA_4 configuration as the major isomer. The *cis*-olefin **62** was also epoxidized to form a separable mixture of the corresponding *cis*-epoxides. Oxidative cleavage with periodate of each epoxide diastereomer afforded the corresponding enantiomerically pure isomer of **33**. The natural 5*S*,6*R*-isomer was converted to dienal **34** by successive Wittig condensations with formylmethylenetriphenylphosphorane. The dienal **34** was transformed into LTA_4 methyl ester by the standard Wittig process. Conversions to LTC_4, LTD_4, and LTE_4 using the triethylamine–methanol conditions was straightforward.

A third route to leukotriene A_4 methyl ester (124) started from 2-deoxy-D-ribose using an intermediate first prepared by the Harvard group (48). Wittig reaction of 2-deoxy-D-ribose and phosphonium ylide **66** (1 equiv.) followed by hydrogenation afforded triol **67a** in 64% yield (Scheme 19). Selective activation of the primary alcohol and treatment with base generated epoxide **32** via the intermediacy of epoxide **31**. Oxidation provided **33**, which was converted to LTA_4 methyl ester in the usual manner. This route was modified to allow the synthesis of the three remaining enantiomerically pure diastereomers of **32**. The enantiomer of **32**, epoxyalcohol **70**, was prepared from triol **67a** by protection of the C-6, C-7 diol, tosylation at C-5, and regenera-

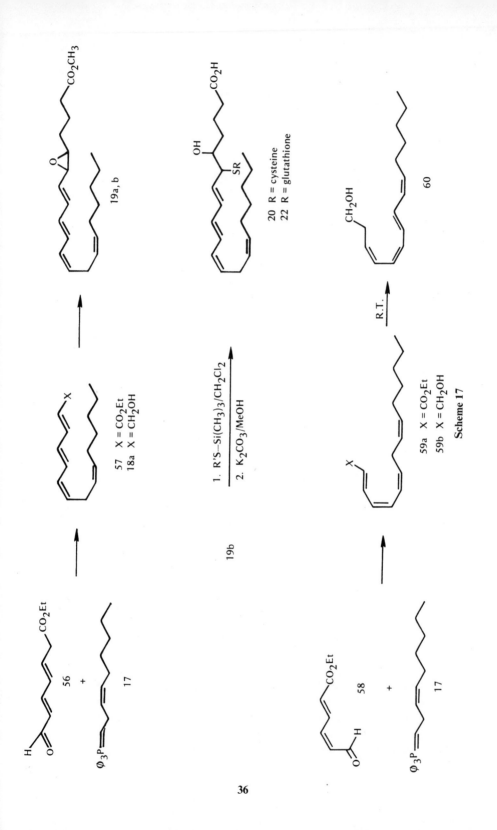

57 X = CO$_2$Et
18a X = CH$_2$OH

19a, b

20 R = cysteine
22 R = glutathione

19b

1. R'S–Si(CH$_3$)$_3$/CH$_2$Cl$_2$
2. K$_2$CO$_3$/MeOH

56

17

58

17

59a X = CO$_2$Et
59b X = CH$_2$OH

60

R.T.

Scheme 17

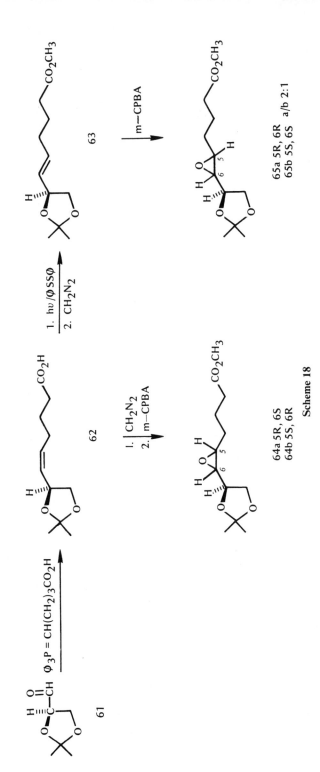

Scheme 18

37

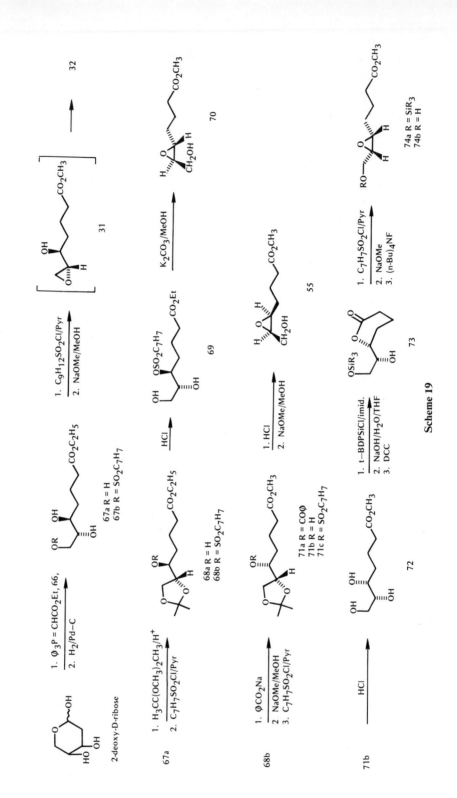

Scheme 19

tion of the diol to afford tosylate **69**. Treatment with base led to oxirane formation with inversion at C-5. The epoxide **70** was then transformed to 5-epi,6-epi-LTA$_4$ methyl ester. Alternatively, inversion at C-5 of ketal tosylate **68b** produced a new ketal tosylate **71c,** which on removal of the protecting group and exposure to base generated *cis*-epoxyalcohol **55**. This substrate was carried on to 6-epi-LTA$_4$ methyl ester. Finally, epoxyalcohol **74b** was prepared by protection of the primary alcohol, lactonization at C-5, tosylation at C-6, and epoxide formation with inversion at C-6.

A fourth route to leukotriene A$_4$ methyl ester was reported by the Merck group (125), which again utilized 2-deoxy-D-ribose and proceeded through C-glycoside **75a** (Scheme 20). Wittig reaction between 2-deoxy-D-ribose and ylide **66** (2 equiv.) produced C-glycoside **75a** in 80% yield. Tosylation of the primary alcohol followed by anion formation and β elimination afforded unsaturated epoxyalcohol **76**. Hydrogenation and treatment with base produced the LTA$_4$ methyl ester intermediate alcohol **33**. The diastereomeric alcohols **70** and **74b** were also prepared from C-glycoside **75a**.

A Fisons group (92) has also utilized 2-deoxy-D-ribose for the synthesis of LTA$_4$ methyl ester in a reaction sequence that intersects the original Harvard synthesis at the key intermediate dibenzoate tosylate (Scheme 21). The dibenzoate of 2-deoxy-D-ribose was reacted with ylide **66** (1.5 equiv.) to afford olefin **78** as a mixture of geometrical isomers ($E:Z$ 83:17). Hydrogenation, ester exchange, and tosylation afforded the known tosylate **30b**.

Stereospecific synthesis of 6-epileukotrienes A$_4$, C$_4$, and D$_4$ has been accomplished (35) starting from D-(+)-mannose (Scheme 22). The glycol

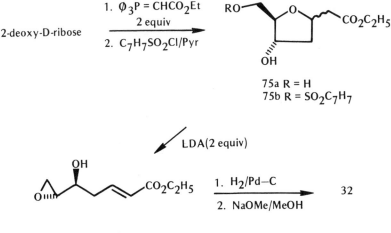

75a R = H
75b R = SO$_2$C$_7$H$_7$

Scheme 20

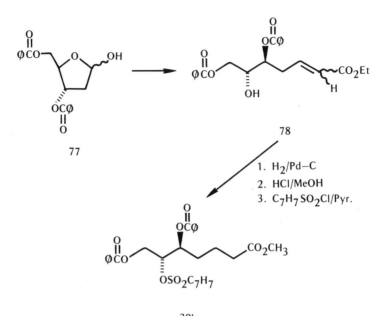

Scheme 21

monoacetonide **80** was prepared by known procedures and was transformed to the corresponding cyclic hemiacetal by hydroxy mercuration and reduction. Wittig condensation and subsequent reduction afforded alcohol **81a,** which was protected as the tetrahydropyranyl ether. Treatment of **81b** with tetra-*n*-butylammonium fluoride followed by base generated hydroxy ester **82a.** Protecting-group exchange afforded tosylate **82d,** which was transformed to *cis*-epoxyaldehyde **84** by the sequence: (1) conversion of the diol ketal to a cyclic orthoacetate, (2) reaction with potassium carbonate to generate the *cis*-epoxide **83,** (3) exposure to trace PyrHTsO⁻ to convert the cyclic orthoacetate to a monoacetate, (4) deacetylation with potassium carbonate, and (5) oxidative glycol cleavage with lead tetraacetate. The aldehyde **84** was converted to 6-epi-LTA$_4$ methyl ester, 6-epi-LTC$_4$, and 6-epi-LTD$_4$ by the standard sequence of reactions. To date, these isomers have not been identified from natural sources.

An alternative approach to the synthesis of chiral epoxide **32** utilizes the recently discovered asymmetric epoxidation procedure of Sharpless (83). Both Sharpless (128) and the Harvard group (53) have reported syntheses of **32** utilizing as substrates different allylic alcohols (Scheme 23). The Sharpless substrate **85a** was obtained by palladium-catalyzed dimerization of butadiene. The Harvard substrate **85b** was obtained in a short reaction

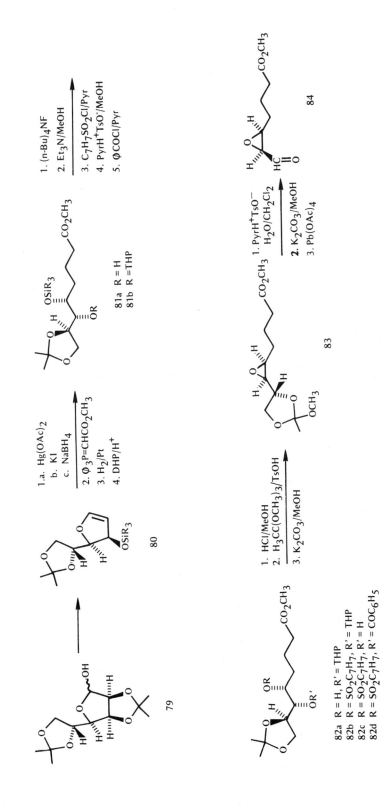

Scheme 22

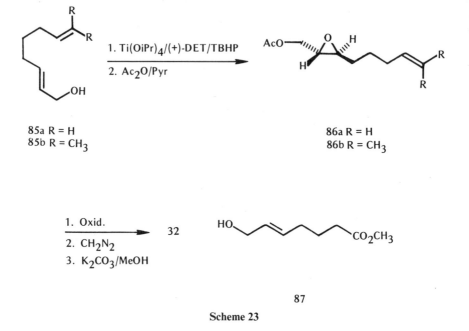

85a R = H
85b R = CH₃

86a R = H
86b R = CH₃

87

Scheme 23

sequence using the components of 1-bromo-3-methyl-2-butene, *tert*-butyl-lithioacetate, and propargyl alcohol. Reaction of alcohols **85a** or **85b** under nearly identical reaction sequences using *tert*-butylhydroperoxide, L-(+)-diethyl tartrate, and titanium isopropoxide afforded the requisite epoxyal-cohols. Conversion to the ester **32** proceeded in four steps. The enantiomeric excess was excellent in each case (95 and 93%, respectively). Yields from the more obvious substrate **87** were not good because of decomposition of the product under the epoxidation conditions.

A biomimetic approach to the synthesis of LTA₄ methyl ester has been reported by Corey *et al.* (32,41). Racemic 5-HPETE was synthesized (40) in a very short reaction scheme from arachidonic acid (Scheme 24). Alternatively, (5*S*)-HPETE was prepared in an enzymic reaction. Thus, reaction of arachidonic acid with potato lipoxygenase afforded after diazomethane treatment (5*S*)-HPETE methyl ester **90a** as the major hydroperoxy product in 10% yield. Conversion of the hydroperoxy ester to the activated peroxytri-fluoromethanesulfonate **90b** in the presence of a sterically hindered base, 1,2,2,6,6-pentamethylpiperidine, led to 1,7-elimination to form LTA₄ methyl ester (33%) and 1,2-elimination to generate dienic ketone **91** (8%). The isolated LTA₄ methyl ester was identical to the previously synthesized epoxide, and was further converted to LTC₄, which was identical to native SRS-A. Sih (3) later reported a similar procedure that gave in addition to **35**

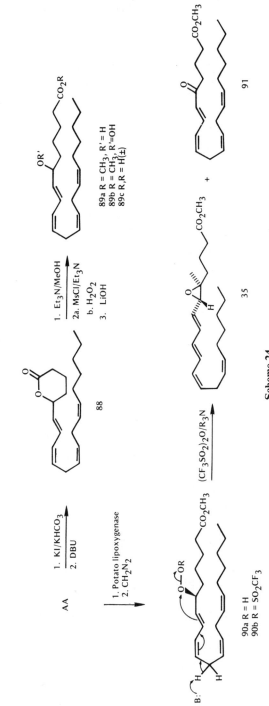

89a R = CH$_3$, R' = H
89b R = CH$_3$, R'=OH
89c R,R = H($\pm$)

1. Et$_3$N/MeOH
2a. MsCl/Et$_3$N
 b. H$_2$O$_2$
3. LiOH

88

91

35

Scheme 24

AA

1. KI/KHCO$_3$
2. DBU

1. Potato lipoxygenase
2. CH$_2$N$_2$

(CF$_3$SO$_2$)$_2$O/R$_3$N

90a R = H
90b R = SO$_2$CF$_3$

and **91** the isomeric epoxide **46**. The use of racemic 5-HPETE has the advantage of ready availability in quantity, but the disadvantage of requiring separation of diastereomers of LTC_4 (or other leukotrienes). The use of (5S)-HPETE provides milligram quantities of the natural SRS-As in a very short reaction sequence.

VI. SYNTHESIS OF LEUKOTRIENE B₄ AND ITS ISOMERS

A. Introduction

Leukotriene B_4 (**5**) (LTB_4), originally isolated by Borgeat and Samuelsson (14), is enzymatically derived from leukotriene A_4. The correct formulation has been demonstrated by synthesis (48) as (5S,12R)-dihydroxy-6-*cis*-8-*trans*-10-*trans*-14-*cis*-eicosatetraenoic acid. Numerous studies have shown LTB_4 to be a biologically active substance, and considerable attention has been focused on the strong possibility that LTB_4 is an endogenous mediator of various *in vivo* inflammatory responses. For example, Ford-Hutchinson *et al.* (65) were the first to demonstrate that LTB_4 stimulated neutrophil aggregation and chemokinesis *in vitro,* as well as induction of leukocyte migration *in vivo.* In addition to the *in vitro* neutrophil response such as aggregation (65), chemokinesis (65,113,146), chemotaxis (69,113,146), degranulation (69,139), hexose transport (11), and cation flux (101), the myotropic effects of LTB_4 on guinea pig parenchymal strips has been reported (144). It has also been shown that LTB_4 induces the secretion of lysosomal enzyme from PMN *in vitro* (112), as well as causing an increase in muscular permeability in the presence of a vasodilator such as PGE_2 (22). Since LTB_4 is the most potent chemokinetic and chemotactic lipoxygenase product so far tested (65,113) (it is at least 100–1000 times as active as the most potent HETE or HPETE, with maximal activity between 0.1 and 1.0 ng/ml), it is reasonable to expect that LTB_4 might be an important mediator both in immediate hypersensitivity reaction and in inflammation. Although thus far no direct proof exists for endogenously formed LTB_4 being involved in *in vivo* inflammatory responses, Goetzl *et al.* (85) have demonstrated that significant levels of LTB_4 have been found in joint aspirates from patients with rheumatoid arthritis and spondyloarthritis. A minireview summarizing various biological data to date has appeared (145).

The rarity of native LTB and the lack of a detailed structural assignment have prompted various studies dealing with detection, activity, structural identification, and synthesis of this important compound, The Harvard group (48,49,55–57) was the first to report the complete elucidation of its structure as well as the preparation of gram quantities of LTB_4 by an efficient, stereoselective total synthesis.

When LTA$_4$ methyl ester **35** is treated with mild acid or exposed to silica gel, six diastereomeric dihydroxy-7,9,11,14-eicosatetraenoic acids are obtained, four of which are 5,6-diols that are readily cleaved by treatment with aqueous periodate. In addition, two diastereomeric 5,12-dihydroxy-6,8,10,14-eicosatetraenoic acids were obtained, which are different from LTB$_4$ and which do not react with periodate. The two diastereomeric 5,12-diols derived from LTA$_4$ possess an all-trans-geometry in the conjugated triene unit as evidenced by comparison of the UV absorption (λ_{max} = 258, 268, 278 nm $\pm$ 0.5) with that of native LTB$_4$ (UV λ_{max} = 260, 270, 280 nm $\pm$ 0.5), as well as by comparison with totally synthetic reference samples (*vide infra*). As mentioned earlier, using naturally derived LTB$_4$, Borgeat and Samuelsson (14,16) were able to determine the configuration to be 5S,12R. This was followed by their prediction that the most probable 6,8,12-triene geometry involved two trans and one cis double bond. The question still remained, however, of the exact stereochemistry (or geometry) of native LTB$_4$. By analysis of the transition state for cation formation that leads to the three possible isomers of LTB$_4$, it was surmised (48) that the most energetically favored should be that affording the 6-*cis*-8-*trans*-10-*trans*-triene **5**, and the least favored should be that which leads to the 6-*trans*-8-*trans*-10-*cis*-isomer **92,** with the 6-*trans*-8-*cis*-10-*trans*-isomer **93** intermediate. The reasoning was that the formation of isomer **92** would involve severe repulsion between the HC(9) and H$_2$C(13) groups, whereas formation of **93** would involve less steric repulsion, principally between the HC(7) and HC(10) groups. The formation of **5** entails relatively little if any steric repulsion (Scheme 25).

On the basis of the preceding analysis, structure **5** was initially favored for LTB$_4$, a supposition that was later proved to be correct by a complete structural elucidation (48,49,55) and the first stereocontrolled total synthesis of LTB$_4$ **5,** as well as the synthesis of isomers **92** and **93.**

B. Synthesis of (5S,12R)-Dihydroxy-6,14-*cis*-8,10-*trans*-Eicosatetraenoic Acid (5) LTB$_4$

The first convergent synthesis of LTB$_4$ **5**(48) was accomplished by coupling C-1–C-6 segment **94** and C-7–C-20 segment **95** (Scheme 26).

The optically active C-1–C-6 segment **94** was constructed starting with readily available 2-deoxy-D-ribose. Thus, reaction of 2-deoxyribose with 2-methoxypropene catalyzed by pyridinium tosylate afforded deoxyribo-pyranose-3,4-acetonide **96** in 60% yield. Reaction of acetonide **96** with a slight excess of [(methoxycarbonyl)methylene]triphenylphosphorane followed by hydrogenation afforded the hydroxy ester intermediate **97** in 95% overall yield. Tosylation of **97** gave the corresponding monotosylate ketal, which was deketalized (HCl, methanol) to a glycol, which was further con-

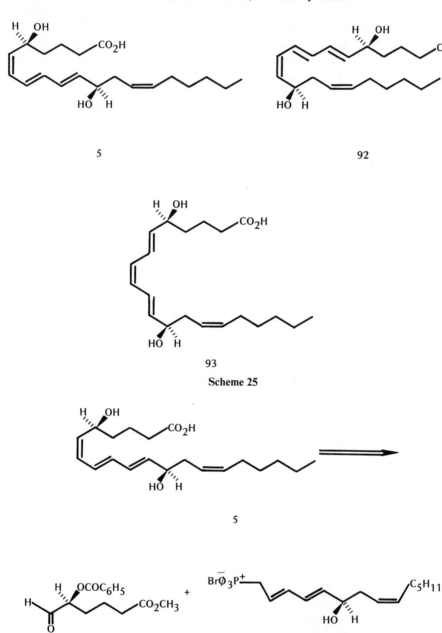

5

92

93

Scheme 25

5

94   +   95

Scheme 26

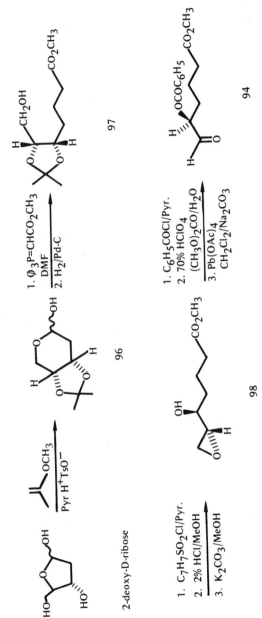

Scheme 27

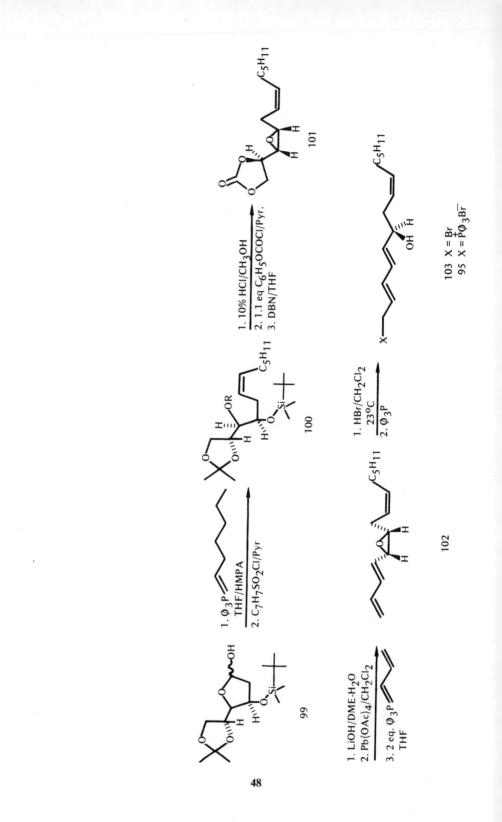

99

1. Φ₃P
THF/HMPA
2. C₇H₇SO₂Cl/Pyr

100

1. 10% HCl/CH₃OH
2. 1.1 eq C₆H₅OCOCl/Pyr.
3. DBN/THF

101

1. LiOH/DME-H₂O
2. Pb(OAc)₄/CH₂Cl₂
3. 2 eq. Φ₃P
THF

102

1. HBr/CH₂Cl₂
23°C
2. Φ₃P

103 X = Br
95 X = ⁺PΦ₃Br⁻

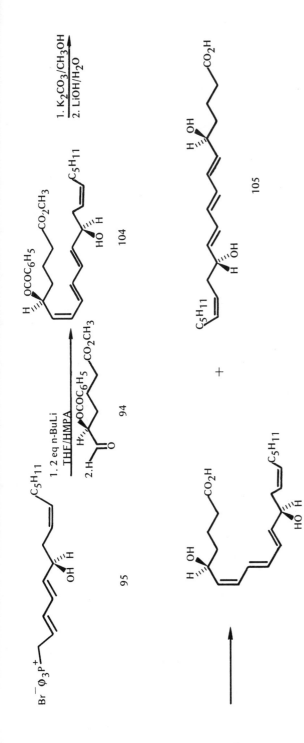

Scheme 28

49

verted with potassium carbonate in methanol to the epoxyester **98** in 90% overall yield from **97**. Epoxyester **98** was next converted to the C-1–C-6 segment, aldehyde ester **94,** in 74% overall yield by a sequence of reactions involving (1) benzylation of the hydroxy group in **98** (2) oxirane-1,2-glycol hydration employing perchloric acid in dimethyl carbonate–water, and (3) cleavage of the resulting 5-benzoyloxy-6,7-dihydroxyheptanoate to the aldehyde ester **94** employing lead tetraacetate in methylene chloride containing sodium carbonate as a buffer (Scheme 27).

The C-7–C-20 segment **95** was prepared in a stereochemically unambiguous manner starting with hemiacetal **99**, which had been synthesized previously (35) starting with D-(+)-mannose in 57% overall yield. A stereospecific Wittig reaction of **99** with *n*-hexylidenetriphenylphosphorane in 9:1 THF–HMPA gave the *cis*-olefin **100** (R = H), which, when treated with an excess of tosyl chloride in neat pyridine, afforded tosylate **100**(R = Ts) in nearly quantitative yield. Deprotection of tosylate **100** with dry HCl and reaction of the resulting triol with phenyl chloroformate followed by reaction of the resulting carbonate with an excess of diazobicyclo[4.3.0]nonene in THF at 75°C provided the *cis*-epoxide **101** in 66% overall yield from **100** (R = Ts). Hydrolysis of the carbonate **101**, cleavage of the resulting 1,2-diol with lead tetraacetate, and reaction of the resulting aldehyde with two equivalents of allylidenetriphenylphosphorane cleanly gave acid-sensitive epoxytriene **102** in 62% overall yield from **101**. Reaction of acid-sensitive epoxytriene **102** with a slight excess of dry hydrogen bromide resulted in stereospecific conversion of this reactive triene to the even less stable bromoalcohol **103**. *In situ* coupling of this intermediate with excess triphenylphosphine in methylene chloride afforded crystalline phosphonium bromide **103** (X = Ph$_3$P$^+$Br$^-$), the C-7–C-20 segment, in 60 to 70% overall yield from **102**. Wittig reaction of the corresponding ylide derived from phosphonium salt **103** by reaction with 2 equivalents of *n*-butyllithium with C-1–C-7 segment–aldehyde ester **94** afforded the desired triene ester **104**. Hydrolysis of the ester groups with potassium carbonate and lithium hydroxide, followed by acidification, proceeded cleanly and afforded leukotriene LTB$_4$ **5** along with ~15% of the readily separable 6-*trans*-isomer **105**, the result of a minor degree of nonselectivity in the coupling step. The synthetic LTB$_4$ **5** obtained via this route was indistinguishable from native LTB$_4$ by spectroscopic comparison (UV, methanol λ_{max} = 260, 270.5, 281 nm ± .05, RP-HPLC, and high-field NMR) as well as by biological comparison of chemotactic activity toward neutrophils and effects on pulmonary tissue. The identity of synthetic LTB$_4$ **5** with native LTB$_4$ and the observed differences (*vide infra*) in the properties of LTB$_4$ **5** compared to those of isomers **92, 93,** and **105,** allowed the first unambiguous assignment of the correct structure for this naturally occurring leukotriene (Scheme 28).

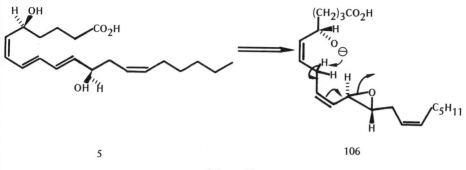

5   106

Scheme 29

Shortly after the first synthesis of LTB$_4$ **5**, the Harvard group (55) reported a second, more efficient and fully stereocontrolled synthesis of **5**. This synthesis, like the first one, was fully convergent, but in addition it was economically very efficient and provided LTB$_4$ **5** as a single isomer in gram amounts. The key step in this improved synthesis makes use of a novel, internally promoted elimination reaction of epoxy acid intermediate **106** (Scheme 29). This reaction, which allows stereospecific generation of the conjugated triene unit, takes advantage of both the *cis*-Δ^6-olefinic linkage and the hydroxy function of LTB$_4$ to provide a low-energy pathway for its formation.

The key intermediate *cis*-triene ester **107** was prepared via a sequence of convergent steps that once again called for the preparation of two major segments: a C-1–C-6 segment (aldehyde ester **94**) and a C-7–C-20 segment (phosphonium salt **108**). Phosphonium salt **108** was prepared starting with 2,3-oxidoundeca-2-*trans*-5-*cis*-dien-1-ol (47,49) (**109**), which was also a key intermediate for the synthesis of LTB$_4$ isomer **93** (see Scheme 33). Collins oxidation of epoxide **109** followed by reaction of the resulting aldehyde with the ylide prepared from the 2-methoxy-2-propyl ester (49) and *n*-butyllithium afforded the cis-olefination product **110** ($X = $ OC(CH$_3$)$_2$OCH$_3$) in 92% yield. Deprotection of this ether by exposure to acetic acid in acetonitrile–water provides, in 72% yield, alcohol **110** ($X = $ OH), which was converted to phosphonium salt **108** via the corresponding tosylate and iodide under standard conditions (Scheme 30).

The second key intermediate, C-1–C-6 fragment **94**, was synthesized from 2-deoxyribose by a modification of the approach developed for the first LTB$_4$ synthesis (see Scheme 27). Wittig reaction of 2-deoxyribose with methoxycarbonylmethylenetriphenylphosphorane in the presence of trace benzoic acid gave triol ester **111**, which was converted to the epoxydiester **112** in 67% overall yield by a four-step reaction sequence involving (1) hydrogenation, (2) selective monotosylation of the primary alcohol, (3) epoxide for-

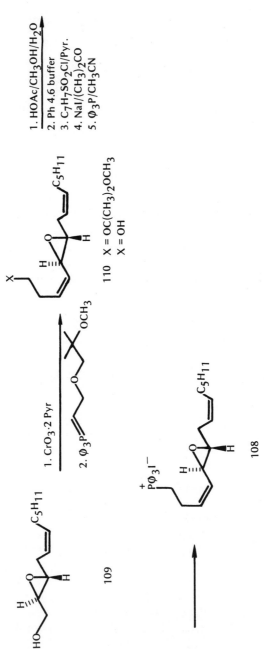

110   X = OC(CH$_3$)$_2$OCH$_3$
         X = OH

1. CrO$_3$·2 Pyr
2. ϕ_3P

109

108

Scheme 30

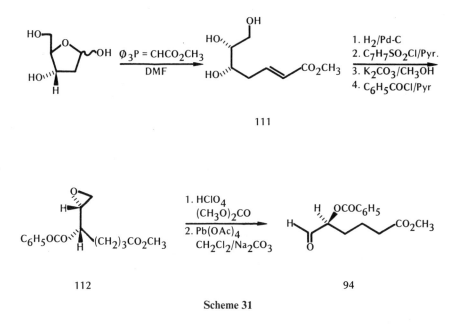

111

112   94

Scheme 31

mation by reaction of the resulting monotosylate with potassium carbonate in methanol, and (4) benzylation. Exposure of the resulting epoxydiester intermediate **112** to 70% perchloric acid in dimethyl carbonate–water followed by the lead tetraacetate cleavage of the resulting diol, provided the C-1–C-6 segment, aldehyde ester **94,** in 77% overall yield (Scheme 31).

Wittig reaction of the ylide derived from the phosphonium salt **108** with aldehyde ester **94** cleanly afforded the all-*cis*-triene diester **107,** which after treatment with methanolic potassium carbonate, hydrolysis, and acidification, generated leukotriene B₄ (**5**) in 75% yield (Scheme 32). No isomers of LTB₄ were detected. The yield of the last "one-pot" three-step process was further improved to greater than 90% simply by substituting potassium *tert*-butoxide–isopropanol for potassium carbonate–methanol. Synthetic LBT₄ obtained via this route was identical in every respect to native LBT₄ and the synthetic LTB₄ obtained by the original route (Scheme 28).

C. Synthesis of LTB₄ Isomers

In order to establish firmly the correct structure of LTB₄ and to rule out even the slightest possibility that natural LTB₄ might be in fact a mixture of stereoisomers, the synthesis was undertaken of the remaining three isomers: 6-*trans*-8-*trans*-10-*cis*-LTB₄ (**92**), 6-*trans*-8-*cis*-10-*trans*-LTB₄ (**93**), and all-*trans*-LTB₄ (**105**). These syntheses also provided material for careful physical

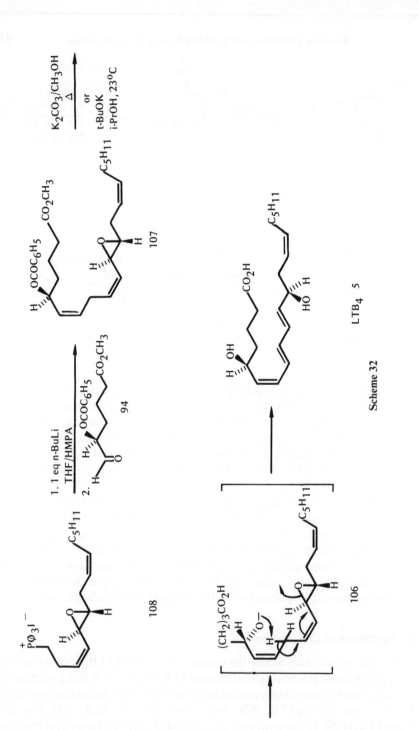

Scheme 32

and biological comparisons of these isomers with natural LTB$_4$. As in the case of the SRS-A work, these syntheses played a key role in the elucidation of structure in complete detail.

D. Synthesis of (5S,12R)-Dihydroxy-6,8-trans-10,14-cis-Eicosatetraenoic Acid (92)

The synthesis of LTB$_4$ stereoisomer 92 (49) was accomplished in an unambiguous and stereospecific manner by the coupling of two key intermediates, functionalized phosphonium salt 113 and methyl (5S,6R)-oxido-7-oxoheptanoate (33). Phosphonium salt 113 was prepared in a multistep sequence starting with 2,5-undecadiyn-1-ol (59) 114, which was converted to phenylurethane intermediate 115 in 75% overall yield by a sequence of reactions involving (1) lithium aluminum hydride reduction, (2) asymmetric epoxidation (138) of the resulting allylic alcohol, (3) Lindlar hydrogenation, and (4) urethane formation by reaction with phenyl isocyanate. Reaction of urethane 115 with perchloric acid followed by protection of the resulting hydroxy carbonate, reductive cleavage of the carbonate, and oxidative glycol cleavage cleanly gave protected aldehyde 116. Wittig reaction of aldehyde 116 with the ylide derived from the 2-methoxy-2-propyl ether of (3-hydroxypropyl)triphenylphosphonium bromide, gave after cleavage of the protecting group, olefinic alcohol 117, free of any trans-isomer. Conversion of 117 to phosphonium salt 113 under standard conditions proceeded cleanly in 84% overall yield. Finally, Wittig reaction of the ylide derived from 113 and aldehyde ester 33 afforded epoxytriene 118 as a single isomer, which was converted to the desired triene-LTB$_4$ isomer 92 in 75% overall yield by a three-step sequence of (1) hydrolysis of the methyl ester, (2) isomerization of the epoxide to the allylic alcohol using a previously developed method (45), and (3) desilylation. This LTB$_4$ isomer, although showing an identical UV absorption to native or synthetic LTB$_4$, was clearly distinguished by RP-HPLC and was found to be biologically inactive as a chemotactic agent for neutrophils and had no effect on pulmonary smooth muscles (Scheme 33).

E. Synthesis of (±)-Dihydroxy-6,10-trans-8,14-cis-Eicosatetraenoic Acid (93) and (5S,12S)-Dihydroxy-6,10-trans-8,14-cis-Eicosatetraenoic Acid (119)

The synthesis of LTB$_4$ isomer 93 as a racemate was first carried out starting from arachidonic acid (1). A previously developed method (44) for selective internal oxygen transfer of peroxy arachidonic acid to the 14,15-double bond was used for the construction of key intermediate 120, which was converted to the desired isomer 93 in a stereochemically controlled

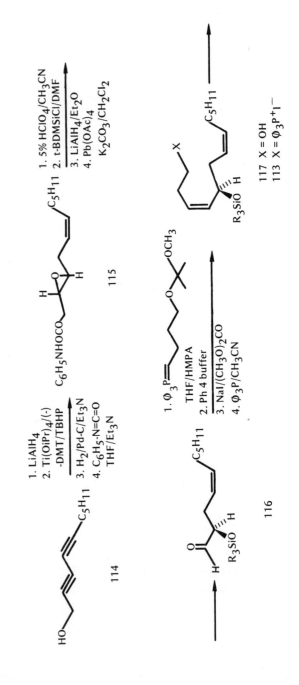

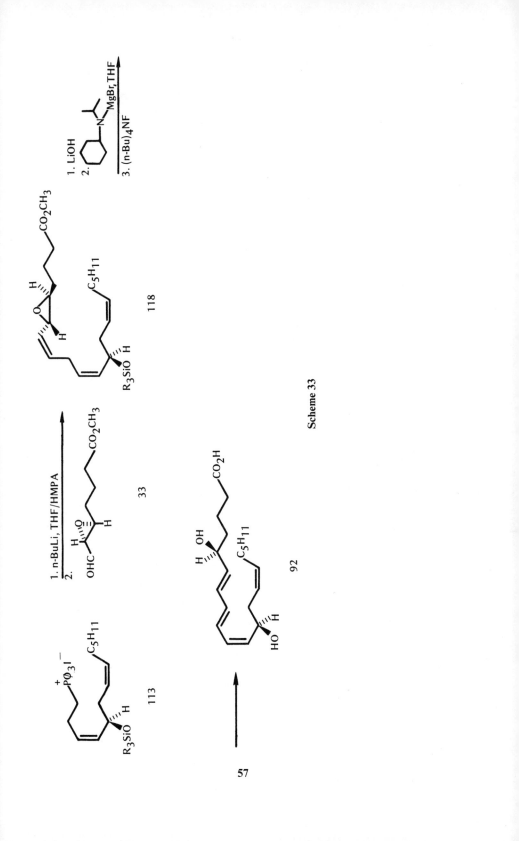

Scheme 33

57

manner employing a minimum number of steps. Conversion of the 14,15-epoxide of arachidonic acid **121** to the corresponding iodolactone followed by elimination and lactone hydrolysis, as described previously for the synthesis of 5-HETE methyl ester (44), afforded the 14,15-epoxide of 5-HETE (**120**). Photosensitized oxygenation of **120** followed by reduction of the resulting hydroperoxide intermediate employing excess triphenylphosphine afforded a mixture of diastereomers **122** and **123** in 55% yield. Deoxygenation of the 14,15-epoxide employing potassium selenocyanate followed by hydrolysis and HPLC purification cleanly gave a mixture of **93** and its diastereomer, which had identical UV absorption (λ_{max} = 258, 268, and 278 nm ± 0.5) (Scheme 34). The less polar diastereomer of **93** was found to be different from synthetic or native LTB$_4$ on the basis of UV, HPLC, and biological evaluation. The more polar racemate, although distinguished by UV, was inseparable by RP-HPLC from LTB$_4$ **5** and showed some chemotactic activity but was inactive in the pulmonary muscle assay.

Because the first synthesis of **93** employed racemic intermediates, it was not possible to determine whether the biologically active compound was the 5S,12S- or the 5S,12R-diastereomer. For this reason an unambiguous synthesis of (5S,12S)-dihydroxy-(6E,10E,8Z,14Z)-eicosatetraenoic acid (**119**) was developed (57). Interestingly, as this work was progressing a Canadian group (21) reported the isolation of a novel metabolite from incubation of (5S)-HETE with blood platelets or (12S)-HETE with leukocytes. It was also reported that this substance could be derived from incubation of arachidonic acid with mixed peripheral blood leukocytes. Furthermore, this metabolite was found to be isomeric with LTB$_4$, having UV λ_{max} absorption of 258, 268, and 278 nm. On the basis of these facts and the data obtained from racemic isomer **93**, it was concluded that the structure of this new metabolite was very likely to be one diastereomer of **93**. Wittig reaction of (5S)-benzoyloxy-5-formylvalerate **94**, prepared as described earlier (48,49), with formylmethylenetriphenylphosphorane cleanly gave key C-1–C-6 segment α,β-unsaturated aldehyde **124**. The C-7–C-20 segment, phosphonium salt **125**, was prepared starting from (2S,3S)-epoxy-(5Z)-undecen-1-ol (**126**), which was prepared by a parallel route previously described (Scheme 33) for the dextro enantiomer **109** (49,55), except that dextro rotatory dimethyl tartrate was used as the chiral director. Collins oxidation of epoxyalcohol **126** followed by Wittig coupling with methylenetriphenylphosphorane provided intermediate epoxydiene **127**, which was converted to hydroxyphosphonium salt **125** ($X = Ph_3P^+Br^-$) by reaction with one equivalent of dry hydrogen bromide followed by *in situ* treatment of the resulting allylic bromide **125** ($X = Br$) with triphenylphosphine. Reaction of phosphonium salt **125** with *n*-butyllithium followed by reaction of the resulting β-oxidoylide with aldehyde **124** gave tetraene ester **128** along with a comparable amount of the isomeric

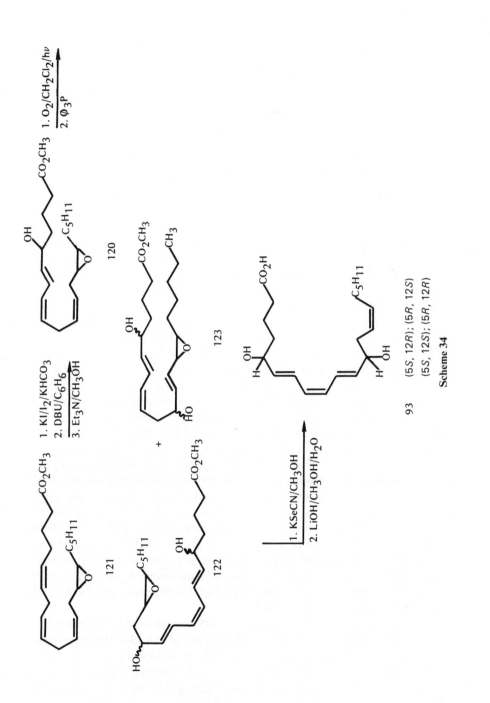

Scheme 34

more polar trans-olefination product, which was readily separable from **128** on silica. Hydrolysis of **128** under standard conditions afforded quantitatively (5S,12S)-dihydroxy-(6E,10E,8Z,14Z)-eicosanoic acid (**119**) (Scheme 35). This metabolite was shown to be identical with native **119** by RP-HPLC, UV, high-field ^{1}H-NMR, and bioassay.

F. Synthesis of the 12R and 12S Forms of 6,8,10-*trans*-14-*cis*-Leukotriene B$_4$ (105 and 129)

It was mentioned earlier that nonenzymatic hydration of LTA$_4$ generated a mixture of two trans-isomers of LTB$_4$ that were diastereomeric at C-12. In order to confirm the structure of these two diastereomeric diols, these last two remaining isomers of LTB$_4$ were synthesized (56) and compared with native LTB$_4$. The key steps of this parallel synthesis made use of (1) a common intermediate for one segment of the final structure, (2) enantiomeric and chiral synthesis of the other segment, and (3) stereospecific coupling of the two segments via a novel β-oxidoylide.

The two key intermediates, β-hydroxyphosphonium salt **130** and dienal ester **131**, had both been prepared previously. β-Hydroxyphosphonium salt **130** was prepared by chiral synthesis from natural S-(−)-malic acid and was a key intermediate in the (12S)-HETE synthesis (43). The dienal **131** was prepared from the ester aldehyde **94** by reaction with 1-lithio-4-ethoxybutadiene, as previously described (46) and as discussed in the synthesis of LTA$_4$. Reaction of β-hydroxyphosphonium salt **130** with *n*-butyllithium and treatment of the resulting β-oxidoylide with dienal **131** afforded all-*trans*-triene ester intermediate **132**. The reaction proceeded in a fully stereospecific manner, and no isomers were detected. Saponification of **132** by exposure to excess potassium carbonate followed by lithium hydroxide gave cleanly all-*trans*-LTB$_4$ isomer **129**, which was found to be homogeneous by RP-HPLC analysis (Scheme 36). The UV absorption (λ_{max} = 259, 269, and 280 nm) and HPLC comparison of this isomer to native or synthetic LTB$_4$ easily distinguished these compounds. Furthermore, synthetic LTB$_4$ isomer **129** was identical by UV and RP-HPLC comparison to one of the diastereomers produced by acid-catalyzed hydrolysis of leukotriene A$_4$ as well as to the by-product obtained in the synthesis of (5S,12S)-dihydroxy-(6E,10E,8Z,14Z)-eicosatetraenoic acid, isomer **119**.

The synthesis of (5S,12R)-LTB$_4$ isomer **105** was achieved by a parallel route employing dienal **131** and hydroxyphosphonium salt **133**. The preparation of **133** required the unnatural form of malic acid [(R)-(+)-isomer] and was accomplished starting with (R,R)-(+)-dimethyl tartrate (natural form) **134**, which was treated with excess saturated hydrogen bromide in acetic acid to give acetyl bromide **135**. Reduction of **135** with *in situ* generated trimethyltin

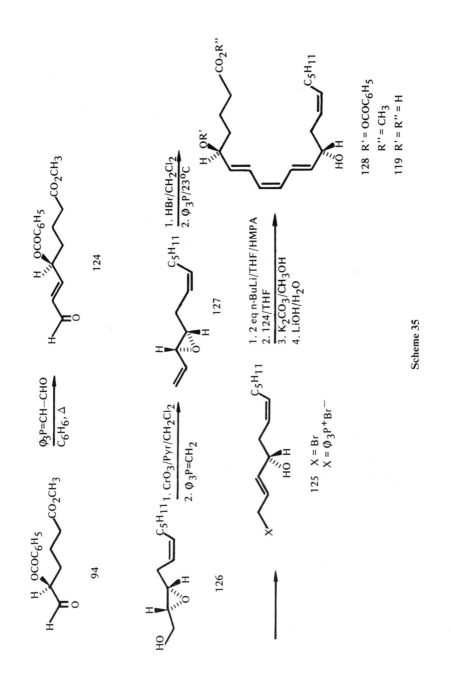

Scheme 35

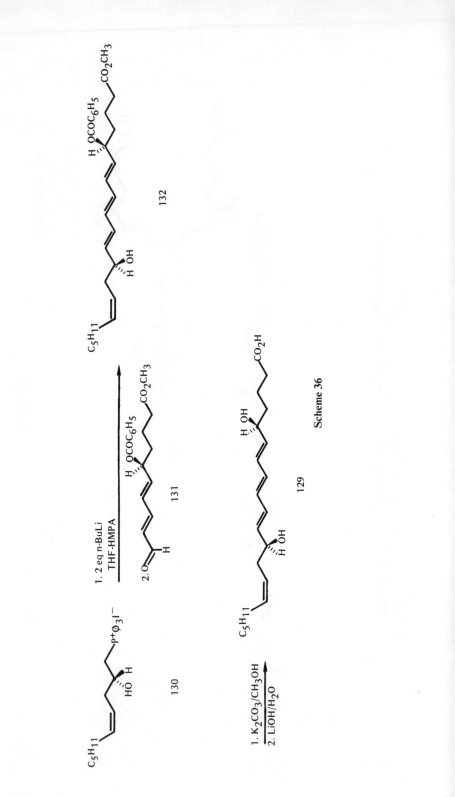

Scheme 36

hydride and deacetylation of the resulting dimethyl acetyl malate afforded after distillation (R)-$(+)$-dimethyl malate **136** in 56% overall yield. The synthesis of phosphonium salt **133** was then carried out following the identical procedure reported earlier (43) for the preparation of phosphonium salt **130**. Wittig condensation of the β-oxidoylide derived from salt **133** by the standard method, and reaction with dienal **131** cleanly gave triene ester **137**, which on hydrolysis gave the (5S,12R)-LTB$_4$ isomer **105** as a single product. This isomer showed UV λ_{max} at 258, 268, and 278 nm in methanol and was indistinguishable from (5S,12R)-*tert-tert-tert*-LTB$_4$ **105** obtained as a minor by-product in the first synthesis of LTB$_4$ **5**. This isomer was also identical to the 5S,12S-diastereomer obtained by nonenzymatic hydration of LTA$_4$ (Scheme 37).

Since the original report of the synthesis of LTB$_4$ as well as isomers **92, 93, 105**, and **129**, only one very recent synthesis of LTB$_4$ has appeared. Once again starting with 2-deoxy-D-ribose, the group at Merck (70) reported a stereospecific synthesis of LTB$_4$ **5** utilizing a novel approach to chiral dienic synthesis. This approach was based on the finding that some C-glycosides possessing a leaving group on the tetrahydrofuran ring, such as compound **138**, can serve nicely as a masked precursor to diene **139** (Scheme 38).

Working from these findings and employing previously described methods (124), glycoside **140** was prepared in 16% overall yield starting with a synthetic precursor to all leukotrienes, 2-deoxy-D-ribose. Removal of the protecting group and subsequent mesylation afforded the key intermediate, glycoside mesylate **141**, which, when treated with sodium ethoxide in ethanol, was cleanly converted to diene **142**. The diene **142** was then converted to phosphonium salt **143** employing a standard procedure. Wittig reaction with aldehyde ester **144** gave a mixture of $\Delta^{6,7}$-*cis*-isomer **145** and $\Delta^{6,7}$-*trans*-isomer **146** in a ratio of 2.5:1. Separation of **145** and **146** by HPLC, followed by removal of the protecting group and hydrolysis, cleanly afforded LTB$_4$ (**5**) in 60% yield (Scheme 39).

G. Synthesis of 14,15-Dehydro-LTB$_4$ (147)

In order to obtain ^{3}H-label LTB$_4$ to facilitate biological studies, the Harvard group (38) has also prepared 14,15-dehydro-LTB$_4$ (**147**). The synthesis of this analog was carried out via a convergent route, again employing a C-1–C-6 segment, aldehyde ester **94**, and a C-7–C-20 segment, phosphonium salt **148**. This salt was prepared in good overall yield starting from (2E)-undecen-5-yn-1-ol (**114**) and employing a sequence of reactions analogous to those used in the preparation of phosphonium salt **108** (see Scheme 30). Wittig coupling of the ylide derived from phosphonium salt **148** with aldehyde ester **94** gave all-*cis*-diene **149** in variable yields of 30 to 50%.

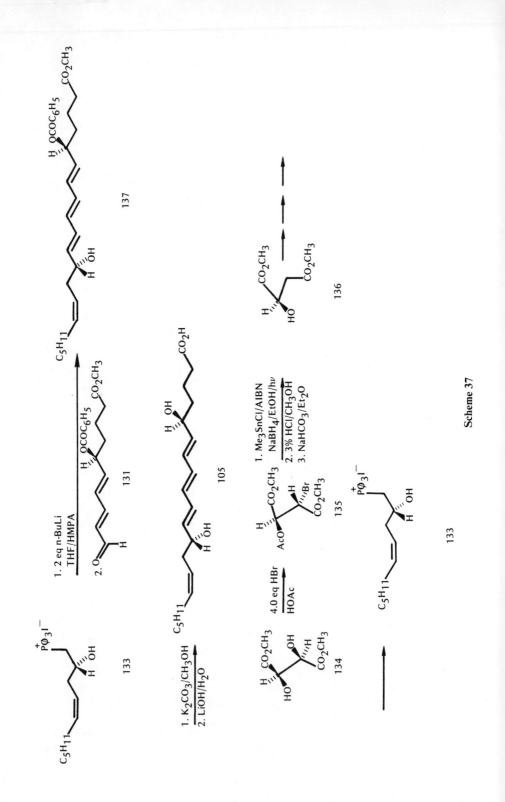

Scheme 37

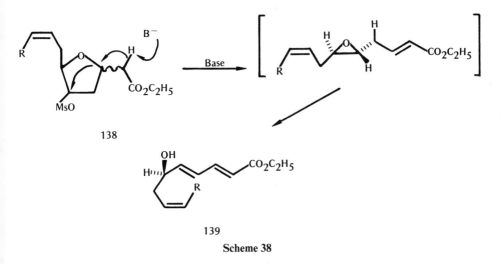

138

139

Scheme 38

Interestingly significant amounts (10–25%) of the strongly UV-active, more polar triene ester **150** were also isolated. Hydrolysis of this compound under standard conditions gave dehydro-LTB$_4$ **147** in quantitative yield. Although the reason for the formation of intermediate **150** was not further investigated, the excess of the ylide used in the reaction or the nature of the workup (THF removal *in vacuo* before workup) may bear some consequence for the observed allylic epoxide opening (Scheme 40).

By analogy to the synthesis of leukotriene B$_4$ (that is, conversion of compound **106** to LTB$_4$; see Scheme 29), it was expected that the conversion of epoxydiene **149** to the desired dehydro-LTB$_4$ **147** would proceed without any problem. However, reaction of compound **149** under various conditions developed for the synthesis of LTB$_4$ gave a rather poor yield (~30%) of dehydro-LTB$_4$ **147**. The major product was not fully characterized but showed a distinct UV absorption of 225 ± 0.5 nm and is probably enyne **151** (Scheme 41).

To circumvent these difficulties, an alternative method was developed. Hydrolysis of diene ester **149** followed by esterification afforded hydroxy ester intermediate **152**. Treatment of **152** with excess DBN followed by the hydrolysis of the methyl ester cleanly generated dehydro-LTB$_4$ **147** in 70% overall yield. The DBN-promoted opening of hydroxy epoxide intermediate **152** provides additional evidence for the original proposal for an internally promoted elimination reaction mechanism in the conversion of epoxide **107** to LTB$_4$ (Scheme 42).

In conclusion, the comparison of synthetic LTB$_4$ with native LTB$_4$ and the observed difference in the properties of the synthetic isomers **92, 93, 105,**

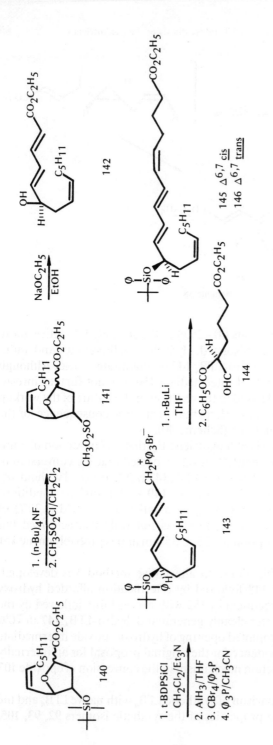

Scheme 39

66

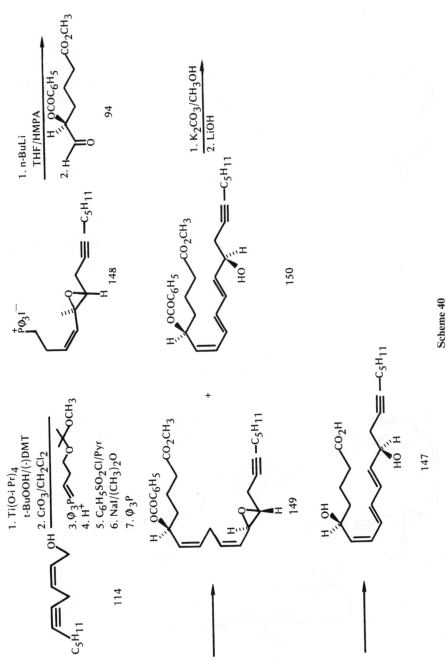

Scheme 40

67

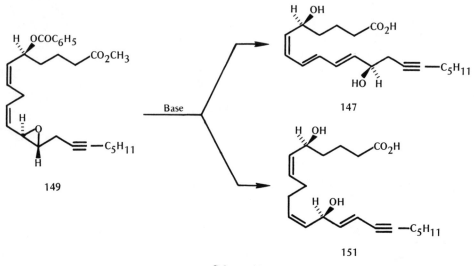

Scheme 41

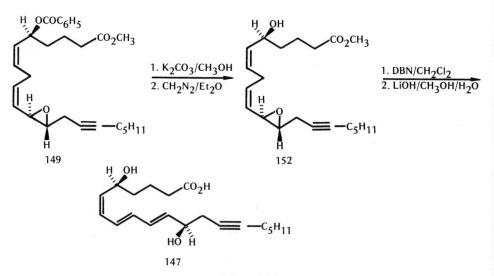

Scheme 42

129, and **147** from that of native or synthetic LTB$_4$ have allowed the unambiguous assignment of the structure of LTB$_4$ and have firmly ruled out the possibility that native LTB$_4$ might exist as a mixture of stereoisomers. The syntheses described are elegant as well as practical and can provide an ample amount of these important compounds, which are bound to produce numerous biological and medical studies of major significance.

VII. SYNTHESIS OF LEUKOTRIENE ANALOGS—MODIFICATION OF THE ω PORTION OF LEUKOTRIENES

A. Synthesis of Leukotriene A Analogs

Since the discovery that the naturally occurring leukotrienes, LTA$_4$, LTB$_4$, LTC, LTD$_4$, and LTE$_4$, are derived via the 5-lipoxygenase pathway, it seems reasonable to speculate whether additional arachidonic acid lipoxygenase metabolites are transformed in a similar manner. Both 12(S)-HPETE and 15(S)-HPETE are known to be generated enzymatically and could, in theory, be predecessors of epoxyeicosatetraenoic acid analogous to leukotriene A$_4$ (i.e., compounds **153** and **154,** respectively). In view of the possibility that these trienic epoxides and their corresponding peptide conjugates might be naturally occurring biologically active eicosanoids, the synthesis of these substances was undertaken (Scheme 43).

The synthesis of the racemic methyl ester of the 11,12-oxido analog **153** (47) started from undecen-2,5-diyn-1-ol (59) (**155**), which was converted to aldehyde **156** in 87% overall yield by a sequence of (1) selective reduction of the 2,3-triple bond with lithium aluminum hydride, (2) epoxidation of the resulting allylic alcohol, (3) cis-hydrogenation, and (4) Collins oxidation. This key intermediate was next converted to the epoxytrienal **157** by reaction with 1-lithio-4-ethoxybutadiene (150) by a standard method discussed earlier. Wittig coupling of trienol **157** with the ylide derived from 5-(triphenylphosphino)pentanoic acid (42), followed by esterification, afforded (±)-11,12-LTA$_4$ isomer **153** in 70% yield (Scheme 44).

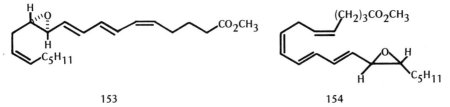

153   154

Scheme 43

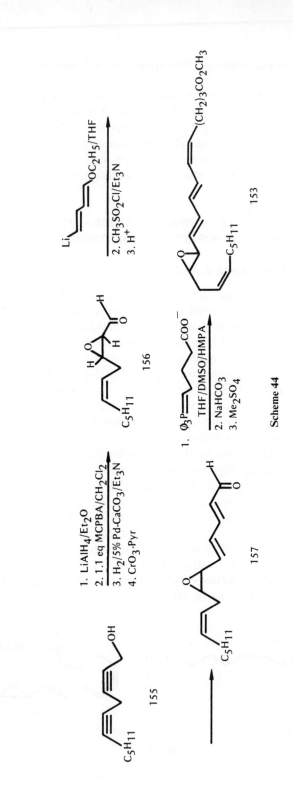

Scheme 44

The synthesis of 14,15-LTA$_4$ methyl ester **154** was carried in optically active form from readily available (15S)-HPETE (10,47) (**158**) (R = H). Reaction of (15S)-HPETE (**158**) [formed from arachidonic acid (**1**) by the Baldwin method (10)] with ethereal diazomethane afforded the corresponding methyl ester **158** (R = CH$_3$), which when treated with 1,2,2,6,6-pentamethylpiperidine and an equivalent of trifluoromethanesulfonic anhydride at low temperature in methylene chloride – ether, gave mixtures of the desired 14,15-methyl ester LTA$_4$ **154**, along with the 15-ketone **159** arising from simple 1,2-elimination of 15-HPETE in ratio of 2:1. Due to the difficulty in chromatographic separation of compounds **154** and **159**, this mixture was immediately treated with sodium borohydride at 0°C, which resulted in reduction of ketone **159** and thus allowed simple chromatographic separation and isolation of 14,15-LTA$_4$ **154** in 40% yield (32). Sih *et al.* (3) repeated this reaction and reported the formation of **154** as well as the 8,10-*cis*-isomer, the latter of which predominated in their hands (Scheme 45).

The S-glutathione conjugates **160** and **162** were prepared by a standard method described earlier for the preparation of the parent LTC$_4$ and LTD$_4$ leukotrienes. From racemic LTA$_4$ isomer **153**, two separable diastereomeric peptide conjugates were obtained in equal amounts, which were separated by RP-HPLC, whereas optically active 14,15-LTA$_4$ methyl ester **154** gave only a single conjugate. Unlike 14,15-conjugate **162**, which was clearly distinguishable by RP-HPLC from the parent LTC$_4$ compound, the diastereomeric conjugates **160** showed almost identical RP-HPLC behavior (Scheme 46).

The S-cysteinylglycyl conjugates **161** and **163** were obtained in an analogous manner by reacting N-trifluoroacetylcysteinylglycine methyl ester (**24**) with the corresponding 11,12- and 14,15-oxides (**153** and **154**), followed by hydrolysis.

Biological evaluation (58) for contractile activities of these analogs and comparison of their activity to that of parent LTC$_4$ and LTD$_4$ has found analogs **160, 161, 162,** and **163** to be minimally active, with potency not even equal to 50% of the maximum histamine response. Thus it seems that by a simple repositioning of the peptide, a total loss of activity is observed, further emphasizing that the position of the peptide moiety at C-6 is of critical importance for contractile activity.

B. Synthesis of (5S)-12-Glutathionyl-6,8,10-*trans*-14-*cis*-Eicosatetraenoic Acid (164)

Employing conditions developed in the original model study for opening of LTA$_4$ via either S$_N$1 or S$_N$2 pathways, the Harvard group (34) was able to synthesize the two diastereomers of leukotriene C$_4$ having the 6-peptide linkage at C-12. Thus, when LTA$_4$ methyl ester (**35**) was allowed to react with

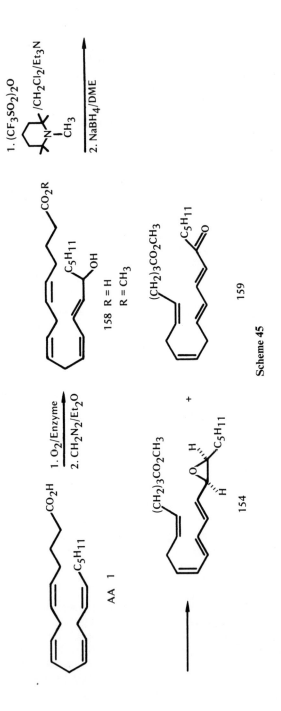

Scheme 45

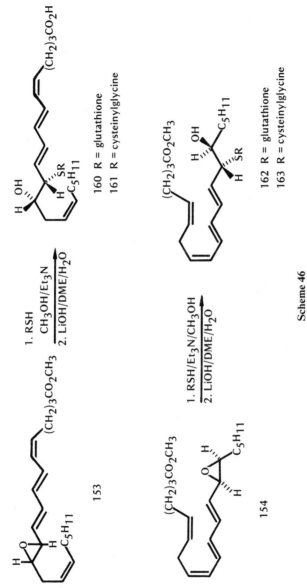

160 R = glutathione
161 R = cysteinylglycine

162 R = glutathione
163 R = cysteinylglycine

Scheme 46

73

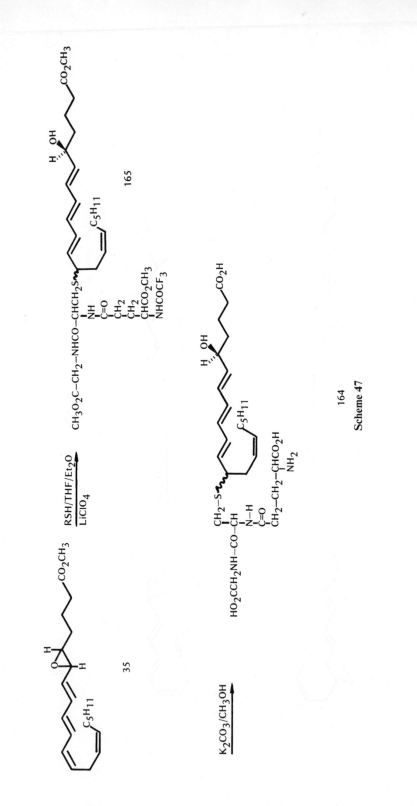

Scheme 47

N-trifluoroacetylglutathione dimethyl ester (25) in the presence of excess anhydrous lithium perchlorate in tetrahydrofuran – ether, a diastereomeric mixture of protected 12-glutathionyl adducts 165 was obtained in excellent yield. Only trace amounts of the S_N2 adduct 76 were obtained. The diastereomers 165 were readily separated by RP-HPLC, and the protecting groups were hydrolyzed using standard conditions to afford pure (5S,12)-glutathionyl-6,8,10-*trans*-14-*cis*-eicosatetraenoic acid derivatives 164. These diastereomers were clearly different from the parent LTC$_4$ as ascertained by RP-HPLC and UV absorption; for example, λ_{max} for 164 = 277 nm ± 0.5, as compared to LTC λ_{max} = 280 nm ± 0.5. Biological evaluation of these analogs and comparison to LTC$_4$ showed that both diastereomers 164 were inactive when tested on guinea pig ileum and on pulmonary strips (58) (Scheme 47).

C. Synthesis of C-15 Hydroxy LTD (166)

In an *in vitro* experiment designed to study the kinetics and characteristics of the inactivation of SRS-A by the action of lipoxygenase, Sirois (141) reported formation of novel SRS analog 166, containing a hydroxy group at C-15. This conjugated tetraenoic analog is a direct product of LTD$_4$ inactivation by lipoxygenase, which requires a specific 1,4-diene unit for its action. Biological evaluation (58) of this analog, and comparison to the parent LTD$_4$ showed only 45% of histamine activity at 0.1 μM. This observation once again strongly argues that the hydrophobicity of the C-7 to C-20 portions of SRS-A is important in retaining maximum activity (Scheme 48).

D. Synthesis of $\Delta^{11,12}$, $\Delta^{14,15}$-Dehydroleukotrienes A, C, and D

A recent European patent (126) by Hoffmann La Roche has disclosed the preparation of (R,S)-all-*trans*-3-(1,3-tetradecadiene-5,8-diyn-1-yl)-1-*trans*-oxiranebutyric acid methyl ester 167 and its conjugates. The route to this analog parallels the original Harvard synthesis of racemic LTA$_4$ 19a,b. Thus, when the ylide of (E,E)-2,4-pentadecadiene-6,9-diyn-1-yl-tetrahydrobromide (168) was condensed with methyl 4-formylbutyrate under standard conditions, a mixture of *cis*- and *trans*-dihydro-epoxides 167 was obtained, which were separated by liquid chromatography (Scheme 49). These workers have claimed compound 167 to be an antagonist of SRS-A and especially useful in the treatment of bronchial asthma at very low dosage.

Following an analogous route for the preparation of LTA$_4$ methyl ester 35 as described earlier, a group at Merck (66) has reported the synthesis of 14,15-dehydro-LTA 169 and the corresponding conjugates 170, 171, and 172 (Scheme 50). The synthesis of 14,15-LTA 169 was accomplished during the

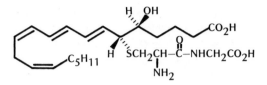

LTD 7

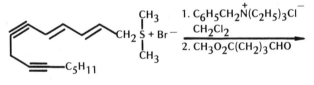

166

Scheme 48

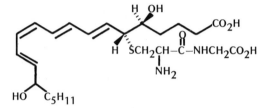

168

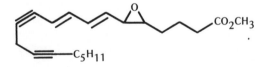

167

Scheme 49

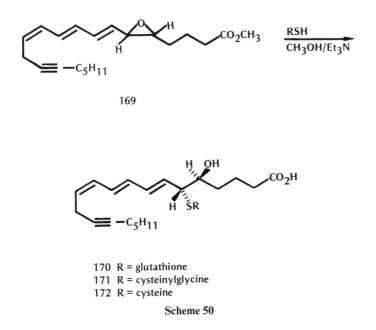

170 R = glutathione
171 R = cysteinylglycine
172 R = cysteine

Scheme 50

preparation of the corresponding sulfone derivatives of LTC_4 and LTD_4 *(vide infra)*.

E. Synthesis of $\Delta^{14,15}$-Dihydroleukotriene A, C, and D

In principle one might also expect that Δ^{14}-dihydroleukotriene A_4 (Δ^{14}-LTA_4 **173**), Δ^{14}-dihydroleukotriene C_4, D_4, and E_4, and 11-*trans*-Δ^{14}-dihydro-leukotriene C_4 could also be derived biosynthetically from Δ^{14}-dihydroara-chidonic acid by the same biosynthetic pathways from which the parent leukotrienes are formed. For this reason the Harvard group (52) has pre-pared Δ^{14}-dihydro LTA **173** and the corresponding conjugates **174** and **175**. Unlike leukotrienes C_4 and D_4, these analogs are not deactivated by soybean lipoxygenase because of the lack of a 1,4-diene unit.

The synthesis of Δ^{14}-dihydro-LTA **173** parallels closely the synthesis of leukotriene A_4 methyl ester (**35**). Wittig reaction of the ylide derived from phosphonium salt **176** with diene aldehyde **34** under standard conditions gave $(5S,6S)$-oxide-$(7E,9E,11Z)$-eicosatrienoate, dihydro-LTA_4 **173** in 67% yield. Similarly to LTA_4 methyl ester (**35**), dihydro-LTA_4 methyl ester **173** was also found to be unstable on silica, and purification was accomplished by deactivation of the silica with triethylamine. Conversion of dihydro-LTA_4 **173** to Δ^{14}-dehydro-LTC_4 and LTD_4 conjugates **174** and **175** using the trieth-

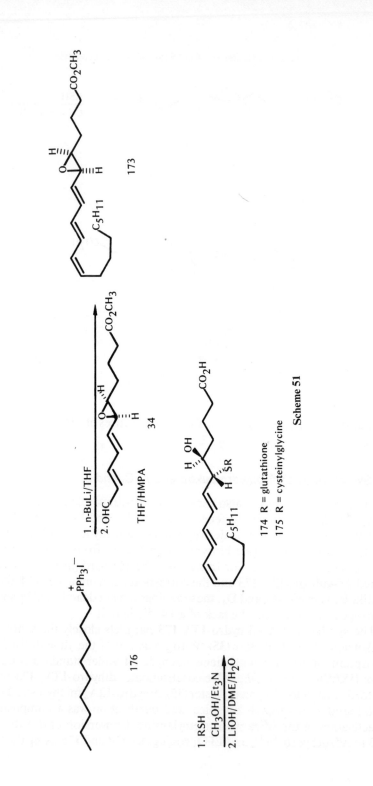

176

1. n-BuLi/THF
2. OHC
THF/HMPA

34

173

1. RSH
   CH₃OH/Et₃N
2. LiOH/DME/H₂O

174 R = glutathione
175 R = cysteinylglycine

Scheme 51

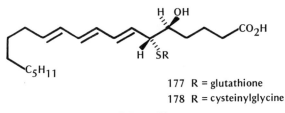

177 R = glutathione
178 R = cysteinylglycine

Scheme 52

ylamine–methanol conditions followed by hydrolysis proceeded in a straightforward manner (Scheme 51).

Small amounts of the Δ^{14}-dihydro-11-*trans*-leukotriene C_4 and D_4 (**177** and **178**) were also isolated (Scheme 52).

Shortly after the completion of this synthesis, Samulesson and Hammarström (134) reported the transformation of 5,8,11-eicosaenoic acid by RBL-1 cells into Δ^{14}-dihydro-LTA$_4$ **173** and the corresponding conjugates **174** and **175**, which he designated as LTA$_3$ for **173**, LTC$_3$ for **174**, and LTD$_3$ for **175**. Biological evaluation (58) of conjugates **174** and **175** showed that the saturation of the 14,15-double bond did not cause a significant decrease in activity when tested on guinea pig ileum and pulmonary parenchymal strips. For example, when compared on a molar basis, Δ^{14}-dihydro-LTD **175** was 66% as effective as the parent LTD$_4$.

F. Synthesis of 7-*trans*-11-*cis*-tetrahydro-LTA$_4$ (179) and the Corresponding Conjugates 180 and 181

In order to establish whether a fully conjugated trienic unit in the parent leukotrienes was necessary for the retention of biological activity, 7-*trans*-11-*cis*-tetrahydro-LTA **179** and the corresponding LTC and LTD conjugates **180** and **181** were prepared (33). The synthesis of these analogs was accomplished starting with 1-nonyne (**182**). Conversion of **182** to 1-bromo-4-tridecene (**183**) by a standard method, followed by Grignard formation (121), coupling with epoxyaldehyde **33**, and reaction of the resulting alcohol with *o*-nitrophenylselenocyanate, afforded selenoepoxide intermediate **184**. Oxidation followed by phenyl selenoxide elimination provided tetrahydro-LTA **179** in excellent overall yield. Conversion of **179** to the corresponding conjugates **181** and **182** was straightforward (Scheme 53).

G. Synthesis of 7-$\Delta^{9,11,14}$-*cis* and 7-$\Delta^{9,11,14}$-*trans*-Hexahydro-LTA (185 and 186) and the Corresponding Conjugates

Employing an analogous route that was developed for the LTA$_4$ synthesis, the Harvard group (33,54) has also prepared 7-*cis*-hexahydro-LTA **185**, 7-

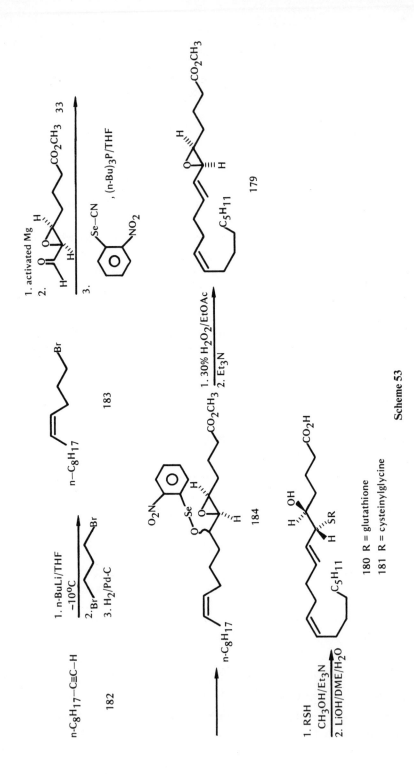

Scheme 53

trans-hexahydro-LTA **186,** and their corresponding conjugates. Thus, Wittig reaction between epoxyaldehyde **33** and ylide **187** in the presence of 10 equivalents of anhydrous lithium iodide in ether produced a mixture of 7-*cis*-hexahydro-LTA **185** and 7-*trans*-hexahydro-LTA **186** in a ratio of 2:1 as determined by ^{1}H-NMR. However, if the same reaction was carried out in THF in the absence of HMPA or lithium iodide, 7-*cis*-hexahydro-LTA **185** was obtained as the major product with only traces ($< 5\%$) of the corresponding trans-isomer **186** (Scheme 54).

The synthesis of pure 7-*trans*-hexahydro-LTA **186** was accomplished in 50% overall yield by a different route in which the 7-*trans* linkage was established by coupling of the epoxyaldehyde **33** and *n*-tridecyl magnesium bromide followed by phenyl selenoxide elimination. Unlike the parent LTA$_4$ methyl ester (**35**), both hexahydro-LTA **185** and **186** were quite stable to purification and did not require triethylamine deactivation of silica gel (Scheme 55).

Reaction of these hexahydro-leukotriene analogs **185** and **186** with protected forms of glutathione or cysteinylglycine under standard conditions of triethylamine – methanol followed by hydrolysis afforded the corresponding conjugates **188** and **189** in excellent yield (Scheme 56).

Evaluation (58) of $\Delta^{9,11,14}$-hexahydro-LTD **189** for contractile activities on guinea pig pulmonary parenchymal strips and ileum, and comparison to the response obtained for the parent leukotrienes, indicated 7-*trans*-$\Delta^{9,11,14}$-hexahydro-LTD **189** to be about 1.5 to 2 logs less active in both the airway and ileum assays. The 7-*trans*-$\Delta^{9,11,14}$-LTC analog **188,** when compared to the parent LTC$_4$ on a molar basis, was 19% as effective as LTC on the pulmonary parenchymal strip and 35% as active on the ileum bioassay. The 7-*cis*-$\Delta^{9,11,14}$-hexahydro-LTD analog **188** was found to exhibit about the same activity as the corresponding 7-*trans*-$\Delta^{9,11,14}$-hexahydro-LTC analog **189,** but the 7-*cis*-$\Delta^{9,11,14}$-hexahydro-LTC analog **188** was found to be appreciably less active when tested on the pulmonary parenchymal strip, yet retaining about the same activity on the ileum. Comparison of the $\Delta^{9,11,14}$-hexahydro analogs of LTD on both assays showed a higher loss of overall activity relative to the parent LTD than that of the $\Delta^{9,11,14}$-hexahydro-LTC analogs relative to the parent LTC.

H. Synthesis of Octahydro-LTA (190)

Because of the preceding observation that the degree of unsaturation in the polyenic chain of the leukotrienes may not always play a critical role in defining biological activity, efforts by the Harvard group (38) and others (151) have been undertaken to prepare fully saturated $\Delta^{7,9,11,14}$-octahydro-LTA **190** and its conjugates. The first and most obvious approaches would have been

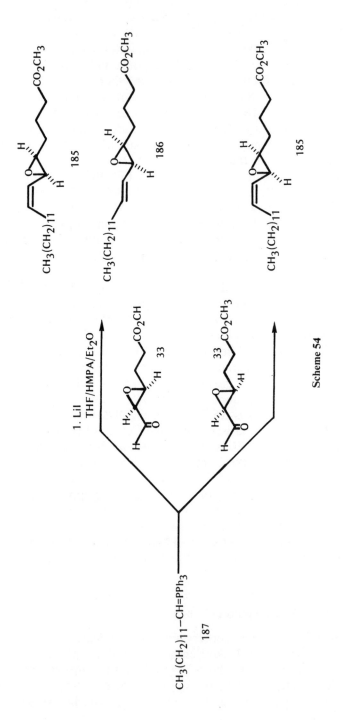

Scheme 54

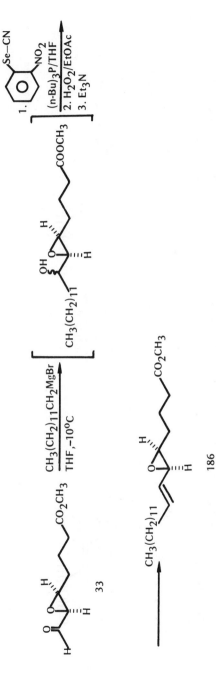

Scheme 55

83

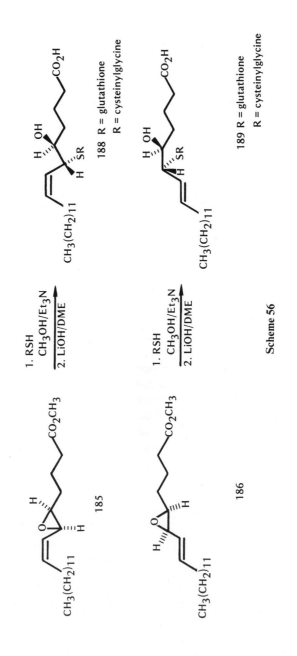

Scheme 56

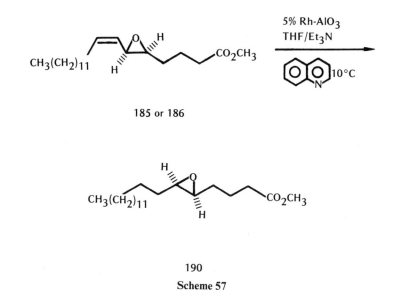

185 or 186

190

Scheme 57

hydrogenation of leukotriene A (LTA) or the hydrogenation of more saturated analogs of LTA such as compounds **173, 179, 185,** and **186.** As expected, because of the very reactive nature and instability of LTA$_4$, various attempts to hydrogenate LTA$_4$ or leukotriene C$_4$ or D$_4$ fully under a variety of conditions failed. However, when the more stable $\omega^{9,11,14}$-hexahydro analogs **185** and **186** were hydrogenated under carefully controlled conditions using 5% rhodium on alumina in the presence of triethylamine and a synthetic isoquinoline in THF, the desired octahydro-LTA **190** was obtained in moderate yields of 40 to 50% (Scheme 57). However, one obvious drawback to this approach is the loss of regiocontrol in the reaction of peptides with the saturated leukotriene A analog.

A nonstereoselective route to octahydro-leukotrienes LTC, LTD, and LTE **191** via a stereoselective sulfenyllactonization reaction has been reported (151). Reaction of **192** with a sulfenyl chloride afforded a mixture of diastereomeric lactones **193.** Separation of diastereomers followed by hydrolysis of the protecting groups afforded the fully saturated analogs of leukotriene C, D, and E **191** (Scheme 58).

Biological evaluation of these fully saturated analogs relative to leukotriene C$_4$ (LTC$_4$) on guinea pig tracheal tissue showed that the erythro compounds are about three orders of magnitude less active and that the threo analogs are essentially inactive. The activity difference between pairs of diastereomers was found to be insignificant.

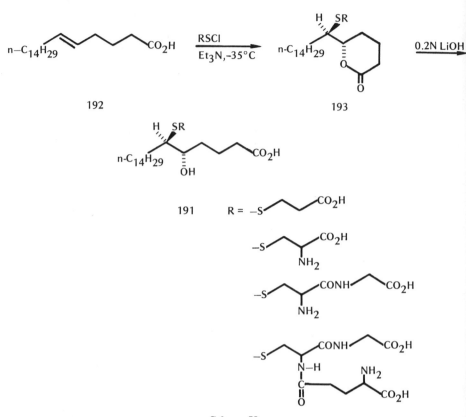

Scheme 58

I. Synthesis of Thio and Methano Analogs of LTA (194 and 195)

In a continuing effort toward rational selection of candidates as possible inhibitors of biosynthetic pathways leading to leukotrienes, both thio analog **194** (51) and methano analog **195** (2,102) have been prepared. Reaction of racemic LTA$_4$ methyl ester **19b** with excess sodium thiocyanate in methanol-containing triethylamine afforded thio analog **194** in 60% yield (51). The racemic LTA$_4$ methyl ester **(19b)** was readily prepared starting with methyl-7-hydroxy-5-heptanate **(196)** by a standard sequence of reaction involving (1) Lindlar hydrogenation, (2) pyridinium chlorochromate oxidation of the resulting allylic alcohol with concurrent isomerization to the *trans*-α,β-unsaturated aldehyde, (3) sodium borohydride reduction, (4) MCPBA epoxidation, (5) oxidation, (6) four-carbon chain extension, and (7) Wittig coupling of the resulting dienal with ylide **17** as described earlier (Scheme 59).

The synthesis of (±)-5,6-methanoleukotriene A$_4$ analog **195,** which is one

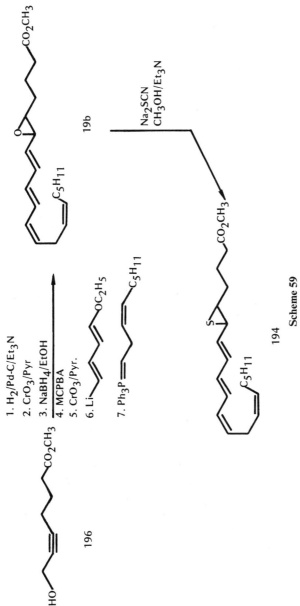

Scheme 59

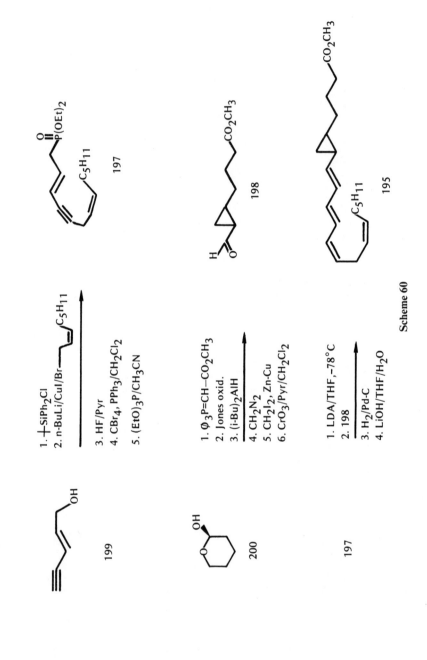

Scheme 60

88

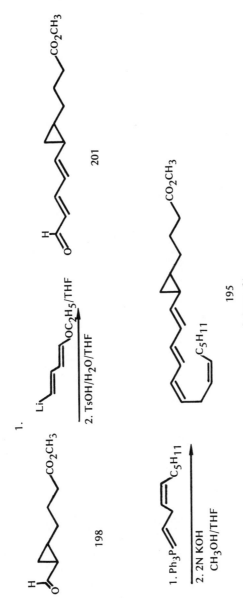

Scheme 61

of the most stable analogs thus far prepared, was reported independently by two groups (2,102). In the first synthesis Nicolaou *et al.* (102) employed a convergent route that made use of a stereocontrolled coupling of the ylide derived from phosphonate **197** with methanoaldehyde **198**. Thus, reaction of the lithium salt of phosphonate **197** with aldehyde **198** followed by selective hydrogenation of the acetylenic linkage and hydrolysis of the corresponding methyl ester generated 5,6-methanoleukotriene A **195**. The phosphonate intermediate **197** was in turn obtained in excellent overall yield starting with pent-2-en-4-yn-1-ol (**199**), by a sequence of reactions involving (1) phenylsilyl ether formation, (2) coupling to (2*E*)-1-bromooct-2-ene, (3) removal of the silyl protecting group, and (4) conversion of the resulting alcohol to the phosphonium salt via an intermediate bromide. The C-1–C-7 segment, methanoaldehyde ester **198**, was prepared from γ-valerolactol (**200**) by a sequence of reactions involving (1) reaction with methyl(triphenylphosphoranylidene) acetate, (2) Jones oxidation of the resulting alcohol, (3) ester reduction, (4) esterification of the resulting allylic alcohol, and (5) cyclopropanation with CH_2I_2-Zn-CuCl followed by oxidation (Scheme 60).

In preliminary studies (102), these workers reported that methano-LTA **195** is a potent and selective inhibitor of leukotriene A biosynthesis.

An alternative synthesis of (±)-methano-LTA **195** was reported by a group at Ono (2). Conversion of methanoaldehyde ester **198** to the corresponding dienal **201**, followed by a sequence from the original Harvard LTA synthesis (see Scheme 11), gave the (±)-methano-LTA analog **195** in good overall yield (Scheme 61). These workers also reported that methano analog **195** exhibited strong 5-lipoxygenase inhibitory activity without inhibiting cycloxygenase or the 12-lipoxygenase.

VIII. SYNTHESIS OF STRUCTURAL ANALOGS OF LEUKOTRIENES C₄, D₄, AND E₄—MODIFICATION OF THE POLAR REGION

As a part of a continuing study of structure–activity relationships of leukotrienes, numerous stereochemical and structural analogs have been prepared (58,89,90) and evaluated for agonist or antagonist activity. In the foregoing sections the synthesis and biological properties of various synthetic leukotriene analogs in which the principle alteration of structure occurred in the ω portion of the C_{20} chain have been outlined. From these studies it was concluded that although the long hydrophobic chain is required for high contractile activity of leukotrienes, the degree of unsaturation and the geometry of the ω portion clearly played a less critical role. Thus small changes in the structure of the ω portions of leukotrienes were not necessarily detrimental to activity. In this section the synthesis and biological data of various analogs where the polar regions of leukotriene systems have been systematically modified (90) is presented. The modifications in the C-1 to C-6 region were the following: (1) changes made in the peptide or amino acid substituents at the C-6 position of the eicosanoid chain, (2) modification of the carboxylic groups in the peptide and eicosanoid chain, (3) removal or modification of the free amino moiety in the peptide section, (4) oxidation of the sulfur attached at C-6, and (5) change in the absolute chirality of carbons 5 and 6. The analogs prepared are listed in Table I and are named relative to the parent leukotriene (LTC_4, LTD_4, LTE_4). Most of these analogs were prepared by a direct modification of the synthetic sequence developed for the synthesis of the parent leukotrienes as described earlier in this chapter. Therefore only a brief comment seems appropriate.

The LTC_4 monoamide **202** was prepared by reaction of N-trifluoroacetyl-LTD dimethyl ester with 15 M ammonium hydroxide followed by hydrolysis of the remaining esters and the N-trifluoroacetyl group. LTD-glycine monoamide **204** was prepared by reaction of LTA with N-trifluoroacetyl-cysteinylglycineamide employing standard conditions of methanol–triethylamine followed by hydrolysis as described earlier for the parent LTD leukotriene. LTD bisamide **203** was prepared from LTD-glycine monoamide by reaction with anhydrous ammonia–ammonium chloride. Deamino-LTD bisamide **204** was prepared by reaction of LTA methyl ester with 2-mercaptopropionylglycine methyl ester followed by reaction with ammonia–ammonium chloride. Deamino-LTD analog **216** was prepared by the hydrolysis of the intermediate ester of analog **204** followed by hydrolysis. LTD-glycine mono-dimethylamide analog **206** was prepared by coupling LTA and N-trifluoro-cysteinylglycine dimethylamide followed by standard hydrolysis. The various dipeptide analogs **207–214** were also prepared by a standard coupling of LTA methyl ester with the appropriate peptides followed by standard hydrolysis procedure. The D-pen analog of LTE (**215**) was prepared by reaction of LTA methyl ester with N-trifluoroacetyl-D-pen-methyl ester following the procedure described for the preparation of leukotriene E. N-acetyl-LTD and LTE, analogs **217** and **218,** were prepared by the reaction of the parent leukotrienes LTD and LTE with acetic anhydride in methanol–water at 0°C. Diastereomeric LTD-sulfoxide analogs **219** and **220** were prepared by reaction of excess sodium periodate with the parent LTD in phosphate buffer–ethanol. The preparation of the corresponding sulfone analogs **221–223** was recently reported by the Merck group (66), employing a recently developed method for sulfur oxidation by Trost (147). Thus, as in the case of the sulfoxides, the parent leukotrienes LTC, LTD, and LTE were directly oxidized by reaction with potassium hydrogen persulfate. The preparation, full characterization, and comparison of these sulfone analogs to the native

TABLE I

Contractile Activities of Leukotriene Analogs; Activity Ratios to LTD on Guinea Pig Tissues

Entry	Compound	Structural variation	Plumonary parenchymal strip EC_{50} ratio[a]	Ileum dose ratio[b]
1	LTD	None	1	1

202	LTD monoamide (C-1)	1	1	0.25
203	LTD bisamide (C-1, Gly)	1, 2	<0.001	<0.002
204	Deamino-LTD bisamide (C-1, Gly)	1, 2, 4	<0.001	<0.002
205	LTD monoamide (Gly)	2	0.10	ND[d]
206	LTD monodimethylamide (Gly)	2	0.006	<0.002
207	D-Ala[c] LTD	3	0.11	0.33
208	L-Ala[c] LTD	3	0.09	0.05
209	Pro[c] LTD	3	0.03	0.03
210	Glu[c] LTD	3	0.02	0.02
211	Val[c] LTD	3	0.008	0.01
212	Homocys[e] LTD	5	0.26	0.20
213	D-Pen[e] LTD	5, 6	<0.001	<0.002
214	D-Cys[e] LTD	6	0.11	0.02
215	D-Pen LTD	5, 6	<0.001	0.005
216	Deamino-LTD	4	0.05	0.20
217	N-Acetyl-LTD	4	0.03	ND
218	N-Acetyl-LTE	4	0.04	0.04
219	LTD-sulfoxide, isomer 1	6	0.10	0.10
220	LTD-sulfoxide, isomer 2	6	−0.001	<0.002
221	LTC sulfone	6		
222	LTD sulfone	6		
223	LTE sulfone	6		
224	6-Epi-LTD	7	0.004	0.005
225	6-Epi-LTC	7	0.005	0.002
226	5-Epi-LTD	8	0.004	0.005
227	5-Dehydroxy-9,12,14,15-hexahydro LTD	9, 10	<0.001	<0.002

[a] Analog/LTD EC_{50} ratio; EC_{50} of LTD = 0.6 nM.
[b] Analog/LTD ratio; LTD reference dose = 0.4 nM.
[c] This amino acid replaced Gly of LTD.
[d] ND, not determined.
[e] This amino acid replaced L-Cys of LTD.

leukotrienes has disproved the evidence presented by Ohnishi and co-workers (104), who claimed that the structure of SRS-A isolated from the peritoneal cells is one in which the sulfur of the thio ether linkage is oxidized (structure **221**) rather than a sulfide. The 6-epi analogs of LTD and LTC (**224** and **225**) were prepared as described earlier in this chapter (see Scheme 22). 5-Epi-LTD (**226**) was prepared by coupling racemic *cis*-LTA$_4$ methyl ester with glutathione, which afforded a mixture of 5- and 6-epi-leukotriene C$_4$. Cleavage of these intermediates with γ-glutamyl transpeptidase followed by RP-HPLC separation afforded 5-epi-LTD analog **226**. Finally, 5-dehydroxy-9,12,14,15-hexahydro-LTD, analog **227** (and its C-6 epimer) were prepared by a coupling of methyl-6-tosyloxy-eicosa-*cis*-11,14-enoate with N-trifluoroacetylcysteinylglycine followed by hydrolysis employing standard procedures.

In general the leukotriene analogs can be categorized into three groups:

1. Analogs equipotent to the parent leukotrienes, which include 14,15-di-hydro-LTC and -LTD, LTD$_4$ amide, and LTC$_4$ sulfone. Although these derivatives demonstrate that the hydrophobic chain, the eicosanoid carboxyl, and the sulfur oxidation state can be altered without loss of activity, the molecular changes are quite simple, and more drastic structural modifications result in loss of activity.

2. Analogs approximately 10 times less potent than the parent leukotrienes, which include 11-*trans*-LTC$_4$, $\Delta^{9,11,14}$-hexahydro-LTD, and LTD-glycylamide, and demonstrate that modification of the triene moiety or the glycine carboxy moiety leads to a loss of activity on the order of 1 log unit.

3. Analogs ≥ 100 times less potent than the parent leukotriene, represented by two structural types. One class involves gross molecular rearrangement such as the 12-glutathionyl analogs or the LTC$_4$ and LTD$_4$ derivatives derived from 8,11- or 15-HPETE. The second class involves small molecular changes such as 5-desoxyl-LTD$_4$ (36), N-acetyl-LTD$_4$, or desamino-LTD$_4$, demonstrating that the 5-hydroxy moiety and the glycine amino group are essential for activity. In conclusion, the evidence obtained in these studies strongly argues for a relative geometrical arrangement of the C$_{20}$ chain and peptide unit in order to retain activity. This observation might further support the possible existence of a true receptor for these native leukotrienes and in particular for LTD$_4$ and LTC$_4$.

IX. SYNTHESIS OF LTB$_4$ ANALOGS

Synthesis of LTB Amides

Considerable indirect evidence has been presented that suggests the existence of a stereospecific receptor for LTB$_4$ on neutrophils (89,139). Because of

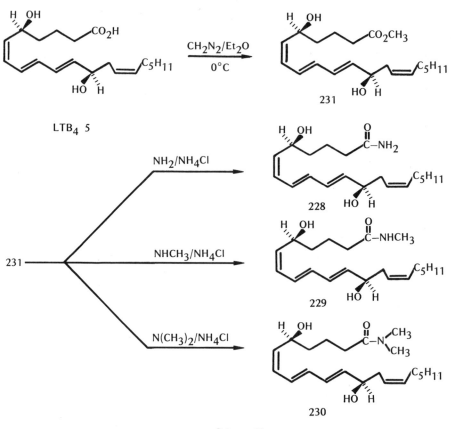

Scheme 62

this possibility several LTB analogs, namely LTB$_4$ amide **228**, LTB$_4$ mono-methylamide **229**, and LTB$_4$ dimethylamide **230**, were prepared by the Harvard group (140) and examined for their antagonistic activity toward LTB$_4$. To date these are the only three analogs of LTB$_4$ reported. The possibility that one of these analogs might show strong antagonistic activity toward LTB$_4$ draws close analogy to previous work (63,91) in the field of prostaglandins, where it was shown that prostaglandin F$_{2\alpha}$ dimethylamide antagonized smooth muscle contraction induced by prostaglandin F$_{2\alpha}$. Clearly an active antagonist of the LTB$_4$ receptor could be potentially useful for modulation of the inflammatory response.

The amide analogs **228–230** (140) were prepared in a straightforward manner. Thus reaction of LTB$_4$ (**5**) with ethereal diazomethane cleanly afforded the corresponding LTB methyl ester **231**, which was without any further purification azeotroped with benzene and reacted with an excess of the appropriate amine under an atmosphere of argon, in a sealed high-pressure test tube. Each reaction was catalyzed by an equivalent of ammonium chloride. After several days at room temperature, nearly quantitative yields of analogs **228–230** were obtained (Scheme 62). All three analogs showed identical UV-absorption spectra, which were further identical to the parent LTB_4 (γ_{max} = 260, 270, and 281.5 nm $\pm$ 0.5), indicating that no isomerization of the conjugated triene has occurred. The purity of each analog was found to be > 95%, as ascertained by RP-HPLC, which cleanly separated these analogs from each other as well as from the parent compound. Preliminary biological evaluation of these analogs demonstrated (140) that one of these compounds, namely the least polar LTB dimethylamide analog **230,** strongly antagonized the degranulation response to LTB_4 at concentrations where it has little or no agnoistic activity. Whether LTB_4 dimethylamide analog **230** is a true antagonist of the LTB_4 receptor or acts by a desensitizing mechanism is not clear yet and will require further study. However, the fact that analog **230** dramatically reduces the response to LTB_4 can at least provide a guide to the development of novel and more specific antagonists.

X. NOVEL LEUKOTRIENES

The ever-growing field of chemistry and biology of leukotrienes is being continuously expanded by newer additions and identification of various leukotrienes derived from oxygenation of arachidonic acid, as well as other eicosanoic acids (100). Hammarström (76) reported an experiment in which mouse mastocytoma cells stimulated with ionophore A23187 in the presence of dihomo-γ-linolenic acid produced a novel leukotriene that was characterized as 8-hydroxy-(9S)-glutathionyl-10,12,14-eicosatrieonic acid LTC_3 **232.** Leukotriene is most likely formed from dihomo-γ-linolenic acid by lipoxygenase transformation to the 8-hydroperoxide followed by conversion to the 8,9-epoxide and conjugation with glutathione (74,75,77). In a similar experiment Rådmark et al. (82) reported the isolation and identification of two new dihydroxy acids obtained from incubation of arachidonic acid with a preparation of human leukocytes. These acids, which contained conjugated triene units and which were characterized as 8,15-dihydroxy-5,9,11,13-eicosatetraenoic acid **233** (8,15-leukotriene B_4) and 14,15-dihydroxy-5,8,10,12-eicosatetraenoic acid **234** (14,15-leukotriene B_4), are obviously derived from initial oxygenation of arachidonic acid at C-15. Diols formed by hydrolysis of 11,12- and 14,15-epoxides of arachidonic acid have also been isolated and reported (105). On treatment of arachidonic acid with mixed human leukocytes, Ford-Hutchinson et al. (28) reported the isolation and characterization of a C_{20}-tetraunsaturated hydroxy acid with hydroxy groups at C-5, C-12, and C-20.

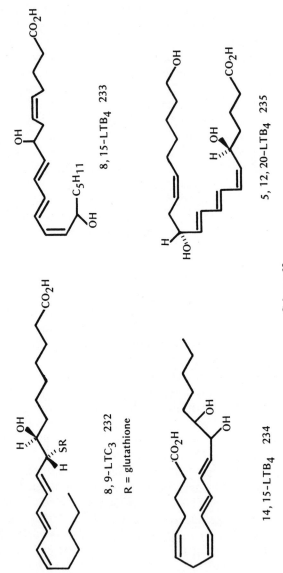

8,9-LTC₃ 232
R = glutathione

8,15-LTB₄ 233

14,15-LTB₄ 234

5,12,20-LTB₄ 235

Scheme 63

The exact structure of this rather unusual metabolite was determined to be 5,12,20-trihydroxy-6,8,10,14-eicosatetraenoic acid 235 (Scheme 63). The effect of this compound on the chemokinesis of human PMN and in the aggregation of rat PMNs was investigated and compared to LTB_4. It was found that compound 235 exhibited a somewhat lesser degree of activity than LTB_4 but was more active than any other monohydroxy derivative of arachidonic acid. No doubt additional families of these metabolites will be found as time progresses, each of them bringing us a step closer to understanding and truly evaluating their roles as possible mediators of inflammation.

REFERENCES

1. Agata, I., Corey, E. J., Hortmann, A. G., Klein, J., Proskow, S., and Ursprung, J. J. (1965). *J. Org. Chem.* 30, 1698–1710.
2. Arai, Y., Konno, M., Shimoji, K., Konishi, Y., Niwa, H., Toda,M., and Hayashi, M. (1982). *Chem. Pharm. Bull.* 30, 379–382.
3. Atrache, V., Pai, J. K., Sok, D. E., and Sih, C. J. (1981). *Tetrahedron Lett.* pp. 3443–3446.
4. Bach, M. K., and Brashler, J. R. (1978). *Life Sci.* 23, 2119–2126.
5. Bach, M. K., Brashler, J. R., and Gorman, R. R. (1977). *Prostaglandins* 14, 21–38.
6. Bach, M. K., Brashler, J. R., Hammarström, S., and Samuelsson, B. (1980). *Biochem. Biophys. Res. Commun.* 93, 1121–1126.
7. Bailey, D. M., and Casey, F. B. (1982). *Annu. Rep. Med. Chem.* 17, 203–217.
8. Bailey, D. M., and Chakrin, L. W. (1981). *Annu. Rep. Med. Chem.* 16, 213–227.
9. Baker, S. R., Jamieson, W. B., McKay, S. W., Morgan, S. E., Rackham, D. M., Ross, W. J., and Shrubsall, P. R. (1980). *Tetrahedron Lett.* pp. 4123–4126.
10. Baldwin, J. E., Davies, D. I., Hughes, L. J., and Gutteridge, N. A. (1979). *J. Chem. Soc., Perkin Trans. 1* pp. 115–121.
11. Bass, D. A., Thomas, M. J., Goetzel, E. J., DeChatelet, L. R., and McCall, C. E. (1981). *Biochem. Biophys. Res. Commun.* 100, 1–7.
12. Bergström, S. (1967). *Science* 157, 382–391.
13. Boot, J. R., Brockwell, A. D. J., Dawson, W., and Sweatman, W. J. F. (1977). *Br. J. Pharmacol.* 59, 444–445P.
14. Borgeat, P., and Samuelsson, B. (1979). *J. Biol. Chem.* 254, 2643–2646.
15. Borgeat, P., and Samuelsson, B. (1979). *Proc. Natl. Acad. Sci. U.S.A.* 76, 2148–2152.
16. Borgeat, P., and Samuelsson, B. (1979). *Proc. Natl. Acad. Sci. U.S.A.* 76, 3213–3217.
17. Borgeat, P., and Samuelsson, B. (1979). *J. Biol. Chem.* 254, 7865–7869.
18. Borgeat, P., and Sirois, P. (1980). *Union Med. Can.* 109, 557.
19. Borgeat, P., and Sirois, P. (1981). *J. Med. Chem.* 24, 121–126.
20. Borgeat, P., Hamberg, M., and Samuelsson, B. (1976). *J. Biol. Chem.* 251, 7816–7820; 252, 8772.
21. Borgeat, P., Picard, S., Vallerand, P., and Sirois, P. (1981). *Prostaglandins Med.* 6, 557–570.
22. Bray, M. A., Cunningham, F. M., Ford-Hutchinson, A. W., and Smith, M. J. H. (1981). *Br. J. Pharmacol.* 73, 258P–259P.
23. Bray, M. A., Ford-Hutchinson, A. W., and Smith, M. J. H. (1981). "SRA-A and Leukotrienes." Wiley, New York.
24. Brocklehurst, W. E. (1953). *J. Physiol. (London)* 120, 16P–17P.

25. Brocklehurst, W. E. (1962). *Prog. Allergy* **6**, 539–558.
26. Bunting, S., Gryglewski, R., Moncada, S., and Vane, J. R. (1976). *Prostaglandins* **12**, 897–913.
27. Burka, J. F. (1981). *N. Engl. Soc. Allergy Proc.* **2**, 62–67.
28. Camp, R. D. R., Fincham, N. J., Ford-Hutchinson, A. W., Mallet, A. I., and Woolard, P. M. (1982). *Br. J. Pharmacol.* **75**, 163P.
29. Clark, D. A., and Marfat, A. (1982). *Annu. Rep. Med. Chem.* **17**, 291–300.
30. Clark, D. A., Goto, G., Marfat, A., Corey, E. J., Hammarström, S., and Samuelsson, B. (1980). *Biochem. Biophys. Res. Commun.* **94**, 1133–1139.
31. Cohen, N., Banner, B. L., and Lopresti, R. J. (1980). *Tetrahedron Lett.* pp. 4163–4166.
32. Corey, E. J., and Barton, A. E. (1982). *Tetrahedron Lett.* pp. 2351–2354.
33. Corey, E. J., and Brion, F. (1981). Harvard University, Cambridge, Massachusetts (unpublished work).
34. Corey, E. J., and Clark, D. A. (1980). *Tetrahedron Lett.* pp. 3547–3548.
35. Corey, E. J., and Goto, G. (1980). *Tetrahedron Lett.* pp. 3463–3466.
36. Corey, E. J., and Hoover, D. (1982). *Tetrahedron Lett.* pp. 3463–3466.
37. Corey, E. J., and Hortmann, A. G. (1965). *J. Am. Chem. Soc.* **87**, 5736–5742.
38. Corey, E. J., and Marfat, A. (1981). Harvard University, Cambridge, Massachusetts (unpublished work).
39. Corey, E. J., Arai, Y., and Mioskowski, C. (1979). *J. Am. Chem. Soc.* **101**, 6748–6749.
40. Corey, E. J., Albright, J. O., Barton, A. E., and Hashimoto, S. (1980). *J. Am. Chem. Soc.* **102**, 1435–1436.
41. Corey, E. J., Barton, A. E., and Clark, D. A. (1980). *J. Am. Chem. Soc.* **102**, 4278–4279.
42. Corey, E. J., Weinshenker, N. M., Schaaf, T. K., and Huber, W. J. (1969). *J. Am. Chem. Soc.* **91**, 5675–5677.
43. Corey, E. J. Niwa, H., and Knolle, J. (1978). *J. Am. Chem. Soc.* **100**, 1942–1943.
44. Corey, E. J., Niwa, H., and Falck, J. R. (1979). *J. Am. Chem. Soc.* **101**, 1586–1587.
45. Corey, E. J., Marfat, A., Falck, J. R., and Albright, J. O. (1980). *J. Am. Chem. Soc.* **102**, 1433–1435.
46. Corey, E. J., Clark, D. A., Goto, G., Marfat, A., Mioskowski, C., Samuelsson, B., and Hammarström, S. (1980). *J. Am. Chem. Soc.* **102**, 1436–1439, 3663.
47. Corey, E. J., Marfat, A., and Goto, G. (1980). *J. Am. Chem. Soc.* **102**, 6607–6608.
48. Corey, E. J., Marfat, A., Goto, G., and Brion, F. (1980). *J. Am. Chem. Soc.* **102**, 7984–7985.
49. Corey, E. J., Hopkins, P. B., Munroe, J. E., Marfat, A., and Hashimoto, S. (1980). *J. Am. Chem. Soc.* **102**, 7986–7987.
50. Corey, E. J., Clark, D. A., Marfat, A., and Goto, G. (1980). *Tetrahedron Lett.* pp. 3143–3146.
51. Corey, E. J., Park, H., Barton, A., and Nii, Y. (1980). *Tetrahedron Lett.* pp. 4243–4246.
52. Corey, E. J., Goto, G., and Marfat, A. (1980). Harvard University, Cambridge, Massachusetts (unpublished work).
53. Corey, E. J., Hashimoto, S., and Barton, A. E. (1981). *J. Am. Chem. Soc.* **103**, 721–722.
54. Corey, E. J., Marfat, A., and Brion, F. (1981). Harvard University, Cambrdige, Massachusetts (unpublished work).
55. Corey, E. J., Marfat, A., Munroe, J., Kim, K. S., Hopkins, P. B., and Brion, F. (1981). *Tetrahedron Lett.* pp. 1077–1080.
56. Corey, E. J., Marfat, A. and Hoover, D. J., (1981). *Tetrahedron Lett.* pp. 1587–1590.
57. Corey, E. J., Marfat, A., and Laguzza, B. C. (1981). *Tetrahedron Lett.* pp. 3339–3342.
58. Drazen, J. M., Lewis, R. A., Austen, K. F., Toda, M., Brion, F., Marfat, A., and Corey, E. J. (1981). *Proc. Natl. Acad. Sci. U.S.A.* **78**, 3195–3198.

59. Eiter, K., Lieb, F., Disselnkötter, H., and Oediger, H. (1978). *Liebigs Ann. Chem.* pp. 658-674.
60. Engineer, D. M., Piper, P. J., and Sirois, P. (1976). *Br. J. Pharmacol.* **57**, 460-461P.
61. Engineer, D. M., Morris, H. R., Piper, P. J., and Sirois, P. (1978). *Br. J. Pharmacol.* **64**, 211-218.
62. Feldberg, W., and Kellaway, C. H. (1938). *J. Physiol. (London)* **94**, 187-226.
63. Fitzpatrick, T. M., Alter, J., Corey, E. J., Ramwell, P. W., Rose, J. C., and Kot, P. A. (1978). *J. Pharmacol. Exp. Ther.* **206**, 139-142.
64. Ford-Hutchinson, A. W. (1984). *Adv. In Inflamm. Res.* **7**, 29-38.
65. Ford-Hutchinson, A. W., Bray, M. A., Doig, M. V., Shipley, M. E., and Smith, M. J. H. (1980). *Nature (London)* **286**, 264-265.
66. Girard, Y., Larue, M., Jones, T. R., and Rokach, J. (1982). *Tetrahedron Lett.* pp. 1023-1026.
67. Gleason, J. G., Bryan, D. B., and Kinzig, C. M. (1980). *Tetrahedron Lett.* pp. 1129-1132.
68. Goetzl, E. J. (1981). *Med. Clin. North Am.* **65**, 809-828.
69. Goetzl, E. J., and Pickett, W. C. (1980). *J. Immunol.* **125**, 1789-1791.
70. Guindon, Y., Zamboni, R., Lau, C. K., and Rokach, J. (1982). *Tetrahedron Lett.* pp. 739-742.
71. Hamberg, M., and Samuelsson, B. (1967). *J. Biol. Chem.* **242**, 5336-5343.
72. Hamberg, M., and Samuelsson, B. (1974). *Proc. Natl. Acad. Sci. U.S.A.* **71**, 3400-3404.
73. Hamberg, M., Svensson, J., and Samuelsson, B. (1975). *Proc. Natl. Acad. Sci. U.S.A.* **72**, 2994-2998.
74. Hammarström, S. (1980). *J. Biol. Chem.* **255**, 7093-7094.
75. Hammarström, S. (1981). *J. Biol. Chem.* **256**, 2275-2279.
76. Hammarström, S. (1981). *J. Biol. Chem.* **256**, 7712-7714.
77. Hammarström, S. (1981). *Biochim. Biophys. Acta* **663**, 575-577.
78. Hammarström, S., Murphy, R. C., Samuelsson, B., Clark, D. A., Mioskowski, C., and Corey, E. J. (1979). *Biochem. Biophys. Res. Commun.* **91**, 1266-1272.
79. Hammarström, S., Samuelsson, B., Clark, D. A., Goto, G., Marfat, A., Mioskowski, C., and Corey, E. J. (1980). *Biochem. Biophys. Res. Commun.* **92**, 946-953.
80. Jakschik, B. A., Falkenhein, S., and Parker, C. W. (1977). *Proc. Natl. Acad. Sci. U.S.A.* **74**, 4577-4581.
81. Johnson, R. A., Morton, D. R., Kinner, J. H., Gorman, R. R., McGuire, J. C., Sun, F. F., Whittaker, N., Bunting, S., Salmon, J., Moncada, S., and Vane, J. R. (1976). *Prostaglandins* **12**, 915-928.
82. Jubiz, W., Rådmark, O., Lindgren, J. A., Malmsten, C., and Samuelsson, B. (1981). *Biochem. Biophys. Res. Commun.* **99**, 976-986.
83. Katsuki, T., and Sharpless, K. P. (1980). *J. Am. Chem. Soc.* **102**, 5974-5976.
84. Kellaway, C. H., and Trethewie, E. R. (1940). *Q. J. Exp. Physiol. Cogn. Med. Sci.* **30**, 121-145.
85. Klickstein, L. B., Shapleigh, G., and Goetzl, E. J. (1980). *J. Clin. Invest.* **66**, 1166-1170.
86. Lewis, R. A., and Austen, K. F. (1981). *Nature (London)* **293**, 103-108.
87. Lewis, R. A., Austen, K. F., Drazen, J. M., Clark, D. A., Marfat, A., and Corey, E. J. (1980). *Proc. Natl. Acad. Sci. U.S.A.* **77**, 3710-3714.
88. Lewis, R. A., Drazen, J. M., Austen, K. F., Clark, D. A., and Corey, E. J. (1980). *Biochem. Biophys. Res. Commun.* **96**, 271-277.
89. Lewis, R. A., Goetzl, E. J., Drazen, J. M., Soter, N. A., Austen, K. F., and Corey, E. J. (1981). *J. Exp. Med.* **154**, 1243-1248.
90. Lewis, R. A., Drazen, J. M., Austen, K. F., Toda, M., Brion, F., Marfat, A., and Corey, E. J. (1981). *Proc. Natl. Acad. Sci. U.S.A.* **78**, 4579-4583.

91. Maddox, Y. T., Ramwell, P. W., Shiner, C. S., and Corey, E. J. (1978). *Nature (London)* **273,** 549–552.
92. Marriott, D. P., and Bantick, J. R. (1981). *Tetrahedron Lett.* pp. 3657–3658.
93. Moncada, S., Gryglewski, R., Bunting, S., and Vane, J. R. (1976). *Nature (London)* **263,** 663–665.
94. Morris, H. R., Taylor, G. W., Piper, P. J., Sirois, P., and Tippins, J. R. (1978). *FEBS Lett.* **87,** 203–206.
95. Morris, H. R., Taylor, G. W., Piper, P. J., and Tippins, J. R. (1979). *Agents Actions, Suppl.* **6,** 27–36.
96. Morris, H. R., Piper, P. J., Taylor, G. W., and Tippins, J. R. (1979). *Br. J. Pharmacol.* **67,** 179–184.
97. Morris, H. R., Taylor, G. W., Piper, P. J., Samhoun, M. N., and Tippins, J. R. (1980). *Prostaglandins* **19,** 185–201.
98. Morris, H. R., Taylor, G. W., Piper, P. J., and Tippins, J. R. (1980). *Nature (London)* **285,** 104–106.
99. Murphy, R. C., Hammarström, S., and Samuelsson, B. (1979). *Proc. Natl. Acad. Sci. U.S.A.* **76,** 4275–4279.
100. Murphy, R. C., Pickett, W. C., Culp, B. R., and Lands, W. E. M. (1981). *Prostaglandins* **22,** 613–622.
101. Naccache, P. H., Sha'afi, R. I., Borgeat, P., and Goetzl, E. J. (1981). *J. Clin. Invest.* **67,** 1584–1587.
102. Nicolaou, K. C., Petasis, N. A., and Seitz, S. P. (1981). *J. Chem. Soc., Chem. Commun.* pp. 1195–1196.
103. Nugteren, D. H. (1975). *Biochim. Biophys. Acta* **380,** 299–307.
104. Ohnishi, H., Kosuzume, H., Kitamura, Y., Yamaguchi, K., Nobuhara, M., and Suzuki, Y. (1980). *Prostaglandins* **20,** 655–666.
105. Oliw, E. H., Lawson, J. A., Brash, A. R., and Oates, J. A. (1981-. *J. Biol. Chem.* **256,** 9924–9931.
106. Orange, R. P., and Austen, K. F. (1969). *Adv. Immunol.* **10,** 105–144.
107. Orange, R. P., and Chang, P. L., (1975). *J. Immunol.* **115,** 1072–1077.
108. Orange, R. P., and Moore, E. G. (1976). *J. Immunol.* **116,** 392–397.
109. Orange, R. P., Murphy, R. C., Karnovsky, M. L., and Austen, K. F. (1973). *J. Immunol.* **110,** 760–770.
110. Orange, R. P., Murphy, R. C., and Austen, K. F. (1974). *J. Immunol.* **113,** 316–322.
111. Örning, L., Hammarström, S., and Samuelsson, B. (1980). *Proc. Natl. Acad. Sci. U.S.A.* **77,** 2014–2017.
112. Palmer, R. M. J., and Yates, D. A. (1981). *Br. J. Pharmacol.* **73,** 260P.
113. Palmer, R. M. J., Stepney, R. J., Higgs, G. A., and Eakins, K. E. (1980). *Prostaglandins* **20,** 411–418.
114. Parker, C. W., Huber, M. M., Hoffman, M. K., and Falkenhein, S. F. (1979). *Prostaglandins* **18,** 673–686.
115. Parker, C. W., Koch, D. A., Huber, M. M., and Falkenhein, S. F. (1980). *Prostaglandins* **20,** 887–907.
116. Piper, P. J. (1980). *Annu. Rep. Med. Chem.* **15,** 69–78.
117. Piper, P. J., Samhoun, M. N., Tippins, J. R., Morris, H. R., and Taylor, G. W. (1980). *Agents Actions* **10,** 541–547.
118. Piper, P. J., Samhoun, M. N., Tippins, J. R., Morris, H. R., Jones, C. M., and Taylor, G. W. (1981). *Int. Arch. Allergy Appl. Immunol.* **66,** 107–112.
119. Piper, P. J., ed. (1981). "SRS-A and Leukotrienes." Wiley, New York.

120. Rådmark, O., Malmsten, C., Samuelsson, B., Clark, D. A., Goto, G., Marfat, A., and Corey, E. J. (1980). *Biochem. Biophys. Res. Commun.* **92**, 954–961.
121. Rieke, R. D., and Bales, S. E. (1974). *J. Am. Chem. Soc.* **96**, 1775–1781.
122. Rokach, J., Girard, Y., Guindon, Y., Atkinson, J. G., Larue, M., Young, R. N., Masson, P., and Holme, G. (1980). *Tetrahedron Lett.* pp. 1485–1488.
123. Rokach, J., Young, R. N., Kakushima, M., Lau, C. K., Seguin, R., Frenette, R., and Guindon, Y. (1981). *Tetrahedron Lett.* pp. 979–982.
124. Rokach, J., Zamboni, R., Lau, C. K., and Guindon, Y. (1981). *Tetrahedron Lett.* pp. 2759–2762.
125. Rokach, J., Lau, C. K., Zamboni, R., and Guindon, Y. (1981). *Tetrahedron Lett.* pp. 2763–2766.
126. Rosenberg, M., and Lederer, F. (1980). European Patent 36663, *U.S. Patent* 4311645.
127. Rosenberg, M., and Neukom, C. (1980). *J. Am. Chem. Soc.* **102**, 5425–5426.
128. Rossiter, B. E., Katsuki, T., and Sharpless, B. K. (1981). *J. Am. Chem. Soc.* **103**, 464–465.
129. Samuelsson, B. (1980). *Atherosclerosis (Berlin)* **5**, 776.
130. Samuelsson, B. (1980). *Trends Pharmacol. Sci.* **1**, 227–230.
131. Samuelsson, B. (1981). *Int. Arch. Allergy Appl. Immunol.* **66**, 98–106.
132. Samuelsson, B. (1981). *Harvey Lect.* **75**, 1–40.
133. Samuelsson, B., and Borgeat, P. (1979). *J. Biol. Chem.* **254**, 2643–2644.
134. Samuelsson, B., and Hammarström, S. (1980). *Prostaglandins* **19**, 645–648.
135. Samuelsson, B., Borgeat, P., Hammarström, S., and Murphy, R. C. (1979). *Prostaglandins* **17**, 785–787.
136. Samuelsson, B., Hammarström, S., Murphy, R. C., and Borgeat, P. (1980). *Allergy* **35**, 375–381.
137. Samuelsson, B., Borgeta, P., Hammarström, S., and Murphy, R. C. (1980). *Adv. Prostaglandin Thromboxane Res.* **6**, 1–18.
138. Samuelsson, B. (1981). *Pure Appl. Chem.* **53**, 1203–1213.
138a. Samuelsson, B., and Paoletti, R., eds. (1982). "Leukotrienes and Other Lipoxygenase Products." Raven Press, New York.
139. Showell, H. J., Naccache, P. H., Borgeat, P., Picard, S., Vallerand, P., Becker, E. L., and Sha-afi, R. I. (1981). *J. Immunol.* **128**, 811–816.
140. Showell, H. J., Otterness, I. C., Marfat, A., and Corey, E. J. (1982). *Biochem. Biophys. Res. Commun.* **105**, 741–747.
141. Sirois, P. (1979). *Prostaglandins* **17**, 395–403.
142. Sirois, P., and Borgeat, P. (1980). *Int. J. Immunopharmacol.* **2**, 281–293.
143. Sirois, P., Engineer, D. M., Piper, P. J., and Moore, E. G. (1979). *Experientia* **35**, 361–363.
144. Sirois, P., Roy, S., Tetrault, J. P., Borgeat, P., Picard, S., and Corey, E. J. (1981). *Prostaglandins Med.* **7**, 327–340.
145. Smith, M. J. H. (1981). *Gen. Pharmacol.* **12**, 211–216.
146. Smith, M. J. H., Ford-Hutchison, A. W., and Bray, M. A. (1980). *J. Pharm. Pharmacol.* **32**, 517–518.
147. Trost, B. M., and Curran, D. P. (1981). *Tetrahedron Lett.* pp. 1287–1290.
148. Walker, I. C., Jones, R. L., and Wilson, N. H. (1979). *Prostaglandins* **18**, 173–178.
149. Walker, J. L. (1973). *Adv. Biosci.* **9**, 235–239.
150. Wollenberg, R. H. (1978). *Tetrahedron Lett.* pp. 717–720.
151. Young, R. N., Coombs, W., Guindon, Y., Rokach, J., Ethier, D., and Hall, R. (1981). *Tetrahedron Lett.* pp. 4933–4936.
152. Advances in Prostaglandin, Thromboxane and Leukotriene Research (eds. Samuelsson, B. and Paoletti, R.), (1981). *9*, Raven Press, New York.

3

Platelet Arachidonate Lipoxygenase

DAVID AHARONY,[1] J. BRYAN SMITH,[2] AND MELVIN J. SILVER

Cardeza Foundation and
Department of Pharmacology
Thomas Jefferson University
Philadelphia, Pennsylvania

[1] Present address: Biomedical Research, Department of Pharmacology, Stuart Pharmaceuticals, A Division of ICI Americas Inc., Wilmington, Delaware 19897.

[2] Present address: Thrombosis Research Center, Temple University, School of Medicine, Philadelphia, Pennsylvania 19140.

THE LEUKOTRIENES

I. INTRODUCTION

The existence of a mammalian lipoxygenase was first recognized in human platelets in 1974 (Hamberg *et al.,* 1974). Since then lipoxygenases have been found in white blood cells, lungs, and kidneys, as discussed elsewhere in this book. The platelet enzyme catalyzes the conversion of arachidonic acid (AA) to 12-L-hydroperoxy-5,8,10,14-eicosatetraenoic acid (12-HPETE), which is reduced intracellularly to the corresponding 12-hydroxy metabolite, 12-HETE (Nugteren, 1975). In platelets from most species examined, a greater portion of AA (either added to platelet suspensions or released endogenously) is oxygenated via the lipoxygenase pathway than via the cyclooxygenase pathway. Although 12-HETE and 12-HPETE have been shown to be strongly chemotactic for neutrophils (Turner *et al.,* 1974; Goetzel *et al.,* 1980), the biological activity of these substances with regard to platelet physiology is still debated. In this chapter our current knowledge of the properties of platelet lipoxygenase will be reviewed. In addition, we will discuss the recent evidence for the relationship between 12-HPETE and platelet function, including its possible role as a modulator of AA metabolism.

A. Platelets and Hemostasis

Platelets are fundamental in hemostasis. They arrest blood loss from a ruptured blood vessel by formation of aggregates. The participation of the metabolites of AA in this process is controlled by the enzymes responsible for its release and oxygenation in platelets (for a recent review, see Silver, 1981). Here we review the mechanisms for the release of AA and the significance of the platelet cyclooxygenase pathway.

B. Platelet Phospholipases

The liberation of AA from platelet phospholipids appears to be governed by several hydrolytic enzymes, the most important of which is probably phospholipase A_2, which hydrolyzes 2-arachidonylphospholipids to yield lysophospholipids and free AA (Bills *et al.,* 1976; McKean *et al.,* 1981). Several other mechanisms for the release of AA from platelet phospholipids have been described (Rittenhouse-Simmons, 1979; Bell *et al.,* 1979; Lapetina and Cuatrecasas, 1979; Lapetina *et al.,* 1981; Smith *et al.,* 1973).

C. Platelet Cyclooxygenase

As soon as AA is freely available in platelets, it is acted on by cyclooxygenase, which catalyzes a double oxygenation as well as a cyclization of the substrate to yield PGG_2, the first prostanoid molecule in prostaglandin biosynthesis. This PGG_2 is converted by the peroxidase component of cyclooxygenase to PGH_2, which then serves as the parent molecule for further transformation into other prostaglandins (Hamberg *et al.*, 1974).

D. Biological Activities of Platelet Prostanoids and Related Substances

Prostanoids can affect platelets in several ways. Prostaglandin endoperoxides and TxA_2 are potent inducers of platelet aggregation and secretion (Hamberg *et al.*, 1974) at submicromolar concentration. Although the evidence for the activity of TxA_2 is indirect because it has not been isolated and tested, the accepted order of potency is $TxA_2 > PGG_2 > PGH_2 > PGH_3 > PGH_1$. It is generally agreed that endoperoxides and TxA_2 mediate the secondary aggregation seen with ADP, epinephrine, and collagen. In addition, prostaglandin endoperoxides and TxA_2 are powerful vasoconstrictors. In contrast to these effects, PGE_1, PGD_2, and prostacyclin (produced in vascular tissues) are potent antiaggregating and antisecretory agents that exert their effects through elevation of platelet cAMP. This subject has been reviewed elsewhere (Smith, 1980).

II. PLATELET LIPOXYGENASE (ARACHIDONATE:OXYGEN OXIDOREDUCTASE)

In addition to its conversion by cyclooxygenase, AA is oxygenated by platelet lipoxygenase to 12-HPETE. Then, 12-HPETE is reduced to the 12-hydroxy compound 12-HETE, which may be isolated from platelets (Nugteren *et al.*, 1975; Siegel *et al.*, 1980). At high concentrations of AA, nonenzymatic formation of trihydroxy and epoxyhydroxy acids also occurs (Jones *et al.*, 1978; Bryant and Bailey, 1979). Figure 1 summarizes the presently known lipoxygenase pathway in human platelets.

A. Mechanism and Specificity

The mechanism of catalysis by platelet arachidonate lipoxygenase is similar to that by soybean lipoxygenase (Hamberg, 1976) except for the regiospecificity of the attack on the fatty acid substrate. The initial step is a stereoisomeric removal of L- but not D-hydrogen at carbon 10 (ω-11) of AA followed by a shift of the C-11 double bond to carbon 10. Active bimolecular oxygen is then attached to carbon 12 (ω-9) of the substrate to yield 12-HPETE (Hamberg and Hamberg, 1980). The hydrogen abstraction as well as molecu-

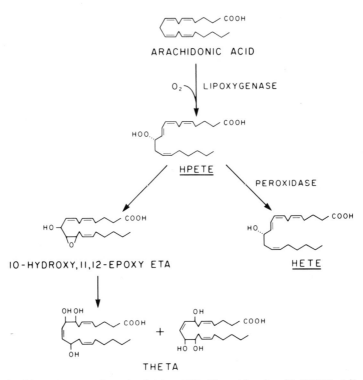

ARACHIDONIC ACID

O_2 LIPOXYGENASE

HPETE

PEROXIDASE

10-HYDROXY,11,12-EPOXY ETA

HETE

+

THETA

Fig. 1. Lipoxygenase pathway in platelets. ETA, Eicosatrienoic acid; THETA, trihydroxy-ETA.

lar oxygen activation are probably mediated by changes in the redox state of iron atoms bound by lipoxygenase (Aharony *et al.,* 1980, 1981a; Greenwald *et al.,* 1980), as proposed (but not proven) in Fig. 2.

Nugteren (1975) tested 10 different long-chain polyunsaturated fatty acids as substrates for bovine platelet lipoxygenase and found that the enzyme prefers 20-carbon acids that have at least two double bonds at positions ω-9 and ω-12, AA being the best substrate. Relative rates of 81, 60, and 60% conversion to product were found for 20:3(5,8,11), 20:3(8,11,14) (DHL), and 20:5(5,8,11,14,17) (EPA), respectively, compared to 20:4(5,8,11,14) (AA), which was considered as 100%. This greater affinity of the enzyme toward AA was later confirmed for human platelet lipoxygenase when K_m values of 16 μM for AA, 24 μM for EPA, and 79 μM for DHL were reported (Wallach and Brown, 1981). In this respect the enzyme differs from soybean lipoxygenase, which prefers 18- to 20-carbon acids as substrates (VanOs *et al.,* 1981; Spaapen *et al.,* 1980).

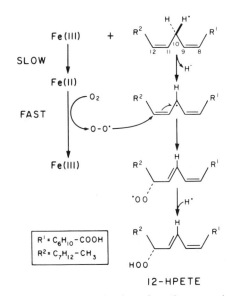

Fig. 2. Proposed mechanism of AA lipoxygenation.

B. Kinetics of Arachidonic Acid Oxygenation

Three methods have been used to measure lipoxygenase activity: (1) a spectrophotometric assay that follows the formation of conjugated diene bonds at 236 nm, (2) an oxygen consumption assay, and (3) an assay in which the formation of radiolabeled products from radioactive substrate is determined after lipid extraction and separation of the metabolites by thin-layer chromatography (TLC). Figure 3 shows the Lineweaver-Burk plot for the changes in initial velocities recorded spectrophotometrically and obtained with increasing concentrations of AA. The K_m for AA obtained by this method was $3.4 \pm 0.9 \ \mu M$ ($n = 8$). Values very similar to this were obtained when the conversion of [^{14}C]AA to 12-[^{14}C]HPETE or oxygen consumption was measured.

The linearity of the reaction of AA oxygenation was tested with four dilutions of the soluble lipoxygenase fraction over several concentrations of the substrate. Figure 4 shows that the V_{max} obtained at saturating concentrations of AA increased linearly with increasing protein concentration in the range of 165 to 1420 μg/ml. The K_m for AA was unchanged.

The relatively low K_m value of 3.4 μM for AA that we obtained for platelet lipoxygenase is comparable to that reported for sheep cyclooxygenase (2.3 μM AA; Hemler *et al.*, 1978) and soybean lipoxygenase type 1 (8.5 μM AA; VanOs *et al.*, 1981). Our K_m value, however, differs from those that have

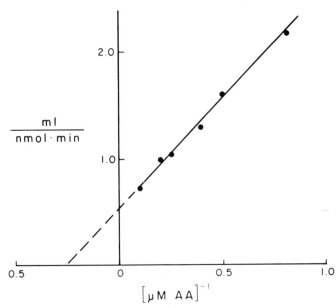

Fig. 3. Lineweaver-Burk plot of AA oxygenation by human platelet lipoxygenase. Reaction was initiated by adding an ethanolic solution of AA, at the indicated concentrations, to the enzyme solution (0.5 mg/ml in 25 mM Tris-HCl, pH 8.0), at 24°C, in a 1-ml cuvet. The increase in absorbance at 236 nm was recorded for the first 80 sec. Changes in initial velocities as a result of increasing AA concentrations were recorded spectrophotometrically, and the amount of 12-HPETE formed was calculated from the extinction coefficient at 236 nm (28,000 Cm-M^{-1}).

been previously reported for different preparations of platelet lipoxygenase, namely, 16 μM AA for detergent-solubilized platelet lipoxygenase (Wallach and Brown, 1981) and 80 μM AA for lipoxygenase activity in platelet cytosol obtained by high-speed centrifugation of freeze-thawed platelets (Siegel *et al.*, 1980). There are at least two reasons for these differences:

1. Lipoxygenase is a unique enzyme that has a lag phase before any observed catalysis starts. This lag period depends on enzyme concentration (Funk *et al.*, 1981), presence of peroxides (Funk *et al.*, 1981; Siegel *et al.*, 1979), and redox state of the free — SH groups of the enzyme. Thus if the lipoxygenase concentration is too low or the — SH groups are covalently modified to — SR or oxidized to — S— S, the lag phase will be prolonged. On the other hand, the presence of as little as 1 μM peroxide can increase the activity up to 100-fold and completely eliminate the lag phase (Hamberg and Hamberg, 1980; Funk *et al.*, 1981). Calculation of the true initial rate must take into account the time of the lag phase.

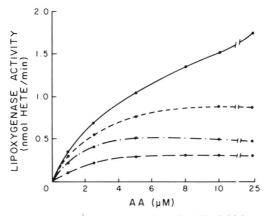

Fig. 4. Lipoxygenase activity versus protein concentration. The initial rate of oxygenation at different concentrations of AA with increasing concentration of enzyme were recorded spectrophotometrically. Conditions are as described in Fig. 3. Protein concentrations (μg/ml): 1420 (———), 700 (-----), 350 (– · –), 165 (– – –).

2. The enzyme reaction is best monitored by a direct assay such as conjugation of diene bonds at 236 nm or oxygen consumption. The radioactive-tracer assay can be used, but only if either total metabolite production or substrate loss are measured, not formation of radioactive 12-HPETE alone. This is because nonenzymatic breakdown of hydroperoxide (Gardner, 1975; Gardner and Jurisnic, 1981) will result in underestimation of the rate of product formation and lead to overestimation of the calculated K_m.

C. Preparation and Some Characteristics of the Enzyme

Platelet lipoxygenase can be conveniently prepared by sonication of washed human platelets suspended in Tris-saline buffer pH 8, containing 5–10 mM dithiothreitol. The sonicate is centrifuged for 30 min at 20,000 g at 4°C, the pellet is discarded, and the supernatant is then centrifuged at 105,000 g for 1 h at 4°C. The supernatant is collected, and most of the enzymatic activity can be precipitated with 25% ammonium sulfate in the cold, keeping the pH basic at all times. The pellet is resuspended in 25 mM Tris-HCl, pH 8, containing 2–5 mM dithiothreitol, and dialyzed for 3 h against the same buffer. The concentrated enzyme solution can be kept at − 60°C for 1 year. Figure 5 shows the pH versus activity profile of human platelet lipoxygenase with AA as substrate. The apparent broad pH optimum is in agreement with data reported before by others (Nugteren, 1975;

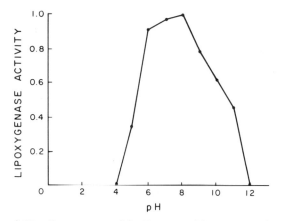

Fig. 5.   Effect of pH on lipoxygenase activity. Enzyme activity was determined spectrophoto-metrically as described in Fig. 3, after preincubation at 0°C for 5 min at the indicated pH. Maximal activity at pH 8 was assigned a value of 1.

Siegel *et al.,* 1980) and implies that intracellular pH is not a regulating factor for platelet lipoxygenase activity.

D. Stability

The soluble platelet lipoxygenase tends to aggregate and to lose activity when freeze-thawed repeatedly (Nugteren, 1977; Wallach and Brown, 1981). The thermostability of lipoxygenase activity is shown in Fig. 6. It can be seen that the enzymatic activity decayed very rapidly at 37°C with a half-life of 20 min versus a half-life of 17 h at 0°C. This low thermostability of the enzyme *in vitro* explains the loss of activity seen when soluble enzyme preparations are freeze-thawed repeatedly.

E. Purification

Platelet lipoxygenase has not yet been purified to homogeneity. It was reported that the enzyme can be obtained in soluble form from the platelet cytosolic fraction (Nugteren, 1975) and also as a particulate enzyme from platelet microsomes (Ho *et al.,* 1977). Fractions with lipoxygenase activity and apparent molecular weights of 100,000, 160,000, and higher were resolved when platelet cytosol was subjected to gel filtration (Nugteren, 1977; Siegel *et al.,* 1980).

We used a combination of gel filtration and affinity columns in an attempt to purify the platelet lipoxygenase. Figure 7 shows the elution pattern when the platelet cytosolic fraction was applied to a Sepharose-4B column and

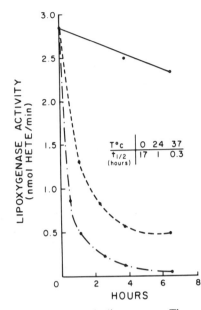

Fig. 6. Thermostability of human platelet lipoxygenase. The enzyme was preincubated at the given temperature for the time indicated (hours). It was then adjusted to room temperature and assayed as described in Fig. 3. Temperatures (°C): 0 (———), 24 (- - -), 37 (– · –).

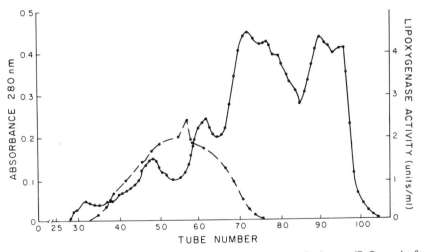

Fig. 7. Gel filtration of platelet cytosol (105,000 g supernatant) on Sepharose-4B. One unit of lipoxygenase activity (- - -) is the amount of enzyme that will cause an increase of absorbance of 0.028 per minute at 236 nm (———).

eluted with 25 mM Tris-HCl, pH 8. It can be seen that lipoxygenase activity was spread over large volumes of the eluate corresponding to proteins with molecular weights ranging from 100,000 to 400,000. These results suggest aggregation of the enzyme or its association with other larger proteins. Tubes 55–60 (Fig. 8), which had the highest activity, were pooled and applied to an AH Sepharose-4B linoleic acid gel. After washing the column with 25 mM Tris buffer, pH 8.2, the activity was eluted with stepwise increases in the ionic strength of the buffer. Figure 8 shows that two peaks of activity were eluted from the column. The first and major peak was eluted with 0.25 M NaCl and contained a total of 9.3 units of lipoxygenase activity. A second peak was eluted with 0.5 M NaCl and had a total of 5.2 units. No more activity or protein was eluted from the column, even with 1.0 M NaCl or 6 M urea.

The total activity eluted from the affinity column represented less than 5% of the initial activity in the cytosol and still contained five different proteins as indicated by SDS–gel electrophoresis of material in the second peak, reduced with 1% mercaptoethanol. A scheme for partial purification of platelet lipoxygenase from platelet cytosol has been published (Siegel *et al.,* 1980). The authors used gel filtration or ion-exchange chromatography to purify the lipoxygenase activity. However, no evidence for homogeneity was presented in this study.

It has been reported that platelet lipoxygenase activity is also associated with the microsomal fraction of platelets (Ho *et al.,* 1977). We and others (Siegel *et al.,* 1980) have confirmed that there are always appreciable amounts of activity associated with the platelet microsomal fraction. These findings may indicate that the so-called soluble lipoxygenase is actually a loosely bound membrane enzyme that can be released from the membrane by detergents or by the physical methods of sonication or freezing and thawing, but even then it remains associated with hydrophobic membrane proteins.

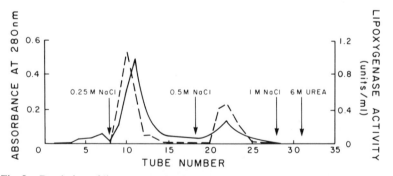

Fig. 8.   Resolution of lipoxygenase (pooled tubes 55–60 from Sepharose-4B column) on affinity column. For details see Fig. 7 and text.

F. Solubilization

A number of detergents were tested to find out whether they would help in the purification of the lipoxygenase activity of platelets. Initially we tested the effects of detergents on the 25% ammonium sulfate fraction obtained from the cytosol of human platelets. The preparations were mixed thoroughly with 1% detergent and then assayed for lipoxygenase activity using radiolabeled AA as a substrate. The results shown in Table I clearly demonstrate that all the detergents studied inhibited the lipoxygenase activity by more than 50%.

We also tried to assess the effect of detergents on the lipoxygenase activity revealed when whole platelets were solubilized in various detergents. Washed platelets were solubilized with 1% detergent solution in saline and centrifuged at 105,000 g for 1 h at 4°C. The supernatant was collected, diluted 1:50 in 25 mM Tris-HCl buffer, pH 8.2, and assayed spectrophotometrically for lipoxygenase activity. Table II shows that all of the detergents tested were inhibitory to some degree, with NP_{40} being the least inhibitory. However, all of the activity extracted from NP_{40}-treated platelets was lost within 5 to 6 h in the cold room, and all attempts to purify this fraction further on a Sepharose-4B column (equilibrated with or without 1% NP_{40}) or on affinity columns were unsuccessful.

G. Iron Dependence

Platelet lipoxygenase probably contains iron and depends on it for its activity (see Fig. 2). It is most likely in the ferric [Fe(III)] form, since ferric iron chelators such as toluene-3,4-dithiol, dithizone, EDTA, EGTA, Ferron, and orthophenanthrolene strongly inhibit the enzymatic activity (Aharony

TABLE I

Inhibition of Lipoxygenase by Detergents Measured by Percentage
Radioactivity in Products[a]

Products[b]	Detergent (1%)				
	None	Tween 30	Tween 80	Triton X-100	NP_{40}
12-HETE	3.1	1.6	0.6	0.6	0.2
12-HPETE	14.6	6.1	4.9	0.3	0.1
AA	75.9	88.2	92.3	96.3	98.9

[a] Results are means of duplicate determinations. Incubation was for 10 min with 10 μM radioactive AA. For other details see text.

[b] Approximately 1–6% of the radioactivity was associated with the origin on the TLC plates and was probably a mixture of nonenzymatic degradation products of 12-HPETE.

TABLE II

Lipoxygenase Activity in Detergent-Solubilized Platelet Preparations

Fraction	Broken Platelets	NP_{40}	DOC^b	Triton X-100
Units/ml^c	14.4	11.6	6.4	7.2
% Recovery	100	80	44	50

^{a} Ultrasonicated at 85 watts, three times in ice bath.
^{b} Deoxycholate.
^{c} Mean of triplicate determinations. For details see text.

et al., 1980, 1981a; Greenwald *et al.,* 1980). Figure 9 shows the concentration-dependent inhibition of lipoxygenase activity by some iron chelators. Toluene-3,4-dithiol strongly complexes with ferric but not ferrous ions (Pistorius *et al.,* 1974). Similar results were obtained with dithizone (not shown), an agent previously reported to be a potent inhibitor of soybean lipoxygenase, an enzyme that probably requires ferric iron (Pistorius *et al.,* 1974). In contrast, little inhibition of platelet lipoxygenase activity was observed with 2,2'-dipyridyl at 50 μM and none with EDTA at 5 mM. (See discussion of inhibition by EDTA below.) The iron-chelating agent *o*-phenanthroline inhibited diene formation by approximately 50% (IC_{50}) at 100 μM (10-fold less active than toluene-3,4-dithiol or dithizone), and analysis of radioactive products confirmed that it inhibited formation of HPETE. In contrast, bathophenanthroline at 100 μM had no effect on the formation of HPETE.

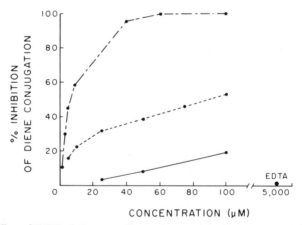

Fig. 9. Effect of Fe(III) chelators on lipoxygenase activity. Enzyme was preincubated for 5 min with the compounds indicated: (- - -) toluene-3,4-dithiol; (-----) *o*-phenanthroline; (———) 2,2-dipyridyl. Enzyme activity was determined as described in Fig. 3 using 10 μM AA as substrate.

In the preceding experiments, EDTA did not inhibit the lipoxygenase activity when preincubated with the enzyme for as long as 10 min. In dialysis experiments, however, all the activity was lost within 4 h when active enzyme fractions were dialyzed at 4°C against 25 mM Tris-HCl buffer, pH 8.2, containing 2 mM EDTA. Control enzyme that was dialyzed against buffer alone lost approximately 15% of its initial activity. Our results are in agreement with those of Greenwald et al. (1980), who found a linear correlation between the logarithm of the stability constants of some ferric iron – chelator complexes and the logarithm of the inhibition constant of the enzymatic activity, where the strongest ferric chelator of the compounds tested (EDTA) was the most potent inhibitor of lipoxygenase. In addition, they showed that ferric but not ferrous chloride could partially protect against the inhibition of activity produced by the chelators. The iron content in lipoxygenase has not been determined, however, since no one has yet purified the enzyme to homogeneity and assayed its iron content.

Studies on the effects of dithizone on lipoxygenase activity in intact platelets did not show selectivity, since it inhibited cyclooxygenase as well as lipoxygenase (data not shown). Thus the chelating agents presently available do not permit selective probing of lipoxygenase in intact cells.

Platelet lipoxygenase, like the lipoxygenase from soybean, also contains free — SH groups, which are essential for enzymatic activity. p-Chloromercurobenzoate (2 mM) (Nugteren, 1977), iodoacetamide (1 mM), N-ethylmaleimide (1 mM), and p-chloromercuroparasulfonate (1 mM) (Siegel et al., 1980) all strongly inhibit the platelet enzyme.

H. Peroxide Activation

The activation of platelet lipoxygenase by its own product 12-HPETE, or by other intracellular peroxides may accelerate the oxygenation of AA via this pathway. It has been reported that 12-HPETE (EC$_{50}$ = 0.33 μM), but not its reduced metabolite 12-HETE, markedly stimulates the initial rate of AA oxygenation and eliminates the lag phase (Siegel et al., 1979b). The lipoxygenase activity is also stimulated by 11-HPETE (EC$_{50}$ = 1.4 μM), whereas both 8- and 9-HPETE are inactive at concentrations up to 50 μM. The activation of platelet lipoxygenase by peroxides has also been shown in intact platelets. Hamberg and Hamberg (1980) showed that a 15-sec preincubation with AA greatly stimulates the conversion of 5,8,11,14,17-[1-^{14}C]eicosapentaenoic acid (EPA) to 12-hydroperoxy EPA. Since AA is a good substrate for both the cyclooxygenase and the lipoxygenase, while EPA is a poor substrate for cyclooxygenase but almost as good as AA for the lipoxygenase, this was interpreted as indicating that peroxides of AA generated via cyclooxygenase stimulated the lipoxygenase activity toward EPA. Indeed, this three- to fourfold stimulation was abolished with concomitant appearance of a 1-min lag phase when 140 μM indomethacin, a cyclooxygenase inhibitor, was preincubated with the platelets (Hamberg and Hamberg, 1980). The conclusions of the study were that PGG_2 formation causes activation of lipoxygenase in intact platelets.

Thus, once sufficient amounts of PGG_2 are generated in platelets, an effect that occurs within 30 sec after platelet stimulation, lipoxygenase activity increases rapidly. Initial generation of 12-HPETE by the lipoxygenase further accelerates its activity, and the enzyme then goes on to generate even greater amounts of the metabolite, for a period of 20 min or more, while TxB_2 production diminishes (Hamberg et al., 1974; Nugteren, 1977).

Although 12-HPETE in high concentrations can inactivate the lipoxygenase in a cell-free system, this may not be the case in intact platelets, where effective removal of this reactive product probably occurs via a peroxidase. In 1979 Siegel et al. reported that aspirin-like drugs inhibit the conversion of 12-HPETE to 12-HETE in intact platelets, and this was interpreted as an inhibition of 12-HPETE peroxidase (Siegel et al., 1979a). It was proposed that drugs like aspirin, indomethacin, ibuprofen, and sulindac have dual effects on platelets, inhibiting both the cyclooxygenase and the peroxidase, thus raising the 12-HPETE to abnormally high levels. The inhibition of platelet aggregation by these drugs was hypothesized to result from the combined effects of abolishing prostaglandin synthesis and accumulation of 12-HPETE.

Peroxidase activity has been shown to depend on the presence of glucose and reduced glutathione (Bryant and Bailey, 1980). In the absence of these cofactors 12-HPETE decomposes nonenzymatically into trihydroxy fatty acids. These authors also have provided evidence for the importance of selenium for the peroxidase activity.

III. INHIBITORS

A. Classification

Presently known inhibitors of platelet lipoxygenase can be divided into seven classes:

1. Fatty acid analogs:
    a. Acetylenic acids (e.g., ETYA)
    b. Product analogs (e.g., 15-HETE)
2. Iron chelators (e.g., 3,4-toluene dithiol, dithizon, and KCN)
3. Phenylhydrazones (e.g., benzoyl chloride phenylhydrazone)
4. Sulfhydryl reagents (e.g., PCMB, NEM)

5. Antioxidants: nordihydroguaiaretic acid
6. Miscellaneous (e.g., Zn^{2+}, Sn^{2+}, and chloropromazine)

The use of one or a combination of these inhibitors may enable the biologist to achieve a better understanding of the function of lipoxygenase in platelets, provided that they can be shown to act selectively and not have other effects on the platelet membrane.

B. Fatty Acid Analogs

Platelet lipoxygenase is not inhibited by cyclooxygenase inhibitors such as aspirin or indomethacin (Hamberg et al., 1974). Both oxygenases, however, are inhibited to different extents by fatty acid acetylenic analogs such as 5,8,11,14-eicosatetraynoic acid (ETYA) (Hamberg et al., 1974). In intact platelets 50% inhibition or more of platelet lipoxygenase was obtained with ETYA at 4.0 μM (Hammarström, 1977a), 10 μM (Hamberg et al., 1974), 2.9 μM (Sun et al., 1980), and as low as 0.7 μM (Dutilh et al., 1980). However, cyclooxygenase was only inhibited by ETYA at the higher concentrations of 8 to 10 μM. An IC_{50} as low as 0.03 μM for inhibition of lipoxygenase activity in the platelet high-speed supernatant has been reported (Sun et al., 1981). We found half-maximal inhibition of a soluble platelet lipoxygenase preparation at 0.1 μM ETYA. A 100-fold increase in ETYA concentration (10 μM), however, was needed to abolish the enzyme activity.

Hammarström (1977) showed that 5,8,11-eicosatriynoic acid, although six times less potent than ETYA as a lipoxygenase inhibitor, is much more selective than ETYA, with an IC_{50} of 24 μM for lipoxygenase compared to 340 μM for cyclooxygenase. He suggested that a fatty acid analog that has carbon 10 attached to two acetylenic carbons is a selective lipoxygenase inhibitor, whereas an acetylenic bond at carbon 14 is not crucial, since the initial lipoxygenase-mediated catalysis occurs at carbon 10. Several studies done with nine different polyacetylenic analogs do not support this suggestion (Wilhelm et al., 1981; Sun et al., 1981). It was found that the acetylenic acid 20:4(4,7,10,13) is a highly selective lipoxygenase inhibitor with considerably less effect on cyclooxygenase. This was demonstrated both in cell-free preparations, where this analog was almost 900 times more potent in inhibiting lipoxygenase compared to cyclooxygenase (Sun et al., 1981), and in intact platelets where it was over 100 times more potent (Wilhelm et al., 1981). The authors interpreted the data as indicating that a methylene carbon at C-10 is not an absolute requirement for inhibition, since the most potent inhibitor of the series did not possess this structure.

Other oxygenated derivatives of fatty acids can inhibit platelet lipoxygenase. It was reported that 15-HPETE is a potent inhibitor of both lipoxygenase and cyclooxygenase in platelets with IC_{50} values of 2.5 and 5.7 μM, respectively (Vanderhoek et al., 1980). Although less potent than its 15-hydroperoxy precursor, 15-HETE was much more selective, inhibiting the lipoxygenase with an IC_{50} of 8.2 μM compared to an IC_{50} of 135 μM for the cyclooxygenase. The mechanism for such selective inhibition, however, is not clear, since the hydroxyl group at carbon 15 is not in the vicinity of carbons 10 or 12, which are involved in the catalysis by platelet lipoxygenase. As the double bonds at positions 8 and 11 and the methylene carbon at C-10 are still intact in 15-HETE, it is possible that it can still be recognized by the platelet lipoxygenase as a substrate, perhaps forming some irreversible complex with the enzyme. Interestingly, both 12-HETE and ricinoleic acid had no effect on platelet lipoxygenase at concentrations up to 300 μM (Vanderhoek et al., 1980).

C. Phenylhydrazones

Search for other selective lipoxygenase inhibitors led to the finding that acetone phenylhydrazone is 10 times more potent in inhibiting the lipoxygenase than the cyclooxygenase in a washed-platelet system (Sun et al., 1980). A series of phenylhydrazone derivatives have now been synthesized and tested on isolated soybean lipoxygenase, platelet lipoxygenase, and cyclooxygenase. Two derivatives, benzoyl chloride phenylhydrazone and ketonmethyl-4-pyridyl-phenylhydrazone, were found to be both potent and highly selective lipoxygenase inhibitors, that worked at submicromolar concentrations (Wallach and Brown, 1981). We also studied the effects of p-isopropyl-benzoyl chloride phenylhydrazone (kindly supplied by Dr. D. P. Wallach, The Upjohn Company) on platelet lipoxygenase and found that it inhibited the enzyme activity in a noncompetitive (K_i 2.8 μM, Fig. 10A) and a time-dependent fashion (Fig. 10B). The mechanism by which these compounds exert their effect may be through iron chelation, since their structures are similar to the iron chelator dithizone and their effects depend on preincubation with the enzyme.

D. Cyanide

Soybean lipoxygenase (Tappel, 1963) as well as bovine platelet lipoxygenase (Nugteren, 1975) were reported to be insensitive to cyanide. However, it has since been shown that both rat testis lipoxygenase and soybean lipoxygenase are sensitive to cyanide inhibition (Shahin et al., 1978). We investigated the effects of potassium cyanide on the activity of human platelet lipoxygenase in a cell-free system as well as in intact platelets. Spectrophoto-

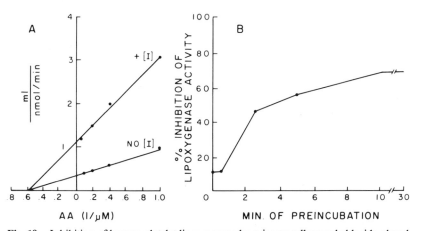

Fig. 10. Inhibition of human platelet lipoxygenase by p-isopropylbenzoyl chloride phenyl-hydrazone (U-28938). Lipoxygenase (0.5 mg/ml) was incubated for 10 min with or without 5 μM U-28938 (I). Reaction was initiated with increasing concentrations of AA. Other conditions were as described in Fig. 3. (A) Lineweaver-Burk plot of the lipoxygenase reaction. (B) Effect of preincubation time on the inhibition of lipoxygenase by (I) at 2.5 μM.

metric assays indicated that KCN inhibited activity of platelet cytosol in a dose-dependent fashion with an IC_{50} of 2 mM. This inhibition was confirmed both by a radiochemical assay that utilized [^{14}C]AA as a substrate and by direct measurement of oxygen consumption by polarography (Aharony *et al.*, 1982b).

E. Antioxidants

The antioxidant nordihydroguaiaretic acid was reported to inhibit the lipoxygenase selectively but not the cyclooxygenase (Hamberg, 1976). Antioxidants probably prevent the activation of oxygen by the enzyme, thus arresting the catalysis at its initial stage.

F. Miscellaneous Inhibitors

In addition to the inhibitors already mentioned, other agents inhibit platelet lipoxygenase. The antiinflammatory drug BW755C was reported to inhibit both the cyclooxygenase and the lipoxygenase (Higgs *et al.*, 1979). At 3.7 mM, Zn^{2+} and Sn^{2+} (but not Ca^{2+}, Mg^{2+}, Cu^{2+}, Fe^{2+}, Ni^{2+}, or Cd^{2+}) completely abolish the enzyme activity (Wallach and Brown, 1981). Chloropromazine at 1 mM was reported to inhibit platelet lipoxygenase activity by 50% (Robak and Dimiec, 1980).

IV. EFFECTS OF LIPOXYGENASE PRODUCTS ON PLATELETS

Since the biological activities of hydroperoxy- and hydroxy fatty acids on other cells are discussed in detail in other chapters of this volume, this discussion is limited to some effects that 12-HPETE exerts on the metabolism and function of platelets.

Hammarström and Falardeau (1977) reported that 12-HPETE inhibits partially purified thromboxane synthetase in a dose-dependent fashion with an IC_{50} of 100 μM, whereas 12-HETE had no such effect. Siegel *et al.* (1979b) found that 12-HPETE also inhibits the metabolism of AA via the cyclooxygenase pathway. The conversion of exogenously added AA to TxB_2 and hydroxyheptadecatrienoic acid (HHT) was reduced by 12-HPETE in a concentration-dependent fashion in intact human platelets ($IC_{50} = 6 \mu M$) or homogenates ($IC_{50} = 3 \mu M$). Siegel *et al.* (1979b) also found that 12-HPETE (100 μM) inhibits collagen or AA-induced platelet aggregation measured in platelet-rich plasma. We have extended these studies (Aharony *et al.*, 1982) to a washed-platelet system (to avoid the binding of 12-HPETE by albumin) and found that 12-HPETE inhibits AA-induced aggregation in a concentration-dependent fashion with an IC_{50} of 2.5 μM. However, TxB_2 and malondialdehyde (MDA) production were inhibited at higher concentrations with IC_{50} values of 15 and 25 μM, respectively. This dissociation of the concentration–response curves actually implies a direct effect of 12-HPETE on platelet aggregation apart from inhibition of cyclooxygenase.

Table III shows the concentrations of 12-HPETE required to produce half-maximal inhibition of platelet aggregation induced by different agonists. Thrombin-induced aggregation was not inhibited by 12-HPETE. Aggregation induced by AA, azo-PGH_2, or epoxymethano-PGH_2 was inhibited by lower concentrations of 12-HPETE than that induced by collagen or thrombin. This together with the fact that higher concentrations of 12-

TABLE III

Concentrations of 12-HPETE (μM) That
Produce Half-Maximal Inhibition of the
Aggregation of Washed Human Platelets

Aggregating agent		IC_{50}
AA	(5 μM)	2.5
Azo-PGH_2	(0.2 μM)	2
Epoxymethano-PGH_2	(1.4 μM)	3
Collagen	(10 μg/ml)	6
Thrombin	(0.2 U/ml)	> 50

HPETE were needed to abolish TxB_2 synthesis implies an antagonistic effect of 12-HPETE on endoperoxide- and/or thromboxane-induced aggregation. The data suggest that under conditions in which platelets accumulate high concentrations of 12-HPETE, their responsiveness to aggregating stimuli might be inhibited.

It was previously reported (Linder *et al.*, 1979) that AA in high concentrations inhibits platelet aggregation and secretion. We used increasing concentrations of radiolabeled AA to induce platelet aggregation and found that diminished aggregation was associated with a marked increase in 12-HETE formation, reflecting an increased formation of 12-HPETE (Aharony *et al.*, 1982a). The ratio of 12-HETE:TxB_2 rose from 3.9 $\pm$ 1.8 at 5 μM AA (maximal aggregation) to 15.1 $\pm$ 5.2 ($p <$ .01) at 50 μM AA (minimal aggregation). This diminished aggregation was not due to lack of thromboxane synthesis, since the concentration of TxB_2 increased over threefold.

The concept that lipoxygenase products inhibit platelet function is not accepted by all researchers, Dutilh *et al.* (1980) showed that AA-induced aggregation is reversed by ETYA at concentrations that block the formation of 12-HETE but not HHT or TxB_2. The authors' interpretation was that this implies that 12-HETE formation actually promotes the irreversibility of thromboxane-induced aggregation. In a later report, however (Dutilh *et al.*, 1981), they showed that both mead acid (5,8,11-eicosatrienoic acid), a good platelet lipoxygenase substrate (Nugteren, 1975), and 12-HETE itself inhibit platelet aggregation. The mechanism of inhibition of aggregation and secretion of human platelets by 12-HPETE is not known at the present time. Although 12-HPETE does not increase cAMP in platelets (D. Aharony, unpublished observations), another HPETE isomer was shown to activate platelet guanylate cyclase (Hidaka and Asano, 1977) and to inhibit platelet diglyceride lipase (Rittenhouse-Simmons, 1980).

In conclusion, metabolites of the platelet lipoxygenase pathway may have a modulatory role that tends to attenuate and finally terminate the effects of the cyclooxygenase products (e.g., aggregation and secretion). Furthermore, although not discussed here, 12-HPETE shares many of the activities attributed to other HPETE isomers on leukocytes (Goetzl *et al.*, 1980), vascular prostacyclin synthetase (Ham *et al.*, 1979) and smooth muscle (Trachte *et al.*, 1979).

ACKNOWLEDGMENTS

This work was supported in part by NIH grant HL-14890 and a fellowship of the Pharmaceutical Manufacturers Association to Dr. Aharony.

REFERENCES

Aharony, D., Smith, J. B., and Silver, M. J. (1980). *Fed. Proc. Fed. Am. Soc. Exp. Biol.* **39,** 424 (abstr.).

Aharony, D., Smith, J. B., and Silver, M. J. (1981a). *Prostaglandins Med.* **6,** 237–242.

Aharony, D., Smith, J. B., and Silver, M. J. (1981b). *Thromb. Haemostasis.* **46,** 834 (abstr.).

Aharony, D., Smith, J. B., and Silver, M. J. (1982). *Biochim. Biophys. Acta* **718,** 193–200.

Aharony, D., Smith, J. B., and Silver, M. J. (1982b). *Experientia* **38,** 1334.

Bell, R. L., Kennerly, D. A., Stanford, N., and Majerus, P. W. (1979). *Proc. Natl. Acad. Sci. U.S.A.* **76,** 3238–3241.

Bills, T. K., Smith, J. B., and Silver, M. J. (1976). *Biochim. Biophys Acta* **424,** 303–314.

Bryant, R. W., and Bailey, J. M. (1979). *Prostaglandins* **17,** 9–18.

Bryant, R. W., and Bailey, J. M. (1980). *Adv. Prostaglandin Thromboxane Res.* **6,** 95–99.

Dutilh, C. E., Haddeman, E., and Ten-Hoor, F. (1980). *Adv. Prostaglandin Thromboxane Res.* **6,** 101–115.

Dutilh, C. E., Haddeman, E., Don, J. A., and Ten-Hoor, F. (1981). *Prostaglandins Med.* **6,** 111–126.

Funk, M. O., Kim, S. H., and Alteneder, A. W. (1981). *Biochem. Biophys. Res. Commun.* **98,** 923–929.

Gardner, H. W. (1975). *J. Agric. Food Chem.* **23,** 124–136.

Gardner, H. W., and Jurisinic, P. A. (1981). *Biochim. Biophys. Acta* **665,** 100–112.

Goetzl, E. J., Hill, H. R., and Gorman, R. R. (1980). *Prostaglandins* **19,** 71–85.

Greenwald, J. E., Alexander, M. S., Fertel, R. H., Beach, C. A., Wong, L. K., and Bianchine, J. R. (1980). *Biochem. Biophys. Res. Commun.* **96,** 817–822.

Ham, E. A., Eagan, R. W., Soderman, P. D., Gale, P. H., and Kuehl, F. A., Jr. (1979). *J. Biol. Chem.* **254,** 2191–2194.

Hamberg, M. (1976). *Biochim. Biophys. Acta* **431,** 651–654.

Hamberg, M., and Hamberg, G. (1980). *Biochem. Biophys. Res. Commun.* **95,** 1090–1097.

Hamberg, M., Svensson, J., and Samuelsson, B. (1974). *Proc. Natl. Acad. Sci. U.S.A.* **71,** 3824–3828.

Hammarström, S. (1977). *Biochim. Biophys. Acta* **487,** 517–519.

Hammarström, S., and Falardeau, P. (1977). *Proc. Natl. Acad. Sci. U.S.A.* **74,** 3691–3695.

Hemler, M. E., Crawford, C. G., and Lands, E. M. (1978). *Biochemistry* **17,** 1772–1779.

Hidaka, H., and Asano, T. (1977). *Proc. Natl. Acad. Sci. U.S.A.* **74,** 3657–3663.

Higgs, G. A., Flower, R. J., and Vane, J. R. (1979). *Biochem. Pharmacol.* **28,** 1959–1961.

Ho, P. P. K., Waters, C. P., and Sullivan, H. R. (1977). *Biochem. Biophys. Res. Commun.* **76,** 398–405.

Jones, R. L., Kerry, P. J., Poyser, N. L., Walker, I. C., and Wilson, N. H. (1978). *Prostaglandins* **16,** 583–590.

Lapetina, E. G., and Cuatrecasas, P. (1979). *Biochim. Biophys. Acta* **573,** 394–402.

Lapetina, E. G., Billah, M. M., and Cuatrecasas, P. (1981). *J. Biol. Chem.* **256,** 5037–5040.

Linder, B. L., Chernoff, A., Kaplan, K. L., and Goodman, D. S. (1979). *Proc. Natl. Acad. Sci. U.S.A.* **76,** 4107–4111.

McKean, M. L., Smith, J. B., and Silver, M. J. (1981). *J. Biol. Chem.* **256,** 1522–1524.

Nugteren, D. H. (1975). *Biochim. Biophys. Acta* **380,** 299–307.

Nugteren, D. H. (1977). *In* "Prostaglandins in Haematology" (M. J. Silver, J. B. Smith, and J. J. Kocsis, eds.), pp. 11–25. Spectrum Publ., New York.

Pistorius, E. K. and Axelrod, B. (1974). *J. Biol. Chem.* **249,** 3183–3186.

Rittenhouse-Simmons, S. (1979). *J. Clin. Invest.* **63,** 580–587.

Rittenhouse-Simmons, S. (1980). *J. Biol. Chem.* **255,** 2254–2262.

Robak, J., and Dimiec, Z. (1980). *Biochim. Biophys. Acta* **620,** 52–54.

Shahin, I., Grossman, S., and Sredni, S. (1978). *Biochim. Biophys. Acta* **529,** 300–308.

Siegel, M. I., McConnell, R. I., and Cuatrecasas, P. (1979a). *Proc. Natl. Acad. Sci. U.S.A.* **76,** 3774–3778.

Siegel, M. I., McConnell, R. T., Abrams, S. L., Porter, N. A., and Cuatrecasas, P. (1979b). *Biochem. Biophys. Res. Commun.* **89,** 1273–1280.

Siegel, M. I., McConnell, R. I., Porter, N. A., and Cuatrescasas, P. (1980). *Proc. Natl. Acad. Sci. U.S.A.* **77,** 308–312.

Silver, M. J. (1981). *Adv. Pharmacol. Chemother.* **18,** 1–47.

Smith, J. B. (1980). *Am. J. Pathol.* **94,** 743–804.

Smith, J. B., Silver, M. J., and Webster, G. R. (1973). *Biochem. J.* **131,** 615–618.

Spaapen, L. J. M., Verhagen, J., Veldnik, G. A., and Vliegenthart, J. F. E. (1980). *Biochim. Biophys. Acta* **618,** 153–162.

Sun, F. F., McGuire, J. C., Wallach, D. P., and Brown, V. R. (1980). *Adv. Prostaglandin Thromboxane Res.* **6,** 111–114.

Sun, F. F., McGuire, J. C., Morton, D. R., Pike, J. E., Sprecher, H., and Kumas, W. H. (1981). *Prostaglandins* **21,** 333–343.

Tappel, A. L. (1963). *In* "The Enzymes" (P. D. Boyer, H. Lardy, and K. Myrbäck, eds.) 2nd rev. ed., Vol. 8, pp. 275–283. Academic Press, New York.

Trachte, G. J., Lefer, A. M., Aharony, D., and Smith, J. B. (1979). *Prostaglandins* **18,** 909–912.

Turner, S. R., Tainer, J. A., and Lynn, W. S. (1974). *Nature (London)* **257,** 680–681.

Vanderhoek, J. Y., Bryant, R. W., and Bailey, J. M. (1980). *J. Biol. Chem.* **255,** 5996–5998.

VanOs, C. P. A., Rijke-Shilder, C. P. M., VanHalbek, H., Verhagen, J., and Vlieganthart, J. F. G. (1981). *Biochim. Biophys. Acta* **663,** 177–193.

Wallach, D. P., and Brown, V. R. (1981). *Biochim. Biophys. Acta* **663,** 361–372.

Wilhelm, T. E., Sankarappa, S. K., Van Rollins, M., and Sprecher, H. (1981). *Prostaglandins* **21,** 323–332.

4

The Lipoxygenases in Leukocytes and Other Mammalian Cells

CHARLES W. PARKER

Howard Hughes Medical Institute Laboratory and Department of Internal Medicine
Division of Allergy and Immunology
Washington University School of Medicine
St. Louis, Missouri

I. GENERAL FEATURES

Lipoxygenases (EC 1.13.11.12) enzymes widely distributed in plants and animals that have the common property of oxidizing unsaturated long-chain fatty acids (and to a lesser extent alcohols, esters, and halides) to hydroperoxy products. [For reviews of plant and animal lipoxygenases, see Galliard (1975), Gibian and Galaway (1978), Nugteren (1977), and Bailey and Chakrin, (1981).] In the oxidation reaction, two oxygen atoms from molecular oxygen are inserted into the fatty acid chain. Lipoxygenases attack fatty acids with at least two double bonds separated by three carbons (cis, cis-1,4-pentadienes), converting them to 1-hydroperoxy-2,4-trans-cis-pentadienes. Lipoxygenases have been known for many years. (The lipoxygenase enzyme from soybeans was one of the first enzymes to be crystallized.)

All of the early studies were conducted with plant enzymes, and until recently, their physiologic role was largely obscure, even in plants. Lipoxy-

THE LEUKOTRIENES

genases from different sources vary considerably in their substrate specificity, pH optima, susceptibility to inhibitors, and the isomeric nature of their products (Galliard, 1975; Gibian and Galaway, 1978; Van Os *et al.*, 1979; Galliard and Phillips, 1971; Christopher *et al.*, 1972; Yamamoto *et al.*, 1980; Roza and Francke, 1973; Nelson *et al.*, 1977; Holman *et al.*, 1969). Purified lipoxygenases from a single source frequently exhibit electrophoretic or molecular weight heterogeneity, suggesting the possible existence of isozymes (Galliard, 1975; Gibian and Galaway, 1978; Bryant *et al.*, 1982), although efforts to distinguish heterogeneity at the level of the genome from other bases for heterogeneity (variable glycosylation, proteolysis, or other forms of posttranslational processing such as phosphorylation) have rarely been attempted (Yamamoto *et al.*, 1980). Even where the necessary interrupted pentadiene structure is present, the susceptibility of a fatty acid to enzymatic attack varies depending on the location of its double bonds and the lipoxygenase. In studies with isomeric octadecanoic acids with 1,4-pentadiene units, many plant lipoxygenases prefer a fatty acid with the unsaturation beginning at the ω-6 position (numbering from the methyl end) for maximal activity (i.e., maximal activity is obtained with linoleic acid, the ω-6,9 octadecadienoic acid). Nonetheless, activity is also seen with many other C-18 dienoic acids, indicating that considerable flexibility in enzyme action is possible (Gibian and Galaway, 1978).

Originally, it appeared that a lipoxygenase from an apparently homogeneous source could insert oxygen at more than one position in a long-chain polyunsaturated acid. However, the lipoxygenases that have purified sufficiently to resolve different enzyme subfractions from one another show marked selectivity for one of the double bonds. For example, when the products formed from linoleic acid (9,12-octadienoic acid) by ordinary preparations of soybean lipoxygenase are chromatographed, the 13-hydroxyperoxy and 9-hydroperoxy isomers are both present in substantial quantities, even though the 13-hydroxyperoxy isomer normally predominates. However, the enzyme can be resolved into at least four subspecies that vary in their pH optima and product specificities. The major subspecies is most active at pH 9.0 and produces the 13-hydroperoxide with little or no 9-isomer. While small amounts of the 9-hydroperoxy product may still be observed, this can probably be attributed to isozymic impurities, autooxidation, or rearrangements during or after the enzymatic reaction. Another form of the enzyme is more active at pH 6–7, and its major product is the 9-hydroperoxy fatty acid (Van Os *et al.*, 1979).

As lipoxygenases have been more extensively studied, additional complexities in enzyme reactivity have been observed. While the major substrate for most lipoxygenases is the free fatty acid, usually in the form of the carboxylate ion, lipoxygenases may act on preferentially esterified fatty acids (Verhue and Francke, 1972). With such enzymes, activity may be demonstrated against fatty acids in phospholipids or triglycerides available either as micellar suspensions or incorporated in membranes (Rapoport *et al.*, 1979). Since most of the fatty acid in tissues is esterified rather than in the form of the free fatty acid, this direct action on fatty acids without their having to be released from ester linkage by lipases or phospholipases has obvious biologic implications. For the most part, however, the unesterified fatty acids are much more susceptible to enzyme action than fatty acids in membranes, and preliminary activation of a phospholipase or lipase is required for efficient oxidation by the enzyme.

Arachidonic acid (AA), which has double bonds at the 5, 8, 11, and 14 positions (numbering from the COOH end), contains three overlapping *cis,cis*-1,4-pentadiene units and is generally a good substrate for lipoxygenases. This is particularly true of the mammalian lipoxygenases, which frequently prefer AA to other unsaturated long-chain fatty acid substrates (Bailey and Chakrin, 1981). Because of the multiplicity of double bonds in AA, six monoperoxy or monohydroxy products, substituted at the 5, 8, 9, 11, 12, or 15 positions, theoretically are possible. All of these have been isolated from mammalian tissues. While the possibility of spontaneous autooxidation has to be kept in mind, a number of different animal lipoxygenases have been clearly identified. These enzymes differ in their distribution in tissue as well as in their site of action on AA. The lipoxygenase isoenzymes from soybeans all contain one atom of nonheme iron per enzyme molecule (Galliard, 1975; Gibian and Galaway, 1978). This iron is firmly attached and not readily removed by chelating agents, but prolonged treatment in the presence of thiols may result in its removal. Direct evidence that the iron is in the active site of the enzyme is not yet available. Nonetheless, by analogy with other oxidizing enzymes that contain iron, this possibility seems highly likely. The iron is presumably involved in the complexing of oxygen, reducing the activation energy of oxygenation.

Once the long-chain fatty acid hydroperoxide has been formed, it may undergo reduction to the corresponding hydroxy fatty acid, further oxidation to dioxygenated or trioxygenated acids, or an addition reaction with intracellular thiols to form a sulfide (Galliard, 1975; Gibian and Galaway, 1978; Bailey and Chakrin, 1981). Tissue extracts frequently contain more monohydroxy- than monoperoxy-eicosatetraenoates. This is partly a result of reduction by peroxidases, although reduction during extraction, storage, or subsequent chromatographic analysis may frequently be a contributing factor. Isomerization or further enzymatic conversions may produce an epoxy, hydroxy fatty acid, or a vinyl ether derivative. Under anaerobic or partially anaerobic conditions, the hydroperoxides may undergo fragmentation or dimerization, and epoxide or carbonyl formation may be promoted.

II. LIPOXYGENASES IN MAMMALIAN TISSUES

Most studies of mammalian lipoxygenases have focused attention on the products formed from AA, because of its general availability as a substrate when tissues are stimulated and its flexibility as a substrate and biosynthetic precursor due to its multiplicity of double bonds. The list of mammalian tissues that metabolize AA to monohydroxy-eicosatetraenoic acids (HETEs) is rapidly growing (Nugteren, 1977; Bailey and Chakrin, 1981; Bryant et al., 1982; Rapoport et al., 1979; Jim et al., 1982; Narumiya et al., 1981; Turk et al., 1982; Goetzl, 1981a,b; Hamberg and Samuelsson, 1974; Borgeat et al., 1976; Borgeat and Samuelsson, 1979a; Goetzl and Sun, 1979; Hammarstrom et al., 1975; Hamberg, 1976; Roberts et al., 1978; Hubbard et al., 1978; Falkenhein et al., 1980; Ford-Hutchinson et al., 1982; Stenson et al., 1980; Stenson and Parker, 1979a; Nugteren, 1975; Doig and Ford-Hutchinson, 1980; Valone et al., 1980; Maas et al., 1982a; Rigaud et al., 1979; Jorg et al., 1982; Rouzer et al., 1980). For example, rabbit polymorphonuclear leukocytes (PMN) produce 5-HETE, human neutrophils 5-,8-,9-,12-, and 15-HETEs, human platelets 12-HETE, human epidermis 12-HETE, guinea pig lung 11,12- and 15-HETEs, rat mast cells 5,11- and 15-HETEs, VX2 carcinoma 11- and 15-HETEs, rabbit reticulocytes 15- and 12-HETEs, human T lymphocytes 5,11,12- and 15-HETEs, RBL-1 cells 5- and 15-HETEs, peritoneal, blood, and lung monocytes 5,12- and 15-HETEs; rat kidneys 8,9- and 12-HETEs; eosinophils 15-HETE.

These observations suggest at least as much flexibility among mammalian lipoxygenases in the oxidation of AA and other long-chain fatty acid substrates as has been demonstrated for the various plant lipoxygenases. 5-Lipoxygenase (5-LO) activity is present and frequently prominent in leukocytes (neutrophils, monocytes, basophils, eosinophils, lymphocytes) and mast cells regardless of the tissue and animal species. Since these cells are the major cellular elements of the immune system and the enzyme can frequently be shown to be rapidly activated when leukocytes respond acutely to extracellular stimuli, one might speculate that 5-LO metabolites may have a special significance for the control of immune reactivity. As will be discussed later, there is evidence that 5-lipoxygenase products may play a dual role in the cellular response, both by promoting the release of important enzymes and nonlipid mediators to the extracellular fluid and through their own direct effects on smooth muscle tone and leukocyte function.

III. 5-LIPOXYGENASE PRODUCTS

The products of 5-lipoxygenases include the following: the 5-hydroperoxide itself, 5-HPETE (5-D-6,8,11,14-hydroperoxy-eicosatetraenoic acid); 5-HETE (5-D-hydroxy-6,8,11,14-eicosatetraenoic acid); leukotriene B_4, a specific isomer of 5,12-diHETE; and leukotriene C_4 (6-S-glutathionyl, 5-hydroxy-7,9,11,14-eicosatetraenoic acid) (Bailey and Chakrin, 1981; Falkenhein et al., 1980; Ford-Hutchinson et al., 1982; Stenson et al., 1980; Stenson and Parker, 1979a; Maas et al., 1982a,b; Goetzl, 1981b; Borgeat and Samuelsson, 1979a,b; Parker et al., 1979, 1980a; Borgeat et al., 1982; Parker, 1980a, 1983; Hammarstrom et al., 1979; Ornig, 1980; Morris, 1980; Samuelsson et al., 1980). Other derivatives are formed when the products just listed are metabolized, including (Ornig, 1980; Parker, 1980a,b; Morris, 1980; Lewis et al., 1980) LTD_4 (the cysteinylglycyl derivative formed from LTC_4 by removal of the γ-glutamyl group); LTE_4 (the cysteinyl derivative formed from LTC_4 by removal of the glycyl group and the γ-glutamyl group); 20-hydroxy-LTB_4 and 20-carboxy-LTD_4 (formed by selective oxidation of LTB_4 at C-20) (Jubiz et al., 1982).

Additional dioxygenated products also have been described particularly from monocytes (Maas et al., 1982a). Leukotrienes C_4 and D_4 produce sustained contractile responses on smooth muscle preparations of the guinea pig ileum, and on central and peripheral airways from several animal species, and are therefore termed slow-reacting substances (SRS) (Parker, 1983; Lewis et al., 1980; Jakschik et al., 1977a). Leukotriene B_4 stimulates locomotion, release of intracellular enzymes (in the presence of cytochalasins), chemotaxis, and aggregation, in leukocytes (Ford-Hutchinson, 1981; Ford-Hutchinson et al., 1981; Feinmark et al., 1981); 5-HETE stimulates lysozomal enzyme release and chemotaxis in these cells (Bailey and Chakrin, 1981; Goetzl, 1981b; Stenson and Parker, 1980). These substances are presently thought to act both intracellularly and extracellularly to promote the inflammatory response. The action of LTB_4 may be exerted through stereospecific receptors on these cells (Kreisle and Parker, 1983), whereas 5-HETE may be acting at least in part through covalent incorporation into membrane lipids (Stenson and Parker, 1979a,b). Some effects of lipoxygenase products may be exerted through cyclic nucleotides, since hydroperoxy fatty acids have been reported to stimulate guanylate cyclase (White et al., 1982). They are produced transiently when leukocytes and mast cells are activated by exogenous stimuli.

The factors controlling the relative amounts of the primary 5-lipoxygenase products are not completely understood. The initial product is almost certainly the 5-hydroperoxide, which spontaneously rearranges to the more highly reactive 5,6-epoxide (leukotriene A) (Radmark et al., 1980). Transformation to LTC_4 is undoubtedly influenced in part by the concentration of intracellular glutathione, which also is an essential constituent of the LTC_4 molecule (Parker et al., 1980b). In addition, an S-transferase enzyme is likely to be involved in transfer of the thiol group to the 5-epoxide or hydroperoxide. Nonetheless, under ordinary circumstances the rate-limiting step in the formation of the SRS appears to be the availability of the 5-hydroperoxide itself, since RBL-1 cells supplied with 5-hydroperoxide extracellularly produce large amounts of LTC_4 (Falkenhein et al., 1980; Parker et al., 1980a). Nonetheless, observations in RBL-1 cells indicate that the potential exists for manipulating the concentration of intracellular thiol and markedly reducing SRS formation without reducing the production of other 5-lipoxygenase products. Enzymes capable of promoting hydroxylation at the 12 position appear to be involved in the biosynthesis of LTB_4 (Borgeat and Samuelsson, 1979b,c). This can explain the selective formation of LTB_4 at the expense of other diastereoisomers of 5,12-diHETE, which are produced primarily by nonenzymatic hydroxylation. The available evidence would suggest that the 5,6-epoxide is required for LTB_4 formation and that 5-HETE is not normally an LTB_4 precursor. Thus, LTB_4 and LTC_4 are both apparently formed primarily through the epoxide. 5-HETE may be formed either by spontaneous hydrolysis of the 5,6-epoxide or enzymatically from peroxidases, which are widely distributed in mammalian cells and may or may not utilize glutathione as a cofactor.

IV. KINETICS OF 5-LIPOXYGENASE PRODUCT FORMATION IN ACTIVATED CELLS

In contrast to many of the other enzymes in the arachidonate cascade, the 5-lipoxygenase is normally in a resting state intracellularly. This is clearly the case not just in the RBL-1 cell line in which most of our lipoxygenase studies have been conducted but also in human peripheral blood polymorphonuclear leukocytes (PMN) (Falkenhein et al., 1980; Stenson and Parker, 1979a; Jakschik et al., 1977b). In these cells the formation of 5-lipoxygenase products is very limited unless the cells are exposed to an exogenous agent that stimulates the cells metabolically. The most effective activating agent is the divalent cation ionophore, A23187. Somewhat different results have been obtained in rat peritoneal PMN, where considerably higher spontaneous 5-lipoxygenase activity has been observed (Borgeat et al., 1976). However, this may be a result of the injection of an inducing agent intraperitoneally to promote leukocyte accumulation (to improve the yield and purity of the cells). In this situation, the enzyme may already have been partially stimulated in vivo. Even in these cells the enzyme is activated further by A23187.

In all of these systems, the formation of 5-lipoxygenase products can be demonstrated by radiochromatography using $[3,6,9,12,15-^3H]AA$ or $[1-^{14}C]AA$ as a biosynthetic precursor. Incorporation of radiolabel into 5-HETE, LTB_4, and LTC_4 can be demonstrated either from exogenous AA in the medium or from AA that has been incorporated intracellularly into membrane lipids by preincubating the cells with AA under conditions in which the cells are not activated (Stenson and Parker, 1979a). The requirement for enzyme activation is particularly evident in RBL-1 cells where large amounts of labeled AA can be provided to otherwise unstimulated cells extracellularly with little or no formation of 5-LO products (Parker, 1983).

As already indicated, A23187 is ordinarily the most effective stimulator of the 5-LO pathway regardless of the leukocyte species and source. A23187 promotes the exchange of divalent cations into and out of cells and is a potent secretogog in many different cell systems. The effectiveness of A23187 depends on the medium containing high micromolar or low millimolar concentrations of Ca^{2+} (Jakschik et al., 1977a). Other divalent cations such as magnesium ion or manganese ion appear to be unable to substitute for Ca^{2+}. Taken together, these observations raise the possibility that the actual stimulus to the enzyme is the intracellular accumulation of ionized calcium. In support of this possibility, the enzyme is stimulated by Ca^{2+} in broken cell preparations (Jakschik et al., 1980; Parker and Aykent, 1982). In contrast, while there is no doubt that A23187 can promote the accumulation of Ca^{2+} intracellularly under the conditions in which it is normally used for 5-LO activation, many other changes are occurring in the cells metabolically. Therefore, a direct role of Ca^{2+} in lipoxygenase activation intracellularly cannot necessarily be assumed.

The study of other activating agents in RBL-1 cells has been relatively unsatisfactory, since these cells do not respond readily to immunologic stimuli, and even potent stimuli to granule release in mast cells such as the polyfunctional amines (e.g., compound 48/80) are relatively ineffective. However, studies in other 5-LO-containing cells indicate that a variety of other extracellular stimuli can increase 5-lipoxygenase activity including phorbol myristate ester, complement-activated zymosan, formylmethionyl oligopeptides, and latex particles in polymorphonuclear leukocytes, mitogenic lectins in lymphoctyes, and antigen–antibody complexes and particulate stimuli in macrophages (Bailey and Chakrin, 1981; Goetzl, 1981b). Nonetheless, it is important to keep in mind that these agents vary considerably in their effectiveness and that, depending on the experimental system, negative results may sometimes be obtained.

V. CHARACTERIZATION OF THE 5-LIPOXYGENASE ENZYME IN RBL-1 CELLS

The most extensive early studies of the 5-lipoxygenase enzyme have been carried out in RBL-1 cells and neutrophils. RBL-1 cells are a rat neoplastic cell line apparently derived from basophils. They were originally used for studies of IgE receptors but subsequently shown to generate SRS on stimulation with A23187 (Jakschik *et al.*, 1977a). They can be maintained as a continuous line in tissue culture and grown in large quantities making them suitable as a preparative source of the enzyme. Originally demonstration of 5-LO activity in broken cell systems was difficult. However, it was later found that enzyme activity could be demonstrated if the cells were broken in medium that contained a chelating agent for divalent cations (Jakschik *et al.*, 1980). In such preparations, very substantial amounts of 5-lipoxygenase activity were present in the cytosol and considerably less in other subcellular fractions. Whether this is the true distribution of the enzyme intracellularly in unactivated cells or whether the enzyme has undergone redistribution in the presence of the chelating agent remains to be established.

In work that is still largely unpublished, we have succeeded in obtaining the enzyme in a highly purified form through a series of column purification techniques including affinity chromatography on arachidonate-coupled Sepharose columns, ion exchange chromatography, gel filtration HPLC, and preparative gel electrophoresis or reverse-phase HPLC. The purified enzyme is obtained with an overall yield of about 20% of the original enzyme activity and is apparently homogeneous by gel filtration HPLC and in discontinuous SDS–polyacrylamide gels. The activity of the purified lipoxygenase can be studied with AA and other long-chain fatty acids either spectrophotometrically by following the increase in absorbancy at 237 nm or by identifying the metabolites formed from AA by thin-layer chromatography (TLC) and reverse-phase HPLC.

As discussed later, 5-HETE and 5-HPETE are prominent products of the purified enzyme. The specific activity of the purified enzyme varies somewhat with the duration of storage, mode of purification, and enzyme preparation. In the absence of an activating agent such as Ca^{2+}, the purified enzyme is ordinarily essentially inactive, at least in dilute solutions. In the presence of 0.5 mM or higher concentrations of Ca^{2+}, the enzyme shows a marked increase in activity (Parker and Aykent, 1982). The activity of the calcium-activated enzyme is greatest at or near neutral pH. At substantial enzyme and substrate concentrations, the addition of Ca^{2+} is associated with a rapid burst of enzyme activity with a slight initial lag followed within 10 to 15 min by total cessation of enzyme activity. Calcium is partially effective as an activating agent even with 0.1% SDS present. The inactive enzyme has MW of about 90,000 by gel filtration, which is similar to independent MW estimates under dissociating conditions in reduced and unreduced SDS–polyacrylamide gels (Parker and Aykent, 1982). Activation of the enzyme by Ca^{2+} is associated with the formation of dimers and higher molecular weight aggregates of the enzyme.

All of the enzyme activity is obtained within or near (see later) the dimeric region. At high enzyme concentrations, the enzyme may be partially active, even without added calcium, and a portion of the enzyme migrates as the dimer on gel filtration HPLC. The partial activation of the enzyme at high protein concentrations seen in the absence of added calcium may depend at least in part on divalent cations present adventitiously in the enzyme preparation, since 1 mM EDTA inactivates the concentrated enzyme. When divalent cations are added in excess of the EDTA present, both CA^{2+} and Mg^{2+} reactivate the enzyme. However, when the EDTA and any divalent cations that might be complxed with it are removed from the enzyme on a HPLC column before adding the divalent cation, only Ca^{2+} restores the enzyme activity. Thus, it appears that the ability of Mg^{2+} to restore activity when EDTA is still present is due to displacement of bound calcium from the EDTA. Attempts to activate the enzyme with purified beef heart calmodulin have been unsuccessful, as have attempts to demonstrate binding of iodinated calmodulin to the enzyme. These observations, taken together with the high degree of purity of the enzyme, suggest that Ca^{2+} is interacting directly with the 5-LO rather than indirectly through a regulatory protein such as calmodulin.

The enzyme is also affected by a variety of neutral and charged lipids including several phospholipids and acylglycerols, particularly the diacylglycerols (DAG).

The effect on the purified enzyme of these lipids has possible implications for the control of enzyme activity in intact cells. While the purified enzyme is stimulated by Ca^{2+}, high (≥ 0.5 mm) concentrations of Ca^{2+} are required. It is doubtful that this level of Ca^{2+} is reached even transiently in activated leukocytes (estimates of free Ca^{2+} concentrations in the cytosol of cells are usually in the range of 10^{-6} to 10^{-7} M). Therefore, there is some reason to doubt whether or not Ca^{2+} is the immediate stimulus to lipoxygenase activation inside cells. One alternative possibility is that rat peritoneal mast cells and platelets undergo very substantial acute rises in DAG and phosphatidic acid after surface stimulation (Kennerly *et al.,* 1979), presumably because of Ca^{2+}-dependent stimulation of phospholipase C and DAG kinase activities. The cellular levels of DAG seen in activated mast cells are well within the range over which the purified RBL-1 cell enzyme is affected by DAG in vitro.

Other changes in intracellular lipids may also be involved in control of the enzyme.

One of the interesting features of the 5-LO in activated leukocytes is the rapid burst of initial activity followed by rapid cessation of activity. In crude homogenates the enzyme is very labile and the use of the protease inhibitors slows the rate of inactivation of the enzyme. The marked susceptibility of the lipoxygenase to proteolytic degradation provides one possible mechanism for this rapid diminution in enzyme activity with time. Another important mechanism may be negative-feedback inhibition of the enzyme by lipoxygenase products. While 15-HETE and 15-HPETE have been reported to inhibit 5-LO (Bailey *et al.,* 1982), our preliminary observations with the RBL-1 enzyme suggest that it is less effective as an inhibitor in this particular system than 5-HETE. Leukotrienes B_4 and C_4 also inhibit enzyme activity, but they are less effective than 5-HETE on a molar basis. Just how general these observations with 5-HETE and 15-HETE will be for other 5-LOs remains to be established. In the PT-18 murine mast cell/basophil cell line, 15-HETE stimulates rather than inhibits the enzyme (Vanderhoek *et al.,* 1982).

We have not studied 5-LO enzymes in other cell types. In a recent study with a partially purified lipoxygenase from rabbit peritoneal PMN, 15-LO but not 5-LO activity was present, and, 15-ketoeicosatetraenoic acid (15-KETE) was a major product (Narumiya *et al.,* 1981). Since 5-LO products ordinarily predominate when rabbit peritoneal leukocytes are stimulated with A23187, it seems possible that the 5-LO enzyme is present originally but is altered during purification. However, the alternative possibility, that 5-LO and 15-LO activities are both present originally in the PMN but the 5-LO activity is lost during purification is probably considerably more likely.

Other than our studies of product inhibition described already, we have not yet carefully studied the purified 5-LO enzyme from the point of view of possible pharmacologic inhibitors of enzyme activity. However, previous studies in intact RBL-1 cells and other cell types have indicated that a variety of agents may affect the activity of the RBL-1 of PMN enzymes including nor-dihydroguaiaretic acid, 5,8,11,14-eicosatetranoic acid (ETYA), other triple unsaturated long-chain fatty acids, vitamin A, platelet-activating factor, and pyrogallol (Bailey and Chakrin, 1981; Falkenhein *et al.,* 1980; Goetzl, 1981b; Jakschik *et al.,* 1977a, 1982; Chilton *et al.,* 1982). In general, nonsteroidal antiinflammatory agents have been found to be more effective cyclooxygenase than lipoxygenase inhibitors, although agents with dual inhibitory activity such as BW-755C are beginning to be identified (Bailey and Chakrin, 1981). The problem of finding truly selective inhibitors of the 5-LO pathway is beginning to be explored in some detail, as discussed elsewhere in this book.

REFERENCES

Bailey, D. M., and Chakrin, L. W. (1981). *Annu. Rep. Med. Chem.* **16**, 213–227.

Bailey, J. M., Low, C. A., Pupillo, M., Bryant, R. W., and Vanderhoek, J. Y. (1982). *In* "Leukotrienes and Other Lipoxygenase Products" (B. Samuelsson and R. Paoletti, eds.), pp. 341–353. Raven Press, New York.

Borgeat, P., and Samuelsson, B. (1979a). *Proc. Natl. Acad. Sci. U.S.A.* **76**, 2148–2152.

Borgeat, P., and Samuelsson, B. (1979b). *J. Biol. Chem.* **254**, 2643–2646.

Borgeat, P., and Samuelsson, B. (1979c). *Proc. Natl. Acad. Sci. U.S.A.* **76**, 3213–3217.

Borgeat, P., Hamberg, M., and Samuelsson, B. (1976). *J. Biol. Chem.* **251**, 7816–7820.

Borgeat, P., Fruteau de Laclos, B., Picard, S., Vallerand, P., and Sirois, P. (1982). *In* "Leukotrienes and Other Lipoxygenase Products" (B. Samuelsson and R. Paoletti, eds.), pp. 45–51. Raven Press, New York.

Bryant, R. W., Bailey, J. M., Schewe, T., and Rapoport, S. M. (1982). *J. Biol. Chem.* **257**, 6050–6055.

Chilton, F. H., O'Flaherty, J. T., Walsh, C. E., Thomas, M. J., Wykle, R. L., DeChatelet, L. R., and Waite, B. M. (1982). *J. Biol. Chem.* **257**, 5402–5407.

Christopher, J. P., Pistorius, E. K., and Axelrod, B. (1972). *Biochim. Biophys. Acta* **284**, 54–62.

Doig, M. V., and Ford-Hutchinson, A. W. (1980). *Prostaglandins* **20**, 1007–1019.

Falkenhein, S. F., MacDonald, H., Huber, M. M., Koch, D., and Parker, C. W. (1980). *J. Immunol.* **125**, 163–168.

Feinmark, S. J., Lindgren, J. A., Claesson, H.-E., Malmsten, C., and Samuelsson, B. (1981). *FEBS Lett.* **136**, 141–144.

Ford-Hutchinson, A. W. (1981). *J. R. Soc. Med.* **74**, 831–833.

Ford-Hutchinson, A. W., Bray, M. A., Cunningham, F. M., Davidson, E. M., and Smith, M. J. H. (1981). *Prostaglandins* **21**, 143–152.

Ford-Hutchinson, A. W., Piper, P. J., and Samhoun, M. N. (1982). *Br. J. Pharmacol.* **76**, 215–220.

Galliard, T. (1975). *In* "The Biochemistry of Plants" (P. K. Stumpf and E. E. Conn, eds.), pp. 335–357. Academic Press, New York.

Galliard, T., and Phillips, D. R. (1971). *Biochem. J.* **124**, 431–437.

Gibian, M. J., and Galaway, R. A. (1978). *In* "Bioorganic Chemistry" (E. E. van Tamelen, ed.), pp. 117–136. Academic Press, New York.

Goetzl, E. J. (1981a). *Biochem. Biophys. Res. Commun.* **101**, 344–350.

Goetzl, E. J. (1981b). *Med. Clin. North Am.* **65**, 809–828.

Goetzl, E., and Sun, F. (1979). *J. Exp. Med.* **150**, 406–411.

Hamberg, M. (1976). *Biochim. Biophys. Acta.* **431**, 651–654.

Hamberg, M., and Samuelsson, B. (1974). *Proc. Natl. Acad. Sci. U.S.A.* **71**, 3400–3404.

Hammarstrom, S., Hamberg, M., Samuelsson, B., Duell, E., Stawiski, M., and Vorhees, J. (1975). *Proc. Natl. Acad. Sci. U.S.A.* **72**, 5130–5134.

Hammarstrom, S., Murphy, R. C., Samuelsson, B., Clark, D. A., Mioskowski, C., and Corey, E. J. (1979). *Biochem. Biophys. Res. Commun.* **91**, 1266–1272.

Holman, R. T., Egwim, P. O., and Christie, W. W. (1969). *J. Biol. Chem.* **244**, 1149–1151.

Hubbard, W. C., Hough, A., Watson, J. T., and Oates, J. A. (1978). *Prostaglandins* **15**, 721.

Jakschik, B. A., Falkenhein, S. F., and Parker, C. W. (1977a). *Proc. Natl. Acad. Sci. U.S.A.* **74**, 4577–4581.

Jakschik, B. A., Kulczycki, A., MacDonald, H. H., and Parker, C. W. (1977b). *J. Immunol.* **119**, 618–622.

Jakschik, B. A., Sun, F. F., Lee, L. H., and Steinhoff, M. M. (1980). *Biochem. Biophys. Res. Commun.* **95**, 103–110.

Jakschik, B. A., DiSantis, D. M., Sankarappa, S. K., and Sprecher, H. (1982). *In* "Leukotrienes and Other Lipoxygenase Products" (B. Samuelsson and R. Paoletti, eds.), pp. 127–135. Raven Press, New York.

Jim, K., Hassid, A., Sun, F., and Dunn, M. J. (1982). *J. Biol. Chem.* **257,** 10294–10299.

Jorg, A., Henderson, W. R., Murphy, R. C., and Klebanoff, S. J. (1982). *J. Exp. Med.* **155,** 390–402.

Jubiz, W., Radmark, O., Malmsten, C., Hansson, G., Lindgren, J., Palmblad, J., Uden, A., and Samuelsson, B. (1982). *J. Biol. Chem.* **257,** 6106–6110.

Kennerly, D. A., Sullivan, T. J., Slywester, P., and Parker, C. W. (1979). *J. Exp. Med.* **150,** 1039–1044.

Kreisle, R. A., and Parker, C. W. (1983). *J. Exp. Med.* **157,** 628–641.

Lewis, R. A., Austen, K. F., Drazen, J. M., Clark, D. A., Marfat, A., and Corey, E. J. (1980). *Proc. Natl. Acad. Sci. U.S.A.* **77,** 3710–3714.

Maas, R. L., Brash, A. R., and Oates, J. A. (1982a). *In* "Leukotrienes and Other Lipoxygenase Products" (B. Samuelsson and R. Paoletti, eds.), pp. 29–44. Raven Press, New York.

Maas, R. L., Turk, J., Oates, J. A., and Brash, A. R. (1982b), *J. Biol. Chem.* **257,** 7056–7067.

Morris, H. R. (1980). *Nature (London)* **285,** 104–105.

Narumiya, S., Salmon, J. A., Cottee, F. H., Weatherly, B. C., and Flower, R. J. (1981). *J. Biol. Chem.* **256,** 9583–9592.

Nelson, M. S., Pattee, H. E., and Singleton, J. A. (1977). *Lipids* **12,** 418–422.

Nugteren, D. H. (1975). *Biochim. Biophys. Acta* **380,** 299–307.

Nugteren, D. H. (1977). *In* "Prostaglandins in Hematology" (M. J. Silver, J. B. Smith, and J. J. Kocsis, eds.), pp. 11–24. Spectrum Publications, Inc., New York.

Orning, L., Hammarstrom, S., and Samuelsson, B. (1980). *Proc. Natl. Acad. Sci. U.S.A.* **77,** 2014–2017.

Parker, C. W. (1980a). *Prostaglandins* **20,** 863–886.

Parker, C. W. (1980b). *In* "Proceedings of the Fourth International Symposium on the Biochemistry of the Acute Allergic Reaction" (E. L. Becker, A. S. Simon, and K. F. Austen, eds.), pp. 23–36. Liss, New York.

Parker, C. W. (1983). *In* "Immunopharmacology of the Lung" (H. H. Newball, ed.), pp. 5–53. Marcel Dekker, New York.

Parker, C. W., and Aykent, S. (1982). *Biochem. Biophys. Res. Commun.* **109,** 1011–1016.

Parker, C. W., Huber, M. M., Hoffman, M. K., and Falkenhein, S. F. (1979). *Prostaglandins* **18,** 673–686.

Parker, C. W., Koch, D., Huber, M. M., and Falkenhein, S. S. (1980a). *Biochem. Biophys. Res. Commun.* **96,** 1037–1043.

Parker, C. W., Fischman, C. M., and Wedner, H. J. (1980b). *Proc. Natl. Acad. Sci. U.S.A.* **77,** 6870–6873.

Rådmark, O., Malmsten, C., Samuelsson, B., Goto, G., Marfat, A., and Corey, E. J. (1980). *J. Biol. Chem.* **255,** 11828–11831.

Rapoport, M., Schewe, T. Wiesner, R., Halangk, W., Ludwig, P., Janicki-Hohne, M., Tanneri, C., Hiebsch, C., and Klatt, D. (1979). *Eur. J. Biochem.* **96,** 545–561.

Rigaud, M., Durand, J., and Breton, J. C. (1979). *Biochim. Biophys. Acta* **573,** 408–412.

Roberts, L. J., Lewis, R. A., Lawson, J. A., Sweetman, B. J., Austen, K. F., and Oates, J. A. (1978). *Prostaglandins* **15,** 717.

Rouzer, C. A., Scott, W. A., Hamill, A. L., and Cohen, Z. A. (1980). *J. Exp. Med.* **152,** 1236–1247.

Roza, M., and Francke, A. (1973). *Biochim. Biophys. Acta* **316,** 76–82.

Samuelsson, B., Borgeat, P., Hammarstrom, S., and Murphy, R. C. (1980). *Adv. Prostaglandin Thromboxane Res.* **6,** 1–18.

Stenson, W. F., and Parker, C. W. (1979a). *J. Clin. Invest.* **64,** 1457–1465.

Stenson, W. F., and Parker, C. W. (1979b). *Prostaglandins* **18,** 285–292.

Stenson, W. F., and Parker, C. W. (1980). *J. Immunol.* **124,** 2100–2104.

Stenson, W. F., Parker, C. W., and Sullivan, T. J. (1980). *Biochem. Biophys. Res. Commun.* **96,** 1045–1052.
Turk, J., Maas, R. L., Brash, A. R., Roberts, L. J., and Oates, J. A. (1982). *J. Biol. Chem.* **257,** 7068–7076.
Valone, F. H., Franklin, M., Sunn, F. F., and Goetzl, E. J. (1980). *Cell. Immunol.* **54,** 390–401.
Vanderhoek, J. Y., Tare, N. S., Bailey, J. M., Goldstein, A. L., Pluznik, D. H. (1982). *J. Biol. Chem.* **257,** 12191–12195.
Van Os, C. P. A., Rijke-Schilder, G. P. M., Vliegenthart, J. F. G. (1979). *Biochimica et Biophysica Acta.* **575,** 479–484.
Verhue, W. M., and Francke, A. (1972). *Biochim. Biophys. Acta* **285,** 43–53.
White, A. A., Karr, D. B., and Patt, C. S. (1982). *Biochem. J.* **204,** 383–392.
Yamamoto, A., Fujui, Y., Yasumoto, K., and Mitsuda, H. (1980). *Lipids* **15,** 1–5.

5

Characterization of Leukotriene Formation

BARBARA A. JAKSCHIK AND CHRISTINE G. KUO

Department of Pharmacology
Washington University
St. Louis, Missouri

I. INTRODUCTION

The structure of slow reacting substance (SRS) remained unknown for more than 40 years following their discovery by Feldberg and Kellaway in 1938. SRS is now known to be a group of compounds belonging to the leukotriene (LT) family (Murphy *et al.*, 1979; Hammarström *et al.*, 1979; Parker *et al.*, 1979a,b; Morris *et al.*, 1980a,b). The past few years have been a period of extraordinarily rapid progress in the field of leukotrienes. The recent advancement in knowledge is partially due to the finding that these compounds are derived from arachidonic acid (Bach *et al.*, 1977; Jakschik *et al.*, 1977) and that the compounds are structurally related because of similar ultraviolet absorption spectra (Morris *et al.*, 1978; Borgeat and Samuelsson, 1979a) and are formed via the 5-lipoxygenase (Borgeat *et al.*, 1976; Borgeat and Samuelsson, 1979b–d; Murphy *et al.*, 1979). Most recently, leukotrienes formed via a 15-lipoxygenase have also been described (Lundberg *et al.*, 1981; Jubiz *et al.*, 1981; Maas *et al.*, 1981, 1982).

Over the past few years we have studied leukotriene formation via the 5-lipoxygenase in a cell-free enzyme system. We obtain this enzyme preparation by homogenizing rat basophilic leukemia (RBL-1) cells under gentle conditions in the presence of EDTA (Steinhoff *et al.*, 1980; Jakschik *et al.*, 1980a). The availability of a simple cell-free enzymatic generating system of leukotrienes allows the study of the formation of these compounds in detail. With such a system, substrate and cofactors can be readily controlled, and one need not be concerned about uptake into tissues or cells.

II. CALCIUM STIMULATION OF THE 5-LIPOXYGENASE

Utilizing this cell-free enzyme system we studied the formation of 5-hydroxyeicosatetraenoic acid (5-HETE) and diHETEs (including LTB_4) by incubating the 10,000 g supernatant with [^{14}C]arachidonic acid. The products formed were separated by thin-layer chromatography and quantitated by liquid scintillation counting of the radioactive bands. When the 10,000 g supernatant was incubated with [^{14}C]arachidonic acid alone, only insignificant amounts of lipoxygenase products were synthesized. Addition of calcium to the incubation mixture markedly stimulated the formation of hydroxy acids (Fig. 1). The two major products observed were 5-HETE and diHETE. These bands were identified by gas chromatography–mass spectrometry. The diHETE band contained a mixture consisting of LTB_4 and its isomers. The enhancement by calcium was dose dependent (Fig. 2). Maximum stimulation was observed on readdition of 0.5 mM calcium. An equivalent stimulation by calcium was observed when EGTA instead of EDTA was used in the preparation. It is difficult to calculate the actual amount of calcium needed to activate the enzyme, as it is very likely that some calcium is chelated by EDTA or EGTA during homogenization. No enhancement of the 5-lipoxygenase activity was observed when magnesium was substituted for calcium. We investigated whether a similar calcium stimulation would occur with the platelet lipoxygenase. When 8000 g supernatant from broken platelets was incubated with [^{14}C]arachidonic acid with or without calcium, no effect of calcium on arachidonate metabolism was observed (Jakschik *et al.*, 1980a). A similar enhancement by calcium occurred when SRS synthesis was studied on the superfused guinea pig ileum (Fig. 3) (Jakschik and Lee, 1980).

The stimulation of this pathway by calcium was suggested earlier when we found that the calcium ionophore A23187 potentiated SRS synthesis from arachidonic acid by RBL-1 cells (Jakschik *et al.*, 1977) as well as diHETE and

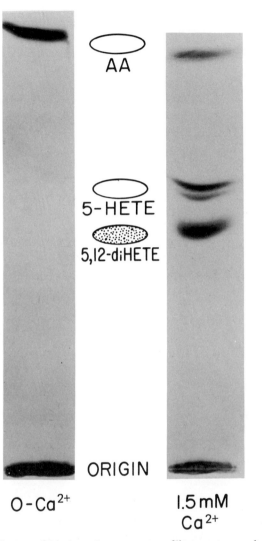

Fig. 1. Autoradiogram of thin-layer chromatograms of lipoxygenase products. Supernatant (10,000 g) of RBL-1 cell homogenates was incubated with 3.3 μM [^{14}C]arachidonic acid (AA) with or without calcium as indicated at 37°C for 20 min. The reaction was stopped by the addition of 1 ml of acetone to precipitate the protein. The pH of the supernatant was adjusted to pH 3.2 to 3.5, and the mixture was extracted twice with 2 ml of chloroform. Thin-layer chromatography was performed in the organic phase of ethyl acetate–2,2,4-trimethylpentane–acetic acid–water (110:50:20:100). The migration of radioactive peaks was determined by autoradiography. (Adapted from Jakschik *et al.*, 1980a.)

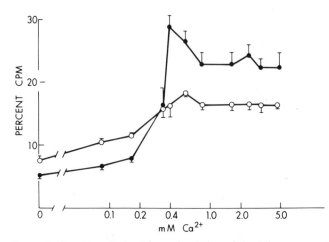

Fig. 2. Concentration-dependent calcium stimulation of the 5-lipoxygenase. For experimental details see legend of Fig. 1. Quantitation was achieved by scraping and liquid scintillation counting. (●——●) 5,12-diHETE; (○——○) 5-HETE. Vertical bars, SEM ($n = 5$–11). (Adapted from Jakschik *et al.*, 1980a.)

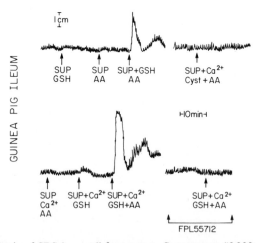

Fig. 3. Biosynthesis of SRS by a cell-free system. Supernatant (10,000 g) of RBL-1 cell homogenate was incubated at 37°C, 15 min, with the agents indicated at the following concentrations: reduced glutathione (GSH) 1 mM, calcium (Ca^{2+}) 2 mM, arachidonic acid (AA) 16 μM, and directly applied to the superfused guinea pig ileum. FPL55712 was applied to the tissue at a concentration of 0.2 μM. (Adapted from Jakschik and Lee, 1980.)

5-HETE formation (Jakschik *et al.,* 1978). A potentiation of 5-HETE and 5,12-diHETE synthesis by A23187 has also been reported by Borgeat and Samuelsson (1979a) for polymorphonuclear leukocytes.

Calcium appears to act at the first step, the 5-lipoxygenase, since in the absence of calcium neither 5,12-diHETE nor 5-HETE were produced in significant amounts. This is further substantiated by the work of Parker *et al.* (1980a). They found that calcium ionophore was not required for SRS synthesis from 5-hydroperoxyeicosatetraenoic acid but was necessary for synthesis from arachidonic acid. Formation of LTB_4 or LTC_4 from LTA_4 also does not require calcium (Jakschik and Kuo, 1982, 1983; Jakschik *et al.,* 1982b). The observed effect of calcium on leukotriene formation is of great interest, as calcium is needed in mast cells and basophils for the release reaction to occur. The increase in intracellular calcium would therefore cause the release of arachidonic acid from phospholipids, activate the 5-lipoxygenase to initiate leukotriene synthesis, and cause histamine release.

III. REQUIREMENT OF REDUCED GLUTATHIONE

The cell-free enzyme system was also utilized to study SRS formation by monitoring contraction of the superfused guinea pig ileum. This work showed very clearly that glutathione is essential for the synthesis of the peptidoleukotrienes (Jakschik and Lee, 1980). If the glutathione was replaced by cysteine, no SRS activity was generated (Fig. 3). Similar results were obtained with cysteinylglycine. The incorporation of glutathione rather than cysteine as such into SRS agrees with our earlier observations with [35S]cysteine (Parker *et al.,* 1979a). A higher percentage of label was incorporated into SRS when RBL-1 cells were grown for 16 h in the presence of [35S]- or [14C]cysteine as compared to a brief exposure (1 h). These experiments had already suggested that cysteine was first incorporated into another compound before utilization in SRS synthesis.

The SRS produced by the cell-free system from RBL-1 cells is a mixture of LTC_4, LTD_4, and sometimes also LTE_4 (Jakschik *et al.,* 1982b). In the original experiments demonstrating generation of SRS by a cell-free system we utilized the 10,000 *g* supernatant. Only recently we realized that most of the enzyme activity responsible for the formation of the peptidoleukotrienes from LTA_4 sediments with 10,000 *g* centrifugation (Fig. 4D) (Jakschik *et al.,* 1982b). Therefore, the whole homogenate generates much larger amounts of SRS activity than the 10,000 *g* supernatant. If one follows the formation of the peptidoleukotrienes with time, one observes mainly LTC_4 during the first few minutes. At approximately 20 to 30 min the predominant species is LTD_4. With longer incubations LTE_4 is also present. Similar observations were reported by Parker *et al.* (1980b) utilizing whole RBL-1 cells and A23187 as the stimulus.

IV. SUBCELLULAR LOCALIZATION OF LEUKOTRIENE-FORMING ENZYMES

The whole homogenate of RBL-1 cells can produce 5-HETE, LTB_4, and its isomers (5,12-diHETEs and 5,6-diHETEs, which are formed by the nonenzymatic breakdown of LTA_4), LTC_4, LTD_4, and LTE_4 (Fig. 4A and B) (Jakschik *et al.*, 1982b). In order to determine the subcellular localization of the individual enzymes, the homogenate was fractionated by centrifugation at 10,000 *g* and 100,000 *g*. The 5-lipoxygenase, LTA synthetase, and LTA hydrolase are soluble enzymes. Their products 5-HETE, LTB_4, and its trans isomers, 5,12-diHETE and 5,6-diHETE, were generated only when arachidonic acid was incubated with the 10,000 *g* or 100,000 *g* supernatant (Fig. 4C and E). No LTB_4 or other diHETEs were formed when arachidonic acid was incubated with the 10,000 *g* and 100,000 *g* pellets. When LTA_4 was added to the 10,000 *g* and 100,000 *g* pellets or supernatants, only the 10,000 *g* and 100,000 *g* supernatants generated LTB_4 (Jakschik and Kuo, 1982, 1983). Egan *et al.* (1983) also observed 5-lipoxygenase activity and Maycock *et al.* (1983) LTA-hydrolase activity in the soluble fraction of RBL-1 cells. However, no careful analysis of all the subcellular fractions was reported.

We had observed earlier (Jakschik *et al.*, 1980a) that RBL-1 cells also generate 12-HETE, which indicates the presence of a 12-lipoxygenase. Borgeat *et al.* (1982) and Lindgren *et al.* (1981) have demonstrated that an isomer of LTB_4 can be formed by double lipoxygenation — that is, the action of the 12-lipoxygenase or 5-lipoxygenase on 5-HETE or 12-HETE, respectively. These investigators also report that the product formed, (5S,12S)-dihydroxyeicosa-6,10-*trans*-8,14-*cis*-tetraenoic acid [(5S,12S)-diHETE], comigrates with LTB_4 on reverse-phase HPLC. Therefore, we methylated the LTB_4 peak obtained from reverse-phase HPLC and applied it to normal-phase HPLC to separate LTB_4 from (5S,12S)-diHETE (Fig. 5). With 10- to 20-min incubations, the LTB_4 peak observed on reverse-phase HPLC contains approximately 20–50% (5S,12S)-diHETE.

Comparing the whole homogenate and 10,000 *g* supernatant for their ability to synthesize the peptidoleukotrienes, we observed that much larger amounts were generated by the whole homogenate than the 10,000 *g* supernatant. This was observed on HPLC analysis as well as on monitoring SRS activity on the guinea pig ileum (Jakschik *et al.*, 1982b). These data indicate that the glutathione transferase ($LTA_4 \rightarrow LTC_4$) and the γ-glutamyl transpeptidase ($LTC_4 \rightarrow LTD_4$) are particulate enzymes present in the 10,000 *g*

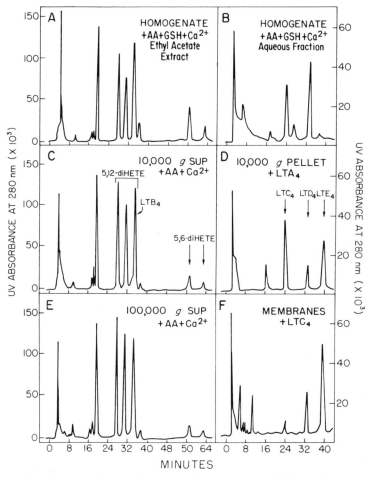

Fig. 4. Subcellular localization of leukotriene-forming enzymes. RBL-1 cell homogenates or fractions thereof were incubated with arachidonic acid (AA) 33 μM, LTA$_4$ 20 μM (hydrolysate of methyl-LTA$_4$), or LTC$_4$, with or without calcium 1.5 mM and glutathione (GSH) 1 mM as indicated at 37°C for 15 min. After the incubation, prostaglandin (PG) B$_2$ was added as internal standard. Samples containing homogenate, 10,000 g pellet, or membranes were precipitated with four volumes of cold absolute ethanol. The supernatant was diluted with distilled water to an ethanol concentration of 5%, pH adjusted to 6 to 6.5, and the samples applied to ODS-C18 concentrator columns (Baker). The 10,000 g and 100,000 g supernatants were diluted six- to eightfold with distilled water and applied directly to Baker columns. The samples were eluted with 1 ml of methanol. Samples that contained dihydroxy acids as well as the peptidoleukotrienes (A, B, and D) were differentially extracted with ethyl acetate at pH 6.4. The ethyl acetate was evaporated and the extract redissolved in methanol–water (1:3). HPLC analysis was performed with a Nucleosil C-18 column, 5-μm particle size (Machery Nagel), flow rate 1 ml/min. Mobile phase, (A, C, and E) methanol–water–acetic acid (68:32:0.05), pH 4.7; (B, D, and F) methanol–water–acetic acid (67:33:0.05), pH 5.4.

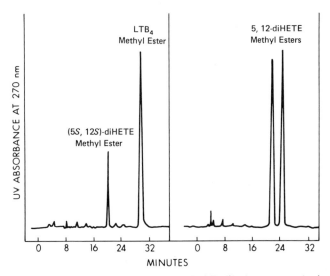

Fig. 5. Separation of methyl-LTB$_4$ from methyl-(5S, 12S)-dihydroxy-*trans, cis*-eicosatetraenoic acid [(5S,12S)-diHETE]. The LTB$_4$ and the 6-trans-5,12-diHETE peaks obtained from reverse-phase HPLC (see legend of Fig. 4) were treated with diazomethane and applied to Nucleosil-50 column, 5-μm particle size (Machery Nagel). Mobile phase, hexane–isopropenol–acetic acid (95:5:0.02), flow rate 1 ml/min.

pellet. We incubated the 10,000 g pellet with LTA$_4$, and LTC$_4$, LTD$_4$, as well as LTE$_4$ were synthesized (Fig. 4D). This confirmed that the glutathione transferase, γ-glutamyl transpeptidase as well as aminopeptidase (LTD$_4$ $\rightarrow$ LTE$_4$) are membrane bound. It was not surprising that in RBL-1 cells the γ-glutamyl transpeptidase and aminopeptidase are particulate enzymes, because these enzymes are known to be membrane-bound in kidney, lung, and liver (Tate *et al.*, 1976). The presence of the glutathione transferase in the 10,000 g pellet was surprising, because this enzyme is usually cytosolic (Wolkoff *et al.*, 1979).

To determine further the localization of the enzymes responsible for the synthesis of the peptidoleukotrienes, we fractionated the 10,000 g pellet by sucrose gradient and obtained a plasma membrane preparation. Figure 4F demonstrates that the membrane fraction efficiently transformed LTC$_4$ to LTD$_4$ and further to LTE$_4$. No significant conversion of LTA$_4$ to LTC$_4$ was observed. The pellet obtained from the sucrose gradient centrifugation contained marked glutathione transferase activity converting LTA$_4$ to LTC$_4$. The conversion of LTC$_4$ to LTD$_4$ was completely inhibited by 20 mM L-serine borate (Kuo *et al.*, 1984). This compound has been reported to inhibit the γ-glutamyl transpeptidase and the conversion of LTC$_4$ to LTD$_4$ (Örning and Hammarström, 1980). Sok *et al.* (1980) demonstrated that L-cysteine blocks the degradation of LTD_4 to LTE_4. Therefore, we incubated the plasma membrane fraction with LTC_4 in the presence of L-cysteine and observed inhibition of LTE_4 formation (Kuo *et al.*, 1984). The conversion of LTC_4 to LTD_4 and further to LTE_4 by the plasma membrane fraction was also monitored by bioassay on the superfused guinea pig ileum (Fig. 6). In these experiments, inhibition of LTD_4 formation by L-serine borate and LTE_4 formation by L-cysteine were also observed. The conversion of LTC_4 to LTD_4 was time and concentration dependent. The time course reached a plateau at approximately 45 min (Kuo *et al.*, 1984). Figure 6 illustrates also that the shape of the contraction of the superfused guinea pig ileum caused by LTC_4 differs from that of LTD_4 and LTE_4. Therefore, if LTC_4 is present alone it can be distinguished from LTD_4 and LTE_4. However, LTD_4 and LTE_4 do not vary in the shape of the contraction but only in potency, LTD_4 being more potent.

The data obtained with the plasma membrane preparation provide evidence that the γ-glutamyl transpeptidase and aminopeptidase are present in this subcellular fraction. It appears that glutamic acid might be removed from LTC_4 as it passes through the membranes to the outside of the cell to form the more potent bronchoconstrictor, LTD_4. This may indicate that the functional significance of LTC_4 may be intracellular and that of LTD_4, extracellular. It is of interest to note that the conversion of LTD_4 to LTE_4 is markedly enhanced when the 10,000 *g* pellet or plasma membrane fraction are used as the enzyme source as compared to the whole homogenate (Fig.

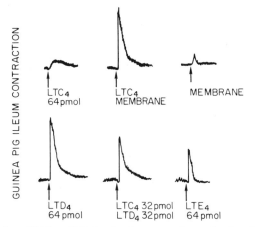

Fig. 6. Conversion of LTC_4 to LTD_4 by the plasma membrane fraction. Plasma membranes obtained from RBL-1 cell homogenates by sucrose gradient centrifugation were incubated with LTC_4 for 15 min. The incubation mixture was applied to the guinea pig ileum superfused with Krebs Henseleit solution and various inhibitors (Steinhoff *et al.*, 1980). The contraction obtained from the incubation mixture was compared to contractions caused by LTC_4, LTD_4, and LTE_4 standards.

4B, D, and F). This suggests that some modulating factors are removed with subcellular fractionation. The exact subcellular localization of the glutathione transferase is under investigation. However, present evidence indicates that the pellet from the sucrose gradient possesses this activity. This fraction is markedly enriched in granules. This raises the possibility that LTC_4 synthesis may be closely linked with granule fusion or the release of its content.

V. KINETIC STUDIES OF 5-HETE, LTA_4, AND LTB_4 SYNTHESIS

In these experiments the biosynthesis of 5-HETE, LTA_4, and LTB_4 were followed with time and varying arachidonic acid concentrations. Because no glutathione is added to the incubation mixture, the 5-lipoxygenase products are expressed as hydroxy acids (no peptidoleukotrienes are formed). In this system, LTA_4 is converted either enzymatically to LTB_4 or nonenzymatically to isomeric 5,12-diHETE and 5,6-diHETE. Therefore, the amount of LTA_4 synthesized is equivalent to the sum of the diHETEs formed. Two different methods to quantitate the products formed from trace-labeled substrate were employed. We used HPLC to quantitate LTA_4 and LTB_4, and thin-layer chromatography to determine 5-HETE and LTA_4 (diHETE band). The amounts of LTA_4 measured by the two methods were equivalent (Jakschik and Kuo, 1983).

When the concentrations of arachidonic acid, the substrate for the 5-lipoxygenase, were varied, we observed changes in the ratios of products formed (Fig. 7). At lower concentrations of arachidonic acid, relatively larger amounts of LTB_4 than of each of the nonenzymatically formed diHETEs were synthesized. The formation of LTB_4 leveled off at 30 μM arachidonic acid, whereas LTA_4 formation leveled off only at 100 μM, and 5-HETE had not reached a plateau at 300 μM arachidonic acid (Fig. 7). It is of interest that 5-HETE only begins to rise steeply at the point when LTB_4 is starting to reach its plateau. These experiments suggest that this enzyme system has a much larger capacity to synthesize 5-HETE and LTA_4 than LTB_4.

These marked differences in 5-HETE, LTA_4, and LTB_4 synthesis with increasing arachidonic concentrations were rather surprising. Although large amounts of LTA_4 were formed, at higher concentrations of arachidonic acid, the amount of LTB_4 synthesized was limited. The accumulation of the nonenzymatically formed diHETEs is also observed when the whole homogenate of RBL-1 cells with glutathione is used and the peptidoleukotrienes LTC_4 and LTD_4 are generated (Jakschik *et al.*, 1982b). This is in contrast to the arachidonate cyclooxygenase pathway, where the endoperoxide synthase, the first step in the cascade, seems to be the rate-limiting step. These findings may suggest that LTA synthase and LTA hydrolase are not tightly

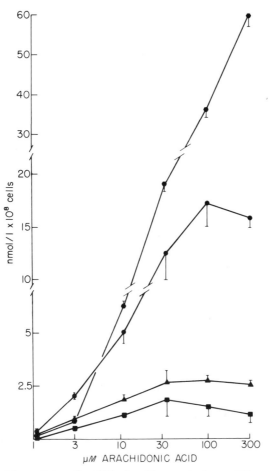

Fig. 7. Effect of the variation of arachidonic acid concentration on 5-lipoxygenase product formation. Supernatant (10,000 g) of RBL-1 cell homogenates was incubated with 1.5 mM calcium and varying concentrations of arachidonic acid as indicated (each sample contained [^{14}C]arachidonic acid as tracer) at 37°C for 15 min. The samples for LTA$_4$ (●) and LTB$_4$ (▲) determinations were processed as described in the legend of Fig. 4. The peaks were collected and liquid scintillation counting performed on aliquots. The LTB$_4$ peak collected from reverse-phase HPLC was methylated and rechromatographed to separate LTB$_4$ from 5S,12S-diHETE (■). The samples for 5-HETE (⬥) determinations were processed as described in the legend of Figs. 1 and 2. The quantities of each product were calculated from the number of counts in each peak (HPLC) or radioactive band (TLC) and adjusted per 1 × 10^8 cells. Vertical bars, SEM (n = 4).

coupled or that a certain cofactor needed for efficient LTB_4 synthesis is missing. We tested a number of agents, some of which are known to enhance hydrolases, but no enhancement of LTB_4 synthesis was observed. The agents tested were NADPH, NADH, 6-methyltetrahydropteridine, and ascorbic acid. In fact, most of these factors decreased LTA_4 formation. It might be argued that in tissues such high concentrations of free arachidonic acid are not available, and therefore, nonenzymatic breakdown of LTA_4 to LTB_4 isomers would be minimal. However, this possibility need not be excluded, since LTB_4 is formed during inflammatory processes, and concentrations of arachidonic acid as high as $100 \ \mu M$ have been observed in inflamed tissue (Hammarström *et al.,* 1975). So far no biological activity has been reported for the nonenzymatically formed isomers of LTB_4, except when tested in very high concentrations (Lewis *et al.,* 1981). Another explanation for the relatively large amounts of LTA_4 synthesized could be that LTA_4 itself has some intracellular action that has not yet been discovered.

The time course of formation (at $30 \ \mu M$ arachidonate) is very similar for 5-HETE, LTA_4, and LTB_4 (Fig. 8). All three compounds reached a plateau between 5 and 10 min, except that the amount of LTA_4 is three times that of LTB_4 and the amount of 5-HETE approximately twice that of LTA_4.

Examining the formation of the double-lipoxygenation product. $(5S,12S)$-diHETE, one finds that only small amounts are formed at low concentrations of arachidonic acid. When the plateau is reached at approximately $10 \ \mu M$ arachidonate, $(5S,12S)$-diHETE constitutes only $20-50\%$ of the LTB_4 peak on reverse-phase HPLC. The time course experiments show that barely detectable levels of $(5S,12S)$-diHETE are present early in the time course (1 min). These results may indicate that this compound is formed only when high concentrations of substrate are available.

To test whether the enzymes were still active when the plateau of the time course was reached, more arachidonic acid was added after 15 min of incubation, and the preparation was allowed to incubate for another 15 min. No further synthesis of LTA_4 or LTB_4 was observed. However, when 10,000 g supernatant was incubated with $167 \ \mu M$ arachidonic acid for 15 min and then more enzyme (10,000 g supernatant) was added and the incubation continued for another 15 min, the second addition of enzyme caused further formation of LTA_4 and LTB_4 (Fig. 9). It was surprising to find that a second addition of arachidonic acid at submaximal substrate concentrations for LTA_4 synthesis did not produce any additional LTA_4 or LTB_4. Judging from the profile of LTA_4 and LTB_4 synthesis shown in Fig. 7, we expected that further addition of arachidonic acid would cause additional formation of LTA_4, because LTA_4 synthesis had not yet reached a plateau at $30 \ \mu M$ arachidonic acid. These data suggested that the 5-lipoxygenase or LTA synthase were inactivated with time by arachidonic acid or its product(s).

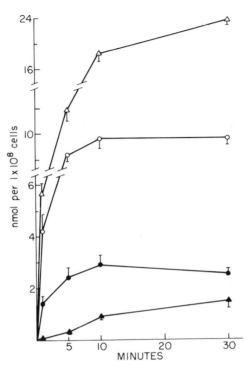

Fig. 8. Time course of 5-HETE (△), LTA₄ (○), and LTB₄ (●) biosynthesis. (▲) (5S,12S)-diHETE. Supernatant (10,000 g) of RBL-1 cell homogenates was incubated with 1.5 mM calcium and 30 μM arachidonic acid (600,000 cpm of [¹⁴C]arachidonate as tracer) for the time indicated. The samples were processed and quantities calculated as described in the legend of Fig. 7. Vertical bars, SEM (n = 3–5).

We further investigated this phenomenon by preincubating 10,000 g supernatant with 10 μM of cold arachidonic acid and 1.5 mM Ca^{2+} at 37°C for various amounts of time. Then 17 μM [¹⁴C]arachidonate was added and the incubation continued for another 15 min. The products formed were analyzed by thin-layer chromatography. As the diHETE band contains LTB₄ and its isomers, it is equivalent to LTA₄. As illustrated in Fig. 10, the formation of LTA₄ and 5-HETE was markedly decreased with time as the preparation was exposed to arachidonic acid at 37°C (Fig. 10B). No such inactivation was observed when the 10,000 g supernatant was preincubated in the presence of calcium without the addition of arachidonic acid (Fig. 10A) (Jakschik and Kuo, 1983). These results present evidence that the 5-lipoxygenase is inactivated by its substrate or product(s). The data also suggest an inactivation of LTA synthase, because, as demonstrated in Fig. 7, the ratio of LTA₄ to 5-HETE increases as the substrate concentration decreases. Therefore, if only

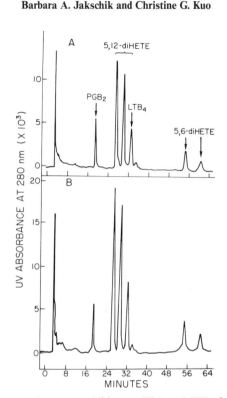

Fig. 9. Effect of repeated enzyme addition on LTA_4 and LTB_4 formation. Supernatant (10,000 g) of RBL-1 cell homogenates was incubated with 1.5 mM calcium and 167 μM arachidonic acid at 37°C for 15 min. At this point another 2 ml of 10,000 g supernatant were added (B) and the incubation allowed to continue for another 15 min. (A) The sample without the second addition of 10,000 g supernatant. The samples were processed as in the legend of Fig. 4. Approximately one-tenth of the sample was applied to reverse-phase HPLC.

the lipoxygenase would be inactivated and not the LTA synthase, more LTA_4 than 5-HETE should be formed during the time course of inactivation. However, the reverse is the case; the ratio of LTA_4 to 5-HETE decreases from 0.8 to 0.4. Therefore, it appears that the LTA synthase is also inactivated. The time course of formation (Fig. 8) shows a slight slope in the plateau for 5-HETE but not LTA_4. This suggests a slower inactivation of the 5-lipoxygenase than the LTA synthase. The inactivation of the enzymes was investigated further by preincubating the 10,000 g supernatant with dihomo-γ-linolenic acid or palmitic acid instead of arachidonic acid. The unsaturated fatty acid, dihomo-γ-linolenic acid, caused an inactivation similar to arachidonate. No enzyme inactivation was observed when the preincubation was performed

A   B

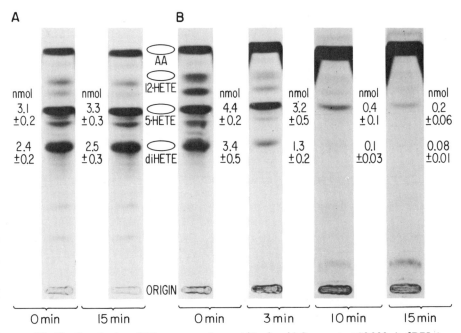

nmol	nmol	nmol	nmol	nmol	nmol
3.1	3.3	4.4	3.2	0.4	0.2
±0.2	±0.3	±0.2	±0.5	±0.1	±0.06
2.4	2.5	3.4	1.3	0.1	0.08
±0.2	±0.3	±0.5	±0.2	±0.03	±0.01

0 min — 15 min — 0 min — 3 min — 10 min — 15 min

Fig. 10.   Inactivation of 5-lipoxygenase by arachidonic acid. Supernatant (10,000 g) of RBL-1 cell homogenates (0.5 ml) was preincubated with 1.5 mM calcium, without (A) or with 10 μM arachidonic acid (AA) (B) at 37 °C for the time indicated. Then [^{14}C]arachidonic acid (17 μM) was added and the incubation continued for 15 min. The samples were processed as described in the legend of Fig. 1. The autoradiogram shows a representative experiment. The data are expressed as mean ± SEM ($n = 3$–5).

with the saturated fatty acid, palmitate (Jakschik and Kuo, 1982b). From earlier experiments we know that the RBL-1 cell system converts dihomo-γ-linolenic acid to monohydroxy acids and only insignificant amounts of dihydroxy acids (Jakschik *et al.,* 1980b), whereas saturated fatty acids are not converted at all. Therefore, these data suggest that a product of arachidonic acid and not the fatty acid itself inactivates the enzymes of the 5-lipoxygenase pathway. In fact, when the 10,000 g supernatant was preincubated with 15-hydroperoxyeicosatetraenoic acid, inactivation of the enzymes occurred. Again, a more pronounced decrease in LTA$_4$ than 5-HETE was observed, which further substantiates a greater inactivation of the LTA synthase than 5-lipoxygenase. These data indicate that hydroperoxide formed from arachidonic acid is probably the inactivating species (Jakschik and Kuo, 1983). Inactivation of the 5-lipoxygenase by peroxides has also been observed by Egan *et al.* (1983).

VI. SUBSTRATE SPECIFICITY FOR LEUKOTRIENE FORMATION VIA THE 5-LIPOXYGENASE

Utilizing a variety of polyenoic fatty acids differing in chain length and in degree and position of unsaturation, we investigated the substrate specificity for the enzymatic production of hydroxy acids (including LTB) and the peptidoleukotrienes. The formation of mono- and diHETE from these various fatty acids was monitored by incubating [^{14}C]fatty acids with the 10,000 g supernatant of RBL-1 cell homogenates in the presence of calcium. The fatty acids that had a double bond at 5,8,11 were readily converted to products that comigrated with 5-HETE and the diHETEs. Thus the 20:3(5,8,11), 20:4(5,8,11,14), 20:5(5,8,11,14,17), and 18:4(5,8,11,14) fatty acids were all excellent substrates for this enzyme system (Fig. 11). Chain length appeared to be less of an influence than the necessity for double bonds at 5,8,11, as evidenced by the striking conversion of Δ^5-fatty acids as compared with the fatty acids with their first double bond at Δ^4, Δ^6, Δ^7, or Δ^8. The latter fatty acids were oxygenated to some extent to monohydroxy acids, but only insignificant amounts of diHETEs were formed.

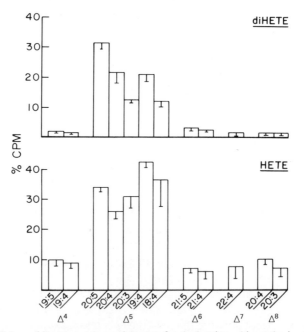

Fig. 11. Fatty acid structural requirement for leukotriene biosynthesis. Supernatant (10,000 g) of RBL-1 cell homogenates (0.5 ml) was incubated with [^{14}C]fatty acid (150,000 cpm) in the presence of 2 mM calcium for 30 min, 37°C. The incubation mixture was extracted and chromatographed as described in the legend of Figs. 1 and 2.

The biosynthesis of the peptidoleukotrienes was monitored on the super-fused guinea pig ileum. A profound contractile response was obtained when 20:3(5,8,11), 20:4(5,8,11,14), 20:5(5,8,11,14,17), and 18:4(5,8,11,14) were used as substrate. Again, all of these fatty acids have unsaturation at 5,8,11. No con-traction resulted when glutathione was omitted from the incubation mix-ture. The SRS receptor antagonist FPL55712 efficiently blocked the contrac-tions (Jakschik *et al.,* 1980b). All of the polyenoic fatty acids tested were converted enzymatically to SRS-like compounds, the activity of which was blocked by FPL55712. However, the SRS activity generated was minimal as compared to the Δ^5-fatty acids. There was a striking parallelism between diHETE formation and generation of detectable SRS activity and the obvi-ous preference for double bonds at positions 5,8,11. This unsaturation re-quirement at 5,8,11 has not been observed with the cyclooxygenase or the 12-lipoxygenase in platelets (Needleman *et al.,* 1981). The conversion of 20:5(5,8,11,14,17) (Hammarström, 1980; Murphy *et al.,* 1981) and of 20:3(5,8,11) (Hammarström, 1981a) has been reported by other investigators by stimulat-ing mouse mastocytoma cells with the calcium ionophore A23187. Ham-marström (1981b) has also demonstrated leukotriene formation from di-homo-γ-linolenic acid, 20:3(8,11,14) by the mouse mastocytoma. However, the relative amounts formed, as compared with arachidonic acid conver-sion, were not stated. It is also not clear whether this leukotriene synthesis was via the 5-lipoxygenase or another lipoxygenase.

Further analysis by HPLC of the products obtained from the conversion of 5,8,11-eicosatrienoic acid by the 5-lipoxygenase-leukotriene pathway showed that this fatty acid can be readily converted to LTA_3 but only insignificant amounts of LTB_3 are formed. This suggests a certain substrate specificity for the LTA hydrolase. Therefore, not only are the three double bonds needed to form the conjugated triene, but the LTA hydrolase also requires the double bond at C-14 to efficiently convert LTA to LTB. No such specificity was observed with the glutathione-S-transferase, the enzyme responsible for the conversion of LTA to LTC (Jakschik *et al.,* 1983). These observations have some pertinent biological implications. 5,8,11-Eicosatrienoic acid accumu-lates in essential fatty acid deficiency. Among the abnormalities observed during this condition is a decrease in inflammatory reactions. Edema for-mation as well as leukocyte infiltration are reduced. This altered response has been attributed to the lack of prostaglandin (PG) production (Ziboh and Hsia, 1972). However, we know now that leukotrienes are important factors in inflammatory processes. The lack of formation of LTB, a potent chemo-tactic factor, could be responsible for the decreased leukocyte infiltration. LTB_4 is also known to cause plasma exudation in the presence of PGE_2 and polymorphonuclear leukocytes (Bray *et al.,* 1981; Wedmore and Williams, 1981). 5,8,11-Eicosatrienoic acid can be converted to peptidoleukotrienes.

These compounds, when derived from arachidonic acid, cause broncho-constriction and plasma exudation. In our hands LTC_3 and LTD_3 (derived from 5,8,11-eicosatrienoic acid) can contract smooth muscle. However, it is not known at the present time whether they can change vascular permeability. The formation of the peptidoleukotrienes with potent bronchoconstrictor activity and the lack of dilator prostaglandins may explain some of the pulmonary complications experienced in essential fatty acid deficiency.

Double bond requirements for this pathway were further studied by utilizing 5,8,14- and 5,11,14-eicosatrienoic acid. The latter fatty acid was not a substrate for the 5-lipoxygenase while 5,8,14-eicosatrienoic acid was converted by the 5-lipoxygenase but not by the LTA-synthetase (Wei *et al.,* 1984). Therefore, the substrate requirements for the 5-lipoxygenase are double bonds at C-5 and C-8, for the LTA synthetase double bonds at C-5, C-8, and C-11 and for the LTA hydrolase double bonds at C-5, C-8, C-11, and C-14. The substrate specificity for the glutatione transferase is not as stringent. Any fatty acid that is converted to LTA will also produce peptidoleukotrienes.

VII. EFFECT OF VARIOUS ACETYLENIC FATTY ACIDS ON LEUKOTRIENE FORMATION

We investigated the effect of a large number of acetylenic acids varying in chain length and in the position and number of the triple bonds on arachidonic acid metabolism by RBL-1 cells (Jakschik *et al.,* 1982a). The effect on the formation of 5-HETE, diHETE, and prostaglandins was monitored by incubating the 10,000 g supernatant with [^{14}C]arachidonate in the presence of the various acetylenic acids and separating the products by thin-layer chromatography. As no glutathione was present during the incubation, the 5-lipoxygenase activity is expressed in the formation of the hydroxy acids and the cyclooxygenase activity as prostaglandins. The effect on the synthesis of the peptidoleukotrienes was tested by monitoring the contractions of the superfused guinea pig ileum. As discussed in the previous section, all of the Δ^5-polyenoic fatty acids tested were excellent substrates for the 5-lipoxygenase. Therefore, we expected the Δ^5-acetylenic acids to be good inhibitors of the 5-lipoxygenase. However, this was not the case. Relatively high concentrations were required for inhibition of the cyclooxygenase as well as 5-lipoxygenase. The Δ^5-acetylenic acids tested were 18:3(5a,8a,11a), 18:4(5a,8a,11a,14a), 19:3(5a,8a,11a), 19:4(5a,8a,11a,14a), 20:3(5a,8a,11a), 20:4(5a,8a,11a,14a), and 21:4(5a,8a,11a,14a). These results may indicate differential requirements of the 5-lipoxygenase at the catalytic site (Δ^5-double bond), and the binding site as the affinity of the Δ^5-acetylenic acids for the enzyme is relatively low.

All the acetylenic acids tested inhibited the formation of peptidoleuko-triienes (SRS). It appears that these compounds directly inhibit the glutathi-one transferase that converts LTA_4 to LTC_4. This conclusion was substan-tiated by the finding that these acetylenic acids block the formation of SRS from LTA_4. The observation that such a large number of acetylenic acids inhibit the glutathione transferase suggests that the inhibition is rather non-specific. It agrees with the observation that glutathione transferases from other tissues have a broad substrate specificity (Jakoby, 1978).

Örning and Hammarström (1980) reported that the 5,8,11-eicosatriynoic acid [(20:3)5a,8a,11a] selectively inhibited LTC_4 biosynthesis by mouse mas-tocytoma cells as compared to its effect on cyclooxygenase or 12-lipoxygen-ase in platelets. The difference in results obtained by these investigators as compared to ours may be partially due to the experimental conditions. They used whole cells and a different cell type, whereas we used a cell-free enzyme system. The preferential inhibition of LTC_4 synthesis may be due in part to the combined action of the acetylenic acid on the 5-lipoxygenase and gluta-thione transferase. We also observed the IC_{50} for the generation of SRS activity to be only one-half of that for the cyclooxygenase, except our values were higher than those reported by Örning and Hammarström.

The Δ^4-acetylenic acids tested are an interesting group of compounds. They do not inhibit the cyclooxygenase or 5-lipoxygenase, but do block the glutathione transferase and therefore the generation of SRS activity (Table I). The potency increases with the carbon chain length of the compound, with 21:4(4a,7a,10a,13a) as the most potent one. The Δ^4-acetylenic acids tested, except for 20:4(4a,7a,11a,14a), also do not have an effect on the 12-lipoxygen-ase in platelets (Sams et al., 1982). The finding that the Δ^4-acetylenic acids block the formation of LTC_4 from its immediate precursor LTA_4 was sub-stantiated by incubating the RBL-1 cell homogenate with LTA_4 and glutathi-one with or without the acetylenic acid. Again, the acetylenic acids blocked

TABLE I

Comparison of the Effect of Δ^4-Acetylenic Acids

Compound	IC_{50} $(\mu M)^a$		
	Cyclooxygenase	5-Lipoxygenase	SRS Activity
16:3(4a,7a,10a)	>60	>60	31 ± 8
19:4(4a,7a,10a,13a)	>55	>55	26 ± 2
20:4(4a,7a,10a,13a)	>50	>50	14 ± 2
21:4(4a,7a,10a,13a)	>50	>50	7 ± 2

[a] IC_{50} is the concentration of acetylenic acid required to cause 50% reduction in activity as compared to the control (Jakschik et al., 1982a).

the formation of SRS activity (Jakschik *et al.*, 1981). These observations make the Δ^4-acetylenic acids valuable tools in the investigation of the role of LTC$_4$ and LTD$_4$ in biological processes.

A more detailed study of the effect of carbon chain length and number of triple bonds was performed with the Δ^8-acetylenic acids. Figure 12 illustrates that the potency of 5-lipoxygenase inhibitors increases with the chain length up to 20 carbons. At least 19 carbons must be present for appreciable inhibition of the 5-lipoxygenase. No such requirements were observed for the cyclooxygenase. Compounds 17:3(8a,11a,14a) and 18:3(8a,11a,14a), which

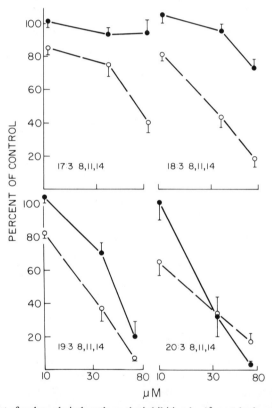

Fig. 12. Effect of carbon chain length on the inhibition by Δ^8-acetylenic acids. Supernatant (10,000 *g*) of RBL-1 cell homogenates was preincubated with the acetylenic acid and 1.5 m*M* calcium at 4°C for 10 min. Then 4 μM [^{14}C]arachidonic acid was added and the mixture incubated for 15 min at 37°C. The samples were extracted and chromatographed as described in the legend of Figs. 1 and 2. (●—●) 5-lipoxygenase; (○---○) SRS activity. Vertical bars, SEM (*n* = 3–8) (Jakschik *et al.*, 1982a).

had no effect on the 5-lipoxygenase, were potent cyclooxygenase inhibitors. A similar effect of carbon chain length was observed with the Δ^6-acetylenic acids; 20:3(6a,9a,12a) was a potent 5-lipoxygenase inhibitor (IC_{50} $15 \pm 2 \, \mu M$), whereas 18:3(6a,9a,12a), 18:4(6a,9a,12a,15a), and 19:4(6a,9a,12a,15a) had no effect on the 5-lipoxygenase. The number of triple bonds present also influenced the extent of the inhibition of the 5-lipoxygenase. The minimum number of triple bonds required seems to be three. Compounds 20:2(8a,11a) and 20:2(10a,13a) had no action on the 5-lipoxygenase, but were good cyclooxygenase inhibitors (IC_{50} 16 ± 2 and $20 \pm 6 \, \mu M$, respectively). With the acetylenic acids having a carbon chain length of 20, the optimal number of triple bonds was three. Increasing the number to four caused a loss of inhibitory activity on the 5-lipoxygenase (Fig. 13). A similar observation was made with the Δ^6-acetylenic acid; 20:3(6a,9a,12a) is a potent 5-lipoxygenase inhibitor (IC_{50} $15 \pm 2 \, \mu M$), and 20:4(6a,9a,12a,15a) is not. Both compounds 20:4(8a,11a,14a,17a) and 20:4(6a,9a,12a,17a) are potent cyclooxygenase inhibitors (IC_{50} 24 ± 3 and $11 \pm 2 \, \mu M$, respectively).

The Δ^7-acetylenic acids were potent inhibitors of the 5-lipoxygenase and cyclooxygenase. Compound 21:3(7a,10a,13a) showed a moderate amount of differential inhibition with the IC_{50} for the cyclooxygenase fourfold higher than that for the 5-lipoxygenase (IC_{50} 14 ± 2 and $3 \pm 0.4 \, \mu M$, respectively).

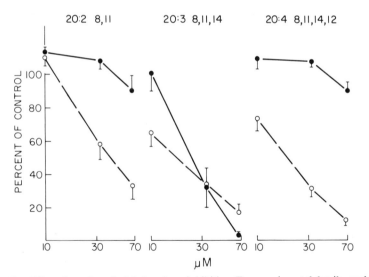

Fig. 13. Effect of number of triple bonds on inhibition. For experimental details, see legend of Fig. 12 (Jakschik *et al.*, 1982a).

The work with these acetylenic fatty acids not only demonstrated that the Δ^4-acetylenic acids are specific inhibitors of SRS formation, as compared to their lack of effect on the cyclooxygenase and 5-lipoxygenase, but also pointed toward marked differences between the 5-lipoxygenase and cyclooxygenase.

VIII. SUMMARY AND CONCLUSION

We have studied leukotriene formation via the 5-lipoxygenase in a cell-free enzyme system obtained from RBL-1 cells. These studies indicated that calcium enhances the 5-lipoxygenase activity and that glutathione is required for LTC_4 synthesis. The calcium stimulation differentiates this pathway from the cyclooxygenase and 12-lipoxygenase in platelets. Further differences between the 5-lipoxygenase and cyclooxygenase were observed in the localization of the enzymes. All the enzymes needed for the conversion of arachidonic acid to LTB_4 are cytosolic, whereas enzymes converting LTA_4 to the peptidoleukotrienes are particulate (10,000 g pellet). In contrast, most of the prostaglandin-forming enzymes seem to be microsomal. The kinetic studies indicated that the rate-limiting enzyme steps are at the level of the conversion of LTA_4 to LTB_4 (LTB hydrolase) or LTC_4 (glutathione transferase). In the prostaglandin pathway the rate-limiting step is at the cyclooxygenase level, the first step in the pathway. The substrate requirement studies with various polyenoic fatty acids showed that double bonds at C-5 and 8 are essential for the 5-lipoxygenase at C-5, C-8, and C-11 for the LTA synthetase, and at C-5, C-8, C-11, and C-14 for the LTA hydrolase. The work with acetylenic acids further differentiated the 5-lipoxygenase from the cyclooxygenase. In general, the potency of the acetylenic acids to inhibit the 5-lipoxygenase increased with carbon chain length up to 20 carbons. A minimum of three triple bonds is necessary for the inhibitory action, and with the 20-carbon compounds the activity decreased when the number of triple bonds increased from three to four. These structure–activity relationships were not observed with the cyclooxygenase. Thus the conditions for and regulation of the enzymatic formation of the biologically potent leukotrienes differ markedly from prostaglandin synthesis.

ACKNOWLEDGMENTS

This work was supported by NIH 2 R01-HL21874-04 and 5P30-CA16217-03.

REFERENCES

Bach, M. K., Brashler, J. R., and Gorman, R. R. (1977). *Prostaglandins* 14, 21–38.

Borgeat, P., and Samuelsson, B. (1979a). *Proc. Natl. Acad. Sci. U.S.A.* 76, 2148–2152.

Borgeat, P., and Samuelsson, B. (1979b). *Proc. Natl. Acad. Sci. U.S.A.* 76, 3213–3217.

Borgeat, P., and Samuelsson, B. (1979c). *J. Biol. Chem.* 254, 2643–2646.

Borgeat, P., and Samuelsson, B. (1979d). *J. Biol. Chem.* 254, 7865–7869.

Borgeat, P., Hamberg, M., and Samuelsson, B. (1976). *J. Biol. Chem.* 251, 7816–7820.

Borgeat, P., Fruteau de Laclos, B., Picard, S., Vallerand, P., and Sirois, P. (1982). *Adv. Prostaglandin, Thromboxane, Leukotriene Res.* 9, 45–51.

Bray, M. A., Cunningham, F. M., Ford-Hutchinson, A. W., and Smith, M. J. H. (1981). *Br. J. Pharmacol.* 72, 483–486.

Egan, R. W., Tischler, A. N., Baptista, E. M., Ham, E. A., Soderman, D. D., and Gale, P. H. (1983). *Adv. Prostaglandin Thromboxane Leukotriene Res.* 11, 151–157.

Feldberg, W. and Kellaway, C. H. (1938). *J. Physiol.* 94, 187–226.

Hammarström, S. (1980). *J. Biol. Chem.* 255, 7093–7094.

Hammarström, S. (1981a). *J. Biol. Chem.* 256, 2275–2279.

Hammarström, S. (1981b). *J. Biol. Chem.* 256, 7712–7714.

Hammarström, S., Hamberg, M., Samuelsson, B., Duell, E., Stawiski, M., and Voorhees, J. (1975). *Proc. Natl. Acad. Sci. U.S.A.* 72, 5130–5134.

Hammarström, S., Murphy, R. C., Samuelsson, B., Clark, D. A., Mioskowski, C., and Corey, E. J. (1979). *Biochem. Biophys. Res. Commun.* 91, 1266–1272.

Jakoby, W. B. (1978). *Adv. Enzymol.* 46, 383–414.

Jakschik, B. A., and Kuo, C. G. (1982). *Adv. Prostaglandin, Thromboxane, Leukotriene Res.* 11, 141–145.

Jakschik, B. A., and Kuo, C. G. (1983). *Prostaglandins,* 25, 767–782.

Jakschik, B. A., and Lee, L. H. (1980). *Nature (London)* 287, 51–52.

Jakschik, B. A., Falkenhein, S., and Parker, C. W. (1977). *Proc. Natl. Acad. Sci. U.S.A.* 74, 4577–4581.

Jakschik, B. A., Lee, L. H., Shuffer, G., and Parker, C. W. (1978). *Prostaglandins* 16, 733–788.

Jakschik, B. A., Sun, F. F., Lee, L. H., and Steinhoff, M. M. (1980a). *Biochem. Biophys. Res. Commun.* 95, 103–110.

Jakschik, B. A., Sams, A. R., Sprecher, H., and Needleman, P. (1980b). *Prostaglandins* 20, 401–410.

Jakschik, B. A., DiSantis, D. M., Sankarappa, S. K., and Sprecher, H. (1981). *Biochem. Biophys. Res. Commun.* 102, 624–629.

Jakschik, B. A., DiSantis, D. M., Sankarappa, S. K., and Sprecher, H. (1982a). *Adv. Prostaglandin, Thromboxane, Leukotriene Res.* 9, 127–135.

Jakschik, B. A., Harper, T., and Murphy, R. C. (1982b). *J. Biol. Chem.* 257, 5346–5349.

Jakschik, B. A., Morrison, A. R., and Sprecher, H. (1983). *J. Biol. Chem.* (in press).

Jubiz, W., Rådmark, O., Malmsten, C., and Samuelsson, B. (1981). *FEBS Lett.* 126, 127–132.

Kuo, C. G., Lewis, M. T., and Jakschik, B. A. (1984). Submitted.

Lewis, R. A., Goetzl, E. J., Drazen, J. M., Soter, N. A., Austin, K. F., and Corey, E. J. (1981). *J. Exp. Med.* 154, 1243–1248.

Lindgren, J. A., Hansson, G., and Samuelsson, B. (1981). *FEBS Lett.* 128, 329–335.

Lundberg, U., Rådmark, O., Malmsten, C., and Samuelsson, B. (1981). *FEBS Lett.* 126, 127–132.

Maas, R. L., Brash, A. R., and Oates, J. A. (1981). *Proc. Natl. Acad. Sci. U.S.A.* 78, 5523–5527.

Maas, R. L., Turk, J., Oates, J. A., and Brash, A. R. (1982). *J. Biol. Chem.* 257, 7056–7067.

Maycock, A. L., Anderson, M. S., DeSousa, D. M., and Kuehl, F. A., Jr. (1982). *J. Biol. Chem.* 257, 13911–13914.

Morris, H. R., Taylor, G. W., Piper, P. J., Sirois, P., and Tippins, J. R. (1978). *FEBS Lett.* **87,** 203–206.

Morris, H. R., Taylor, G. W., Piper, P. J., Samhoun, M. N., and Tippins, J. R. (1980a). *Prostaglandins* **19,** 185–201.

Morris, H. R., Taylor, G. W., Piper, P. J., and Tippins, J. R. (1980b). *Nature (London)* **285,** 104–106.

Murphy, R. C., Hammarström, S., and Samuelsson, B. (1979). *Proc. Natl. Acad. Sci. U.S.A.* **76,** 4275–4279.

Murphy, R. C., Pickett, W. C., Culp, B. R., and Lands, W. E. M. (1981). *Prostaglandins* **22,** 613–622.

Needleman, P., Wyche, A. A., LeDuc, L. E., Jakschik, B. A., Sankarappa, S. K., and Sprecher, H. (1981). *Prog. Lipid Res.* **20,** 415–422.

Örning, L., and Hammarström, S. (1980). *J. Biol. Chem.* **255,** 8023–8026.

Parker, C. W., Jakschik, B. A., Huber, M. G., and Falkenhein, S. F. (1979a). *Biochem. Biophys. Res. Commun.* **89,** 1186–1192.

Parker, C. W., Huber, M. G., Hoffman, M.K., and Falkenhein, S. F. (1979b). *Prostaglandins* **18,** 673–686.

Parker, C. W., Koch, D., Huber, M. M., and Falkenhein, S. F. (1980a). *Biochem. Biophys. Res. Commun.* **94,** 1037–1043.

Parker, C. W., Falkenhein, S. F., and Huber, M.M. (1980b). *Prostaglandins* **20,** 863–886.

Sams, A. R., Sprecher, H., Sankarappa, S. K., and Needleman, P. (1982). *Adv. Prostaglandin, Thromboxane, Leukotriene Res.* **9,** 19–28.

Sok, D. E., Pai, J. K., Atrache, V., and Sih, C. J. (1980). *Proc. Natl. Acad. Sci. U.S.A.* **77,** 6481–6485.

Steinhoff, M. M., Lee, L. H., and Jakschik, B. A. (1980). *Biochim. Biophys. Acta* **618,** 28–34.

Tate, S. S., Thompson, G. A., and Meister, A. (1976). *In* "Glutathione Metabolism and Function" (T. M. Arias and W. B. Jakoby, eds.), pp. 45–55. Raven Press, New York.

Wedmore, C. V. and Williams, T. J. (1981). *Nature (London)* **289,** 646–650.

Wei, Y. F., Sprecher, H., Morrison, A. R., and Jakschik, B. A. (1984). Submitted.

Wolkoff, A. W., Weisinger, R. A., and Jakoby, W. B. (1979). *Prog. Liver Dis.* **6,** 214–224.

Ziboh, V. A., and Hsia, S. L. (1972). *J. Lipid Res.* **13,** 458.

6

Inhibitors of Leukotriene Synthesis and Action

Department of Hypersensitivity Diseases Research
The Upjohn Company, Kalamazoo, Michigan

I. INTRODUCTION

The rapidly emerging literature on the multiple actions of extremely low concentrations of the leukotrienes should suffice to justify the need for compounds that can inhibit the formation or action of these substances. Specifically, the evidence available to date suggests strongly that the leukotrienes may be major contributors to the elicitation of the symptoms of asthma. In addition, evidence is rapidly accumulating to suggest that they may play a key role in other pulmonary conditions such as acute respiratory

THE LEUKOTRIENES

distress. It must be emphasized, however, that all these presumptions about the actions of the leukotrienes are at least partly based on indirect evidence. Specifically, it is known that leukotrienes can be formed by the affected tissues under conditions resembling those of disease and, furthermore, that the administration of leukotrienes to animals or in some cases to humans can mimic some of the symptoms of the disease. Another necessary element in the proof of the proposed role of the leukotrienes is the demonstration that the selective inhibition of the formation of leukotrienes in patients with disease results in the alleviation of the symptoms of the disease. Such proof requires the availability of selective inhibitors that are active *in vivo.*

In considering the pathway leading to leukotriene synthesis, one might naturally ask which step in the pathway would be the most desirable one to inhibit. The answer to this question is determined in part by the intended uses of the inhibitor. For example, if the intent is to prove the role of leukotrienes in disease, one would naturally want a compound that is as selective as possible in its action. This means, by definition, that compounds that will inhibit arachidonate mobilization, or compounds that have a dual action on the 5-lipoxygenase and on the cyclooxygenase are not particularly desirable. However, if the primary goal is therapeutic, compounds with a dual action may have their place. It must be kept in mind, however, that inhibition of the cyclooxygenase may have its bad points in addition to the beneficial ones. For example, inhibition of PGI_2 production may, under certain circumstances, aggravate conditions just as much as the inhibition of thromboxane or PGD_2 formation may be of help.

The evidence to date indicates that the activation of the arachidonate cascade involves the mobilization of arachidonate from membrane phospholipids. Once arachidonate is mobilized, the cells further metabolize the released arachidonate in one of the several manners in which the particular cells are programmed to do so. Thus it follows that, if a given pathway of arachidonate metabolism is blocked by use of a selective inhibitor, the cells will funnel the mobilized arachidonate into the pathway(s) that remain open. This tendency has been utilized to increase formation of leukotrienes in experimental systems by blocking the cyclooxygenase with a nonsteroidal antiinflammatory compound. By analogy, we can anticipate that inhibition of the 5-lipoxygenase might increase formation of products of other pathways of arachidonate metabolism. Depending on the cells being inhibited and the desired end result, such augmented production may have beneficial or deleterious consequences. For example, hyperproduction of thromboxane may be undesirable, whereas hyperproduction of PGI_2 may be desirable.

Going further down the pathway, one has to decide whether formation of both the thiol ether leukotrienes and LTB_4 are to be inhibited, or whether inhibition is to be selective for one of these pathways. If inhibition of formation of all leukotrienes is to be achieved, the choice of sites for inhibition is limited to the 5-lipoxygenase and the LTA_4 synthetase. On the other hand, if selective inhibition is desired, the site of inhibition would have to be the LTA_4: glutathione S-transferase (LTC synthetase) on the one hand, and the LTB_4 synthetase on the other. As will be discussed in more detail in a later section of this chapter, however, glutathione S-transferases are important drug detoxification enzymes, and the potential cross-reactivity between the leukotriene-synthesizing reaction and drug detoxification could lead to serious toxicity problems.

Finally, there is the potential for antagonizing leukotriene *action* by interfering with the binding of the leukotrienes to their receptors. This approach offers both opportunities and challenges, however, since the descriptions of these receptors, which are just now appearing in print (Bruns *et al.,* 1983; Krell *et al.,* 1983; Krilis *et al.,* 1983), make it quite apparent that there are a whole family of such receptors, and that there are differences in selectivity, binding constants, and tissue distribution among the members of this class. Clearly, selective antagonists *within* the class of leukotriene receptors would be expected to have different effects from compounds that antagonize these receptors as a class.

Previous chapters in this book have focused on the structure, biosynthesis, and actions of the leukotrienes. It is the purpose of this chapter to review the rapidly emerging knowledge on the biochemical and pharmacologic control of the synthesis and actions of these potent molecules. The information is considered, as far as possible, in the context of the specific enzymes in the pathway that may be affected by any given agent. In some instances, and especially in the case of the glutathione S-transferases, brief consideration will also be given to the properties of these enzymes.

II. NONSELECTIVE INHIBITORS

By far most of the inhibitors of leukotriene synthesis (or action) that have been described have been reported to inhibit SRS-A. In many cases such reports have preceded the elucidation of the structure of the leukotrienes and, further, have come from groups whose primary interest it has been to develop agents that might have therapeutic utility without any a priori concern for the specific mode of action of the agent being developed. In many cases, such agents were reported to inhibit simultaneously the release of preformed mediators (Lichtenstein and Adkinson, 1969; Orange *et al.,* 1970; Malley and Baecher, 1971; Broughton *et al.,* 1974; Burka and Eyre, 1977; El-Azab and Stewart, 1977; Diamantis *et al.,* 1979; Buckle *et al.,* 1979; Welton *et al.,* 1981a; Armour *et al.,* 1982; Weichman *et al.,* 1982) or the action of such mediators on smooth muscle assay systems (Possanza *et al.,* 1975; Ashack *et al.,* 1980; Ali *et al.,* 1982a,b). More recently, some of these compounds have received further attention, and their mode of action has been elucidated. These will be considered in the appropriate sections later in this review.

A. "Universal" Inhibitors of Arachidonate Metabolism — ETYA

5,8,11,14-Eicosatetraynoic acid (ETYA) is a structural analog of arachidonic acid in which all the ethylenic double bonds are replaced with acetylenic (triple) bonds (see Table I). The compound has been invaluable as a general-purpose inhibitor of arachidonate metabolism (Bach *et al.,* 1977). Although the assumption has often been made that it is a "dual" inhibitor of both the cyclooxygenase and the lipoxygenase pathways, its actions are in fact much more complex. For example, doses that block both the cyclooxygenase and the 5-lipoxygenase have been reported not to affect the platelet 12-lipoxygenase (Morris *et al.,* 1979; Busse *et al.,* 1982). In other reports, doses that inhibited prostaglandin production did not affect SRS-A formation (Engineer *et al.,* 1978) and actually stimulated 5-HETE production (Borgeat *et al.,* 1982). Even more interesting are reports that suggest additional sites of action. Bokoch and Reed (1981) reported that, in guinea pig polymorphonuclear leukocytes (PMNs) challenged with the calcium ionophore A23187, $5-10 \ \mu M$ concentrations of ETYA resulted in the *increased* formation of 5-HETE, while the production of LTB_4 was inhibited. Hunter *et al.* (1982) reported that ETYA as well as indomethacin and in fact even arachidonic acid can combine with the AA subtype of guinea pig liver glutathione *S*-transferase. Other steps in arachidonate mobilization have also been shown to be subject to inhibition by ETYA.

B. Inhibitors Affecting Both the Cyclooxygenase and the Lipoxygenases

Several nonsteroidal antiinflammatory compounds (NSACs) have been described that range all the way from compounds that appear to be truly specific for inhibiting the cyclooxygenase on the one hand, to compounds that, in addition to inhibiting this enzyme, also inhibit various lipoxygenases. As already noted, compounds with little if any lipoxygenase-inhibitory activity often potentiate leukotriene formation (Burka and Eyre, 1975; Weichman *et al.,* 1982; Engineer *et al.,* 1978; Walker *et al.,* 1980). Noteworthy among the compounds that have a dual action are phenidone (Blackwell and Flower, 1978), BW755c and analogs thereof (Randall *et al.,* 1980; Piper and Temple, 1981; Patterson *et al.,* 1981), and benoxaprofen (Walker *et al.,* 1980; Dyer *et al.,* 1982). In general, these compounds appear to be approximately equipotent in inhibiting the cyclooxygenase and the lipoxygenases. Their

5-lipoxygenase inhibitory activity is largely based on indirect observations such as the ability of the compounds to inhibit leukocyte infiltration into irritated sites (Higgs *et al.,* 1981). There are occasional paradoxical reports in the literature suggesting that, in certain systems, compounds that are generally believed to be devoid of lipoxygenase-inhibiting activity are active on the lipoxygenase pathway (Paajanen *et al.,* 1982). It remains to be established if such observations are due to peculiarities of dosing or to idiosyncrasies of the animals being used.

C. Inhibitors That Are Nonselective among the Lipoxygenases

A variety of compounds that are known to be antioxidants have been shown to inhibit the lipoxygenases. The best studied among these is, in all likelihood, nordihydroguaiaretic acid (NDGA), which has been used proto-typically as an inhibitor of lipoxygenases that does not inhibit the cyclooxy-genase (Walker *et al.,* 1980; Morris *et al.,* 1980). In general, a difference in susceptibility was observed between inhibition of 5-HETE formation, IC_{50} 3 μM, and inhibition of leukotriene synthesis, IC_{50} 30 μM (Walker *et al.,* 1980).

Another group of compounds that have been reported to be selective for the lipoxygenases are flavonoids (Baumann *et al.,* 1980; Fiebrich and Koch, 1979; Hope *et al.,* 1982). Potency of these molecules is variable, ranging from an IC_{50} of 0.2 μM for quercetin acting on the 5-lipoxygenase (Hope *et al.,* 1983) to concentrations in the millimolar range for compounds like silychris-tin acting on soybean lipoxygenase (Fiebrich and Koch, 1979). There is also a fair level of selectivity in that 3',4',5,7-tetrahydroxyethyl quercetin is at least 12 times more potent in inhibiting rat spleen 5-lipoxygenase than it is in inhibit-ing the cyclooxygenase. Similarly, quercetin is reportedly at least 20 times more active against the 5-lipoxygenase than it is against human platelet 12-lipoxygenase. It is interesting that quercetin is also a potent inhibitor of the release of preformed mediators from mast cells, although its mode of action in that setting is believed to be the inhibition of calcium mobilization. More recently, another related compound, a chromone (Baicalein), has been reported to be a selective inhibitor of platelet lipoxygenase (Sekiya and Okuda, 1982). The level of selectivity is approximately sevenfold compared to platelet cyclooxygenase, and no data on activity on other lipoxygenases were reported.

Sulfasalazine has been used for many years in the management of inflam-matory bowel disease. The original rationale for its synthesis was the attempt to combine the antibacterial action of sulfa drugs with the antiinflamma-tory action of salicylates. However, a recent report suggested that this com-pound may be a selective inhibitor of the lipoxygenases in mucosal tissue (Stenson and Lobs, 1982). There is a suggestion in that report that one of the breakdown products of sulfasalazine, 5-aminosalicylic acid, may be a selective inhibitor of LTB_4 formation without affecting 5-HETE formation. The concentrations of sulfasalazine that were required were in the millimolar range. Although these concentrations may occur in bowel contents, they are far higher than the concentrations of the same compound that are required for inhibiting platelet cyclooxygenase. Sulfasalazine is not truly selective since it was shown to inhibit the soybean lipoxygenase at a similar concentration (Sircar *et al.*, 1983).

Nafazatrom, a naphthyloxymethylpyrazolinone derivative, has been reported to be a selective lipoxygenase inhibitor. Data on selectivity for one lipoxygenase compared to another were not furnished, however (Honn and Dunn, 1982; Busse *et al.*, 1982). The compound is a free radical scavenger (Sevilla *et al.*, 1983) which may explain its mode of action.

Wallach and Brown (1981a) have reported that a series of phenylhydrazones are potent inhibitors of various lipoxygenases. Results were reported for the soybean lipoxygenase, platelet lipoxygenase, and seminal vesicle cyclooxygenase, so that there are no direct data available on activity of these compounds on a 5-lipoxygenase. It is interesting, however, that relative potencies for these three enzymes varied considerably. Thus, 1-(*p*-isopropylphenyl)-chloromethyl-phenylhydrazone had a molar inhibition constant of 2.7×10^{-8} *M* for the soybean enzyme, 2.8×10^{-7} *M* for the platelet enzyme, and 7.8×10^{-5} *M* for the cyclooxygenase.

Attempts have been made to find selective lipoxygenase inhibitors by the suitable incorporation of acetylenic bonds into analogs of arachidonic acid. One such molecule, 5,8,11-eicosatriynoic acid, has been reported to be a selective inhibitor of the platelet 12-lipoxygenase, although no data on its activity on other lipoxygenases were supplied (Hammarström, 1977). Other efforts of this type have also been reported (Wilhelm *et al.*, 1981; Sun *et al.*, 1981).

Sera from various species have been reported to contain an inhibitor of lipoxygenase as determined by polarographic analysis using the soybean lipoxygenase (Saeed *et al.*, 1980; Collier *et al.*, 1981). Activity appeared to be located in Cohn fractions III, IV, and V but not in fractions II or VI. No further characterization of these materials has been reported.

III. SELECTIVE INHIBITORS

The enzymatic sequence leading to the synthesis of the leukotrienes is summarized in Fig. 1. A summary of the compounds that are considered in this section, their known or presumed sites of action, and reported potencies can be seen in Table I.

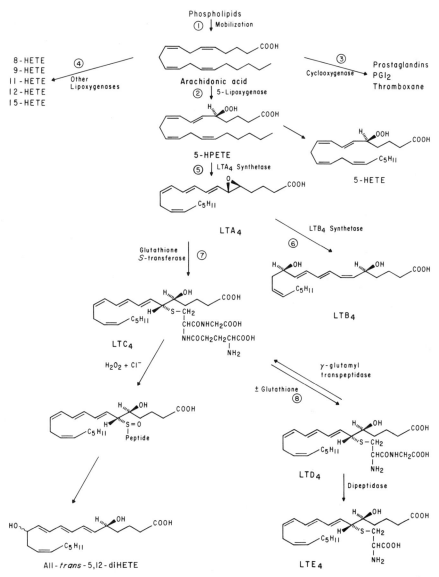

Fig. 1.   Schematic for arachidonate metabolism via the 5-lipoxygense. Circled numbers refer to reaction designations in Table I.

TABLE I

Representative Inhibitors of Leukotriene Synthesis

Name	Structure	Identified sites of action[a]	Comments	Usual ID$_{50}$ values	References (Representative)
5,8,11,14-Eicosatetraynoic acid (ETYA)	$CH_3-(CH_2)_4-C\equiv C-CH_2-C\equiv C-CH_2-C\equiv C-CH_2-C\equiv C-(CH_2)_4-COOH$	1, 2, 3, 4, 5, 7	Nonselective; structural analog of arachidonic acid	$\sim 10^5\ \mu M$	Bach et al. (1977); Engineer et al. (1978); Bokoch and Reed (1981)
Code #3585	*(structure: 4-fluorophenyl / F_3C-phenyl cyclohexyl $-NH-(CH_2)_3-CO-$ · HCl)*	1	—	$0.5\ \mu M$	Wallach and Brown (1981b)
BW755C	*(structure: CF_3-phenyl, NH_2, N-pyrazoline)*	2, 3, 4	—	$5\ \mu M$	Higgs et al. (1981); Randall et al. (1980)
Nordihydroguaiaretic acid (NDGA)	*(structure: two catechol rings $-CH_2-CH-CH-CH_2-$ with $CH_3\ CH_3$)*	2, 4	—	$3\ \mu M$	Walker et al. (1980); Bokoch and Reed (1981)
Quercetin	*(structure: flavonoid with multiple OH groups)*	2, 4	Lipoxygenase; independently also inhibits histamine release	$0.2\ \mu M$ for 5-LPO $5\ \mu M$ for 12-LPO	Hope et al. (1983)
Nafazatrom	*(structure: naphthalene $-O-CH_2-CH_2-N-$ pyrazolone, CH_3, $=O$)*	2, 4(?)	—	$3\ \mu M$	Honn and Dunn (1982)
Code #2893	*(structure: $(CH_3)_2-CH-O-CH_2-CH_2-$ / phenyl $-C=N-NH-$ phenyl, Cl)*	2, 3, 4	—	$0.03-8\ \mu M$ depending on enzyme used	Wallach and Brown (1981a)
5,6-Dehydroarachidonic acid	*(structure: $C_5H_{11}-$ chain $C\equiv C-$ ... $-COOH$)*	2	Irreversible?	$0.5-10\ \mu M$ depending on preincubation time	Corey and Munroe (1982); Sok et al. (1982)

5,6-Methano-LTA$_4$		2	—	3 μM (PMNs)	Koshihara et al. (1982); Arai et al. (1982)
15-HETE		2 (4)	Note *induction* of 5-lipoxygenase in some mast cells lines!	6 μM	Vanderhoek et al. (1980)
Sulfasalazine		2	Active on *Platelet* cyclooxygenase as well	1 mM	Stenson and Lobs (1982)
5-Aminosalicylic acid		5?	—	1 mM	Stenson and Lobs (1982)
Diethylcarbamazine		5	—	5 μM in mastocytoma cells; 5 mM in guinea pig lung	Mathews and Murphy (1982); Engineer et al. (1978)
LTB$_4$ Dimethylamide			LTB-Receptor antagonist; partial agonist	0.003–0.01 μM	Showell et al. (1982)
Bilirubin		7	Liver enzyme but not RBL enzyme	1 μM	Kaplowitz et al. (1975); Bach et al. (1982a); Brashler et al. (1983)
17β-estradiol-3-sulfate		7	Both liver and RBL enzymes	50 μM to 1 mM	Ohl and Litwack (1977); Bach et al. (1982a); Brashler et al. (1983)
Buthionine sulfoximine			Inhibits glutathione biosynthesis	<200 μM at 14 h pretreatment	Rouzer et al. (1981a)

(Continued)

171

TABLE I (continued)

Name	Structure	Identified sites of action[a]	Comments	Usual ID$_{50}$ values	References (Representative)
FPL55712			Selective end organ antagonist, short duration of action	~1 μM	Augstein et al. (1973); Welton et al. (1981a)
FPL59257			Selective end organ antagonist, somewhat longer duration of action than FPL55712	5 μM	Sheard (1981); Sheard et al. (1982)
Piriprost (U-60,257)		2;	5-Lipoxygenase inhibitor: selective end organ antagonist	3 μM	Bach et al. (1982b, 1983); Sun and McGuire (1983)

[a] Numbers refer to enzymatic steps as defined in Fig. 1.

A. Structure–Activity Approach to Leukotriene Antagonists

The elucidation of the structures of the leukotrienes and their total chemical synthesis was followed by attempts to develop antagonists based on studies of structure–activity correlation. A number of such studies have been carried out, in which the role of the carboxylate, the double-bond structure, the peptide portion, and the oxidation state of the thiol ether sulfur atom (Lewis *et al.*, 1981a, 1982; Baker *et al.*, 1981, 1982; Young *et al.*, 1981; Tsai *et al.*, 1982; Girard *et al.*, 1982; Jones *et al.*, 1982) have been examined. These studies depended in their evaluation on an examination of biologic activity, since receptor assays for the leukotrienes were not available. None of the compounds that have been reported showed any antagonist action.

More recently, results with more extensively modified leukotriene analogs have been reported. One of these, 4R, 5S, 6Z-nor LTD_1 is a relatively weak antagonist of LTC_4, LTD_4, and LTE_4 *in vitro* and also antagonized both the pulmonary smooth muscle and the microvascular permeability effects of LTD_4 *in vivo*. The compound did not antagonize histamine, carbachol, $PGF_{2\alpha}$, or KCl, however (Wasserman *et al.*, 1983). Other molecules in which the 11-Z olefin in leukotrienes was replaced by a benzene ring, were either inhibitors of leukotriene biosynthesis or end organ antagonists (Cohen *et al.*, 1983).

Similar studies in the LTB_4 series have centered around stereochemical isomers of LTB_4 (Lewis *et al.*, 1981b; Palmblad *et al.*, 1982). The only exception is the observation that LTB_4 dimethylamide appears to be a competitive inhibitor of LTB_4 (Showell *et al.*, 1982). The specific case of an analog of LTA_4 that is an inhibitor of the 5-lipoxygenase will be considered in a later section.

B. Arachidonate Mobilization

Arachidonate is not present in the cells as the free fatty acid. Rather it is primarily bound in the 2 position of glycerol of various phospholipids in the cell membrane. The exact biochemical sequence of events leading to arachidonate mobilization is not completely resolved. There are good examples of situations where mobilization depends on a phospholipase A_2, whereas in other circumstances a combination of a phosphoinositide-specific phospholipase C combined with a diacylglycerol lipase appears to be involved. A selective inhibitor of this latter enzyme has been described (Sutherland and Amin, 1982). As discussed in the introduction, the inhibition of arachidonate mobilization would be generally expected to affect a good deal more than the synthesis of the leukotrienes. It must be stressed, however, that even this generalization may not hold in all cases. Thus there is evidence for the selective *induction* of the formation of different metabolites, for example, with the prostaglandin-generating factor of anaphylaxis (Steel *et al.,* 1982). It is therefore reasonable to expect that selective inhibition at this step in the synthesis could also take place.

The inhibitors that have been described thus far are not selective, however. Best known are the corticosteroids (e.g., Burka and Flower, 1979), whose mode of action is now believed to be the induced formation of lipomodulin (Hirata *et al.,* 1980). Mepacrine and *p*-bromophenacyl bromide have also received considerable attention as so-called selective inhibitors (e.g., Burka and Flower, 1979; Hofmann *et al.,* 1982). However, neither of these compounds is even remotely selective. Mepacrine has been known for a long time to bind to nucleic acids, to be a frameshift mutagen or an antimutagen depending on the circumstances, and to have a large number of other properties. *p*-Bromophenacyl bromide is an alkylating agent and alkylates histidine. A series of compounds that are inhibitory to hog pancreas phospholipase A_2 have been described (Wallach and Brown, 1981b). Although these compounds inhibited the arachidonate cascade both *in vivo* and *in vitro,* it is clear that their action is not selective for one branch of the cascade over another.

C. 5-Lipoxygenase Inhibitors

The 5-lipoxygenase of rat basophil leukemia cells (RBL) has been studied in cell-free preparations by Jakschik *et al.* (1980). The most striking property of this enzyme is that it requires calcium for activity. Details of Dr. Jakschik's work are reported in Chapter 5 of this book and will therefore not be amplified here. Several synthetic organic molecules of various structural classes have been reported to inhibit the 5-lipoxygenase (e.g., Honn and Dunn, 1982; Casey *et al.,* 1983), although the true specificity of these molecules for the 5-lipoxygenase has not been demonstrated. In addition to these compounds, three types of fatty acids have been shown to have selective action on the 5-lipoxygenase. These are certain acetylenic analogs of arachidonate, the 5,6-methano analog of LTA_4, and 15-HETE, the product of oxygenation of arachidonate with the 15-lipoxygenase.

1. Acetylenic Analogs of Arachidonate

The double bond at position 5 is required for the action of the 5-lipoxygenase. Thus replacement of the 5,6 double bond with an acetylenic triple bond resulted in a compound that was a selective inhibitor (Sok *et al.,* 1982; Corey and Munroe, 1982). The inhibition was reported to be irreversible, and its expression was reported to be time dependent. Inactivation of 50% was achieved in 5 min with 10 μM inhibitor and in 2 min with 30 μM. Data on other activities of this compound are thus far sketchy, and its selectivity of action remains to be demonstrated. A somewhat related molecule, 4,5-dehydroarachidonic acid, has been shown to be a potent and irreversible inhibitor. This compound is an analog of 4-hydroperoxy, 4,5-dehydroarachidonic acid, which is believed to be the intermediate in the inhibition of the 5-lipoxygenase by 5,6-dehydroarachidonic acid (Corey *et al.*, 1983).

2. Carba Analogs of 5-HPETE and LTA₄

Both the 5-hydroxymethyleicosatetraenoic acid (HPETE in which the peroxide function is replaced by CH_2OH) and the 5,6-methano-LTA_4 (LTA_4 in which the epoxy oxygen is replaced by a CH_2 group) have been prepared (Arai *et al.*, 1982). Both compounds are reported to inhibit the 5-lipoxygenase of guinea pig PMNs, with IC_{50} values of 100 and 3 μM for the HPETE and LTA_4 analogs, respectively. The specificity of action of the latter compound was further described by Koshihara *et al.* (1982). They compared the IC_{50} values of this compound to those of a series of analogs that differed in the stereochemistry of the double bonds, the derivatization of the carboxylic acid as the methyl ester, and the introduction of an acetylenic bond at position 11 in a cell-free preparation in which both 5-lipoxygenase and cyclooxygenase were determined. A potency ratio of approximately 25 was achieved with IC_{50} values for the 5-lipoxygenase in the 30–40 μM range. This series was examined further (Arai *et al.*, 1983) and certain analogs with 11- or 12-methyl substituents and 5-keto or 5,6-epithio functions also had significant activity. The optimal location of the methano bridge for the inhibition of the 5-lipoxygenase was shown to be at the 5,6 position.

3. 15-HETE

Vanderhoek *et al.* (1980) reported that 15-HETE was a selective inhibitor of the 5-lipoxygenase in rabbit PMNs, with an IC_{50} of 5.7 μM. As subsequently confirmed by Goetzl (1982a), and further developed by Bailey *et al.* (1982), the inhibition was essentially specific for the 5-lipoxygenase on the one hand and for 15-HETE on the other. The 15-hydroxyeicosatrienoic acid was approximately equipotent to 15-HETE, whereas the corresponding dienoic acid was much less active. The observation was also extended to include T cells. By contrast, Maclouf *et al.* (1982) reported that 12-HPETE, but not 12-HETE was a potent *stimulator* of the 5-lipoxygenase of human leukocytes. This raises the possibility that platelet contamination, which is virtually impossible to rule out entirely, may indirectly contribute to the observed 5-lipoxygenase activity of peripheral blood leukocytes by virtue of the stimulated production by platelet-derived 12-HPETE. In more recent studies the group at George Washington University have reported that 15-HETE, rather than inhibiting the 5-lipoxygenase of mast cells, actually stimulated the enzyme in these cells (Vanderhoek *et al.*, 1982). Clearly, the actions of the hydroxy acids as regulators of the lipoxygenase pathways are complex and as yet poorly understood.

D. LTA$_4$ Synthetase

Little is known about the properties of this enzyme. Thus far it has generally been studied in combination with other reactions in the sequence, and activity of a potential inhibitor on this particular reaction has been deduced by a process of elimination. Thus if a compound inhibits LTB$_4$ formation and does not inhibit 5-HETE formation from endogenously or exogenously supplied arachidonate, it is presumed to inhibit either the LTA$_4$ synthetase or the LTA$_4$ hydrolase (LTB$_4$ synthctasc), or both. Similarly, if conversion of arachidonate to 5-HETE is unaffected, and the conversion of exogenously supplied LTA$_4$ to thiol ether leukotrienes is unaffected and yet the synthesis of these substances from arachidonate is inhibited, the presumption is that the LTA$_4$ synthetase is inhibited.

As previously noted, 5-aminosalicylic acid, the breakdown product of sulfasalazine, was reported (Stenson and Lobs, 1982) to inhibit the formation of 5,12-dihydroxyeicosatetraenoic acids while leaving 5-HETE formation unaffected. This observation remains to be confirmed and, if true, the specific site of inhibition (i.e., the LTA$_4$ synthetase versus the LTB$_4$ synthetase step) elucidated.

There are data from two sources that polyacetylenic fatty acids may inhibit the LTA$_4$ synthetase. Jakschik *et al.* (1981) reported that a group of long-chain acids with multiple acetylenic bonds could inhibit the synthesis of the thiol ether leukotrienes without affecting the 5-lipoxygenase in the same cell-free enzyme preparation from RBL cells. The most potent of these compounds was 21:4(4,7,10,13), for which the IC$_{50}$ for thiol ether leukotriene formation was 7 μM, whereas 5-lipoxygenase was unaffected by 50 μM concentrations. This information does not distinguish between inhibition of the LTA$_4$ synthetase and inhibition of the LTC$_4$ synthetase, however. Evidence that the acetylenic analog of arachidonate, ETYA, could selectively inhibit the LTA$_4$ synthetase came from studies by Bokoch and Reed (1981). A comparison of the nonselective lipoxygenase inhibitor, NDGA, with ETYA in guinea pig PMNs revealed (see Fig. 2) that, whereas NDGA inhibited the formation of 5-HETE, (5*S*,12*S*)-all-*trans*-diHETE, and LTB$_4$ in parallel, ETYA inhibited the formation of the two dihydroxy acids in parallel (IC$_{50}$ around 50 μM) while formation of 5-HETE was actually increased.

There have been isolated reports in the medical literature for some 18 years (Mallen, 1965) that diethylcarbamazine, a well-established antifilarial compound, could help in the management of intractable asthma. The initial association that led to these early therapeutic trials was the yet earlier obser-

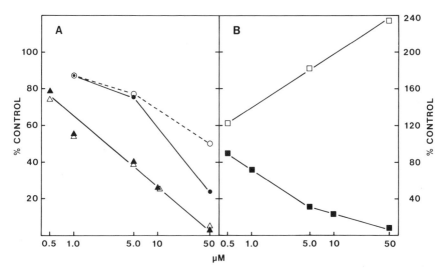

Fig. 2. Selective inhibition of LTA_4 synthetase in guinea pig PMNs by ETYA. Results with NDGA are included for comparison. (A) ETYA (○, ●); NDGA (△, ▲). Open symbols, LTB_4; closed symbols, (5S,12S)-all-*trans*-diHETE. (B) 5-HETE production; ETYA (□); NDGA (■). Note difference in ordinate between the two panels. (Data adapted from Bokoch and Reed, 1981.)

vation that the compound was of benefit in the management of eosinophilic lung disease, a condition that may often have a parasitic infestation as an underlying cause. This clinical observation led to the investigation of the effect of diethylcarbamazine on the release or production of the mediators of anaphylaxis in anaphylactically challenged rodents (Orange *et al.,* 1968a,b). It became apparent that high concentrations of this agent (IC_{50} 15 mg/kg given ip within minutes of the time of anaphylactic challenge) could selectively inhibit the formation of SRS-A, while release of the preformed mediators (histamine) was unaffected. The observation was subsequently extended to anaphylactically challenged human lung fragments and to monkey lung where both the release of histamine and the production of SRS-A were inhibited in tandem (Orange *et al.,* 1971). Furthermore, it became clear that the inhibitory action of diethylcarbamazine was independent of the nature of the immunoglobulin that was used to prepare the animals for the anaphylactic challenge; both IgE-dependent production and production elicited with the heat-stable IgG_a could be inhibited (Orange and Austen, 1971). Activity has also been extended to bovine anaphylaxis (Burka and Eyre, 1975), where an IC_{50} in the neighborhood of 1 mM was reported. An investigation of the structural specificity of the inhibitory action of diethylcarbamazine (Orange and Austen, 1968) revealed an absolute requirement for the presence of the carboxamide residue in the molecule. In contrast, the ring system in the molecule could be replaced by pipecolamide, isonicotinic acid hydrazide, and a number of other aryl and heteroaryl systems. Engineer *et al.* (1978) and Piper and Temple (1981) reported that, in perfused guinea pig lung, inhibition of leukotriene synthesis and of histamine release by diethylcarbamazine occurred in parallel, while prostaglandin formation was only very slightly inhibited.

With the elucidation of the structure of the leukotrienes, this old compound received renewed attention. Mathews and Murphy (1982) reported that in a mastocytoma cell line, diethylcarbamazine caused a dose-dependent inhibition of the formation of LTC_4, LTB_4, and the biologically inactive isomers of LTB_4 (IC_{50} in the neighborhood of 5 μM), while the formation of 5-HETE was actually increased by 27%. It is noteworthy that, in that cell line, diethylcarbamazine was markedly more active than it had been previously found to be.

E. LTA$_4$: Glutathione S-Transferase

1. Glutathione S-Transferases in General

The glutathione *S*-transferases (GSH STs) are a family of enzymes that are quite ubiquitous in mammalian cells. Liver is a particularly rich source, and the GSH STs represent a significant part of the total protein content of liver. At least six forms of the enzyme have been identified in both rat and human liver. These differ in isoelectric point, although they appear to have very nearly the same molcular weight. The different forms of GSH ST are at least partially antigenically cross-reactive, particularly in the case in human liver.

The GSH STs can catalyze a large range of reactions, which can be represented in the following schematic fashion:

a. $GSH + RCH_2X \rightarrow RCH_2SG + HX$
b. $GSH + ArX \rightarrow ArSG + HX$
c. $GSH + R^1CH=CHR^2 \rightarrow R^1CH_2CH(SG)R^2$
d. $GSH + R^1CH \!-\! CHR^2 \rightarrow R^1CH(OH)CH(SG)R^2$
        $\overset{\displaystyle\diagdown\,O\,\diagup}{}$
e. $GSH + R^1COCH_2CH_2CH \parallel CHR^2 \rightarrow R^1COCH=CHCh_2CH_2R^2 + GSH$

In these equations R^1 and R^2 are any aliphatic residue, Ar is an aromatic residue, and G represents the glutathione sequence aside from the explicitly depicted sulfur atom. In example (e), the shift of the double bond into conjugation with the carbonyl oxygen has been described for the case of $\Delta^{4,5}$-androstanedione. Good summaries of these reactions are available (e.g., see Jakoby and Habig, 1980). The different forms of GSH ST differ somewhat in their substrate specificity, so that in all likelihood, any single form of the enzyme is not capable of carrying out all of the reactions listed. We showed earlier that crude high-speed supernatants from homogenized rat liver are capable of catalyzing the condensation of the lithium salt of LTA_4 and gluta-thione (Bach *et al.,* 1981). More recently, the affinity purified mixed GSH STs were fractionated by chromatofocusing into at least 10 distinct enzyme activities and the capacity of these fractions to synthesize LTC_4 from LTA_4 was compared to their activity when 2,4-dinitrochlorobenzene (DNCB) was used as the substrate. Although there were some differences in relative activity, these were generally minor and all the fractions converted LTA_4 to LTC_4 at a rate, on a molar basis, which was 0.00001 to 0.00003 times the rate of reaction with DNCB. The rate of reaction with LTA_4 in the most selective fraction was only 0.0001 times the rate of reaction of the same fraction with DNCB (M. K. Bach, unpublished results).

The large range of substrate specificities of the GSH STs is also reflected in a similarly large range of substances that can inhibit the action of these enzymes on any given substrate. Among the compounds that have been reported to be inhibitory are aprotic solvents (Aitio and Bend, 1979), bromo-sulfophthaleins (Baars *et al.,* 1982), and other organic anions including indo-cyanine green, bilirubin (Kaplowitz *et al.,* 1975), bile acids (Pattison, 1981; Vessey and Zakim, 1981), steroid sulfates (Ohl and Litwack, 1977), and as already noted, ETYA and arachidonate (Hunter *et al.,* 1982). In addition to these, heavy metals are highly inhibitory, with inhibition constants in the micromolar range (Reddy *et al.,* 1981) and so are organotin and organoger-manium compounds (Henry and Byington, 1976). A number of the inhibi-tors that have been reported to inhibit the reaction of glutathione with such aryl halides as 1,2-dichloro-4-nitrobenzene or DNCB also inhibit the gener-ation of LTC_4 from LTA_4 by the enzymes in rat liver cytosol (Bach *et al.,* 1982a).

2. *LTA₄: Glutathione* S-*Transferase of RBL Cells*

Although liver homogenates can convert LTA_4 to LTC_4, this organ is not ordinarily associated with the formation of leukotrienes in the body. As is implied by their name, the leukotrienes are believed to be largely derived from leukocytes. Considerable attention has been given to cell-free prepara-tions from leukocytes, which can catalyze the formation of these com-pounds. The most extensive studies in this regard have used RBL cells, ever since Jakschik and Lee (1980) reported that homogenates of these cells could carry out the conversion of arachidonate to LTC and LTD. The conversion of LTA_4 to thiol ether leukotrienes was found to require a particulate enzyme that was localized in the 100,000 *g* pellet fraction of the homogenates (Jaks-chik *et al.,* 1982). The same homogenates of RBL cells also contain a soluble GSH ST activity that can be detected by use of the aryl halide substrates (Brashler *et al.,* 1983). At least 10 forms of GSH ST were identified in the soluble fraction by chromatofocusing and one form which eluted around pH 6.4 accounted for over 40% of the total activity (Bach, unpublished results). The total high-speed supernatant fraction is incapable of converting LTA_4 to LTC_4. By contrast, the particulate enzyme fraction, which does catalyze this reaction, is virtually inactive when it is tested with the aryl halide substrates (Brashler et al., 1983). There are other examples in the literature of particulate forms of GSH ST (Friedberg et al., 1979; Morgenstern et al., 1980), but in contrast to the particulate enzymes in liver, which have the same substrate specificity and pH optimum as the soluble enzymes, the particulate enzyme in RBL cells has a distinctly different substrate specificity than the soluble enzymes of these cells.

The particulate LTC_4-synthesizing enzyme from RBL cells has been solubilized by use of the nonionic detergent, Triton X-100. Activity of the enzyme is also markedly increased in the presence of this detergent. A comparison of the susceptibility of the LTC-synthesizing reaction to inhibition by a variety of compounds that are inhibitory to the soluble GSH ST(s) of these cells has revealed numerous differences, further documenting that the two enzymes are truly distinct (Brashler et al., 1983). The possibility that certain tetracetylenic, long-chain acids that inhibit LTC_4 formation may in fact act on this enzyme (Jakschik et al., 1981) has been previously noted.

3. Glutathione Depletion

In addition to inhibiting the glutathione S-transferase that catalyzes the reaction of glutathione with LTA_4, the same goal can be achieved by depleting the cells or tissues of glutathione. Parker et al. (1980) have depleted RBL cells of glutathione by incubating them with an alternative substrate for GSH ST. Concentrations in the range of 3 to 10 mM cyclohex-2-ene-1-one or diethylmaleate caused a nearly total inhibition of thiol ether leukotriene synthesis with only little if any effect on the formation of the other products of 5-lipoxygenase in the cells. Rouzer et al. (1981a,b, 1982) employed a selective inhibitor of glutathione synthesis. Preincubation of macrophages with 0.2 mM buthionine sulfoximine for 30 min resulted in a 90% reduction in the incorporation of ^{35}S into glutathione. The half-time for the decrease in cellular pools of glutathione was approximately 2.5 h. Challenge of cells that had been preincubated with this inhibitor for as long as 14 h resulted in no significant changes in the formation of cyclooxygenase products by the cells, a threefold increase in the formation of HETEs, and a nearly total inhibition of the formation of thiol ether leukotrienes without affecting cell viability.

F. Further Conversions of LTC₄

Although the responses of different organs and species differ, LTD_4 is generally at least as active as is LTC_4. In many cases it is actually orders of magnitude more active. The conversion of LTC_4 to LTD_4 is effected by γ-glutamyl transpeptidase, an enzyme that is ubiquitous and is involved in glutathione metabolism in general. The specific enzyme that is responsible for this conversion in leukotriene-generating cells has not been studied in detail. While it may be tempting to speculate that it resembles the ordinary γ-glutamyl transpeptidase, the results from the GSH ST studies (see earlier) should inject a note of caution; here too, the conversion of LTC_4 to LTD_4 as the conversion of LTA_4 to LTC_4 earlier, is not a detoxification or metabolism step, in that the product is as active as is the substrate. The possibility must therefore be kept in mind that a distinctly different and possibly a regulated enzyme may be involved.

Pharmacologically speaking, there is little reason to want to inhibit the conversion of LTC_4 to LTD_4, since the two substances are so nearly equipotent. Three inhibitors have been investigated, however, in experiments that were designed to demonstrate that the biosynthesis of LTD_4 proceeds via LTC_4 as an intermediate. The inhibitors are high concentrations of serine borate (Örning and Hammarström, 1980), the fraudulent substrate for the enzyme o-carboxyphenyl-γ-D-glutamyl hydrazine (Bach et al., 1981; Morris et al., 1982), and the antibiotic inhibitor Acivicin (Bach et al, 1981). Although inhibition of the conversion was observed in two of these studies (Örning and Hammarström, 1980; Morris et al., 1982), it was not observed in the third.

The conversion of LTD_4 to LTE_4 is effected by a dipeptidase. The properties of this enzyme are currently under investigation, but no inhibitor studies have been reported thus far. There is little justification for seeking such inhibitors from any practical point of view. Recently it was reported (Lee et al., 1982) and confirmed (Goetzl, 1982b) that human PMNs that have been activated with phorbol esters rapidly convert LTC_4 to more polar products and to a biologically inactive isomer of 5,12-diHETE. The compounds with increased polarity have been identified as the sulfoxides of LTC_4. This oxidation involves halide and hydrogen peroxide, and was inhibited by azide and by catalase.

G. End Organ Antagonists

1. Miscellaneous Compounds

Compounds of different functional classes have been reported to inhibit the end organ spasmogenic action of the leukotrienes. With few exceptions, these compounds are not particularly selective in their actions and, in fact, inhibit the spasmogenic actions of other agonists as well. For example, rotenone and a series of related compounds were reported to inhibit the contractions elicited with crude preparations of SRS-A on the guinea pig ileum at concentrations ranging between 1 and 5 × 10^{-8} g/ml (Ashack *et al.*, 1980). The same compounds also inhibited contractions caused by histamine, serotonin, and acetylcholine at concentrations that were only 2 to 10 times greater, however. Ali *et al.* (1982a,b) have described a large series of imido sulfamides that were somewhat selective against SRS-A–induced contractions. The basis of selectivity in this case was a comparison of the effect of the compounds on SRS-A–induced contractions to their action on KCl-induced contractions. The order of selectivity was small and the potency of the compounds was lower than that of the chromone carboxylic acids (see later). Nor was there any characterization of the kinetics of the antagonistic action.

3-*i*-Butyryl-2-*i*-propylpyrazolo[1,5-*a*]pyridine, KC 404, was recently described as a highly potent and apparently selective leukotriene antagonist (Nishino *et al.*, 1983). The compound was active against crude SRS-A on the guinea pig ileum at 0.2 μg/ml while at least 15 times more compound was required to antagonize 5-hydroxytryptamine, histamine, bradykinin, and acetylcholine. Bronchodilator action, *in vitro*, was seen with guinea pig tissue at 5 ng/ml. The compound was active against SRS-A *in vivo* at 1.4 μg/kg (iv) while antagonism of histamine required 0.5 mg/Kg. Even intraduodenal administration resulted in antagonistic action against SRS-A at 1.4 μg/kg while antagonism of histamine and acetylcholine required a five-fold higher dose. Inhibition of mediator release was observed both *in vivo* and *in vitro*, but the doses which were required were several orders of magnitude greater.

2. FPL55712 and Analogs

Augstein *et al.* (1973) described a chromone carboxylic acid, FPL55712, which is a highly selective, potent inhibitor of leukotriene-induced contractions of the guinea pig ileum. The IC_{50} was 2.3 × 10^{-8} M and kinetic analysis gave a Schild plot with a slope of just slightly less than 1.0, suggesting that the compound may be a competitive inhibitor. Since that time, this compound has become the prototypic end organ antagonist for the leukotrienes, and, in fact, the ability to inhibit the response of an unknown substance by "appropriate" concentrations (generally below 2 μM *in vitro*) of this compound is viewed by many as one of the criteria for the functional identification of the substance as a thiol ether leukotriene (Levi and Burke, 1980; Feniuk *et al.*, 1982). Many of the earlier data on this compound have been reviewed (Chand, 1979).

More recent data have cast some doubt on the utility of FPL55712 as a diagnostic for leukotriene-dependent responses. On the one hand, there are several documented instances where some leukotriene-dependent responses were not antagonized by this compound (Drazen *et al.*, 1980) or where the susceptibility to antagonism was variable (Krell *et al.*, 1983). On the other hand, FPL55712 was found to inhibit responses which were caused by other agonists in certain cases. For example, the same antagonism was seen to leukotrienes, vasopressin and the thromboxane A_2-mimetic, U-46,619, when changes in pressure in the isolated guinea pig heart were measured (Kennedy et al., 1983).

The activity of FPL55712 in vivo has been less convincing. To begin, the compound has an extremely short half-life (O'Donnell and Welton, 1982), which may explain why doses in the range of 1 mg/kg are required to demonstrate efficacy. It may be of interest that the duration of action was considerably longer when the compound was given by aerosol rather than being administered intravenously (O'Donnell and Welton, 1982). Because FPL55712 is also an effective inhibitor of histamine release (Welton et al., 1981b), it becomes difficult to differentiate between the action of the compound in preventing the elicitation of mediators and its action in preventing their effects. Nonetheless, attempts have been made to demonstrate the efficacy of FPL55712 both in a canine model of asthma (Wanner et al., 1975) and in human disease (Ahmed et al., 1980, 1981; Lee et al., 1981). In these studies, the antigen-induced decrease in the tracheal mucus velocity was largely inhibited by pretreatment with the drug. However, effects of FPL55712 on expiratory flow (FEV_1) in intractable asthmatics were less convincing (Lee et al., 1981).

Efforts have been made to develop better or longer-acting analogs of FPL55712. Studies at the Fisons Pharmaceutical Company have resulted in the synthesis of FPL59257, which differs from FPL55712 in that the carboxylate residue is replaced by a propionate, and the hydroxyl function on the second carbon of the glycerol bridge between the two cyclic moieties is replaced by a hydrogen (Sheard, 1981; Sheard et al., 1982). On the guinea pig ileum, FPL59257 is approximately one-tenth as active as is FPL55712. However, it has the advantage of a considerably longer duration of action in vivo. The activities of both FPL55712 and FPL59257 on the response of normal human volunteers to aerosols of synthetic leukotrienes have been reported (Holroyde et al., 1982). At a dose of 3 mg/ml given as an aerosol between 15 and 10 min before aerosol challenge with leukotrienes, both compounds appeared to reduce the magnitude and the duration of the drop in flow at residual volume plus 1.5 liters, which was caused by the administered leukotrienes.

There are several reports suggesting that, aside from inhibiting the action of leukotrienes, FPL55712 may have other pharmacologic actions. Chasin and Scott (1978) reported that FPL55712 inhibited rat brain cyclic AMP and cyclic GMP phosphodiesterases with IC_{50} values of 3 and 13 μM, respectively. This compares very favorably with the activities of such known inhibitors of these enzymes as papaverine (1.3 and 56 μM, respectively) or theophylline (130 and 310 μM, respectively). Welton *et al.* (1981b) reported that the compound caused a dose-dependent inhibition of thromboxane formation in human platelets (IC_{50} 6.5 μM), which is comparable to that of 1-nonylimidazole, a known potent inhibitor of this enzyme. Finally, Krell *et al.* (1981) reported bizarre effects of FPL55712 on pulmonary tissues. Specifically, it enhanced responses to histamine (parenchyma and trachea) or carbamylcholine (trachea) in a dose-dependent fashion in the 10^{-7} to 10^{-5} M range while relaxing the basal tone of the muscle.

H. Piriprost, U-60,257, A New and Specific Inhibitor with Several Sites of Action

We found piriprost (U-60,257, or 6,9-deepoxy, 6,9-(phenylimino)$\Delta^{6,8}$-prostaglandin I_1) in the course of a search for selective inhibitors of leukotriene biosynthesis. The synthesis of this compound has been described by H. W. Smith *et al.* (1982).

1. In Vitro *Activities*

The new compound, U-60,257, inhibited the formation of the thiol ether leukotrienes in ionophore A23187-challenged rat peritoneal mononuclear cells with an IC_{50} of 4.6 μM. Thromboxane B_2 formation, which was used to monitor the effect of the compound on the cyclooxygenase pathway, was unaffected except at relatively high concentrations of the inhibitor, where there was a slight increase in production (Bach *et al.,* 1982b). The inhibitory activity of U-60,257 did not require a preincubation with the cells. Furthermore, when cells that had been incubated with U-60,257 were centrifuged, the medium removed, and the cells resuspended in fresh buffer in the absence of the inhibitor, the inhibitory activity gradually disappeared over a 15- to 30-min period. Readdition of fresh inhibitor at that time restored the inhibition. Neither prostacyclin nor its stable analog, PGI_1 inhibited leukotriene formation in the ionophore-stimulated system. This was to be expected, since that system is independent of changes in intracellular cyclic nucleotide levels. These data indicate that U-60,257 is a selective inhibitor of leukotriene formation in the sense that the compound does not affect the cyclooxygenase-dependent branch of the arachidonate cascade.

In addition to this level of selectivity, U-60,257 is also selective in the sense that it inhibits the production of leukotrienes without affecting the release of preformed mediators of anaphylaxis. Thus when fragments of human lung were sensitized with reagin-containing serum and were then challenged with ragweed antigen E, the release of histamine that ensued was unaffected by the incorporation of the inhibitor into the incubations, while the release of leukotrienes was inhibited in a dose-dependent fashion with an IC_{50} of approximately 5 μM (Bach *et al.,* 1983).

Two specimens of lung became available at thoracotomy from asthmatic patients who had a known and well-characterized atopic response to birch pollen and horse dander. *In vitro* challenge of lung fragments from these patients elicited the production of large amounts of various eicosanoids, but when challenge occurred in the presence of U-60,257, the formation of the products of the 5-lipoxygenase was reduced by more than 90%. Interestingly, the contractions of bronchioles from these same patients, which could be elicited with antigen, were completely prevented when U-60,257 was added to the otherwise ineffective mixture of indomethacin and an antihistamine which were present in the muscle bath (Dahlén *et al.,* 1983). Thus U-60,257 differs from the inhibitors of mediator release that have been described thus far, both because of its selective action against newly produced mediators and because it does not suffer from the liability of inducing tachyphylaxis against its own action.

The effects of U-60,257 on leukotriene formation were elucidated before the era of radioimmunoassays for the leukotrienes. Thus it was necessary to demonstrate that the addition of the compound to the smooth muscle bath in which leukotrienes are assayed did not inhibit the response of the tissue to preformed leukotrienes. This was the case when the concentrations of U-60,257 that were added reflected the amounts of inhibitor that would be present in the incubations in which inhibition of mediator production was being measured. In contrast, when concentrations of U-60,257 similar to those that inhibited leukotriene formation were added directly to the smooth muscle bath, the response to leukotrienes was inhibited selectively, without affecting responses to histamine, acetylcholine, or bradykinin. The inhibition was difficult to reverse once it was expressed. Therefore, in order to quantitate it, recourse was taken to the use of a superfusion arrangement. In this mode of operation, a continuous stream of buffer is pumped over the tissue, and agonists or antagonists are injected into that stream. Thus the duration of exposure is brief and inhibitory activity is more readily reversible. The incorporation of U-60,257 into the superfusion stream caused a parallel shift in the dose–response curves for leukotrienes. The data could be used to calculate a Schild plot (Arunlakhshana and Schild, 1959) the slope of which was 1.0, suggesting that the inhibition was competitive.

In addition to affecting the production of the thiol ether leukotrienes and to inhibiting the response of smooth muscle preparations to their agonist action, U-60,257 also inhibited the release of lysosomal enzymes from human PMNs, as well as the production of superoxide anion by these cells (R. J. Smith *et al.,* 1982). The IC_{50} values for these actions were dependent on the nature of the secretion-initiating stimulus. When the calcium ionophore A23187 was used, IC_{50} values were comparable to those found for the inhibition of leukotriene synthesis. On the other hand, when the chemotactic peptide, formylmethionylleucylphenylalanine was used, distinctly higher concentrations of the inhibitor were required.

2. In Vivo *Activities*

The anaphylactically challenged guinea pig has long been a favorite laboratory animal model for the study of the anaphylactic reaction. The high sensitivity of the guinea pig to histamine, however, has made it difficult to detect effects due to other mediators in this model. Now, however, Ritchie *et al.* (1981) have described a pharmacologic modification of this model that permits the identification of anaphylaxis-inducing factors in addition to histamine. Specifically, ovalbumin-immunized guinea pigs are treated with an antihistamine to block the response to any histamine that may be released. In addition, the animals are pretreated with an inhibitor of the cyclooxygenase pathway of arachidonate metabolism to prevent contributions by prostaglandins, prostacyclin, or thromboxane. Cholinergic responses are inhibited by administration of atropine, and finally, a bolus injection of arachidonate is given immediately prior to challenge with antigen. Under these conditions, the magnitude of the bronchospasm increases from the inhibited level that can be seen in the presence of the antihistamine, until it reaches approximately the same level as would be seen in uninhibited animals. The selective end organ antagonist FPL55712 is an effective inhibitor of this pharmacologically manipulated response (Bach *et al.,* 1982b), suggesting that leukotriene production may account for a significant portion of the response. When guinea pigs were pretreated with U-60,257 intravenously, the presumably leukotriene-dependent response could again be inhibited with an IC_{50} in the range of 1 to 10 mg/kg. The administration of U-60,257 by the aerosol route is many orders of magnitude more effective, although the procedures that are being employed preclude a calculation of the actual dose that is being delivered to the animals (Bach, unpublished).

Aerosol challenge of *Ascaris*-responder rhesus monkeys with *Ascaris* antigen represents another animal model of anaphylaxis. In this model each animal is used numerous times over a period of many years, and thus its response to antigen in the absence of inhibitors serves as a historic control for the response that can be seen when pretreatment with an inhibitor is employed. The model permits the detailed analysis of the usual parameters of pulmonary function. In practice, changes in total lung resistance (R_L) and dynamic lung compliance (C_{dyn}) are the most indicative of the anaphylactic response. When *Ascaris*-responder monkeys were pretreated with U-60,257 given by aerosol and then challenged with *Ascaris* antigen, their response to

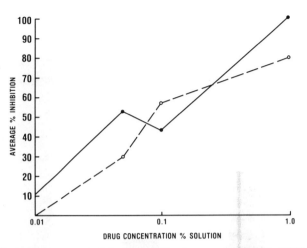

Fig. 3. Effect of pretreatment of *Ascaris*-sensitive rhesus monkeys with U-60,257 on subsequent changes in pulmonary parameters on challenge with aerosols of *Ascaris* antigen. Treatments consisted of 15 breaths of an aerosol of a neutralized aqueous solution of U-60,257 of the concentrations indicated. Results are the inhibition of changes in total lung resistance (R_L, solid line) and dynamic lung compliance (C_{dyn}, broken line), comparing responses in treated animals to the historic control values in the same animals when they were challenged with antigen without pretreatment. (Adapted from Johnson *et al.*, 1982.)

the antigen was blocked in a dose-dependent fashion (Fig. 3; Johnson *et al.*, 1982). The actual doses of the inhibitor that were inhaled by the monkeys can be calculated from the concentration of inhibitor in the aerosilized solution, the number of breaths administered (15), and the known volume of liquid that is aerosolized with each breath. Such a calculation leads to the conclusion that, at the highest concentration employed, a total of approximately 3 μg of U-60,257 was inspired by the animals.

Histamine plays an important role in anaphylaxis in the monkey, just as it does in the guinea pig. Therefore, it was of interest to investigate the effect of combinations of an antihistamine and U-60,257 on the anaphylactic response in the monkey model. As shown in Fig. 4, a marked synergistic effect was observed (Johnson *et al.*, 1982). This suggests that exceedingly low concentrations of U-60,257, when administered by the aerosol route, can effectively inhibit the leukotriene-dependent portion of the anaphylactic response.

3. Mode of Action Studies

An initial examination of the effect of U-60,257 on the 5-lipoxygenase was carried out using 0.1 mM exogenously supplied arachidonate and human PMNs. It was found that the amount of 5-HETE and 5,12-diHETE that were

Michael K. Bach

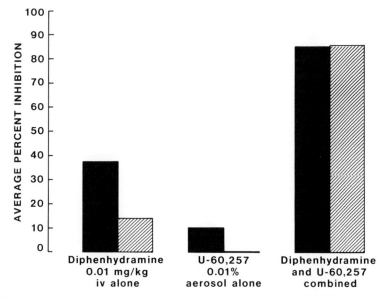

Fig. 4. Synergistic action of diphenhydramine and U-60,257 in inhibiting responses of rhesus monkey to aerosolized *Ascaris* antigen. Black bars, R_L; crosshatched bars, C_{dyn}. Diphenhydramine was administered iv and U-60,257 by aerosol. (Reproduced from Johnson *et al.* 1982, by permission.)

produced in the presence of low concentrations of the inhibitor were actually increased, and only when the inhibitor concentration was raised to 0.1 m*M* was the production of the products of the 5-lipoxygenase inhibited. This observation suggested that the primary site of inhibition may be past the LTA$_4$ synthetase step and possibly was the LTC$_4$ synthetase reaction. An examination of the effect of U-60,257 on crude rat liver glutathione *S*-transferase activity revealed that these enzymes were markedly inhibited both when aryl halides were used as substrates and when the conversion of LTA$_4$ to LTC$_4$ was monitored (Bach *et al.*, 1982b).

The story changed as a consequence of further studies. It was found (Sun and McGuire, 1983) that when the concentration of arachidonate during incubation of human PMNs with U-60,257 was reduced, there was a profound *inhibition* of the production of both 5-HETE and LTB$_4$ (Fig. 5), thus indicating that, under more physiologic conditions, the 5-lipoxygenase may indeed be inhibited by this compound. On the other hand, even though GSH STs of rat liver are inhibited by U-60,257, the LTC$_4$ synthetase of RBL cells was recently found not to be inhibited even when very high concentrations of this compound were used (M. K. Bach and J. R. Brashler, unpublished observations). This would suggest that U-60,257 is primarily a 5-lipoxygen-

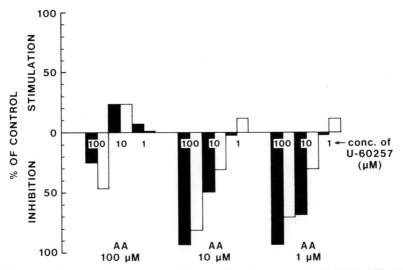

Fig. 5. Inhibition of 5-lipoxygenase of human PMN leukocytes by U-60,257. LTB$_4$ (■); 5-HETE (□). Results are presented for cells that were challenged with the calcium ionophore in the presence of increasing concentrations of free arachidonic acid (AA: numbers along bottom of graph). The concentrations of U-60,257 that were employed are shown near the abscissa. Note that there was enhanced production of lipoxygenase products when low concentrations of U-60,257 were added to cells in the presence of high concentrations of arachidonate. (Reproduced from Sun and McGuire, 1983.)

ase inhibitor. However, recent observations (E. Razin, personal communication) in a murine bone marrow-derived mast cell culture that produces large amounts of leukotriene C$_4$ (Razin *et al.*, 1982) revealed that, under certain conditions, the formation of 5-HETE and LTB$_4$ proceeded unimpeded in those cells in the presence of U-60,257, while the formation of LTC$_4$ was inhibited. Thus we are left with the possibility that this inhibitor may possess dual sites of action. Its primary site of action in different species or different cell types appears to be the 5-lipoxygenase although a secondary action on the LTC synthetase in some instances has not been ruled out.

IV. CONCLUDING REMARKS

The development of inhibitors of leukotriene synthesis is in its infancy. The utility of the rational design of compounds that may act, selectively, on single steps in the pathway still remains to be proven, since the compounds that have been found thus far have certainly not been derived from any detailed knowledge of the substrate specificity, receptor characteristics, or the structures of the activated intermediates involved. Considerable work remains to be done on the properties of the enzymes involved in the biosynthesis of the leukotrienes, the regulatory interactions that may affect their activity in intact tissues, and the differences between the enzymes in different cells, tissues, and species. The possibility that a single compound may affect more than one step in the pathway, and that its primary site of action may be different in different though very closely related cell types, raises potentially serious reservations for the efforts to define the sites of action of inhibitors by comparing their activity in totally unrelated systems. The observations on the unexpected actions (or lack of action) of ETYA in guinea pig PMNs also amplify this cautionary note.

Finally, the need for inhibitors of leukotriene formation—selective or nonselective—is presently based on hypotheses and indirect evidence. It remains to be demonstrated that treatment of disease with such agents has beneficial effects. Only if this can be achieved can one conclude that the leukotrienes are truly major contributors to the symptomatology of disease.

ACKNOWLEDGMENTS

The author wishes to thank Drs. G. A. Higgs of the Wellcome Research Laboratories, Dr. Philip Sheard of the Fisons Laboratories, Dr. Barry M. Weichman of the Smith Kline and French Laboratories, Dr. Ann F. Welton of Hoffmann La Roche, Incorporated, and Drs. H. G. Johnson, R. J. Smith, and F. F. Sun of The Upjohn Company for making the results of experiments available before publication.

REFERENCES

Ahmed, T., Greenblatt, D. W., Birch, S. Marchette, B., and Wanner, A. (1980). *Am. Rev. Respir. Dis.* **121,** Supp. 4, 106.
Ahmed, T., Greenblatt, D. W., Birch, S., Marchette, B., and Wanner, A. (1981). *Am. Rev. Respir. Dis.* **124,** 110–114.
Aitio, A., and Bend, J. R. (1979). *FEBS Lett.* **101,** 187–190.
Ali, E. F., Dandridge, P. A., Gleason, J. G., Krell, R. D., Kruse, C. H., Lavanchy, P. G., and Snader, K. M. (1982a). *J. Med. Chem.* **25,** 947–952.
Ali, E. F., Gleason, J. G., Hill, D. T., Krell, R. D., Kruse, C. H., and Lavanchy, P. G. (1982b). *J. Med. Chem.* **25,** 1235–1240.
Arai, Y., Konno, M., Shimoji, K., Konishi, Y., Niwa, H., Toda, M., and Hayashi, M. (1982). *Chem. Pharmacol. Bull.* **30,** 379–382.
Arai, Y., Shimoji, K., Konno, M., Konishi, Y., Okuyama, S., Iguchi, S., Hayashi, M., Miyamoto, T., and Toda, M. (1983). *J. Med. Chem.* **26,** 72–78.
Armour, C. L., Hughes, J. M., Seale, J. P., and Temple, D. M. (1982). *J. Pharm. Pharmacol.* **34,** 401–402.
Arunlakhshana, O., and Schild, H. O. (1959). *Br. J. Pharmacol. Chemother.* **14,** 48–58.

Ashack, R. J., McCarty, L. P., Malek, R. S., Goodman, F. R., and Peet, N. P. (1980). *J. Med. Chem.* **23**, 1022–1026.

Augstein, J., Farmer, J. B., Lee, T. B., Sheard, P., and Tattersall, M. L. (1973). *Nature (London), New Biol.* **245**, 215–217.

Baars, A. J., Jansen, M., Arnoldussen, S., de Lussanet de la Sablonière, K. L., and Breimer, D. O. (1982). *Experientia* **38**, 426–427.

Bach, M. K., Brashler, J. R., and Gorman, R. R. (1977). *Prostaglandins* **14**, 21–38.

Bach, M. K., Brashler, J. R., Johnson, H. G., and McNee, M. L. (1981). *In* "SRS-A and Leukotrienes" (P. J. Piper, ed.), pp. 161–180. Wiley, New York.

Bach, M. K., Brashler, J. R., Morton, D. R., Steel, L. K., Kaliner, M. A., and Hugli, T. E. (1982a). *In* "Leukotrienes and Other Lipoxygenase Products" (B. Samuelsson and R. Paoletti, eds.), pp. 103–114. Raven Press, New York.

Bach, M. K., Brashler, J. R., Smith, H. W., Fitzpatrick, F. A., Sun, F. F., and McGuire, J. C. (1982b). *Prostaglandins* **23**, 759–771.

Bach, M. K., Brashler, J. R., Fitzpatrick, F. A., Griffin, R. L., Iden, S. S., Johnson, H. G., McNee, M. L., McGuire, J. C., Smith, H. W., Smith, R. J., Sun, F. F., and Wasserman, M. A. (1983). *Adv. Prostaglandin, Thromboxane, Leukotriene Res.* **11**, 39–44.

Bailey, J. M., Bryant, R. W., Low, C. E., Pupillo, M. B., and Vanderhoek, J. Y. (1982). *Cell. Immunol.* **67**, 112–120.

Baker, S. R., Boot, J. R., Jamieson, W. B., Osborne, D. J., and Sweatman, W. J. F. (1981). *Biochem. Biophys. Res. Commun.* **103**, 1258–1264.

Baker, S. R., Boot, J. R., and Osborne, D. J. (1982). *Prostaglandins* **23**, 569–577.

Baumann, J., von Bruchhausen, F., and Wurm, G. (1980). *Prostaglandins* **20**, 627–639.

Blackwell, G. J., and Flower, R. J. (1978). *Prostaglandins* **16**, 417–425.

Bokoch, G. M., and Reed, P. W. (1981). *J. Biol. Chem.* **256**, 4156–4159.

Borgeat, P., Fruteau de Laclos, B., Picard, S., Drapeau, J., Vallerand, P., and Corey, E. J. (1982). *Prostaglandins* **23**, 713–724.

Brashler, J. R., Bach, M. K., and Morton, D. R., II (1983). *Fed. Proc., Fed. Am. Soc. Exp. Biol.* **42**, Abstract 6379.

Broughton, B. J., Chaplen, P., Knowles, P., Lunt, E., Pain, D. L., Wooldridge, K. R. H., Ford, R., Marshall, S., Walker, J. L., and Maxwell, D. R. (1974). *Nature (London)* **251**, 650–652.

Bruns, R. F., Thomsen, W. J., and Pugsley, T. A. (1983). *Life Sci.* **33**, 645–653.

Buckle, D. R., Outred, D. J., Ross, J. W., Smith, H., Spicer, B. A., and Gasson, B. C. (1979). *J. Med. Chem.* **22**, 158–168.

Burka, J. F., and Eyre, P. (1975). *Int. Arch. Allergy Appl. Immunol.* **49**, 774–781.

Burka, J. F., and Eyre, P. (1977). *Can. J. Physiol. Pharmacol.* **55**, 904–908.

Burka, J. F., and Flower, R. J. (1979). *Br. J. Pharmacol.* **65**, 35–41.

Busse, W. D., Mardin, M., Gruetzmann, R., Dunn, J. R., Theodoreau, M., Sloane, B. F., and Honn, K. V. (1982). *Fed. Proc., Fed. Am. Soc. Exp. Biol.* **41**, Abstract 8464.

Casey, F. B., Appleby, B. J., and Buck, D. C. (1983). *Prostaglandins* **25**, 1–11.

Chand, N. (1979). *Agents Actions* **9**, 133–140.

Chasin, M., and Scott, C. (1978). *Biochem. Pharmacol.* **27**, 2065–2067.

Cohen, N., Rosenberger, M., Lovey, A. J., Aig, E., Banner, B. L., Lopresti, R. J., and Weber, G. (1983). Abstracts, Division of Med. Chem., Am. Chem. Soc. August, 1983, Washington, D.C.

Collier, H. O. J., Drew, M., Hammond, M.D., and Saeed, S. A. (1981). *In* "SRS-A and Leukotrienes" (P. J. Piper, ed.), pp. 181–195. Wiley, New York.

Corey, E. J., Kantner, S. S., and Landsbury Jr., P. T. (1983). *Tetrahedron Lett.* **24**, 265–268.

Corey, E. J., and Munroe, J. E. (1982). *J. Am. Chem. Soc.* **104**, 1752–1754.

Dahlén, S.-E., Hansson, G., Hedqvist, P., Björck, T., Granström, E., and Dahlén, B. (1983). *Proc. Natl Acad. Sci. (U.S.A.)* **80**, 1712–1716.

Diamantis, W., Sofia, R. D., Gordon, R., and Ludwig, B. J. (1979). *Arzneim.-Forsch.* **29,** 998–1004.

Drazen, J. M., Austen, K. F., Lewis, R. A., Clark, D. A., Goto, G., Marfat, A., and Corey, E. J. (1980). *Proc. Natl Acad. Sci. U.S.A.* **77,** 4354–4358.

Dyer, R. D., Safford, S. E., and Carter, G. W. (1982). *Fed. Proc., Fed. Am. Soc. Exp. Biol.* **41,** Abstract 7490.

El-Azab, J., and Stewart, P. B. (1977). *Int. Arch. Allergy Appl. Immunol* **55,** 350–361.

Engineer, D. M., Niederhauser, U., Piper, P. J., and Sirois, P. (1978). *Br. J. Pharmacol.* **62,** 61–66.

Feniuk, L., Kennedy, I., and Whelan, C. J. (1982). *J. Pharm. Pharmacol.* **34,** 586–588.

Fiebrich, F., and Koch, H. (1979). *Experientia* **35,** 1548–1550.

Friedberg, T., Bentley, P., Stasiecki, P., Glatt, H. R., Raphael, D., and Oesch, F. (1979). *J. Biol. Chem.* **254,** 12028–12033.

Girard, Y., Larue, M., Jones, T. R., and Rokach, J. (1982). *Tetrahedron Lett.* **23,** 1023–1026.

Goetzl, E. J. (1982a). *Biochem. Biophys. Res. Commun.* **101,** 344–350.

Goetzl, E. J. (1982b). *Biochem. Biophys. Res. Commun.* **106,** 270–275.

Hammarström, S. (1977). *Biochim. Biophys. Acta* **487,** 517–519.

Henry, R. A., and Byington, K. H. (1976). *Biochem. Pharmacol.* **25,** 2291–2295.

Higgs, G. A., Palmer, R. M. J., Eakins, K. E., and Moncada, S. (1981). *Mol. Aspects Med.* **4,** 275–301.

Hirata, F., Schifmann, E., Venkatasubramanian, K., Salomon, D., and Axelrod, J. (1980). *Proc. Natl Acad. Sci. U.S.A.* **77,** 2533–2536.

Hofmann, S. L., Prescott, S. M., and Majerus, P. W. (1982). *Arch. Biochem. Biophys.* **215,** 237–244.

Holroyde, M. C., Altounyan, R. E. C., Cole, M., Dixon, M., and Elliott, E. V. (1982). *In* "Leuko-trienes and Other Lipoxygenase Products" (B. Samuelsson and R. Paoletti, eds.), pp. 237–242. Raven Press, New York.

Honn, K. V., and Dunn, J. R. (1982). *FEBS Lett.* **139,** 65–68.

Hope, W. C., Welton, A. F., Fiedler-Nagy, C., Batula-Bernardo, C., and Coffey, J. W. (1983). *Biochem. Pharmacol.* **32,** 367–371.

Hunter, F. E., Jr., Irwin, C., and Weissman, J. D. (1982). *Fed. Proc., Fed. Am. Soc. Exp. Biol.* **41,** Abstract 1484.

Jakoby, W. B., and Habig, W. H. (1980). *In* "Enzymatic Basis of Detoxification" (W. B. Jakoby, ed.), Vol. 2, pp. 63–94. Academic Press, New York.

Jakschik, B. A., and Lee, L.-H. (1980). *Nature (London)* **287,** 51–52.

Jakschik, B. A., Sun, F. F., Lee, L.-H., and Steinhof, M. M. (1980). *Biochem. Biophys Res. Commun.* **95,** 103–110.

Jakschik, B. A., DiSantis, D. M., Sankarappa, S. K., and Sprecher, H. (1981). *Biochem. Biophys. Res. Commun.* **102,** 624–629.

Jakschik, B. A., Harper, T., and Murphy, R. C. (1982). *J. Biol. Chem.* **257,** 5346–5349.

Johnson, H. G., McNee, M. L., Bach, M. K., and Smith, H. W. (1983). *Int. Arch. Allergy Appl. Immunol.* **70,** 169–173.

Jones, T., Masson, P., Hamel, R., Brunet, G., Holme, G., Girard, Y., Larue, M., and Rokach, J. (1982). *Prostaglandins* **24,** 279–289.

Kaplowitz, N., Kuhlenkamp, J., and Clifton, G. (1975). *Proc. Soc. Exp. Biol. Med.* **149,** 234–237.

Kennedy, I., Whelan, C. J., and Wright, G. (1983). *Br. J. Pharmacol.* **79,** 218 p.

Koshihara, Y., Murota, S. I., Petasis, N. A., and Nicolaou, K. C. (1982). *FEBS Lett.* **143,** 13–16.

Krilis, S., Lewis, R. A., Corey, E. J., and Austen, K. F. (1983). *J. Clin. Invest.* **71,** 909–915.

Krell, R. D., Tsai, B. S., Berdonlay, A., Barone, M., and Giles, R. E. (1983). *Prostaglandins* **25,** 171–178.

Krell, R. D., Osborn, R., Falcone, K., and Vickery, L. (1981). *Prostaglandins* **22,** 423–432.

Lee, C. W., Lewis, R. A., Corey, E. J., Barton, A., Oh, H., Tauber, A. I., and Austen, K. F. (1982). *Proc. Natl. Acad. Sci. U.S.A.* **79,** 4166–4170.

Lee, T. H., Walport, M. J., Wilkinson, A. H., Turner-Warwick, M., and Kay, A. B. (1981). *Lancet* 2, 304–305.

Levi, R., and Burke, J. A. (1980). *Eur. J. Pharmacol.* **62**, 41–49.

Lewis, R. A., Drazen, J. M., Austen, K. F., Toda, M., Brion, F., Marfat, A., and Corey, E. J. (1981a). *Proc. Natl Acad. Sci. U.S.A.* **78**, 4579–4583.

Lewis, R. A., Goetzl, E. J., Drazen, J. M., Soter, N. A., Austen, K. F., and Corey, E. J. (1981b). *J. Exp. Med.* **154**, 1243–1248.

Lewis, R. A., Drazen, J. M., Figueiredo, J. C., Corey, E. J., and Austen, K. F. (1982). *Int. J. Immunopharmacol.* **4**, 85–90.

Lichtenstein, L. M., and Adkinson, N. F. (1969). *J. Immunol.* **103**, 866–868.

Maclouf, J., Fruteau de Laclos, B., and Borgeat, P. (1982). *Proc. Natl. Acad. Sci. U.S.A.* **79**, 6042–6046.

Mallen, M. S. (1965). *Ann. Allergy* **23**, 534–537.

Malley, A., and Baecher, L. (1971). *J. Immunol.* **107**, 586–588.

Mathews, W. R., and Murphy, R. C. (1982). *Biochem. Pharmacol.* **31**, 2129–2132.

Morgenstern, R., Majer, J., Depierre, J. W., and Ernster, L. (1980). *Eur. J. Biochem.* **104**, 167–174.

Morris, H. R., Piper, P. J., Taylor, G. W., and Tippins, J. R. (1979). *Br. J. Pharmacol.* **66**, 452 p.

Morris, H. R., Piper, P. J., Taylor, G. W., and Tippins, J. R. (1980). *Prostaglandins* **19**, 371–383.

Morris, H. R., Taylor, G. W., Jones, C. M., Piper, P. J., Samhoun, M. N., and Tippins, J. R. (1982). *Proc. Natl. Acad. Sci. U.S.A.* **79**, 4838–4842.

Nishino, K., Ohkubo, H., Ohashi, M., Hara, S., Kito, J., and Irikura, T. (1983). *Jap. J. Pharmacol.* **33**, 267–278.

O'Donnell, M., and Welton, A. F. (1982). *Fed. Proc., Fed. Am. Soc. Exp. Biol.* **41**, Abstract 3221.

Ohl, V. S., and Litwack, G. (1977). *Arch. Biochem. Biophys.* **180**, 186–190.

Orange, R. P., and Austen, K. F. (1968). *Proc. Soc. Exp. Biol. Med.* **129**, 836–841.

Orange, R. P., and Austen, K. F. (1971). *Int. Arch. Allergy Appl. Immunol.* **41**, 79–85.

Orange, R. P., Valentine, M. D, and Austen, K. F. (1968a). *Proc. Soc. Exp. Biol. Med.* **127**, 127–132.

Orange, R. P., Valentine, M. D, and Austen, K. F. (1968b). *J. Exp. Med.* **127**, 767–782.

Orange, R. P., Stechschulte, D. J., and Austen, K. F. (1970). *J. Immunol.* **105**, 1087–1095.

Orange, R. P., Austen, W. G., and Austen, K. F. (1971). *J. Exp. Med.* **127**, 136(S)–148(S).

Örning, L., and Hammarström, S. (1980). *J. Biol. Chem.* **255**, 8023–8026.

Paajanen, H., Männistö, J., and Uotila, P. (1982). *Prostaglandins* **23**, 731–741.

Palmblad, J., Udén, A. M., Lindgren, J.-A., Rådmark, O., Hansson, G., and Malmsten, C. L. (1982). *FEBS Lett.* **144**, 81–83.

Parker, C. W., Fischman, C. M., and Wedner, J. H. (1980). *Proc. Natl. Acad. Sci. U.S.A.* **77**, 6870–6873.

Patterson, R., Pruzansky, J. J., and Harris, K. E. (1981). *J. Allergy, Clin. Immunol.* **67**, 444–449.

Pattison, N. R. (1981). *Biochem. Biophys. Res. Commun.* **102**, 403–410.

Piper, P. J., and Temple, D. M. (1981). *J. Pharm. Pharmacol.* **33**, 384–386.

Possanza, G. J., Bauen, A., and Stewart, P. B. (1975). *Int. Arch. Allergy Appl. Immunol.* **49**, 789–795.

Randall, R. W., Eakins, K. E., Higgs, G. A., Salmon, J. A., and Tateson, J. E. (1980). *Agents Actions* **10**, 553–555.

Razin, E., Mencia-Huerta, J. M., Lewis, R. A., Corey, E. J., and Austen, K. F. (1982). *Proc. Natl. Acad. Sci. U.S.A.* **79**, 4665–4667.

Reddy, C. C., Scholz, R. W., and Massaro, E. J. (1981). *Toxicol. Appl. Pharmacol.* **61**, 460–468.

Ritchie, D. M., Sierchio, J. N., Capetola, R. J., and Rosenthale, M. E. (1981). *Agents Actions* **11**, 396–401.

Rouzer, C. A., Scott, W. A., Griffith, O. W., Hamill, A. L., and Cohn, Z. A. (1981a). *Clin. Res.* **29**, 492A.

Rouzer, C. A., Scott, W. A., Griffith, O. W., Hamill, A. L., and Cohn, Z. A. (1981b). *Proc. Natl. Acad. Sci. U.S.A.* **78**, 2532–2536.

Rouzer, C. A., Scott, W. A., Griffith, O. W., Hamill, A. L., and Cohn, Z. A. (1982). *Proc. Natl. Acad. Sci. U.S.A.* **79**, 1621–1625.

Saeed, S. A., Drew, M., and Collier, H. O. J. (1980). *Eur. J. Pharmacol.* **67**, 169–170.

Sekiya, K., and Okuda, H. (1982). *Biochem. Biophys. Res. Commun.* **105**, 1090–1095.

Sevilla, M. D., Neta, P., and Marnett, L. J. (1983). *Biochem. Biophys. Res. Commun.* **115**, 800–806.

Sheard, P. (1981). *In* "SRS-A and Leukotrienes" (P. J. Piper, ed.), pp. 209–218. Wiley, New York.

Sheard, P., Holroyde, M. C., Ghelani, A. M., Bantik, J. R., and Lee, T. B. (1982). *In* "Leukotrienes and Other Lipoxygenase Products" (B. Samuelsson and R. Paoletti, eds.), pp. 229–235. Raven Press, New York.

Showell, H. J., Otterness, I. G., Marfat, A., and Corey, E. J. (1982). *Biochem. Biophys. Res. Commun.* **106**, 741–747.

Sircar, J. C., Schwender, C. F., and Carethers, M. E. (1983). *Biochem. Pharmacol.* **32**, 170–172.

Smith, H. W., Bach, M. K., Alexander, A. W., Johnson, H. G., Major, N. J., and Wasserman, M. A. (1982). *Prostaglandins* **24**, 543–546.

Smith, R. J., Sun, F. F., Bowman, B. J., Iden, S. S., Smith, H. W., and McGuire, J. C. (1982). *Biochem. Biophys. Res. Commun.* **109**, 943–949.

Sok, D.-E., Han, C.-Q., Pai, J.-K., and Sih, C. J. (1982). *Biochem. Biophys. Res. Commun.* **107**, 101–108.

Steel, L. K., Bach, D., and Kaliner, M. A. (1982). *J. Immunol.* **129**, 1233–1238.

Stenson, W. F., and Lobs, E. (1982). *J. Clin. Invest.* **69**, 494–497.

Sun, F. F., and McGuire, J. C. (1983). *Prostaglandins* **26**, 211–221.

Sun, F. F., McGuire, J. R., Morton, D. R., Pike, J. E., Sprecher, H., and Kunau, W. H. (1981). *Prostaglandins* **21**, 333–343.

Sutherland, C. A., and Amin, D. (1982). *J. Biol. Chem.* **257**, 14006–14010.

Tsai, B. S., Bernstein, P., Nacia, R. A., Conaty, J., and Krell, R. D. (1982). *Prostaglandins* **23**, 489–506.

Vanderhoek, J. Y., Bryant, R. W., and Bailey, J. M. (1980). *J. Biol. Chem.* **255**, 10064–10065.

Vanderhoek, J. Y., Tare, N. S., Bailey, J. M., Goldstein, A. L., and Pluznik, D. H. (1982). *Int. J. Immunopharmacol.* **4**, 349.

Vessey, D. A., and Zakim, D. (1981). *Biochem. J.* **197**, 321–325.

Walker, J. R., Boot, J. R., Cox, B., and Dawson, W. (1980). *J. Pharm. Pharmacol.* **32**, 866–867.

Wallach, D. P., and Brown, V. R. (1981a). *Biochim. Biophys. Acta* **663**, 361–372.

Wallach, D. P., and Brown, V. J. R. (1981b). *Biochem. Pharmacol.* **30**, 1315–1324.

Wanner, A., Zarzecki, S., Hirsch, J., and Epstein, S. (1975). *J. Appl. Physiol.* **39**, 950–957.

Wasserman, M. A., Weichman, B. M., Osborn, R. R., Woodward, D. F., Ku, T. W., and Gleason, J. G. (1983). Abstracts, Division of Med. Chem., Am. Chem. Soc., August, 1983, Washington, D.C.

Weichman, B. M., Hosteley, L. S., Bostick, S. P., Mucitelli, R. M., Krell, R. D., and Gleason, J. G. (1982). *J. Pharmacol. Exp. Ther.* **221**, 295–302.

Welton, A. F., Hope, W. C., Crowley, H. J., and Salvador, R. A. (1981a). *Agents Actions* **11**, 345–351.

Welton, A. F., Hope, W. C., Tobias, L. D., and Hamilton, J. G. (1981b). *Biochem. Pharmacol.* **30**, 1378–1382.

Wilhelm, T. E., Sankrappa, S. K., Van Rollins, M., and Sprecher, H. (1981). *Prostaglandins* **21**, 323–332.

Young, R. N., Coombs, W., Guindon, Y., Rokach, J., Ethier, D., and Hall, R. (1981). *Tetrahedron Lett.* **22**, 4933–4936.

7

Lipoxygenase Products: Mediation of Inflammatory Responses and Inhibition of Their Formation

P. BHATTACHERJEE AND K. E. EAKINS

Department of Pharmacology
The Wellcome Research Laboratories
Beckenham, Kent, England

I. INTRODUCTION

Arachidonic acid, a 20-carbon polyunsaturated fatty acid, is the most common fatty acid present in cellular phospholipids. The liberation of arachidonic acid from esterified pools is an essential prerequisite (Lands and Samuelsson, 1968; Vonkeman and Van Dorp, 1968) for the generation of metabolic products via the enzymes cyclooxygenase (prostaglandins and thromboxane A_2) and lipoxygenase (leukotrienes).

During the 1970s, prostaglandins have been assigned major roles as medi-

195

ators of the inflammatory response. These compounds not only reproduce the signs of inflammation but also synergize with other mediators such as histamine and bradykinin. For example, prostaglandins sensitize pain receptors to potentiate pain induced by histamine and bradykinin (Ferreira, 1972) and also potentiate the edema caused by these agents (Williams and Peck, 1977). Prostacyclin (PGI$_2$) and thromboxane A$_2$ are also thought to be involved in the maintenance of hemodynamic balance, with thromboxane A$_2$ aggregating platelets (Hamberg *et al.,* 1975; Moncada and Vane, 1977) and contracting vascular smooth muscle (Moncada *et al.,* 1976a; Svensson and Hamberg, 1976), and prostacyclin opposing these actions (Moncada *et al.,* 1976b; Bunting *et al.,* 1976). The leukotrienes (B$_4$, C$_4$, and D$_4$) are products of the lipoxygenase pathway of arachidonic acid metabolism and possess several biological properties associated with the inflammatory response; for example, leukotriene B$_4$ is a potent chemotactic substance, both *in vivo* and *in vitro,* and in addition has the property of increasing vascular permeability. Leukotrienes C$_4$ and D$_4$ are also thought to be involved in immediate hypersensitivity reactions and asthmatic conditions.

In this chapter we will principally deal with the biological effects of hydroxy derivatives (excluding cysteine-containing leukotrienes) of the lipoxygenase pathway of arachidonic acid metabolism and the pharmacological consequences of lipoxygenase inhibition.

II. METABOLISM OF ARACHIDONIC ACID

The pathways of oxidation of arachidonic acid by cyclooxygenase and lipoxygenase have been reviewed (Grandström, 1976; Samuelsson, 1983) and are therefore only outlined here.

A. Cyclooxygenase Pathway

The cyclooxygenase enzyme system is a microsomal multienzyme complex that catalyzes the oxidation of arachidonic acid to unstable endoperoxide intermediates (PGG$_2$ and PGH$_2$), which are subsequently metabolized to the stable prostaglandins (PGE$_2$; PGF$_{2\alpha}$), prostacyclin, thromboxane A$_2$, 12-hydroxy-5,8,10-heptadecatrienoic acid (HHT), and malondialdehyde (Fig. 1). The nature of the product or mixture of products formed will depend on the cell type (see the review by Salmon and Flower, 1983).

B. Lipoxygenase Pathway

Lipoxygenation of arachidonic acid was first reported in platelets, which were found to synthesize 12-L-hydroperoxy-5,8,10,14-eicosatetraenoic acid

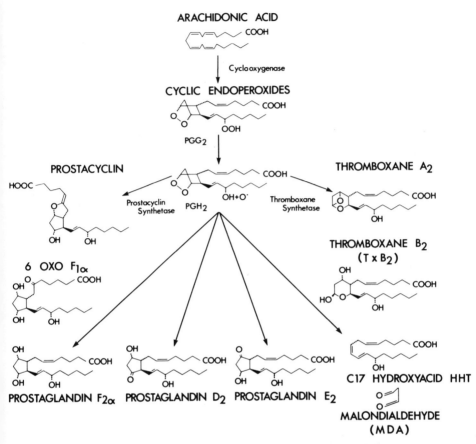

Fig. 1.   The cyclooxygenase pathway of arachidonic acid metabolism.

(12-HPETE), which is then reduced by glutathione peroxidase to 12-L-hy-droxy-5,8,10,14-eicosatetraenoic acid (12-HETE; Hamberg and Samuelsson, 1974; Nugteren, 1975). Other lipoxygenase enzymes and incomplete operation of the cyclooxygenase pathway may also give rise to 11- and 15-HETEs (Fig. 2).

The synthesis of lipoxygenase products has been reported in a number of tissues including leukocytes such as polymorphonuclear leukocytes (PMN) (Borgeat et al., 1976; Borgeat and Samuelsson, 1979a), macrophages (Fels et al., 1982; Hsueh and Sun, 1982), and basophilic leukemia cells (Jakschik and Lee, 1980), lung (Jakschik et al., 1980), and platelets (Nugteren, 1975). Polymorphonuclear leukocytes produce a number of HETEs of which 5-HETE is the major product (Borgeat et al., 1976; Goetzl and Sun, 1979). Lipoxygenation occurs following abstraction of hydrogen at position 7 (yielding either 5-

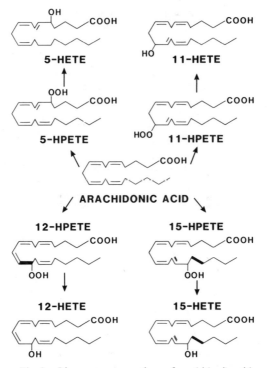

Fig. 2. Lipoxygenase reactions of arachidonic acid.

or 9-HETE), position 10 (yielding either 8- or 12-HETE), or position 13 (yielding either 11- or 15-HETE), followed by peroxidation with molecular oxygen at the appropriate position. These reactions always give rise to the L-isomer in enzymic reactions and show a substantial preference for the 5-, 12-, and 15-products.

The formation of 5-HPETE is also the first step in a pathway (Fig. 3) that gives rise to a family of compounds containing a conjugated triene structure, named the leukotrienes (Samuelsson *et al.*, 1979). The 5,6-epoxide leuko-triene A$_4$ (LTA$_4$), formed from 5-HPETE (Borgeat and Samuelsson, 1979c; Rådmark *et al.*, 1980b) can be nonenzymically hydrolyzed to diastereomers of 5,6-dihydroxyeicosatetraenoic acid (5,6-diHETE), and 6,8,10-trans-14-cis-diastereomers of 5,12-diHETE or can be enzymically converted to (5S,12R)-dihydroxy-6,14-*cis*-8,10-*trans*-eicosatetraenoic acid [leukotriene B$_4$ (LTB$_4$); Borgeat and Samuelsson, 1979a,b,d; Rådmark *et al.*, 1980b]. Both of the products of chemical hydrolysis have little biological activity compared to enzymically formed isomer (Malmsten *et al.*, 1980; Ford-Hutchinson *et al.*, 1981).

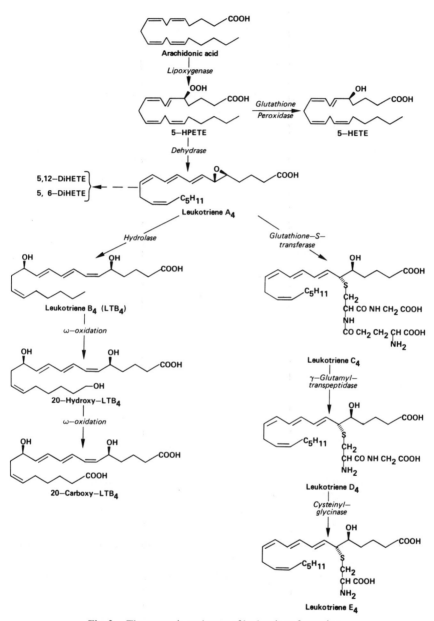

Fig. 3.   The enzymic pathways of leukotriene formation.

Alternatively, the addition of glutathione to LTA_4 by glutathione-S-transferase results in the formation of LTC_4, which can then be converted to the cysteinylglycyl adduct (LTD_4) by removal of the terminal glutamine by γ-glutamyl transpeptidase. Leukotriene D_4 can be further metabolized to the cysteinyl adduct LTE_4 (Hammarström and Samuelsson, 1980; Murphy et al., 1979; Morris et al., 1980; Lewis et al., 1980a,b; Örning et al., 1980; Parker et al., 1980). Morris et al. (1980) have suggested that the slow-reacting substance produced in anaphylaxis (SRS-A) is LTD_4, although it is likely that SRS-A is a mixture of LTC_4, LTD_4, and LTE_4.

Human PMN have been shown to form novel metabolites of LTB_4 by ω oxidation (Lindgren et al., 1981; Hansson et al., 1981). These metabolites are $(5S,12R)$-20-trihydroxyeicosatetraenoic acid (20-hydroxy-LTB_4), which can be further metabolized to the 20-carboxy acid (20-carboxy-LTB_4).

The formation of another series of compounds containing a conjugated triene structure via a 14,15-epoxide intermediate analogous to LTA_4 has been reported in human PMN (Jubiz et al., 1981; Lundberg et al., 1981) and in porcine leukocytes (Maas et al., 1982). Although the stereochemistry of the isomers of these compounds has not been described, they have been termed 8,15-LTB_4 and 14,15-LTB_4 (Lundberg et al., 1981; Rådmark et al., 1982).

III. PATHOPHYSIOLOGICAL PROPERTIES OF LIPOXYGENASE PRODUCTS

A. Vascular Permeability

The mono- and dihydroxy products of the 5-lipoxygenase pathway alter vascular permeability to varying degrees and interact with both PGs and other vasoactive agents to enhance the magnitude of their effect.

Intradermal injections of LTB_4 (0.1–1.0 μg) result in exudation of plasma protein into the extravascular spaces of rabbit skin. The magnitude of the increased vascular permeability is small but significant and is greater than that produced by high doses (10–20 μg) of 5-, 12-, or 15-HPETE (Eakins et al., 1980; Higgs et al., 1981; Bray et al., 1981b). Furthermore, LTB_4 enhances the increase in vascular permeability caused by both bradykinin and PGE_2. In the hamster cheek pouch preparation, local application of LTB_4 similarly caused a dose-dependent increase in vascular permeability (Björk et al., 1982) that was potentiated by nanomolar concentrations of PGE_1.

In the rabbit eye, intraocular injection of 25 to 400 ng of LTB_4 or higher doses of the monohydroxy products (5-HETE, 12-HETE, 5-HPETE) did not affect the integrity of the ocular vascular bed (Bhattacherjee et al., 1982). In contrast, arachidonic acid, PGE_1, PGE_2, $PGF_{2\alpha}$, PGI_1, and bradykinin all profoundly increased vascular permeability. Thus it would appear that LTB_4 and the cyclooxygenase products complement each other in increasing vascular permeability in some tissues such as skin and cheek pouch, but not in the eye, where only the cyclooxygenase products affect the permeability of the anterior uvea.

B. Leukocyte Function

Polymorphonuclear leukocytes (PMN) possess powerful mechanisms for host defense and are important in the elaboration and amplification of the inflammatory response, and if these defensive mechanisms are uncontrolled, loss of functional activity and tissue damage will occur. A prerequisite for PMN accumulation at an inflammatory site is the local generation of chemoattractants. Stimulated locomotion is manifest by an increase in rate of movement (chemokinesis) and in directional control (chemotaxis).

Chemotactic factors such as the complement cleavage product, C5a and the formylmethionylleucylphenylalanine (FMLP) and bacterial-derived chemoattractants, cause leukocyte locomotion via specific receptors on the leukocyte membrane (Chenoweth and Hugli, 1978; Williams *et al.*, 1977; Aswanikumar *et al.*, 1977). Following ligand – receptor interaction, the leukocyte undergoes a sequence of reactions that has been characterized as a stimulus secretion coupling (Korchak and Weissmann, 1980; Smolen and Weissmann, 1980). During this process intracellular concentrations of free calcium increase in PMN, leading to adherence and accumulation. Subsequently, superoxide anions are generated, and the hydrolytic and proteolytic enzymes of the lysosomal granules are extruded (Goldstein *et al.*, 1974, 1975). In common with the effects of C5a and FMLP (Naccache *et al.*, 1979a,b), LTB_4 mobilizes calcium ions bound to plasma membranes, thereby raising the intracellular calcium levels (Sha'afi *et al.*, 1981; Naccache *et al.*, 1981). This effect is also stereospecific and is mimicked by the 20-hydroxylated LTB_4 (Naccache *et al.*, 1982). Structure – activity studies on the chemotactic activity of LTB_4 indicated that human PMN possess receptors on the surface membrane that are specific for LTB_4 (Goetzl and Picket, 1981). These studies were subsequently confirmed in binding studies (Goldman and Goetzl, 1982).

Ford-Hutchinson *et al.*, (1980) originally reported that LTB_4 was a potent chemokinetic and aggregating agent on human and rat PMN, respectively. Leukotriene B_4 was found to be 100 times more potent as a chemokinetic agent than any of the mono-HETEs or HPETEs examined for chemokinetic activity on rabbit, rat, and human PMN and was clearly chemotactic on human PMN (Fig. 4; Palmer *et al.*, 1980). Other workers independently reported that LTB_4 is both chemokinetic and chemotactic (Goetzl and

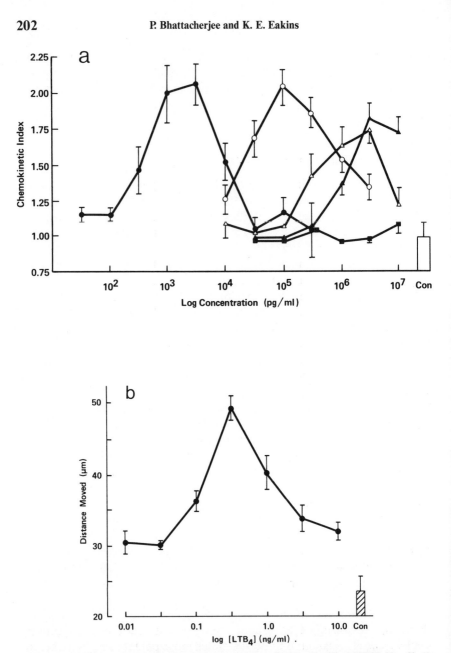

Fig. 4. (a) Human leukocyte chemokinetic activity of LTB$_4$ (●—●), 5-HETE (○—○), 11-HETE (▲—▲), 12-HETE (△—△), and 15-HETE (□—□). Each point is the mean ± SD ($n = 6$) of a single experiment. The background level of migration was 0.15 mm. (b) Human neutrophil chemotactic activity of LTB$_4$. Each point is the mean ± SD of three measurements on each of three replicate filters ($n = 9$). (Reproduced from Palmer *et al.*, 1980).

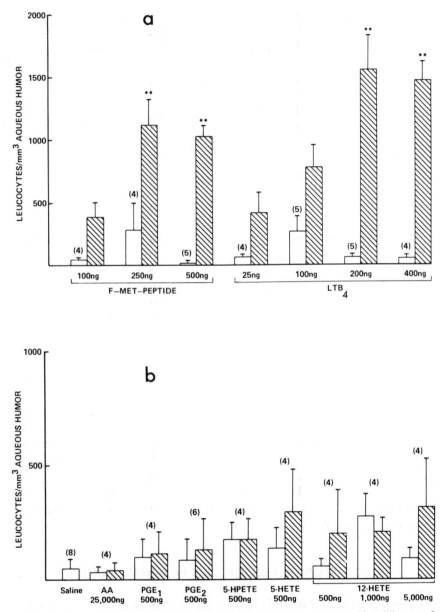

Fig. 5. *In vivo* chemotactic activity expressed as leukocyte counts per cubic millimeter of aqueous humor 4 h after injection, into the anterior chamber of rabbit eyes, of (a) F-Met-peptide and LTB$_4$ and (b) arachidonic acid metabolites. Vertical bars, ± SEM; □ control; ▨ test; **$p <$ .01. Numbers of animals tested are given in parentheses. (Reproduced from Bhattacherjee *et al.,* 1981.)

Picket, 1980; Malmsten *et al.*, 1980; Lewis *et al.*, 1981). These activities of LTB_4 are stereospecific, the activity mainly residing in the *cis – trans – trans*-triene structure (Lewis *et al.*, 1981; Malmsten *et al.*, 1980; Ford-Hutchinson *et al.*, 1981).

Leukotriene B_4 also causes leukocyte accumulation *in vivo* following intracameral administration in the rabbit eye (Fig. 5; Bhattacherjee *et al.*, 1981), intradermal administration both in rabbits (Higgs *et al.*, 1981; Lewis *et al.*, 1981) and in monkeys (Lewis *et al.*, 1981), and intraperitoneal administration in guinea pigs (Smith *et al.*, 1980). It has been subsequently reported that intracutaneous injection of small amounts of LTB_4 in humans resulted in transient wheal and flare followed by dermal infiltration of PMN (Soter *et al.*, 1983).

Increased adherence of leukocytes to the vascular endothelium of the hamster cheek pouch preparation following superfusion with small amounts of LTB_4 was observed by Bray *et al.* (1981a). These workers further demonstrated that LTB_4 could also induce leukocyte accumulation in both human and rabbit skin. Interestingly, PGE_2 was ineffective on its own in the rabbit skin but was found to potentiate the leukocyte accumulation observed following LTB_4 alone. A transient neutropenia was observed following intravenous injection of LTB_4 into the rabbit (Bray *et al.*, 1981a; O'Flaherty *et al.*, 1982). Leukotriene B_4 but not 5-HETE has also been reported to release lysozyme and β-glucuronidase from PMN treated with cytochalasin B (Goetzl and Pickett, 1980; Palmer and Yeats, 1981; Palmblad *et al.*, 1982). Although LTB_4 is the most potent of all lipoxygenase products in the release of lysomal enzymes, it is less active than C5a and FMLP.

The first lipoxygenase product reported to possess chemotactic activity for human PMN *in vitro* was 12-HETE (Turner *et al.*, 1975). Goetzl and Sun in 1979 confirmed this observation and reported that a number of HETEs were both chemokinetic and chemotactic for human PMN. The HPETEs are generally more potent chemokinetic agents for rabbit and human PMN than their corresponding HETE, with the notable exception of the 5- products on human PMN and the 12- products on rabbit PMN, where they were equiactive (Palmer *et al.*, 1980).

IV. FORMATION OF LEUKOTRIENES IN VARIOUS TISSUES

As described in Section II, B, leukocytes metabolize arachidonic acid by the 5-lipoxygenase pathway to mono- and dihydroxy products, of which LTB_4 is the most active biologically.

Other lipoxygenase pathways have also been described. For example, rabbit and human PMN form 15-HPETE via a 15-lipoxygenase pathway

(Narumiya *et al.*, 1982; Borgeat *et al.*, 1983). There are also reports of an interaction between the product formed by 12-lipoxygenase in platelets and 5-lipoxygenase in PMN (Maclouf *et al.*, 1982; Marcus *et al.*, 1982); thus incubation of platelets together with PMN resulted in the formation of increased amounts of both 5-HETE and LTB_4, suggesting a stimulatory effect of 12-HETE on the 5-lipoxygenase pathway in PMN (Maclouf *et al.*, 1982). Hemoglobin was also shown to catalyze conversion of 15-HPETE to 8,15-diHETE and 14,15-diHETE via a free-radical process (Sok *et al.*, 1983). Other tissues that are able to form mono- and dihydroxy lipoxygenase metabolites of arachidonic acid include normal and psoriatic skin (Hammarström *et al.*, 1975, 1979), blood vessels (Greenwald *et al.*, 1979), kidney (Van Praag *et al.*, 1980), ocular tissues (Williams *et al.*, 1983), and bone marrow-derived mast cells (Mencia-Huerta *et al.*, 1983).

Leukotriene B_4 has been identified in inflammatory exudates including synovial fluid from patients with arthritis or spondyloarthritis (Klickstein *et al.*, 1980; Davidson *et al.*, 1982), from patients with gout (Rae *et al.*, 1982), and in blister fluid from human psoriatic skin (Brain *et al.*, 1982). Leukotriene B_4 has now also been identified in carrageenan-induced inflammatory exudates using a specific radioimmunoassay (Simmons *et al.*, 1983).

There are fewer reports on lipoxygenase products as opposed to cyclooxygenase products in inflammatory exudates, partly because of the great difficulties encountered in the measurement of lipoxygenase products in biological fluids. Following the development of a highly specific radioimmunoassay by Salmon *et al.* (1982a), it is now possible to measure accurately the amounts of LTB_4 in inflammatory exudates. Further studies by Salmon and co-workers drew attention to the difficulties found in determining reliable, quantitative estimates of LTB_4 in inflammatory exudates, since these cells are capable of rapidly accumulating the LTB_4 (Salmon *et al.*, 1982b) and rapidly metabolizing it to 20-hydroxy-LTB_4 and 20-carboxy-LTB_4 (Hansson *et al.*, 1981; Lindgren *et al.*, 1982; Salmon *et al.*, 1982b).

V. LIPOXYGENASE INHIBITION AND ITS CONSEQUENCES

The discovery that aspirin and other nonsteroidal antiinflammatory drugs selectively inhibit prostaglandin synthesis (Vane, 1971; Smith and Willis, 1971; Ferreira *et al.*, 1971) led Vane (1971) to propose that inhibition of prostaglandin biosynthesis accounted for the therapeutic and toxic effects of the aspirin-like drugs.

In contrast, the antiinflammatory corticosteroids do not have a direct effect on arachidonate-metabolizing enzymes but rather interfere with the release of fatty acids from cell membrane phospholipids (Gryglewski *et al.*,

1975; Nijkamp *et al.*, 1976), possibly by inducing the synthesis of an anti-phospholipase A_2 protein termed macrocortin (Flower and Blackwell, 1979; Blackwell *et al.*, 1982) or lipomodulin (Hirata *et al.*, 1980). The overall effect of the steroid is to prevent arachidonic acid peroxidation resulting from either the cyclooxygenase or the lipoxygenase pathway.

Other compounds are known to be dual inhibitors of both pathways of arachidonate metabolism, being equally active in inhibiting both cyclooxy-genase and lipoxygenase activity. Thus the overall biochemical effect of these dual inhibitors resembles that of the antiinflammatory steroids in preventing the formation of all of the peroxidation products of arachidonate metabolism. The antioxidant, nordihydroguaiaretic acid (NDGA), was the first compound to be reported to inhibit 12-HETE synthesis in platelets at concentrations lower than those required to inhibit the cyclooxygenase pathway (Hamberg, 1976). This compound also inhibits lipoxygenase from such diverse sources as soybean (Tappel *et al.*, 1953) and PMN (Showell *et al.*, 1980), and it inhibits Ca^{2+} influx induced by FMLP (Naccache *et al.*, 1979b), the respiratory burst induced by serum-treated zymosan (Rossi *et al.*, 1981), degranulation induced by PAF (Smith and Bowman, 1982), and degranula-tion and chemotaxis induced by calcium ionophore A23187, by FMLP, and by C5a (Showell *et al.*, 1980).

The substrate analog, eicosatetraynoic acid (ETYA), inhibits both path-ways of arachidonic acid metabolism with similar potency (Hamberg and Samuelsson, 1974). However, this compound does not apparently act by inhibiting the initial oxygenation reaction at the 5 position, but rather by inhibiting leukotriene formation at a subsequent step (Hamberg and Samu-elsson, 1974; Bokoch and Reed, 1981). Other acetylenic analogs of arachi-donic acid also inhibit lipoxygenase, provided they possess olefinic bonds in or adjacent to the 5, 8, and 11 positions (Hammarström, 1977; Smith *et al.*, 1981; Sun *et al.*, 1981; Wilhelm *et al.*, 1981; Jakschik *et al.*, 1981). Although some of these analogs show selectivity for certain lipoxygenases, they all charac-teristically exhibit a similar lack of activity against the initial oxygenation at the 5 position. High oral doses of either ETYA (Walker *et al.*, 1976) or NDGA (Higgs and Mugridge, 1982) were found to inhibit the appearance of prosta-glandins in the inflammatory exudates in rats without effecting leukocyte infiltration.

In 1978, phenidone (1-phenyl-3-pyrazolidin) was reported to inhibit both the cyclooxygenase and lipoxygenase pathways in guinea pig lungs and horse platelets (Blackwell and Flower, 1978). These observations led to the discov-ery of a series of pyrazoline derivatives that are dual inhibitors of both pathways of arachidonic acid metabolism (Higgs *et al.*, 1979). 3-Amino-1-[*m*-(trifluoromethyl)-phenyl]-2-pyrazoline (BW755C) is perhaps the most extensively studied member of this series and has been shown to inhibit the formation of cyclooxygenase and lipoxygenase products in PMN and other tissues at low concentrations (Randall *et al.*, 1980; Rådmark *et al.*, 1980a; Williams *et al.*, 1983; Casey *et al.*, 1983). In experimental inflammation induced in rat by carrageenan, BW755C inhibited both edema and leukocyte accumulation without potentiating these responses at any dose. This antiinflammatory profile resembled that of dexamethasone more than indomethacin, which was found to enhance the accumulation of PMN at low doses before inhibiting their accumulation at higher doses (Fig. 6; Higgs *et al.*, 1980). There are other reports of enhancement of PMN migration by low doses of flurbiprofen (Adams *et al.*, 1977) and indomethacin (Srinivasan *et al.*, 1980).

The effects of different antiinflammatory agents on both LTB_4 concentrations and PMN accumulation in inflammatory exudates have been studied by Salmon *et al.* (1983). BW755C did not reduce LTB_4 concentration and leukocyte accumulation in parallel, thus the highest dose used (100 mg/kg po) abolished the appearance of LTB_4 in the exudate while reducing the PMN counts by only 55%. These effects were similar to the results obtained with the steroidal antiinflammatory agent, dexamethasone. In contrast, the cyclooxygenase inhibitors indomethacin and flurbiprofen were found to reduce PMN in this exudate without affecting LTB_4 levels, indicating that LTB_4 is not the only mediator involved in chemotactic events in this model of inflammation.

Benoxaprofen and timegadine have also been found to be dual inhibitors of cyclooxygenase and lipoxygenase (Walker and Dawson, 1979; Ahnfelt-Ronne and Arrigoni-Martelli, 1982; Dawson *et al.*, 1982; Casey *et al.*, 1983). It is of interest that whereas benoxaprofen is considerably more potent as a cyclooxygenase inhibitor than as an inhibitor of lipoxygenase, it has greater inhibitory actions on monocyte accumulation in inflammatory exudates than other known cyclooxygenase inhibitors (Meacock and Kitchen, 1976, 1979). 6,9-Deepoxy-6,9-(phenylimino)-$\Delta^{6,8}$-prostaglandin I_1 (U-60257) has been found to be a specific inhibitor of LTC_4 and LTD_4 formation (Bach *et al.*, 1982, 1983), and also to inhibit LTB_4 formation by A23187-activated PMN (Smith *et al.*, 1982).

It is well known that FPL55712 is an antagonist of the actions of leukotrienes C_4, D_4, and E_4 (Welton *et al.*, 1981a; Bach *et al.*, 1979) to inhibit histamine release (Welton *et al.*, 1981b; Krell *et al.*, 1980) and has recently been found to inhibit selectively the 5-lipoxygenase pathway in homogenates of rat basophilic leukemia cells (Casey *et al.*, 1983). This compound has not been studied on leukocyte accumulation in experimental models of inflammation.

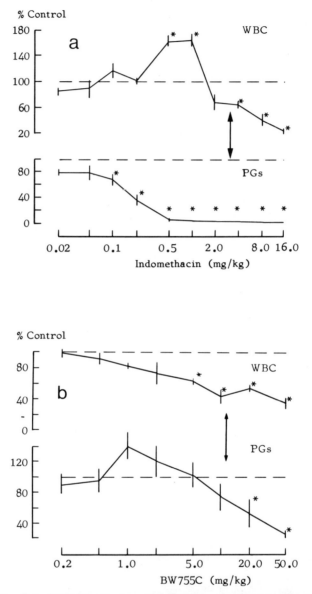

Fig. 6. The effect of (a) indomethacin and (b) BW755C on total leukocyte numbers (WBC) and prostaglandin concentration (PGs) per milliliter of carrageenan-induced inflammatory exudates. In both (a) and (b), three doses per 24 h were given. *$p < .05$, compared with control values. The arrows indicate the dose required to inhibit carrageenan-induced edema by 50% in separate experiments. (Reproduced from Higgs *et al.*, 1980.)

VI. CONCLUSIONS

Metabolism of arachidonic acid by the 5-lipoxygenase pathway leads to the formation of biologically active products. The discovery of novel products formed by other pathways suggests that the complete range of arachidonic acid metabolites formed *in vivo* has yet to be described. For example, the 5S,12S)-stereoisomer of LTB$_4$ (Borgeat *et al.*, 1981) and (5S,15S)-diHETE (Borgeat *et al.*, 1983) have been shown to be formed enzymically. Furthermore, interactions between products of different pathways of arachidonic acid metabolism are still largely unknown, as 12-HETE formed by platelets stimulates the 5-lipoxygenase pathway in PMN (Marcus *et al.*, 1982; Borgeat *et al.*, 1983). Thus it seems that our knowledge of arachidonic acid metabolism is not yet complete.

Of the lipoxygenase products described so far, LTB$_4$ is the most potent chemokinetic, chemotactic, and degranulating stimulus *in vitro* for human PMN (Palmer *et al.*, 1980; Ford-Hutchinson *et al.*, 1980). Leukotriene B$_4$ also causes PMN accumulation (Bhattacherjee *et al.*, 1981; Higgs *et al.*, 1981; Lewis *et al.*, 1981), margination (Dahlén *et al.*, 1981; Bray *et al.*, 1981a), and transient neutropenia (Bray *et al.*, 1981a), and it increases vascular permeability alone or in the presence of prostaglandin E$_1$ *in vivo* (Wedmore and Williams, 1981; Higgs *et al.*, 1981; Björk *et al.*, 1982; Bray *et al.*, 1981b). In addition, LTB$_4$ has been detected in inflammatory exudates in various forms of experimental inflammation and clinical inflammatory diseases (Klickstein *et al.*, 1980); Rae *et al.*, 1982; Brain *et al.*, 1982; Simmons *et al.*, 1983). Therefore, LTB$_4$ fulfills the criteria of mediator of inflammation. Prostaglandins also produce various signs of inflammation and in addition synergize with other mediators (see the reviews by Ferreira and Vane, 1979; Higgs *et al.*, 1983). These observations indicate a therapeutic potential for compounds that modulate either the formation or actions of metabolites of arachidonic acid.

Both the selective cyclooxygenase inhibitors and dual inhibitors of arachidonic acid metabolism are equally effective in inhibiting increased vascular permeability and PMN accumulation. For instance, indomethacin, flurbiprofen, and BW755C all inhibit leukocyte accumulation and prostaglandin formation *in vivo* (Higgs *et al.*, 1980). Salmon *et al.* (1983) have reported a lack of correlation between inhibition of PMN accumulation and LTB$_4$ formation by indomethacin, flurbiprofen, and BW755C. These observations suggest that the reduction in PMN accumulation by these compounds is due to mechanisms other than inhibition of LTB$_4$ formation. More studies of this nature are required to establish the relative importance of lipoxygenase products in the initiation and amplification of the cellular phase of inflammation. At present, the available evidence suggests their participation rather than a pivotal role in inflammatory responses.

REFERENCES

Adams, S. S., Burrows, C. A., Skeldon, N., and Yates, D. B. (1977). *Curr. Med. Res.* **5,** 11–16.
Ahnfelt-Ronne, I., and Arrigoni-Martelli, E. (1982). *Biochem. Pharmacol.* **3,** 2619–2624.
Aswanikumar, S., Corcoran, B. A., Schiffmann, E., Day, AS. R., Freer, R. J., Showell, M. J., Becker, E. L., and Pert, C. B. (1977). *Biochem. Biophys. Res. Commun.* **74,** 810–817.
Bach, M. K., Brashler, J. R., Brooks, C. D., and Neerken, A. J. (1979). *J. Ummunol.* **122,** 160–165.
Bach, M. K., Brashler, J. R., Smith, H. W., Fitzpatrick, F. A., Sun, F. F., and McGuire, J. C. (1982). *Prostaglandins* **23,** 759–771.
Bach, M. K., Brashler, J. R., Fitzpatrick, F. A., Griffin, R. L., Iden, S. S., Johnson, H. G., McGuire, J. C., Smith, H. W., Smith, R. J., Sun, F. F., and Wasserman, M. A. (1983). *Adv. Prostaglandin, Thomboxane, Leukotriene Res.* **11,** 39–44.
Bhattacherjee, P., Hammond, B. R., Salmon, J. A., Stepney, R., and Eakins, K. E. (1981). *Eur. J. Pharmacol.* **73,** 21–28.
Bhattacherjee, P., Hammond, B. R., Salmon, J. A., and Eakins, K. E. (1982). *Adv. Prostaglandin, Thromboxane, Leukotriene Res.* **9,** 325–330.
Björk, J., Hedqvist, P., and Arfors, K. E. (1982). *Inflammation* **6,** 189–200.
Blackwell, G. J., and Flower, R. J. (1978). *Prostaglandins* **16,** 417–425.
Blackwell, G. J., Carnuccio, R., Di Rosa, M., Flower, R. J., Langham, C. S. J., Parente, L., Persico, P., Russel-Smith, N. C., and Stone, D. (1982). *Br. J. Pharmacol.* **76,** 185–194.
Bokoch, G. M., and Reed, P. W. (1981). *J. Biol. Chem.* **256,** 4156–4159.
Borgeat, P., and Samuelsson, B. (1979a). *Proc. Natl. Acad. Sci. U.S.A.* **76,** 2148–2152.
Borgeat, P., and Samuelsson, B. (1979b). *J. Biol. Chem.* **254,** 2643–2646.
Borgeat, P., and Samuelsson, B. (1979c). *Proc. Natl. Acad. Sci. U.S.A.* **76,** 3213–3217.
Borgeat, P., and Samuelsson, B. (1979d). *J. Biol. Chem.* **254,** 7865–7869.
Borgeat, P., Hamberg, M., and Samuelsson, B. (1976). *J. Biol. Chem.* **251,** 7816–7820.
Borgeat, P., Picard, S., Vallerand, P., and Sirois, P. (1981). *Prostaglandins Med.* **6,** 557–570.
Borgeat, P., Fruteau de Laclos, B., and Maclouf, J. (1983). *Biochem. Pharmacol.* **32,** 381–387.
Brain, S. D., Camp, R. D., Black, A. B., Wollard, P. M., Mallet, A. I., and Greaves, M. W. (1982). *Lancet* **2,** 762–763.
Bray, M. A., Ford-Hutchinson, A. W., and Smith, M. J. H. (1981a). *Prostaglandins* **22,** 213–222.
Bray, M. A., Cunningham, F. M., Ford-Hutchinson, A. W., and Smith, M. J. H. (1981b). *Br. J. Pharmacol.* **72,** 483–486.
Bunting, S., Gryglewski, R., Moncada, S., and Vane, J. R. (1976). *Prostaglandins* **12,** 897–913.
Casey, F. B., Appleby, B. J., and Buck, D. C. (1983). *Prostaglandins* **25,** 1–11.
Chenoweth, D. E., and Hugli, J. E. (1978). *Proc. Natl. Acad. Sci. U.S.A.* **75,** 3943–3947.
Dahlén, S. E., Björk, J., Hedqvist, P., Arfors, K.-E., Hammarström, S., Lindgren, J.-A., and Samuelsson, B. (1981). *Proc. Natl. Acad. Sci. U.S.A.* **78,** 3887–3891.
Davidson, E. M., Rae, S. A., and Smith, M. J. H. (1982). *J. Pharm. Pharmacol.* **34,** 410.
Dawson, W., Boot, J. R., Janette, H., and Walker, J. R. (1982). *Eur. J. Rheumatol. Inflammation* **5,** 61–68.
Eakins, K. E., Higgs, G. A., Moncada, S., Salmon, J. A., and Spayne, J. A. (1980). *J. Physiol. (London)* **307,** 71P.
Fels, A. O., Pawlowski, N. A., Cramer, E. B., King, T. K., Cohn, Z. A., and Scott, W. A. (1982). *Proc. Natl. Acad. Sci. U.S.A.* **79,** 7866–7870.

Ferreira, S. H. (1972). *Nature (London)* **240**, 200–203.
Ferreira, S. H., and Vane, J. R. (1979). *In* "Anti-inflammatory Drugs" (J. R. Vane and S. H. Ferreira, eds.), pp. 348–398. Springer-Verlag, Berlin, and New York.
Ferreira, S. H., Moncada, S., and Vane, J. R. (1971). *Nature (London) New Biol.* **231**, 237–239.
Flower, R. J., and Blackwell, G. J. (1979). *Nature (London)* **278**, 456–459.
Ford-Hutchinson, A. W., Bray, M. A., Doig, M. V., Shipley, M. E., and Smith, M. J. H. (1980). *Nature (London)* **286**, 264–265.
Ford-Hutchinson, A. W., Smith, M. J. H., and Bray, M. A. (1981). *J. Pharm. Pharmacol.* **33**, 332.
Goetzl, E. J., and Pickett, W. C. (1980). *J. Immunol.* **125**, 1789–1791.
Goetzl, E. J., and Pickett, W. C. (1981). *J. Exp. Med.* **153**, 482–487.
Goetzl, E. J., and Sun, F. F. (1979). *J. Exp. Med.* **150**, 406–411.
Goldman, D. W., and Goetzl, E. J. (1982). *J. Immunol.* **129**, 1600–1604.
Goldstein, I. M., Horn, J. M., Kaplan, H. B., and Weissmann, G. (1974). *Biochem. Biophys. Res. Commun.* **60**, 807–812.
Goldstein, I. M., Hoftstein, S. T., and Weissmann, G. (1975). *J. Immunol.* **115**, 665–780.
Granström, E. (1976). *In* "Prostaglandins and Thromboxanes" (F. Berti, B. Samuelsson, and G. P. Velo, eds.), pp. 65–74. Plenum, New York.
Greenwald, J. E., Bianchine, J. R., and Wong, L. K. (1979). *Nature (London)* **281**, 588–589.
Gryglewski, R. J., Panczenko, B., Korbut, R., Grodzinske, L., and Ocetkeiwicz, A. (1975). *Prostaglandins* **10**, 343–355.
Hamberg, M. (1976). *Biochem. Biophys. Res. Commun.* **431**, 651–654.
Hamberg, M., and Samuelsson, B. (1974). *Proc. Natl. Acad. Sci. U.S.A.* **71**, 3400–3404.
Hamberg, M., Svensson, J., and Samuelsson, B. (1975). *Proc. Natl. Acad. Sci. U.S.A.* **72**, 2994–2998.
Hammarström, S. (1977). *Biochim. Biophys. Acta* **487**, 517–519.
Hammarström, S., and Samuelsson, B. (1980). *FEBS Lett.* **122**, 83–86.
Hammarström, S., Hamberg, H., Samuelsson, B., Duell, E. A., Stawiski, M., and Voorhees, J. J. (1975). *Proc. Natl. Acad. Sci. U.S.A.* **72**, 5130–5134.
Hammarström, S., Lindgren, J. A., Marcelo, C., Duell, E. A., Anderson, T. F., and Voorhees, J. J. (1979). *J. Invest. Dermatol.* **73**, 180–183.
Hansson, G., Lindgren, J. A., Dahlén, S.-E., Hedqvist, P., and Samuelsson, B. (1981). *FEBS Lett.* **130**, 107–112.
Higgs, G. A., and Mugridge, K. G. (1982). *Br. J. Pharmacol.* **76**, 284P.
Higgs, G. A., Flower, R. J., and Vane, J. R. (1979). *Biochem. Pharmacol.* **12**, 1959–1961.
Higgs, G. A., Eakins, K. E., Mugridge, K. G., Moncada, S, and Vane, J. R. (1980). *Eur. J. Pharmacol.* **66**, 81–86.
Higgs, G. A., Salmon, J. A., and Spayne, J. A. (1981). *Br. J. Pharmacol.* **74**, 429–433.
Higgs, G. A., Moncada, S., and Vane, J. R. (1983). *In* Anti-Rheumatic Drugs" (E. C. Huskisson, ed.), pp. 11–36. Praeger, New York.
Hirata, F., Schiffman, E., Venkatasubramanian, K., Salomon, D., and Axelrod, J. (1980). *Proc. Natl. Acad. Sci. U.S.A.* **77**, 2533–2536.
Hsueh, W., and Sun, F. F. (1982). *Biochem. Biophys. Res. Commun.* **106**, 1085–1091.
Jakschik, B. A., and Lee, L. H. (1980). *Nature (London)* **287**, 51–52.
Jakschik, B. A., Sun, F. F., Lee, L. H., and Steinhoff (1980). *Biochem. Biophys. Res. Commun.* **95**, 103–110.
Jakschik, B. A., Di Santis, D. M., Sankarappa, S. K., and Sprecher, H. (1981). *Biochem. Biophys. Res. Commun.* **102**, 624–629.
Jubiz, W., Radmark, O., Lindgren, J. A., Malmsten, C., and Samuelsson, B. (1981). *Biochem. Biophys. Res. Commun.* **99**, 976–986.
Klickstein, L. B., Shapleigh, C., and Goetzl, E. J. (1980). *J. Clin. Invest.* **66**, 1166–1170.

Korchak, H. M., and Weissmann, G. (1980). *Biochim. Biophys. Acta* **601**, 180–194.

Krell, R. D., McCoy, J., Osborn, R., and Chakrin, L. W. (1980). *Int. J. Immunpharm.* **2**, 56–62.

Lands, W. E. M., and Samuelsson, B. (1968). *Biochem. Biophys. Acta.* **164**, 426–429.

Lewis, R. A., Austen, K. F., Drazen, J. M., Clark, D. M., Marfat, A., and Corey, E. J. (1980a). *Proc. Natl. Acad. Sci. U.S.A.* **77**, 3710–3714.

Lewis, R. A., Drazen, J. M., Austen, K. F., Clark, D. M., and Corey, E. J. (1980b). *Biochem. Biophys. Res. Commun.* **96**, 271–277.

Lewis, R. A., Goetzl, E. J., Drazen, J. M., Soter, N. A. Austen, K. F., and Corey, E. J. (1981). *Proc. Natl. Acad. Sci. U.S.A.* **78**, 4579–4583.

Lindgren, J. A., Hansson, G., and Samuelsson, B. (1981). *FEBS Lett.* **128**, 329–335.

Lindgren, J. A., Hansson, G., Claesson, H. E., and Samuelsson, B. (1982). *Adv. Prostaglandin Thromboxane Leukotriene Res.* **9**, 53–60.

Lundberg, V., Rådmark, O., Malmsten, C., and Samuelsson, B. (1981). *FEBS Lett.* **126**, 127–132.

Maas, R. L., Brash, A. R., and Oates, J. A. (1982). *Adv. Prostaglandin, Thromboxane, Leukotriene Res.* **9**, 29–44.

Maclouf, J., Fruteau de Laclos, B., and Borgeat, P. (1982). *Proc. Natl. Acad. Sci. U.S.A.* **79**, 6042–6046.

Malmsten, C. L., Palmblad, J., Uden, A. M., Rådmark, O., Engstedt, L., and Samuelsson, B. (1980). *Acta Physiol. Scand.* **110**, 449–451.

Marcus, A. J., Brockman, M. J., Safier, L. B., Ullman, H. L., Islam, N., Serhan, C. N., Rutherford, L. E., Korchak, H. M., and Weissmann, G. (1982). *Biochem. Biophys. Res. Commun.* **109**, 130–137.

Meacock, S. C. R., and Kitchen, E. A. (1976). *Agents Actions* **6**, 320–325.

Meacock, S. C. R., and Kitchen, E. A. (1979). *J. Pharm. Pharmacol.* **31**, 366–370.

Mencia-Huerta, J. M., Razin, E., Ringel, E. W., Corey, E. J., Hoover, D., Austen, K. F., and Lewis, R. A. (1983). *J. Immunol.* **130**, 1885–1890.

Moncada, S., and Vane, J. R. (1977). *In* "New Biochemical Aspects of Prostaglandins and Thromboxanes" (N. Kharasch and J. Fried. eds.), pp. 155–177. Academic Press, New York.

Moncada, S., Needleman, P., Bunting, S., and Vane, J. R. (1976a). *Prostaglandins* **12**, 323–336.

Moncada, S., Gryglewski, R. J., Bunting, S., and Vane, J. R. (1976b). *Nature (London)* **263**, 663–665.

Morris, H. R., Taylor, G. W., Piper, P. J., Samhoun, M. N., and Tippins, J. R. (1980). *Prostaglandins* **19**, 185–201.

Murphy, R. C., Hammarström, S., and Samuelsson, B. (1979). *Proc. Natl. Acad. Sci. U.S.A.* **76**, 4275–4279.

Naccache, P. H., Showell, H. J., Becker, E. L., and Sha'afi, R. I. (1979a). *Biochem. Biophys. Res. Commun.* **87**, 292–299.

Naccache, P. H., Showell, H. J., Becker, E. L., and Sha'afi, R. I. (1979b). *Biochem. Biophys. Res. Commun.* **89**, 1224–1230.

Naccache, P. H., Sha'afi, R. I., Borgeat, P., and Goetzl, E. J. (1981). *J. Clin. Invest.* **67**, 1584–1587.

Naccache, P. H., Molski, T. F., Becker, E. L., Borgeat, P., Picard, S., Vallerand, P., and Sha'afi, R. I. (1982). *J. Biol. Chem.* **257**, 8608–8611.

Narumiya, S., Salmon, J. A., Flower, R. J., and Vane, J. R. (1982). *Adv. Prostaglandin, Thromboxane, Leukotriene Res.* **9**, 77–82.

Nijkamp, F. P., Flower, R. J., Moncada, S., and Vane, J. R. (1976). *Nature (London)* **263**, 479–482.

Nugteren, D. H. (1975). *Biochim. Biophys. Acta* **380**, 299–307.

O'Flaherty, J. T., Thomas, M. J., Cousart, S. L., Salzer, W. L., and McCall, C. E. (1982). *J. Clin. Invest.* **69**, 993–998.

Örning, L., Hammarström, S., and Samuelsson, B. (1980). *Proc. Natl. Acad. Sci. U.S.A.* **77**, 2014–2017.

Palmblad, J., Hafström, I., Malmsten, C. L., Udén, A.-M., Radmark, O., Engstedt, L., and Samuelsson, B. (1982). *Adv. Prostaglandin, Thromboxane, Leukotriene Res.* **9,** 293–299.
Palmer, R. M. J., and Yeats, D. A. (1981). *Br. J. Pharmacol.* **73,** 260P.
Palmer, R. M. J., Stepney, R., Higgs, G. A., and Eakins, K. E. (1980). *Prostaglandins* **20,** 411–418.
Parker, C. W., Falkenheim, S. F., and Humber, M. M. (1980). *Prostaglandins* **20,** 836–886.
Rådmark, O., Malmsten, C., and Samuelsson, B. (1980a). *FEBS Lett.* **110,** 213–215.
Rådmark, O., Malmsten, C., Samuelsson, B., Clark, D. A., Goto, G., Marfat, A., and Corey, E. J. (1980b). *Biochem. Biophys. Res. Commun.* **92,** 954–961.
Rådmark, O., Lundberg, W., Jubiz, W., Malmasten, C., and Samuelsson, B. (1982). *Adv. Prostaglandin, Thromboxane, Leukotriene Res.* **9,** 61–70.
Rae, S. A., Davidson, E. M., and Smith, M. J. H. (1982). *Lancet* **2,** 1122–1124.
Randall, R. W., Eakins, K. E., Higgs, G. A., Salmon, J. A., and Tateson, J. E. (1980). *Agents Actions* **10,** 553–555.
Rossi, F., Della Bianca, V., and Bellavite, P. (1981). *FEBS Lett.* **127,** 183–187.
Salmon, J. A., and Flower, R. J. (1983). *In* "Hormones in Blood" (C. H. Gray and V. H. T. James, eds.), Vol. 5, pp. 137–165. Academic Press, New York.
Salmon, J. A., Simmons, P. M., and Palmer, R. M. J. (1982a). *Prostaglandins* **24,** 225–235.
Salmon, J. A., Simmons, P. M., and Palmer, R. M. J., (1982b). *FEBS Lett.* **146,** 18–22.
Salmon, J. A., Simmons, P. M., and Moncada, S. (1983). *J. Pharm. Pharmacol.* **35,** 808–813.
Samuelsson, B. (1983). *Science* **220,** 568–569.
Samuelsson, B., Borgeat, P., and Murphy, R. C. (1979). *Prostaglandins* **17,** 785–787.
Sha'afi, R. I., Molski, T. F. P., Borgeat, P., and Goetzl, E. J. (1981). *J. Cell. Physiol* **108,** 401–408.
Showell, H. J., Naccache, P. H., Sha'afi, R. I., and Becker, E. L. (1980). *Life. Sci.* **27,** 421–426.
Simmons, P. M., Salmon, J. A., and Moncada, S. (1983). *Biochem. Pharmacol.* **32,** 1353–1359.
Smith, J. B., and Willis, A. L. (1971). *Nature (London)* **231,** 235–237.
Smith, M. J. H., Ford-Hutchinson, A. W., and Bray, M. A. (1980). *J. Pharm. Pharmacol.* **32,** 517–518.
Smith, R. J., and Bowman, B. J. (1982). *Biochem. Biophys. Res. Commun.* **104,** 1495–1501.
Smith, R. J., Sun, F. F., Bowman, B. J., Iden, S. S., Bowman, B. J., Sprecher, H., and McGuire, J. C. (1981). *Clin. Immunol. Immunopathol.* **20,** 157–159.
Smith, R. J., Sun, F. F., Bowman, B. J., Iden, S. S., Smith, H. W., and McGuire, J. C. (1982). *Biochem. Biophys. Res. Commun.* **109,** 943–949.
Smolen, J. E., and Weissmann, G. (1980). *Biochem. Pharmacol.* **29,** 533–538.
Sok, D. E., Chung, T., and Sih, C. J. (1983). *Biochem. Biophys. Res. Commun.* **110,** 273–279.
Soter, N. A., Lewis, R. A., Corey, E. J., and Austen, K. F. (1983). *J. Invest. Dermatol.* **80,** 115–119.
Srinivasan, B. D., Kulkarni, P. S., and Eakins, K. E. (1980). *Adv. Prostaglandin Thromboxane Res.* **7,** 861–864.
Sun, F. F., McGuire, J. C., Morton, D. R., Pike, J. E., Sprecher, H., and Kunau, W. H. (1981). *Prostaglandins* **21,** 333–343.
Svensson, J., and Hamberg, M. (1976). *Prostaglandins* **12,** 943–949.
Tappel, A. L., Lundberg, W. O., and Boyer, P. D. (1953). *Arch. Biochem. Biophys.* **42,** 293–304.
Turner, S. R., Tainer, J. A., and Lynn, W. S. (1975). *Nature (London)* **257,** 680–681.
Vane, J. R. (1971). *Nature (London)* **231,** 232–235.
Van Praag, D., Farber, S. J., and Stanley, D. (1980). *Fed. Proc., Fed. Am. Soc. Exp. Biol.* **39,** 1897.
Vonkeman, H., and Van Dorp, D. A. (1968). *Biochim. Biophys. Acta* **164,** 430–432.
Walker, J. R., and Dawson, W. (1979). *J. Pharm. Pharmacol.* **31,** 778–780.
Walker, J. R., Smith, M. J. H., and Ford-Hutchinson, A. W. (1976). *Agents Actions* **6,** 602–606.
Wedmore, C. V., and Williams, T. J. (1981). *Nature (London)* **289,** 646–648.
Welton, A. F., Hope, W. C., Tobias, L. D., and Hamilton, J. G. (1981a). *Biochem. Pharmacol.* **30,** 1378–1382.

Welton, A. F., Crowley, H. J., Miller, D. A., and Yaremko, B. (1981b). *Prostaglandins* **21,** 287–296.
Wilhelm, T. E., Shankarappa, S. K., Van Rollins, M., and Sprecher, H. (1981). *Prostaglandins* **21,** 323–332.
Williams, L. T., Snyderman, R., Pike, M. C., and Lefkowitz, R. J. (1977). *Proc. Natl. Acad. Sci. U.S.A.* **74,** 1204–1208.
Williams, R. N., Bhattacherjee, P., and Eakins, K. E. (1983). *Exp. Eye Res.* **36,** 397–401.
Williams, T. J., and Peck, M. J. (1977). *Nature (London)* **270,** 530–532.

8

Biological Actions of the Leukotrienes

PRISCILLA J. PIPER

Department of Pharmacology,
Institute of Basic Medical Sciences,
Royal College of Surgeons of England,
London, England

I. INTRODUCTION

The actions of slow-reacting substances (SRS) on smooth muscle have been studied by biologists since Feldberg and Kellaway (1938) observed that injection of snake venom into perfused lungs caused the release of material that caused a slow, long-lasting contraction of rabbit jejunum. Early studies described in the literature have been carried out using crude effluent or, at best, partially purified material. Besides being generated by snake venom (phospholipase A$_2$), SRS was produced during antigen challenge of various tissues from animals that had previously been sensitized, including guinea pig lung and rat peritoneum (Brocklehurst, 1960; Orange et al., 1970). The

SRS generated immunologically became known as slow-reacting substance of anaphylaxis (SRS-A) and was considered to be the most intriguing SRS on account of the similarities between the bronchoconstriction of anaphylaxis (in the guinea pig) and asthma in humans. Renewed interest in the structure of SRS occurred following the observation that the output of SRS was increased in the presence of cyclooxygenase inhibitors or fatty acid substrates for lipoxygenase, which suggested a link between SRS and arachidonic acid (Walker, 1973; Jakschik *et al.*, 1977; Piper *et al.*, 1979). The studies with exogenous fatty acids such as arachidonic or eicosapentaenoic acid indicated the presence of a family of similar SRSs that were derived from the individual fatty acids (Bach and Brashler, 1974; Piper *et al.*, 1979).

There was an important advance in the study of the structure of SRS when it was shown that HPLC could be used to purify these labile, naturally occurring substances (Morris *et al.*, 1978) and that the purified material showed UV absorbance with λ_{max} 280 nm, indicating the presence of a modified conjugated triene moiety in the molecule. After purification by HPLC, a number of chemical and biological tests demonstrated that SRS generated immunologically and nonimmunologically from various species, including humans, were indistinguishable (Morris *et al.*, 1979a). At this time the major problem in determining the structure of these substances was that, although they had very potent biological actions, they were released only in extremely small quantities.

Study of the metabolism of arachidonic acid by rabbit polymorphonuclear leukocytes (PMNs) led to the discovery of a family of arachidonic acid metabolites (hydroxy acids) whose formation was initiated by the action of a 5-lipoxygenase (Borgeat *et al.*, 1976; Borgeat and Samuelsson, 1979a,b). Like SRS-A, the hydroxy acid molecules possessed triene chromophores, and an unstable compound, 5,6-oxido-7,9,11,14-eicosatetraenoic acid, was intermediate in their formation (Borgeat and Samuelsson, 1979b). Samuelsson *et al.* (1979) introduced the term "leukotriene" to describe compounds produced by this metabolic pathway that possessed a conjugated triene chromophore in the molecule. Since analogous compounds can be derived from 5,8,11-eicosatrienoic acid, 5,8,11,14,17-eicosapentaenoic acid, and 5,8,11,14-eicosatetraenoic acid (arachidonic acid), a subscript has been used to describe the total number of double bonds in the molecule (Samuelsson and Hammarström, 1980). Leukotrienes include the slow-reacting substances; for instance, the SRS generated from murine mastocytoma cells by A23187 was characterized and described as LTC_4 (Hammarström *et al.*, 1979; Murphy *et al.*, 1979; Samuelsson *et al.*, 1979), and the major biological activity of guinea pig SRS-A is LTD_4 (Morris *et al.*, 1980b). This chapter will mainly discuss the properties of the leukotrienes derived from arachidonic acid.

II. LEUKOTRIENE B₄ AND LEUKOTRIENES WITH AMINO ACID RESIDUES AT C-6

The formation of leukotrienes by a 5-lipoxygenase is described in detail in Chapter 5. On account of their chemical structure and biological reactions, the leukotriene metabolites of LTA_4 can be divided into two groups: the dihydroxy acids and C-6 amino acid-substituted leukotrienes. As a general rule, the presence of the sulfur linkage and amino acid residue at C-6 is necessary for smooth muscle-stimulating activity, whereas the dihydroxy acids are highly chemotactic and chemokinetic but have little smooth muscle-stimulating action (Table I).

Formation of Leukotrienes in Various Tissues

The leukotrienes formed by individual cells or tissues depend on the enzymes present in the tissue and the incubation conditions used. For example, rat basophilic leukemia cells incubated with the calcium ionophore A23187 are a rich source of LTD_4 (Morris *et al.*, 1980a), but alteration of incubation conditions yields $(5S,12R)$-*cis,trans,trans*-LTB_4 and its isomers, $(5S,12S)$-all-*trans*-LTB_4, $(5S,12R)$-all-*trans*-LTB_4, and 5-HETE, but little LTD_4 (Ford-Hutchinson *et al.*, 1982). Human SRS-A consists of LTC_4 and

TABLE I

Pharmacological Actions of Leukotrienes

Leukotriene	Pharmacological actions
Dihydroxy acid LTB_4	Aggregation of PMNs
	Chemotaxis (PMNs)
	Chemokinesis of PMNs
	Exudation of plasma
	Translocation of Ca^{2+}
	Stimulation of phospholipase A_2 (PLA_2) (guinea pig lung)
C-6 Amino Acid-substituted LTs: LTC_4, LTD_4, LTE_4, LTF_4	Contraction of smooth muscle
	Constriction of small airways
	Contraction of guinea pig parenchyma
	Secretion of mucus
	Leakage from postcapillary venules
	Edema formation
	Vasoconstriction
	Coronary arterial constriction
	Stimulation of PLA_2 (guinea pig lung)
	Antagonism by FPL55712

LTD_4 (Lewis *et al.*, 1980), and rat SRS-A contains LTC_4, LTD_4, and LTE_4 (Lewis *et al.*, 1980); murine mastocytoma cells lack γ-glutamyl transpeptidase (γ-GT) (see later) and form LTC_4 (Murphy *et al.*, 1979). It is of interest that in addition to LTD_4, effluent from guinea pig lungs during antigen challenge also contained appreciable amounts of LTB_4 (Morris *et al.*, 1979b). γ-Glutamyl transpeptidase acts on LTC_4 to convert it to the cysteinylglycinyl derivative, LTD_4. This reaction occurs fairly rapidly and may be demonstrated as a change in the profile of the response to LTC_4 in a superfused cascade of assay tissues. Inhibition of γ-GT with δ-D-O-carboxyphenylhydrazine inhibits the change in response by preventing the conversion of LTC_4 to LTD_4 (Morris *et al.*, 1982) (Fig. 1). Guinea pig lung contains sufficient γ-GT to convert tens of nanomoles per minute of LTC_4 to LTD_4, which probably accounts for the fact that the major biological activity of guinea pig SRS-A (assayed on guinea pig ileum) is LTD_4 (Morris *et al.*, 1980b, 1982). Anderson *et al.* (1982) have shown that γ-GT can act on LTE_4 to reincorporate glutamic acid into the molecule and form LTF_4. In some biological systems, LTD_4 is more active than LTC_4 (Lewis *et al.*, 1980; Piper *et al.*, 1981), but generally the conversion of LTC_4 to LTF_4 results in loss of biological activity and probably represents part of the pathway for metabolism and degradation of the leukotrienes.

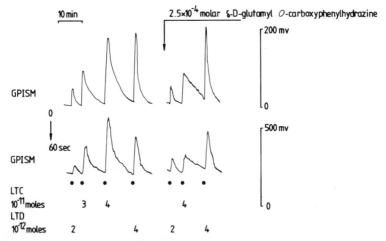

Fig. 1. Activation of LTC_4, during superfusion over smooth muscle strip from guinea pig ileum (GPISM). LTC_4 and LTD_4 were superfused over six strips; results with the first and sixth strips are shown, the time lag between them being 60 sec. (Left) In the first strip 40 pmol of LTC_4 caused contraction equivalent in height to that produced by 4 pmol of LTD_4. In the last strip this had increased significantly. (Right) In the presence of 0.25 mM δ-D-glutamyl-O-carboxyphenylhydrazine (added at arrow), the contraction elicited by 40 pmol of LTC_4 was reduced to the equivalent of that elicited by approximately 2 pmol of LTD_4, and the duration of the response increased. (From Morris *et al.*, 1982, with permission.)

In addition to the variation in leukotrienes present in different SRS, Ohnishi *et al.* (1980) identified the SRS produced from rat peritoneal cells as a leukotriene with a sulfone rather than sulfide linkage at C-6. This suggested that sulfones as well as sulfides may be constituents of SRS-A. Luekotriene sulfones have now been chemically synthesized (Girard *et al.*, 1982) and shown to possess biological activity that closely resembles that of the leukotriene sulfides and is antagonized by FPL55712 (Jones *et al.*, 1982).

III. PHARMACOLOGICAL ACTIONS OF THE LEUKOTRIENES

A. Gastrointestinal Smooth Muscle

As will be described in subsequent sections, the C-6 amino acid-substituted leukotrienes have potent actions on a variety of smooth muscle preparations. The action of leukotrienes occurs at various receptor sites in tissues. Using the antagonist presently available (FPL55712), these receptors have been partially characterized (Drazen *et al.*, 1980; Krell *et al.*, 1983). For many years guinea pig ileum *in vitro* has been used to assay SRS-A (Brocklehurst, 1960), and leukotrienes C_4, D_4, and E_4 are thousands of times more active than histamine on this preparation, the relative order of potency being $LTD_4 > LTC_4 > LTE_4$ (Lewis *et al.*, 1980; Piper *et al.*, 1981). Guinea pig ileum is very sensitive to leukotrienes and will respond to picomole doses.

Rat stomach strip (Piper and Samhoun, 1982) and guinea pig uterus (Weichman and Tucker, 1982) are also contracted by leukotrienes but are less sensitive than guinea pig ileum. These contractile responses are all antagonized by the SRS-A and leukotriene antagonist, FPL55712.

B. Airways

Leukotrienes are generated in lung tissue during anaphylaxis and are collectively responsible for the biological activity of SRS-A from human and guinea pig lung. Leukotrienes C_4 and D_4 are potent constrictors of isolated airway smooth muscle, whereas LTE_4 is less potent. There is considerable variation among species in the responses of airways to leukotrienes; they are thousands of times more active than histamine in respiratory smooth muscle from human and guinea pig lung (Dahlén *et al.*, 1980; Lewis *et al.*, 1980; Piper *et al.*, 1981) but are less active on monkey trachea (Smedegård *et al.*, 1982) and have little or no action in rat, cat, or dog (Krell *et al.*, 1981). Leukotrienes C_4 and D_4 are about equiactive in contracting human isolated bronchus, guinea pig trachea, and guinea pig parenchymal strips, but less active on human parenchymal strips (Dahlén *et al.*, 1980; Samhoun and

Piper, 1983). In guinea pig lung, leukotrienes B_4, C_4, D_4, and E_4 activate a phospholipase (probably phospholipase A_2) and stimulate the release of cyclooxygenase products (Piper and Samhoun, 1982; Samhoun and Piper, 1983). The products released are mainly thromboxane A_2 (TxA_2), together with other prostaglandin-like substances. The released TxA_2 plays an important role in the bronchoconstrictor actions of leukotrienes given intravenously to guinea pigs *in vivo* and in contractions of superfused parenchymal strips *in vitro*. Thromboxane A_2 is a potent bronchoconstrictor and augments the constrictor actions of the leukotrienes (Fig. 2). In these preparations leukotriene-induced bronchoconstriction is inhibited by indomethacin or thromboxane synthetase inhibitors. However, when leukotrienes are administered by aerosol, they appear to have a direct action that is not reduced by indomethacin (Hamel *et al.*, 1982; Weichman *et al.*, 1982). Leukotriene B_4 is a potent constrictor of guinea pig parenchymal strips *in vitro* (Sirois *et al.*, 1981), an action that is dependent on the generation of TxA_2 (Piper and Samhoun, 1981; Sirois *et al.*, 1982) and causes bronchoconstriction in guinea pig *in vivo*, which is blocked by indomethacin (Hamel and Ford-Hutchinson, 1983). Leukotriene B_4-induced constriction differs from that of LTC_4 and LTD_4 in that it easily develops tachyphylaxis and is not antagonized by FPL55712. Although the contraction of guinea pig parenchyma induced by LTE_4 is also dependent on the generation of TxA_2, it is of much longer duration than contractions due to LTC_4 and LTD_4 (Samhoun and Piper, 1983).

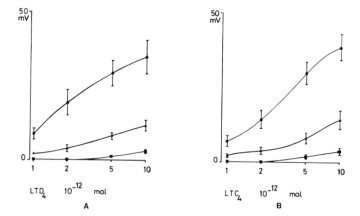

Fig. 2.   Inhibition of contractions of guinea pig parenchymal strips due to 1–10 pmol of (A) leukotriene D_4 (LTD_4) and (B) LTC_4 by carboxyheptylimidazole alone (▲, 24 μM) and CHI plusFPL 55712 (■, 1.9 μM). Uninhibited control contraction (●). Bars represent SEM from eight experiments. Ordinates: 50 mV. Abscissae: doses of LTD_4 and LTC_4 (pmol). (From Piper and Samhoun, 1982, with permission.)

The involvement of TxA_2 in the actions of leukotrienes does not occur in human lung tissue or when leukotrienes are given to guinea pigs by aerosol (Hamel et al., 1982; Weichman et al., 1982; Samhoun and Piper, 1983). Inhalation of leukotriene D_4 produces long-lasting changes in pulmonary mechanics that are antagonized by the leukotriene antagonist FPL55712. Human parenchymal tissue is less sensitive to leukotrienes than guinea pig parenchyma. Leukotriene B_4 also contracts human isolated bronchus, but again, tachyphylaxis rapidly develops (Samhoun and Piper, 1983). In guinea pig trachea, leukotriene-induced contractions are potentiated in the presence of indomethacin, perhaps on account of the release of a constrictor lipoxygenase product or inhibition of release of dilator prostaglandins (Adcock and Garland, 1980; Piper and Tippins, 1982).

Leukotrienes C_4 and D_4 have selective actions on the small airways of the lung and, although they produce a modest fall in specific airway conductance, cause a preferential reduction in compliance (Drazen et al., 1980). In one initial study, when given by aerosol to two normal human volunteers, LTC_4 and LTD_4 had bronchoconstrictor activity (Holroyde et al., 1981). In another study, inhaled LTC_4 was much more potent than histamine in causing long-lasting reduction in expiratory volume and causing wheezing and tightness of the chest (Weiss et al., 1982). Although coughing has been described after LTC_4 inhalation (Holroyde et al., 1981), Weiss et al. (1982) reported that, in contrast to histamine, LTC_4 showed no signs of acting on central airways.

The long duration of the leukotriene-induced effects resembles those seen in asthma and suggests a role for these substances as mediators of allergic airway constriction.

C. Secretion of Mucus

Indirect evidence based on the ability of the leukotriene antagonist FPL55712 to reverse the slowing of mucociliary transport in patients undergoing antigen provocation suggested that leukotrienes might impair airway clearance by stimulating mucous secretion (Ahmed, et al., 1981). Leukotrienes C_4 and D_4 cause secretion of mucins into the lumen of the cat trachea *in vivo*, but these effects can only be demonstrated with concentrations greater than those required to cause exudation of plasma in the skin (Peatfield et al., 1982; Richardson, et al., 1983). The effects of LTC_4 and LTD_4 are weaker than those of other agonists such as adrenoceptor or cholinergic agonists or prostaglandins. Although LTC_4 and LTD_4 stimulated output of mucins from human bronchial strips cultured *in vitro* (Marom et al., 1982), leukotrienes do not stimulate mucus secretion from cat trachea *in vitro* (Peatfield et al., 1982). This suggests a reflex mechanism might be involved in the leukotriene-induced secretion of mucus *in vivo*, although no changes in blood pressure or respiration indicative of reflex action could be seen during administration of leukotrienes. From these observations it seems that leukotrienes are not potent agonists of mucus secretion and are only likely to be among the mediators that influence secretion of mucins into inflamed airways.

D. Microvasculature

When injected intradermally into guinea pig skin, leukotrienes C_4 and D_4 cause exudation of plasma as measured by extravasation of ^{131}I-labeled albumin and of Evan's or Coomassie blue dye (Lewis *et al.,* 1980; Peck *et al.,* 1981). Leukotriene C_4 is much weaker than LTD_4 in stimulating plasma exudation on account of its vasoconstrictor action (see later). Leukotriene E_4 also induces exudation of plasma but is less potent than LTC_4 and LTD_4. In guinea pig skin, leukotriene-induced exudation of plasma is potentiated by vasodilator prostaglandins such as prostaglandin E_2 or I_2 (Peck *et al.,* 1981).

In addition to causing plasma leakage, leukotrienes C_4 and D_4 are unusual compounds in also having a vasoconstrictor action in guinea pig skin. Leukotriene C_4 is the most active constrictor, causing blanching at injection sites (Drazen *et al.,* 1980; Peck *et al.,* 1981), and the LTC_4-induced vasoconstriction is sufficient to mask the exudation of plasma. The potentiation of plasma exudation by prostaglandins is probably due to reversal of leukotriene-induced vasoconstriction. Considerable species variation occurs in the action of leukotrienes in the microvasculature of the skin; in human skin, LTC_4 and LTD_4 are potent vasodilators and produce wheal and flare responses at low concentrations (Bisgaard *et al.,* 1982; Camp *et al.,* 1982). Leukotriene B_4 also produces vascular permeability changes when injected into rabbit, rat, and guinea pig skin in the presence of a vasodilator prostaglandin (Bray *et al.,* 1981a). This action of LTB_4 is dependent on the presence of neutrophils and may result from the interaction of PMNs with the vascular endothelium (Wedmore and Williams, 1981).

The C-6 amino acid-substituted leukotrienes, LTC_4, LTD_4, and LTE_4, are also active in the terminal vascular bed of the hamster cheek pouch *in vivo,* where they cause plasma leakage from postcapillary venules and vasoconstriction in the terminal arterioles (Dahlén *et al.,* 1981). In this preparation the leukotriene-induced vasoconstriction is equivalent to that of angiotensin II. However, plasma leakage and vasoconstriction are not interrelated, since leukotrienes have virtually no vasoconstrictor action at doses that cause near-maximum plasma exudation. Leukotrienes are at least 1000 times as potent as histamine in causing plasma leakage, which is thought to be a result of a direct action on the endothelial lining in the postcapillary venules. Leukotriene B_4 also caused exudation of plasma but was less active than LTC_4, LTD_4, and LTE_4. The response to LTB_4 was slow in onset and, as in the skin, dependent on adhering PMNs in the vascular bed (Bjork *et al.*, 1982).

Leukotriene B_4 is a potent chemotactic and chemokinetic agent for PMNs, its isomers $(5S,12R)$-all-*trans*-LTB_4 and $(5S,12S)$-all-*trans*-LTB_4 being less active (Ford-Hutchinson *et al.*, 1980; Goetzl and Pickett, 1980; Smith *et al.*, 1980). The peptidolipid leukotrienes do not share this action. Leukotriene B_4 has comparable biological activity to other potent chemotactic agents such as the synthetic peptide, formylmethionylleucylphenylalanine, the complement-derived peptide C_{5a}, and platelet-activating factor.

Leukotriene B_4 is also chemotactic for eosinophils. The accumulation of leukocytes also occurs when LTB_4 is administered *in vivo* into rabbit skin (Bray *et al.*, 1981b), guinea pig peritoneal cavity (Smith *et al.*, 1980), rabbit eye (Bhattacherjee *et al.*, 1981), hamster cheek pouch (Bray *et al.*, 1981b), and abraded skin of human forearm (Bray *et al.*, 1981b). Chemoattraction of leukocytes appears to be the main action of LTB_4 in the microvasculature, since exudation of plasma usually requires higher concentrations of LTB_4 and is dependent on the presence of PMNs. It is of interest that LTD_4 has no action on cell migration *in vitro* but that falls in leukocyte counts occur in rats and monkeys following administration of LTD_4 (Feuerstein *et al.*, 1981; Casey *et al.*, 1982; Smedegård *et al.*, 1982).

E. Cardiovascular System

Leukotrienes C_4 and D_4 have potent effects in the cardiovascular system. These actions show some species variation, sometimes involve release of cyclooxygenase products, and also differ according to the route of administration. When given intravenously (iv) in the guinea pig, LTC_4 and LTD_4 cause an initial hypertensive response, which is probably reflex in origin resulting from bronchoconstriction, followed by long-lasting hypotension (Drazen *et al.*, 1980; Piper *et al.*, 1981). When leukotrienes are given intraarterially (ia), the hypertensive phase is less marked but the hypotension more prolonged. Cyclooxygenase products are probably involved in this response, since indomethacin inhibits the hypertension and shortens the duration of the hypotension. In conscious guinea pigs, after a brief pressor phase, LTD_4 (given iv) causes a long-lasting hypotensive effect that is accompanied by reflex bradycardia (Lux *et al.*, 1983). In this preparation indomethacin prolongs the hypotensive phase. In spontaneously hypertensive rats, LTD_4 causes an initial hypotension, then brief hypertension, followed by prolonged hypotension in doses that do not reduce the blood pressure of normotensive rats (Feuerstein *et al.*, 1981). Changes in blood pressure are also accompanied by changes in heart rate. The long-lasting hypotension was attenuated by indomethacin. Leukotrienes have different effects in the cardiovascular system of the cat; when given iv, LTC_4, LTD_4, and LTE_4 all cause dose-related increases in blood pressure, LTE_4 being less potent than LTC_4 or LTD_4 (Feniuk et al., 1983). In primates (Macaca irus), LTC_4 administered into the right atrium cause a transient rise in mean arterial pressure followed by long-lasting hypotension during which cardiac output is reduced. Right and left atrial pressures are similarly affected, reflecting increased resistance in both pulmonary and systemic vascular beds (Smedegård et al., 1982). Although histamine has similar actions, these are of much shorter duration than LTC_4 effects. When given by aerosol, LTC_4 evokes long-lasting changes in pulmonary function, including increase in pulmonary arterial pressure, but has only small pressor effects on systemic arterial pressure (Smedegård et al., 1982). In another species of monkey (M. mulatta), LTD_4 given by inhalation has less effect but shows a decrease in mean arterial pressure after iv injection (Casey et al., 1982). Leukotriene D_4 is a potent pulmonary and systemic vasoconstrictor in the newborn lamb and causes an initial hypotensive response, which is probably mediated by a cyclooxygenase product (Yokochi et al., 1982).

Leukotrienes have actions on cardiac function and are potent vasoconstrictors in the coronary circulation in vivo and in vitro, and, as with other actions of leukotrienes, species differences occur. In guinea pig isolated perfused hearts (constant pressure), LTC_4 and LTD_4 cause marked reduction in coronary flow (Fig. 3) (Burke et al., 1982; Letts and Piper, 1982). A decrease in contractility occurs with the reduction in flow, but no arrhythmias or changes in heart rate. The reduction in flow is due to a direct vasoconstrictor action in the coronary circulation, since neither LTC_4 nor LTD_4 have any direct action on spontaneously beating atria or driven ventricular strips (Letts and Piper, 1982). As in guinea pig skin, LTC_4 is the most active vasoconstrictor. In rat hearts, LTD_4 causes a similar reduction in flow but reduces the spontaneous heart rate to a greater extent than contractility, indicating an action on conductivity in this species (Letts and Piper, 1983). Leukotriene E_4 has similar actions in guinea pig and rat hearts but is 10–15 times less active (Letts and Piper, 1983). In rabbit and cat isolated hearts, LTC_4 and LTD_4 also has potent actions in reducing coronary flow (Letts and Piper, 1983). Leukotriene B_4 has no action in perfused hearts of any species. The actions of leukotrienes in guinea pig and rat hearts are antagonized by FPL-55712. Indomethacin partially inhibits the actions of LTC_4 and LTD_4 in guinea pig hearts but has no action in rat, rabbit, or cat (Letts and Piper, 1982; Letts et al., 1983).

The vasoconstrictor cyclooxygenase product generated by leukotrienes in guinea pig heart is unidentified, because there was no evidence of release of thromboxane A_2 into the heart effluent and a thromboxane synthetase in-

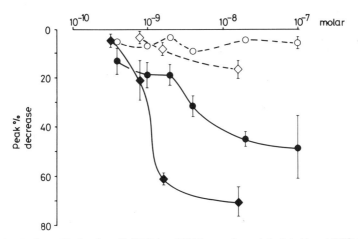

Fig. 3. Actions of leukotriene C_4 (LTC$_4$) and LTD$_4$ on guinea pig isolated heart. LTC$_4$ (◆) and LTD$_4$ (●) caused dose-related reduction in coronary flow. LTC$_4$ (2.0×10^{-8} M) caused a maximum reduction of $71 \pm 6\%$, whereas the maximum reduction produced by LTD$_4$ (1.6×10^{-8} M) was $45 \pm 2\%$. Effects on rate: LTC$_4$ (◇); LTD$_4$ (○). Vertical axis, peak percentage reduction. Horizontal axis, log dose of LTC$_4$ and LTD$_4$. Vertical bars, SEM ($n = 3$–5 per dose). (From Letts and Piper, 1982, with permission.)

hibitor does not affect leukotriene actions in the heart (Letts and Piper, 1983). The effects of LTC$_4$ and LTD$_4$ on coronary circulation of guinea pig hearts may contribute to the hypotensive effects seen *in vivo.*

In anesthetized greyhounds where the left anterior descending coronary artery is perfused with carotid blood, intracoronary injections of LTD$_4$ cause long-lasting dose-related reductions in mean coronary flow (Letts *et al.*, 1983) (Fig. 4). Leukotriene D$_4$ administered by this route has little effect on systemic arterial blood pressure, heart rate, or cardiac output, although LTD$_4$-induced falls in coronary flow are associated with slight increases in *dp/dt*. After administration of LTD$_4$, small discrete hemorrhages develop on the surface of the heart, mainly along the large coronary arteries, although there was no evidence of vascular leakage (Evan's blue dye) or structural damage. Intracoronary injections of LTC$_4$ and LTD$_4$ in similar preparations of pig are more potent in causing prolonged reduction in coronary flow than in the dog (Letts *et al.*, 1983) (Fig. 5). Leukotrienes cause a slight transient decrease in *dp/dt* but have little other action on cardiovascular parameters. Indomethacin does not affect leukotriene-induced reduction in coronary flow in dogs or pigs (Letts *et al.*, 1983). In both dog and pig, LTD$_4$ is more active than angiotensin. Leukotriene D$_4$ also shows very potent vasoconstrictor actions in the coronary circulation of the sheep and produced local coronary constriction and impaired ventricular contraction resulting from

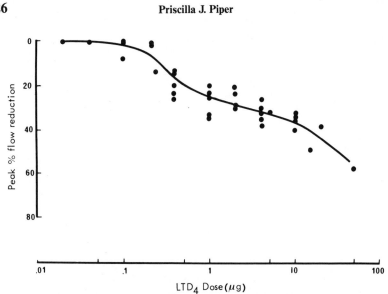

Fig. 4. Percentage reduction in flow in the anterior descending coronary artery of the greyhound following bolus injections of LTD$_4$ into the blood perfusing the artery.

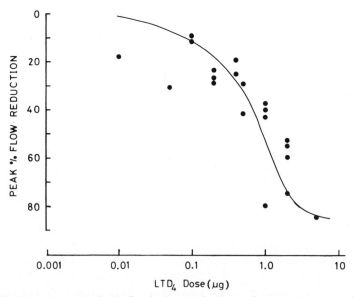

Fig. 5. Percentage reduction in flow in the anterior descending coronary artery of the pig following bolus injections of LTD$_4$ into the blood perfusing the artery. (From Letts *et al.*, 1983, with permission.)

the myocardial ischemia (Michelassi *et al.,* 1982). The biological activity of LTD_4 rapidly disappears in contact with circulating blood (P. J. Piper, unpublished), and LTC_3 has been shown to be rapidly degraded in monkeys and guinea pigs *in vivo* (Hammarström, 1982), so that leukotrienes do not appear to be circulating hormones, which makes their local actions in individual vascular beds of special interest. For instance, the C-6 amino acid-substituted leukotrienes exhibit potent vasoconstrictor actions in the coronary circulation of all species so far investigated, and they have been shown to act directly on isolated coronary arteries (Kito *et al.,* 1981). A 5-lipoxygenase system is present in porcine coronary arteries, and the vessels generate a leukotriene-like substance when challenged by A23187 (Piper *et al.,* 1983b). The possibility therefore exists of leukotrienes being generated from vascular tissue in pathological conditions and acting locally to cause vasoconstriction.

F. Biological Responses of Leukotriene Sulfones

Sulfones of LTC_4, D_4, E_4, and F_4 are potent constrictors of indomethacin-treated guinea pig trachea *in vitro,* being about equiactive with leukotriene sulfides (Jones *et al.,* 1982). The sulfones also cause bronchoconstriction in guinea pigs *in vivo,* LTC_4-sulfone being less active than the sulfide. As with leukotriene sulfides, responses to sulfones are of slow onset and long duration, and are partially reversed by FPL55712. Although the release of leukotriene sulfones has not yet been confirmed, they may be released in and contribute to the signs of various allergic conditions.

IV. CONCLUSIONS

Leukotrienes are a novel group of arachidonic acid metabolites that have biological actions often more potent than those of previously known agonists such as histamine. These actions (see Table I) suggest that leukotrienes may have a role in various pathological conditions. The potent chemotactic and chemokinetic actions of LTB_4, which are dependent on the presence of PMNs, suggest that LTB_4 has a role in inflammatory conditions and tissue damage. Evidence has been provided for this by the detection of LTB_4 in synovial fluid from patients with rheumatoid arthritis (Goetzl and Pickett, 1980) and gout (Rae *et al.,* 1982), and the release of LTB_4 together with mono-HETEs from abraded lesional areas of skin of psoriatics (Brain *et al.,* 1983). Leukotrienes C_4 and D_4 cause changes in pulmonary mechanics — including reduction in expiratory flow, tightness of the chest, and wheezing — that are of slow onset and long duration, suggesting that these leukotrienes may have a role in respiratory diseases such as asthma. Leukotrienes may also act with other mediators to contribute to secretion of mucus in inflamed airways. The vasoconstrictor actions of LTC_4 and LTD_4 on the coronary circulation of various species suggest that they may be involved in conditions such as myocardial ischemia and angina. From these observations it will be of great interest to investigate the effects of leukotriene antagonists and lipoxygenase inhibitors in these disease states.

REFERENCES

Adcock, J. J., and Garland, L. G. (1980). *Br. J. Pharmacol.* **69**, 167–169.

Ahmed, T., Greenblatt, D. W., Birch, S., Marchette, B., and Wanner, A. (1981). *Am. Rev. Respir. Dis.* **124**, 110–114.

Anderson, M. E., Allison, D. R. D., and Meister, A. (1982). *Proc. Natl. Acad. Sci. U.S.A.* **79**, 1088–1091.

Bach, M. K., and Brashler, J. R. (1974). *J. Immunol.* **113**, 2040–2044.

Bhattacherjee, P., Hammond, B., Salmon, J. A., Stepney, R., and Eakins, K. E. (1981). *Eur. J. Pharmacol.* **73**, 21–28.

Bisgaard, H., Kristensen, J., and Sondergaard, J. (1982). *Prostaglandins* **23**, 797–801.

Bjork, J., Hedqvist, P., and Arfors, K.-E. (1982). *Inflammation* **6**, 189–200.

Borgeat, P., and Samuelsson, B. (1979a). *J. Biol. Chem.* **254**, 7865–7869.

Borgeat, P., and Samuelsson, B. (1979b). *Proc. Natl. Acad. Sci. U.S.A.* **76**, 3213–3217.

Borgeat, P., Hamberg, M., and Samuelsson, B. (1976). *J. Biol. Chem.* **251**, 7816–7820.

Brain, S. D., Camp, R. D. R., Dowd, P. M., Kobza Black, A., Woollard, P. M., Mallet, A. I., and Greaves, M. W. (1983). *In* "Leukotrienes and Other Lipoxygenase Products" (P. J. Piper, ed.), pp. 248–254. Wiley, Chichester.

Bray, M. A., Cunningham, F. M., Ford-Hutchinson, A. W., and Smith, M. J. H. (1981a). *Br. J. Pharmacol.* **72**, 483–486.

Bray, M. A., Ford-Hutchinson, A. W., and Smith, M. J. H. (1981b). *In* "SRS-A and Leukotrienes" (P. J. Piper, ed.), pp. 253–270. Wiley, Chichester.

Brocklehurst, W. E. (1960). *J. Physiol. (London)* **151**, 416–435.

Burke, J. A., Levi, R., Guo, Z.-G., and Corey, E. J. (1982). *J. Pharmacol. Exp. Ther.* **221**, 235–241.

Camp, R. D. R., Coutts, A. A., Greaves, M. W., Kay, A. B., and Walport, M. J. (1982). *J. Invest. Dermatol.* **78**, 329.

Casey, L., Clarke, J., Fletcher, J., and Ramwell, P. W. (1982). *In* "Leukotrienes and Other Lipoxygenase Products" (B. Samuelsson and R. Paoletti, eds.), pp. 201–210. Raven Press, New York.

Dahlén, S.-E., Hedqvist, P., Hammarström, S., and Samuelsson, B. (1980). *Nature (London)* **228**, 484–486.

Dahlén, S.-E., Bjork, J., Hedqvist, P., Arfors, K.-E., Hammarström, S., Lindgren, N.-A., and Samuelsson, B. (1981). *Proc. Natl. Acad. Sci. U.S.A.* **78**, 3887–3891.

Drazen, J. M., Austen, K. F., Lewis, R. A., Clark, D. A., Goto, G., Marfat, A., and Corey, E. J. (1980). *Proc. Natl. Acad. Sci. U.S.A.* **77**, 4354–4358.

Feldberg, W., and Kellaway, C. H. (1938). *J. Physiol. (London)* **94**, 187–226.

Feniuk, L., Kennedy, I., and Whelan, C. J. (1983). *In* "Leukotrienes and Other Lipoxygenase Products" (P. J. Piper, ed.), pp. 108–112. Wiley, Chichester.

Feuerstein, G., Zukowska-Grojec, Z., and Kopin, I. J. (1981). *Eur. J. Pharmacol.* **76**, 107–110.

Ford-Hutchinson, A. W., Bray, M. A., Doig, M. V., Shipley, M. E., and Smith, M. J. H. (1980). *Nature (London)* **286**, 264–265.

Ford-Hutchinson, A. W., Piper, P. J., and Samhoun, M. N. (1982). *Br. J. Pharmacol.* **76**, 215–220.

Girard, Y., Larue, M., Jones, T. R., and Rokach, J. (1982). *Tetrahedron Lett.* **23**, 1023–1026.

Goetzl, E. J., and Pickett, W. C. (1980). *J. Immunol.* **125**, 1789–1791.

Hamel, R., and Ford-Hutchinson, A. W. (1983). Prostaglandins (in press).

Hamel, R., Masson, P., Ford-Hutchinson, A. W., Jones, T. R., Brunet, G., and Piechuta, H. (1982). *Prostaglandins* **24**, 419–432.

Hammarström, S. (1982). *In* "Leukotrienes and Other Lipoxygenase Products" (B. Samuelsson and R. Paoletti, eds.), pp. 83–101. Raven Press, New York.

Hammarström, S., Murphy, R. C., Samuelsson, B., Clark, D. A., Mioskowski, C., and Corey, E. J. (1979). *Biochem. Biophys. Res. Commun.* **91**, 1266–1272.

Holroyde, M. C., Altounyan, R. E. C., Cole, M., Dixon, M., and Elliott, E. V. (1981). *Lancet* **2**, 17–18.

Jakschik, B. A., Falkenhein, S., and Parker, C. W. (1977). *Proc. Natl. Acad. Sci. U.S.A.* **74**, 4577–4581.

Jones, T., Masson, P., Hamel, R., Brunet, G., Holme, G., Girard, Y., Larue, M., and Rokach, J. (1982). *Prostaglandins* **24**, 279–291.

Kito, G., Okuda, H., Ohkawa, S., Terao, S., and Kikuchi, K. (1981). *Life Sci.* **29**, 1325–1332.

Krell, R. D., Osborn, R., Vickery, L., Falcone, K., O'Donell, M., Gleason, J., Kinzig, C., and Bryan, D. (1981). *Prostaglandins* **22**, 387–409.

Krell, R. D., Tsai, B. S., and Giles, R. E. (1983). *In* "Leukotrienes and Other Lipoxygenase Products" (P. J. Piper, ed.), pp. 222–233. Wiley, Chichester.

Letts, L. G., and Piper, P. J. (1982). *Br. J. Pharmacol.* **76**, 169–176.

Letts, L. G., and Piper, P. J. (1983). *In* "Leukotrienes and Other Lipoxygenase Products" (B. Samuelsson and R. Paeoletti, eds.), pp. 391–396. Raven Press, New York.

Letts, L. G., Piper, P. J., and Newman, D. L. (1983). *In* "Leukotrienes and Other Lipoxygenase Products" (P. J. Piper, ed.), pp. 94–107. Wiley, Chichester.

Lewis, R. A., Drazen, J. M., Austen, K. F., Clark, D. A., and Corey, E. J. (1980). *Biochem. Biophys. Res. Commun.* **96**, 271–277.

Lux, W. E., Feuerstein, G., Smith, G. P., and Faden, A. I. (1983). *In* "Leukotrienes and Other Lipoxygenase Products" (P. J. Piper, ed.), pp. 338–342. Wiley, Chichester.

Marom, Z., Shelhamer, J. H., Bach, M. K., Morton, D. R., and Kaliner, M. (1982). *Am. Rev. Respir. Dis.* **126**, 449–451.

Michelassi, F., Landa, L., Hill, R. D., Lowenstein, E., Watkins, W. D., Petkau, A. J., and Zapol, W. M. (1982). *Science* **217**, 841–843.

Morris, H. R., Taylor, G. W., Piper, P. J., Sirois, P., and Tippins, J. R. (1978). *FEBS Lett.* **87**, 203–206.

Morris, H. R., Piper, P. J., Taylor, G. W., and Tippins, J. R. (1979a). *Br. J. Pharmacol.* **67**, 179–184.

Morris, H. R., Taylor, G. W., Piper, P. J., and Tippins, J. R. (1979b). *Agents Actions, Suppl.* **6**, 27–36.

Morris, H. R., Taylor, G. W., Piper, P. J., Samhoun, M. N., and Tippins, J. R. (1980a). *Prostaglandins* **19**, 185–201.

Morris, H. R., Taylor, G. W., Piper, P. J., and Tippins, J. R. (1980b). *Nature (London)* **285**, 104–106.

Morris, H. R., Taylor, G. W., Jones, C. M., Piper, P. J., Samhoun, M. N., and Tippins, J. R. (1982). *Proc. Natl. Acad. Sci. U.S.A.* **79**, 4838–4842.

Murphy, R. C., Hammarström S., and Samuelsson, B. (1979). *Proc. Natl. Acad. Sci. U.S.A.* **76**, 4275–4279.

Ohnishi, H., Kosuzume, H., Kitamura, Y., Yamaguchi, K., Nobuhara, M., and Suzuki, Y. (1980). *Prostaglandins* **20**, 655–666.

Orange, R. P., Stechschulte, D. J., and Austen, K. F. (1970). *J. Immunol.* **105**, 1087–1095.

Peatfield, A. C., Piper, P. J., and Richardson, P. S. (1982). *Br. J. Pharmacol.* **77**, 391–393.

Peck, M. J., Piper, P. J., and Williams, T. J. (1981). *Prostaglandins* **21**, 315–321.

Piper, P. J., and Samhoun, M. N. (1981). *Prostaglandins* **21**, 793–803.

Piper, P. J., and Samhoun, M. N. (1982). *Br. J. Pharmacol.* **77**, 267–275.

Piper, P. J., Tippins, J. R., Morris, H. R., and Taylor, G. W. (1979). *Agents Actions, Suppl.* **4**, 37–48.

Piper, P. J., Samhoun, M. N., Tippins, J. R., Williams, T. J., Palmer, M. A., and Peck, M. J. (1981). *In* "SRS-A and Leukotrienes" (P. J. Piper, ed.), pp. 81–99. Wiley, Chichester.

Piper, P. J., Letts, L. G., Tippins, J. R., and Barnett, K. (1983a). *In* "Leukotrienes and Other Lipoxygenase Products" (P. J. Piper, ed.), pp. 299–306. Wiley, Chichester.

Piper, P. J., Letts, L. G., and Galton, S. A. (1983b). *Prostaglandins* **25**, 591–599.

Rae, S. A., Davidson, E. M., and Smith, M. J. H. (1982). *Lancet* **2**, 1122–1124.

Richardson, P. S., Peatfield, A. C., Jackson, D. M., and Piper, P. J. (1983). *In* "Leukotrienes and Other Lipoxygenase Products" (P. J. Piper, ed.), p. 178–187. Wiley, Chichester.

Samhoun, M. N., and Piper, P. J. (1983). *In* "Leukotrienes and Other Lipoxygenase Products" (P. J. Piper, ed.), pp. 161–177. Wiley, Chichester.

Samuelsson, B., and Hammarström, S. (1980). *Prostaglandins* **19**, 645–648.

Samuelsson, B., Borgeat, P., Hammarström, S., and Murphy, R. C. (1979). *Prostaglandins* **17**, 785–787.

Sirois, P., Roy, S., and Borgeat, P. (1981). *Prostaglandins Medicine* **5**, 429–444.

Sirois, P., Roy, S., Borgeat, P., Picard, S., and Vallerand, P. (1982). *Prostaglandins, Leukotrienes Medicine* **8**, 157–170.

Smedegård, G., Hedqvist, P., Dahlén, S.-E., Revenas, B., Hammarström, S., and Samuelsson, B. (1982). *Nature (London)* **295**, 327–329.

Smith, M. J. H., Ford-Hutchinson, A. W., and Bray, M. A. (1980). *J. Pharm. Pharmacol.* **32**, 517–518.

Walker, J. L. (1973). *Adv. Biosci.* **9**, 235–239.

Wedmore, C. V., and Williams, T. J. (1981). *Nature (London)* **289**, 646–650.

Weichman, B. M., and Tucker, S. S. (1982). *Prostaglandins* **24**, 245–253.

Weichman, B. M., Muccitelli, R. M., Osborn, R. R., Holden, D. A., Gleason, J. C., and Wasserman, M. A. (1982). *J. Pharmacol. Exp. Ther.* **222**, 202–208.

Weiss, J. W., Drazen, J. M., Coles, N., McFadden, E. R., Weller, P. W., Corey, E. J., Lewis, R. A., and Austen, K. F. (1982). *Science* **216**, 196–198.

Yokochi, K., Olley, P. M., Sideris, E., Hamilton, F., Huhtanen, D., and Coceani, F. (1982). *In* "Leukotrienes and Other Lipoxygenase Products" (B. Samuelsson and R. Paoletti, eds.), pp. 211–214. Raven Press, New York.

9

Biochemical and Cellular Characteristics of the Regulation of Human Leukocyte Function by Lipoxygenase Products of Arachidonic Acid

DONALD G. PAYAN, DANIEL W. GOLDMAN, AND EDWARD J. GOETZL

Howard Hughes Medical Institute and
Division of Allergy and Immunology, University of California
San Francisco

THE LEUKOTRIENES

I. GENERATION AND DEGRADATION OF LIPOXYGENASE
PRODUCTS OF ARACHIDONIC ACID IN LEUKOCYTES

The recognition of the roles of lipoxygenase products of arachidonic acid in hypersensitivity reactions (Bach *et al.,* 1979; Higgs *et al.,* 1979; Goetzl, 1980b; Samuelsson, 1980; Lewis and Austen, 1981) led to the structural definition of numerous potent lipid factors, which had been identified previously only in terms of mediator activity. Many of the lipoxygenase products can now be quantified precisely by optical and immunochemical techniques (Levine *et al.,* 1980; Lindgren *et al.,* 1982; Salmon *et al.,* 1982). Lipoxygenation of the arachidonic acid released by phospholipases from membrane phospholipids generates one or more hydroperoxyeicosatetraenoic acids (-OOHETEs) in each type of leukocyte (Fig. 1) (Borgeat and Samuelsson, 1979a; Goetzl and Sun, 1979; Jubiz *et al.,* 1981; Lundberg *et al.,* 1981). The compound 5-OOHETE is the exclusive intermediate in the generation by leukocytes of a family of complex 5-hydroxyeicosatetraenoic acids (5-HETEs), termed leukotrienes (LTs), that contain additional polar substituents and three conjugated double bonds (Fig. 1) (Samuelsson, 1980, 1981). The highly reactive 5,6-epoxyeicosa-7,9-*trans*-11,14-*cis*-tetraenoic acid (LTA$_4$) is derived from 5-OOHETE (Borgeat and Samuelsson, 1979b). LTA$_4$ is hydrated enzymatically to form (5S,12R)-dihydroxyeicosa-6,14-*cis*-8,10-*trans*-tetraenoic acid (LTB$_4$), which is a potent stimulus of the migration and other functions of leukocytes *in vitro* and *in vivo* (Ford-Hutchinson *et al.,* 1980; Palmer *et al.,* 1980; Goetzl and Pickett, 1980). LTA$_4$ also combines enzymatically with glutathione to yield (5S)-hydroxy-6-sulfidoglutathionyl-7,9-*trans*-11,14-*cis*-ETE (LTC$_4$), which is converted peptidolytically to (5S)-hydroxy-6-sulfidocysteinylglycine-ETE (LTD$_4$) and subsequently to (5S)-hydroxy-6-sulfidocysteine-ETE (LTE$_4$) (Örning and Hammarström, 1980).

Potent contractile and vasoactive factors, LTC$_4$, LTD$_4$, and LTE$_4$ represent the principal constituents of the slow-reacting substance of anaphylaxis (SRS-A) generated by immunological stimulation of human lung and other tissues (Piper and Vane, 1971; Austen *et al.,* 1974; Bach *et al.,* 1979; Lewis *et al.,* 1979; Drazen *et al.,* 1980). Similarly, 15-OOHETE is transformed to a postulated 14,15-epoxide, which is converted to multiple isomers of 14,15-diHETE and of 8,15-diHETE (Maas *et al.,* 1981; Samuelsson, 1982). Although 12-OOHETE may be as reactive as the initial metabolites of the 5-lipoxygenase and 15-lipoxygenase pathways, the only complex products that have been identified definitively are several trihydroxyeicosatrienoic acids. The 5-lipoxygenation of 12-HETE or the 12-lipoxygenation of 5-HETE generates (5S,12S)-dihydroxyeicosa-8,14-*cis*-6,10-*trans*-tetraenoic acid (8-*cis*-LTB$_4$), which in some instances represents a natural product of the cooperative synthetic activities of leukocytes and platelets. The pathways of generation

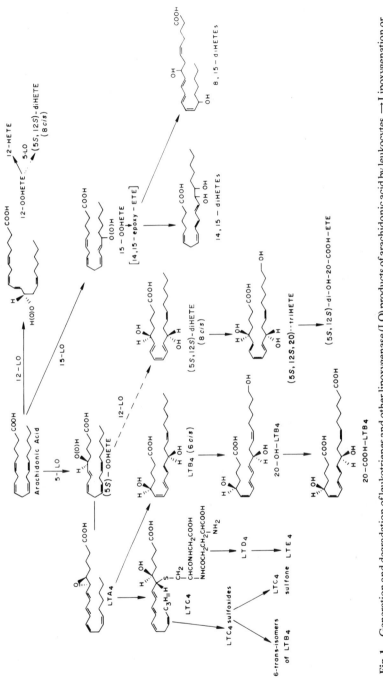

Fig. 1. Generation and degradation of leukotrienes and other lipoxygenase (LO) products of arachidonic acid by leukocytes. → Lipoxygenation or conversion; ---> second lipoxygenation.

and the predominant products of lipoxygenation of arachidonic acid differ both with the class of leukocytes and with the species of origin (Table I). Human granulocytes all produce a substantial quantity of 5-HETE, which is the major mono-HETE of neutrophils and basophils (Goetzl and Sun, 1979; Jakschik and Lee, 1980). In contrast, human (Table I) and murine eosinophils (Turk et al., 1982, 1983) and human peripheral blood T lymphocytes (Goetzl, 1981) generate more 15-HETE than 5-HETE, and 12-HETE/11-HETE is the most prominent mono-HETE product of murine mixed spleen cells, rabbit alveolar macrophages, and canine mastocytoma cells (Table I).

Similar differences are apparent with respect to the leukotriene products. LTB_4 predominates in human neutrophils and T lymphocytes, as well as in murine mixed spleen cells (Borgeat and Samuelsson, 1979a; Goetzl, 1981). In contrast, rabbit alveolar macrophages, dog mastocytoma cells, and human basophils generate approximately equal amounts of the C-6 peptidoleukotrienes and of LTB_4 (Table I). The major C-6 peptidoleukotriene product of the mastocytoma cells and alveolar macrophages is LTC_4, whereas the quantity of LTD_4 far exceeds that of LTC_4 in human and rat basophils after the initial 10 min of incubation (Jakschik and Lee, 1980). The levels pre-

TABLE I

Lipoxygenation of Arachidonic Acid in Leukocytes

Type of leukocyte	Lipoxygenase products (ng/10^6 leukocytes; mean)[a]					
	15-HETE	12-HETE	5-HETE	LTC_4	LTD_4	LTB_4
Human neutrophils	19.8	26.7	89.2	—[b]	—	10.5
Human eosinophils	145.0	43.6	58.0	2.8	—	7.2
Human T lymphocytes	122.0	54.9	64.6	—	—	3.8
Mouse spleen cells	28.2	76.4	32.2	—	—	2.4
Rabbit alveolar macrophages	196.0	243.0	120.0	8.3	4.7	13.8
Dog mastocytoma cells	355.0	409.0	168.0	10.9	6.6	9.3
Human leukemic basophils[c]	31.6	53.8	62.4	0.7	9.4	8.5

[a] 2×10^6–2.6×10^7 leukocytes were incubated in 2 ml of Hanks' solution–0.1 g % ovalbumin for 45 min at 37°C with 100 μg/ml of arachidonic acid. The products were resolved and quantified by optical density as described (Goetzl, 1981); the values were corrected for losses utilizing the level of recovery of 8-[^{3}H]HETE. Each value is the mean of the results of two (mouse spleen cells and dog mastocytoma cells) or three separate analyses that were performed in duplicate.

[b] No product was detected.

[c] Leukocytes were obtained from three patients with chronic myelocytic leukemia, who had basophilia of 17, 35, and 59%, and the basophils were purified to over 90% by centrifugation on metrizamide gradients as described (Paterson et al., 1976).

sented are those attained by the addition of exogenous [^{14}C]arachidonic acid, which is required in order to obtain quantities of each metabolite sufficient for accurate analysis by optical and radiochemical techniques. Specific or other stimuli generally have increased significantly the amount of each compound generated, without altering the relative distribution of the products. The recent development of sensitive radioimmunoassays for specific lipoxygenase products (Levine et al., 1980; Lindgren et al., 1982; Salmon et al., 1982) may now permit reliable assessments of the quantities of mediators in the absence of exogenous arachidonic acid and at cell concentrations relevant to the functional activation of purified and mixed populations of leukocytes.

Leukotrienes are converted to mediators with different activities and are degraded by both oxidative reactions and peptidolysis in leukocytes (Fig. 1). Eosinophils (Goetzl, 1982) and neutrophils (Lee et al., 1982) that have been stimulated to maximum oxidative activity convert approximately one-third of LTC$_4$ to two isomeric sulfoxides and a sulfone of LTC$_4$, and two isomers of 6,8,10-trans-14-cis-LTB$_4$ (all-trans-LTB$_4$) in 10 min at 37°C. The rate of oxidative conversion is decreased by sodium azide, which inhibits eosinophil and neutrophil peroxidases, and by catalase, which destroys H$_2$O$_2$. Partially purified eosinophil peroxidase converts LTC$_4$ to the same products in a reaction that is dependent on the addition of H$_2$O$_2$ and sodium iodide. The peptidolytic transformation of LTC$_4$ to LTD$_4$ by eosinophils and neutrophils occurs at a rate of 10% or less of that of the peroxidative conversions and is independent of the state of activation of oxidative metabolism. LTB$_4$ and 8-cis-LTB$_4$ are converted by a distinct oxidative mechanism to the respective 20-OH derivatives and then to the 20-COOH derivatives, but the molecular mechanisms of the reactions have not been delineated (Fig. 1).

II. REGULATION OF LIPOXYGENASE PATHWAYS BY ENDOGENOUS FACTORS AND PHARMACOLOGICAL AGENTS

Both endogenous factors and pharmacological agents are capable of modulating the lipoxygenation of arachidonic acid in leukocytes with different degrees of specificity. Normal concentrations of vitamin E are required for optimum rates of 5-lipoxygenation, as well as cyclooxygenation, of arachidonic acid in leukocytes, presumably in order to prevent oxidative damage to the enzymes (Goetzl, 1980a). At higher concentrations of vitamin E, which can be achieved in vivo by the administration of pharmacological doses, both 5-lipoxygenation and cyclooxygenation are suppressed significantly (Chan et al., 1980; Ali et al., 1980; Gweber et al., 1980). The cellular level and composition of substrates for oxygenation are influenced by several factors. For example, it is possible to replace arachidonic acid with eicosa-pentaenoic acid in membrane phospholipids, by appropriate dietary manipulation, so that 5-lipoxygenation then yields the mediators LTB_5, LTC_5, and LTD_5, which are generally less potent than the corresponding metabolites of arachidonic acid (Hammarström, 1980; Goetzl and Pickett, 1981). Products of other pathways of lipoxygenation may exert feedback control on the rate of 5-lipoxygenation. The products 15-OOHETE and 15-HETE inhibit 5-lipoxygenation in neutrophils and T lymphocytes and 12-lipoxygenation in platelets, at concentrations attained in stimulated cells, without inhibiting cyclooxygenation (Vanderhoek et al., 1980a,b; Goetzl, 1981). In basophils and mast cells of some species, 15-HETE enhances the rate of 5-lipoxygenation. In some circumstances, 15-HETE also may suppress the activity of the phospholipase(s) that release arachidonic acid.

Pharmacological agents also generally lack selectivity in the inhibition of lipoxygenation of arachidonic acid. Of the acetylenic class of antagonists, eicosatriynoic acid preferentially suppresses lipoxygenation as compared to cyclooxygenation, whereas octadecadiynoic acid exhibits the opposite specificity (Vanderhoek and Lands, 1973; Hammarström, 1977). Similarly, nordihydroguaiaretic acid and benoxaprofen are only moderately more potent as inhibitors of lipoxygenation than cyclooxygenation (Tappel et al., 1953; Walker and Dawson, 1979). Reports of the capacity of aspirin and indomethacin to block the conversion of various OOHETEs to the corresponding HETEs remain to be confirmed with isolated enzyme systems (Siegel et al., 1980a,b).

III. LIPOXYGENASE PRODUCTS OF ARACHIDONIC ACID AS MEDIATORS OF PMN-LEUKOCYTE AND MONOCYTE FUNCTION

A. Migration, Adherence, Degranulation, and the Expression of Receptors

The earliest results of in vitro studies of the leukocyte-directed activities of lipoxygenase products of arachidonic acid demonstrated that mono-HETEs (Goetzl et al., 1977; Goetzl and Sun, 1979; Snyderman and Goetzl, 1981) and LTB_4 (Ford-Hutchinson et al., 1980; Goetzl et al., 1980a, 1981b; Goetzl and Pickett, 1980; Palmer et al., 1980) stimulate the chemotaxis of PMN leukocytes and eosinophils, but not of monocytes. In modified Boyden micropore filter chambers, LTB_4 evokes neutrophil and eosinophil chemotactic responses in vitro that attain 50% of maximal levels at concentrations of 3×10^{-9} and 10^{-8} M, respectively, and achieve a peak equal in magnitude to the maximal responses to C5a and the N-formylmethionyl peptides (Ford-

Hutchinson *et al.*, 1980; Goetzl and Pickett, 1980; Palmer *et al.*, 1980). A rank order of chemotactic potency is manifested, such that $LTB_4 \gg$ 5-HETE $\gg$ 8-HETE $=$ 9-HETE $>$ 11-HETE $=$ 12-HETE, whereas 15-HETE, LTC_4, LTD_4, and trihydroxyeiocsatrienoic acids are not chemotactic. Acetylation of the hydroxyl groups or alterations in the double bonds of the triene portion of LTB_4 reduce the chemotactic potency for PMN leukocytes (Goetzl and Pickett, 1981), which indicates that both the free hydroxyl groups and the sequence of conjugated double bonds are functionally critical determinants. The PMN-leukocyte chemotactic potency of LTB_4 also exceeds by several fold that of the diHETEs generated by the 15-lipoxygenase pathway (Jubiz *et al.*, 1981) and of the 20-OH and 20-COOH derivatives of LTB_4 (Samuelsson, 1982), suggesting that ω oxidation may represent one pathway for inactivation of LTB_4.

The compounds LTB_4 and 5-HETE also stimulate the random migration of PMN leukocytes in the absence of a concentration gradient, a phenomenon termed chemokinesis (Goetzl and Pickett, 1980; Goetzl *et al.*, 1980a). The preincubation of suspensions of neutrophils with maximally chemotactic concentrations of LTB_4 at 37°C induces a stimulus-specific state of unresponsiveness (termed deactivation) to subsequent homologous chemotactic stimulation that is functionally similar to that established by other stimuli (Goetzl *et al.*, 1981a).

At concentrations approximately 3- to 10-fold higher than those required to stimulate maximum chemotaxis, LTB_4 evokes a wide range of PMN-leukocyte responses that are independent of migration. Neutrophil and eosinophil adherence to Sephadex G-25 columns is increased by LTB_4 in a concentration-dependent manner and attains 175–200% of the control level at $3 \times 10^{-8}\ M\ LTB_4$ (Pickett *et al.*, 1982). Also, LTB_4 elicits PMN-leukocyte aggregation, as assessed by standard platelet aggregometry techniques (Ford-Hutchinson *et al.*, 1982). The maximal lysosomal degranulation of PMN leukocytes stimulated by LTB_4 is only 25–30% of that achieved by C5a or N-formylmethionine peptides (Goetzl and Pickett, 1980). The compounds LTB_4 and 5-HETE, but not LTC_4, LTD_4, or 15-HETE, enhance the expression of C3b receptors on human neutrophils (Goetzl *et al.*, 1980a) and eosinophils (Nagy *et al.*, 1982) *in vitro*, with lesser increases in IgG-Fc receptors, as assessed by rosetting techniques.

B. Receptors for LTB₄

A distinct subset of human PMN-leukocyte receptors for LTB_4 has been defined by both conventional techniques and methods utilizing acetone at $-78°C$ to extract the unbound and nonreceptor-bound $[^3H]LTB_4$. LTB_4 is bound stereospecifically by 26,000 to 40,000 receptors per PMN leukocyte, which have a K_D of 10.8–13.9 nM. Analyses of competitive inhibition of the binding of [^{3}H]LTB$_4$ to PMN leukocytes by analogs of LTB$_4$ and other chemotactic factors revealed a close correlation between the chemotactic potency of related 5-lipoxygenase products and their capacity to inhibit the binding of [^{3}H]LTB$_4$ (Goldman and Goetzl, 1982). Concentrations of (5S,12S)-all-*trans*-LTB$_4$ and of 5-HETE 100 times higher than LTB$_4$ are required to inhibit by 50% the binding of [^{3}H]LTB$_4$ to PMN leukocytes, which reflects the 100-fold greater chemotactic potency of LTB$_4$ than the other 5-hydroxyl-containing compounds. In contrast, maximally chemotactic concentrations of C5a and N-formylmethionyl peptides fail to inhibit the binding of [^{3}H]LTB$_4$ to PMN leukocytes. LTC$_4$ inhibits PMN-leukocyte chemotactic responses to LTB$_4$ preferentially, as compared with those elicited by other chemotactic factors. However, optimally active concentrations of LTC$_4$ do not interfere with the binding of [^{3}H]LTB$_4$ to PMN leukocytes, which suggests that the functional consequences of the interaction of LTC$_4$ with PMN leukocytes are mediated by a subset of recognition sites that are independent of LTB$_4$ receptors (Goetzl, 1983). This possibility is supported by the observation that LTC$_4$ alone augments the adherence of PMN leukocytes to surfaces.

The level of non-receptor binding of [^{3}H]LTB$_4$ to human PMN leukocytes exceeds that of peptide chemotactic factors and is greater than that of receptor binding at concentrations higher than 25 nM (Goldman and Goetzl, 1982). It is possible that the increased concentrations of lipoxygenase products in regions of leukocyte membranes other than receptors may augment other functions, especially those stimulated maximally by concentrations substantially higher than that required for optimum chemotaxis.

C. Biochemical Concomitants of Cellular Activation

Numerous studies have demonstrated that LTB$_4$ and mono-HETEs modify a wide range of biochemical events in neutrophils and eosinophils. LTB$_4$ and 5-HETE stimulate the influx of calcium and the uptake of hexose into PMN leukocytes, whereas only LTB$_4$ triggers the mobilization of calcium from intracellular stores (Naccache *et al.,* 1981; Bass *et al.,* 1982). At concentrations lower than those required to evoke an optimum chemotactic response, some HETEs increase the level of guanosine 3',5'-cyclic monophosphate (cyclic GMP) in PMN leukocytes to a maximum value within 1 min and for as long as 20 min (Goetzl *et al.,* 1980b). These effects may be part of the biochemical sequence of leukocyte activation, but neither the mechanisms of coupling to activation nor the order of events have been elucidated.

IV. INTERACTIONS OF LIPOXYGENASE AND CYCLOOXYGENASE PRODUCTS OF ARACHIDONIC ACID IN THE MODULATION OF PMN-LEUKOCYTE FUNCTION

The primary effects of cyclooxygenase products on PMN-leukocyte function are limited to the stimulation of chemokinesis and alterations in adherence to surfaces (Goetzl *et al.*, 1979; Spagnulo *et al.*, 1980; Boxer *et al.*, 1980; Weissman *et al.*, 1980). However, both prostaglandins and thromboxane A_2 mediate and modulate the effects of leukotrienes and other lipoxygenase products (Fig. 2). The chemotactic responses of neutrophils and eosinophils to LTB_4 are inhibited by equimolar concentrations of LTC_4 and LTD_4 (Pickett *et al.*, 1982). Nanomolar concentrations of PGD_2 and 10- to 30-fold higher concentrations of PGE_2 evoke chemokinesis and enhance the chemotactic responses to LTB_4 and other stimuli (Goetzl *et al.*, 1979), whereas higher concentrations of each inhibit chemotaxis in association with elevations in the intraleukocyte level of adenosine $3',5'$-cyclic monophosphate (cyclic AMP).

The two compounds LTB_4 and LTC_4 augment PMN-leukocyte adherence to Sephadex G-25 with the same time course and achieve an identical maximum level of adherence, but LTB_4 is three- to sixfold more potent than LTC_4. The enhanced adherence achieved by optimum concentrations of LTC_4 and LTB_4 are suppressed by a mean of approximately 73 and 35%, respectively ($n = 5$), when the PMN leukocytes are preincubated for 10 min at 37°C with 5 μM indomethacin, suggesting the involvement of a cyclooxygenase product of arachidonic acid. The generation of thromboxane A_2 by PMN leukocytes was stimulated two- to threefold by LTC_4, as assessed by radioimmunoassay and quantification of isolated thromboxane B_2, whereas the maximum level of stimulation by LTB_4 was only 40% or less of that achieved

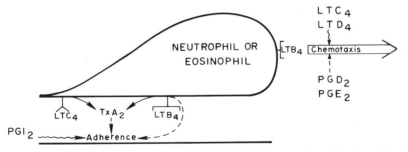

Fig. 2.   Interactions of lipoxygenase and cyclooxygenase products of arachidonic acid in the modulation of PMN-leukocyte function. PG, prostaglandin; Tx, thromboxane; → generation; ---> enhancement; ↝ inhibition.

by LTC$_4$ (Goetzl *et al.,* 1983). Similar concentrations of exogenous thromboxane A$_2$ had been demonstrated previously to augment PMN-leukocyte adherence (Spagnulo *et al.,* 1980). Thus LTB$_4$ increases PMN-leukocyte adherence predominantly by a direct effect, whereas LTC$_4$ stimulates the generation of thromboxane A$_2$ by PMN leukocytes, which accounts for most of the effect of LTC$_4$ on adherence (Fig. 2). PGI$_2$ inhibits PMN-leukocyte adherence, in large part because of an elevation in the intraleukocyte level of cyclic AMP (Boxer *et al.,* 1980).

V. LIPOXYGENASE PRODUCTS OF ARACHIDONIC ACID AS INTRACELLULAR FUNCTIONAL CONSTITUENTS

That some endogenous lipoxygenase products of arachidonic acid may be functionally critical intraleukocyte constituents was suggested initially by the capacity of lipoxygenase inhibitors to suppress a variety of PMN-leukocyte activities, including migration, hexose transport, aggregation, and degranulation (Goetzl *et al.,* 1979, 1980c; Weissman *et al.,* 1980; Naccache *et al.,* 1981; Bass *et al.,* 1982), and by the finding that 5-OOHETE and 5-HETE were capable in some instances of restoring the suppressed activities. The results of similar studies of the participation of products of the 5-lipoxygenation of endogenous arachidonic acid in the activation of T-lymphocyte function are reviewed in Section VI. While the mechanisms of the 5-lipoxygenase dependence of some PMN-leukocyte and T-lymphocyte functions have not been identified, two distinct possibilities have been proposed. Reactive intermediates such as 5-OOHETE can covalently derivatize intracellular PMN-leukocyte peptides, proteins, and other substituents critical to cell function, some of which have been recovered by standard chromatographic procedures from specifically stimulated cells (Goldman and Goetzl, 1981). An alternative hypothesis is based on the observation that leukocytes reincorporate into cellular phospholipids a variable percentage of the 5-HETE generated, but not 12-HETE or LTB$_4$ (Stenson and Parker, 1979). This specific reacylation of phospholipids would alter the properties of the plasma membrane, possibly at the sites of prior deacylation.

VI. LIPOXYGENASE PRODUCTS OF ARACHIDONIC ACID AS MEDIATORS OF T-LYMPHOCYTE FUNCTION

A. Pathways of Lipoxygenation

The results of the first studies of the lipoxygenation of arachidonic acid in human peripheral blood lymphocytes indicated the presence of a 5-lipoxygenase pathway, which was stimulated by the addition of a nonspecific mitogen (Kelly and Parker, 1979). More recently, further definition of the lipoxygenase pathways in highly purified human T lymphocytes has established that arachidonic acid is converted to 15-HETE, 12-HETE, 11-HETE, 5-HETE, LTB_4, and several structural isomers of LTB_4 (Goetzl, 1981) (Table I). The 5-lipoxygenase activity of the T lymphocytes, but not the cyclooxygenase activity, was inhibited noncytotoxically by concentrations of 15-HETE and 15-OOHETE similar to those achieved in stimulated T lymphocytes (Goetzl, 1981), as had been demonstrated for the 5-lipoxygenase of PMN leukocytes (Vanderhoek et al., 1980b) and the 12-lipoxygenase of platelets (Vanderhoek et al., 1980a).

B. T Lymphocyte Migration

The modulation of human T-lymphocyte migration by lipoxygenase metabolites differs from that of PMN leukocytes in two respects. First, T-lymphocyte migration is enhanced only by LTB_4 and 5-HETE, but not by other mono-HETEs at concentrations that evoke PMN-leukocyte responses (Payan and Goetzl, 1981). Second, LTB_4 stimulates T-lymphocyte chemokinesis but not chemotaxis, whereas the response of PMN leukocytes includes both chemotactic and chemokinetic components (Payan and Goetzl, 1981). That the maximum stimulation of human T-lymphocyte chemokinesis and of human PMN-leukocyte chemotaxis are attained by similar concentrations of LTB_4, suggests a fundamental difference in patterns of cellular migration, rather than a stimulus-dependent phenomenon. This contention is supported by the finding that the T lymphocytes also responded chemokinetically but not chemotactically to concanavalin A and to α-thioglycerol (Payan and Goetzl, 1981). Inhibition of both lipoxygenase and cyclooxygenase activities suppressed human T-lymphocyte random migration and chemokinetic responses to several stimuli, whereas inhibition of cyclooxygenase activity alone suppressed only the chemokinetic response to exogenous arachidonic acid, implying that lipoxygenation of endogenous arachidonic acid is a basic prerequisite of lymphocyte motility (Payan and Goetzl, 1981). Micromolar concentrations of 15-OOHETE and 15-HETE, but not 11-HETE, inhibit the rate of 5-lipoxygenation of arachidonic acid in T lymphocytes selectively, without influencing cyclooxygenation (Goetzl, 1981; Bailey et al., 1982). Concentrations of 15-OOHETE and 15-HETE, which are achieved in mitogen-stimulated T lymphocytes and which effectively inhibit the 5-lipoxygenation of arachidonic acid, suppressed both random migration and chemokinesis (Payan and Goetzl, 1981). Maximum suppression of human T-lymphocyte chemokinesis and of random migration was attained at concentrations of 15-HETE as low as 1 to 3 μg/ml, which inhibit maximally the

5-lipoxygenation of arachidonic acid in the T lymphocytes. The effects of 15-HETE on T-lymphocyte migration and 5-lipoxygenase activity are reversed partially by washing the lymphocytes. That the functional effects of 15-HETE on T lymphocytes are attributable predominantly to the inhibition of 5-lipoxygenation of endogenous arachidonic acid was confirmed by the finding that exogenous 5-OOHETE restored lymphocyte chemokinesis to nearly optimal levels in the continued presence of fully inhibitory concentrations of 15-HETE. The 5-lipoxygenation of endogenous arachidonic acid thus appears to be critical to the functional activation of human T-lymphocytes, as well as PMN leukocytes and monocytes.

C. Regulation of the Proliferation of T Lymphocytes and Mononuclear Leukocytes and the Generation of Lymphokines

The generation of lymphokine activity by cultures of T lymphocytes or mixed mononuclear leukocytes stimulated with either mitogen or antigen is suppressed specifically by immunologically relevant concentrations of purified synthetic leukotrienes. The elaboration of leukocyte inhibitory factor (LIF) activity by T lymphocytes and mononuclear leukocytes stimulated with phytohemagglutinin (PHA) is inhibited in a concentration-dependent manner by 10^{-9}–10^{-6} M LTB_4. LTC_4 also suppressed the generation of LIF activity, but exhibited approximately 50% of the potency of LTB_4. The specificity of the suppression of LIF activity by leukotrienes was demonstrated by the lack of effect of 15-HETE and $(5S,12S)$-LTB_4.

The proliferation of PHA-stimulated T lymphocytes and mononuclear leukocytes also is suppressed specifically by distinct products of the lipoxygenation of arachidonic acid, as assessed by the incorporation of [^{3}H]thymidine. LTB_4 inhibits significantly the proliferation of T lymphocytes and, in this respect, is different from human C3a and the terminal octapeptide of C3a, which exert a selective suppressive effect on the generation of LIF without influencing proliferation (Payan et al., 1982, 1983). Thus the initial results demonstrate that products of the 5-lipoxygenation and 15-lipoxygenation of arachidonic acid are not only important mediators of immediate-type hypersensitivity states, but also may modulate significantly immune responses and delayed-type hypersensitivity by their specific effects on T-lymphocyte function.

The accumulated observations of specific regulation of human T-lymphocyte function by concentrations of mast cell or basophil products of the oxygenation of arachidonic acid attained in vitro suggest that immunoregulation may be one of the major in vivo roles of lipid mediators of immediate hypersensitivity responses (Fig. 3). The principal cyclooxygenase metabolite

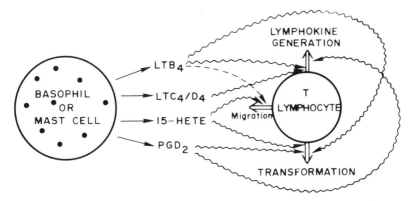

Fig. 3.   Regulation of human T-lymphocyte function by basophil or mast cell-derived products of the oxygenation of arachidonic acid. → Generation; ---> stimulation; ⤳ suppression.

of mast cells and human lung tissue, PGD_2, (Schulman *et al.*, 1981; Lewis *et al.*, 1981), is more potent than PGE_2 in suppressing lymphokine generation and transformation. Both leukotrienes B_4 and C_4 suppress lymphokine generation, whereas only LTB_4 inhibits transformation and stimulates chemokinesis. Another major product of mast cells and basophils, 15-HETE (Table I), suppresses migration (Payan and Goetzl, 1981) and transformation (Bailey *et al.*, 1982), but not lymphokine generation. The interactive effects of mixtures of the different mediators, which may exist *in vivo,* will provide further insights into the mechanisms of immunoregulation by the products of oxygenation of arachidonic acid.

REFERENCES

Ali, M., Gudbranson, C. G., and MacDonald, J. W. D. (1980). *Prostaglandins Med.* **4**, 79–85.

Austen, K. F., Lewis, R. A., Stechschulte, D. J., Wasserman, S. I., and Leid, R. W. (1974). *In* "Progress in Immunology II" (L. Brent and J. Holborow, eds.), Vol. 2, pp. 61–71. North-Holland Publ., New York.

Bach, M. K., Brashler, J. R., Brooks, C. D., and Neerken, J. A. (1979). *J. Immunol.* **122**, 160–165.

Bailey, J. M., Low, C. A., Pupillo, M., Bryant, R. W., and Vanderhoek, J. Y. (1982). *In* "Leukotrienes and Other Lipoxygenase Products" (B. Samuelsson and R. Paoletti, eds.), pp. 341–353. Raven Press, New York.

Bass, D. A., O'Flaherty, J. T., Goetzl, E. J., DeChatelet, L. R., and McCall, C. E. (1981). *Prog. Lipid Res.* **20**, 735–737.

Borgeat, P., and Samuelsson, B. (1979a). *J. Biol. Chem.* **254**, 7865–7868.

Borgeat, P., and Samuelsson, B. (1979b). *Proc. Natl. Acad. Sci. U.S.A.* **76**, 3213–3217.

Boxer, L. A., Allen, J. M., Schmidt, M., Yoder, M., and Baehner, R. L. (1980). *J. Lab. Clin. Med.* **95**, 672–678.

Chan, A. C., Allern, C. E., and Hegarty, P. V. J. (1980). *J. Nutr.* **110**, 66–73.

244 Donald G. Payan, Daniel W. Goldman, and Edward J. Goetzl

Drazen, J. M., Austen, K. F., Lewis, R. A., Clark, D. A., Soto, G., Marfat, A. M., and Corey, E. J. (1980). *Proc. Natl. Acad. Sci. U.S.A.* **77,** 4354–4358.
Ford-Hutchinson, A. W., Bray, M. A., Doig, M. V., Shipley, M. E., and Smith, M. J. H. (1980). *Nature (London)* **286,** 264–265.
Ford-Hutchinson, A. W., Rackham, A., Zamboni, R., Rokach, J., and Roy, S. (1983). *Prostaglandins* **25,** 24–37.
Goetzl, E. J. (1980a). *Nature (London)* **288,** 183–185.
Goetzl, E. J. (1980b). *N. Engl. J. Med.* **303,** 822–825.
Goetzl, E. J. (1981). *Biochem. Biophys. Res. Commun.* **101,** 344–350.
Goetzl, E. J. (1982). *Biochem. Biophys. Res. Commun.* **106,** 270–275.
Goetzl, E. J. (1983). *Fed. Proc. Fed. Am. Soc. Exp. Biol.* **42,** 3128–3131.
Goetzl, E. J., and Pickett, W. C. (1980). *J. Immunol.* **125,** 1789–1791.
Goetzl, E. J., and Pickett, W. C. (1981). *J. Exp. Med.* **153,** 482–487.
Goetzl, E. J., and Sun, F. F. (1979). *J. Exp. Med.* **150,** 406–411.
Goetzl, E. J., Woods, J. M., and Gorman, R. R. (1977). *J. Clin. Invest.* **59,** 179–183.
Goetzl, E. J., Weller, P. F., and Valone, F. H. (1979). *Adv. Inflammation Res.* **14,** 157–167.
Goetzl, E. J., Brash, A. R., Tauber, A. I., Oates, J. A., and Hubbard, W. C. (1980a). *Immunology* **39,** 491–501.
Goetzl, E. J., Hill, H. R., and Gorman, R. R. (1980b). *Prostaglandins* **19,** 71–85.
Goetzl, E. J., Weller, P. F., and Sun, F. F. (1980c). *J. Immunol.* **124,** 926–933.
Goetzl, E. J., Boeynaems, J. M., Oates, J. A., and Hubbard, W. C. (1981a). *Prostaglandins* **22,** 279–288.
Goetzl, E. J., Goldman, D. W., and Valone, F. H. (1981b). *Kroc Found. Ser.* **14,** 169–182.
Goetzl, E. J., Brindley, L. L., and Goldman, D. W. (1983). *Immunology* **50,** 35–41.
Goldman, D. W., and Goetzl, E. J. (1981). *Fed. Proc. Fed. Am. Soc. Exp. Biol.* **40,** 1004.
Goldman, D. W., and Goetzl, E. J. (1982). *J. Immunol.* **129,** 1600–1604.
Gweber, E. T., Trewyn, R. W., and Cornwell, D. G. (1980). *Res. Commun. Chem. Pathol. Pharmacol.* **28,** 361–376.
Hammarström, S. (1977). *Biochim. Biophys. Acta* **487,** 517–519.
Hammarström, S. (1980). *J. Biol. Chem.* **255,** 7093–7094.
Higgs, G. A., Moncada, S., and Vane, J. R. (1979). *Adv. Inflammation Res.* **1,** 413–418.
Jakschik, B. A., and Lee, L. H. (1980). *Nature (London)* **287,** 51–52.
Jubiz, W., Rådmark, O., Lindgren, J. A., Malmsten, C., and Samuelsson, B. (1981). *Biochem. Biophys. Res. Commun.* **99,** 976–980.
Kelly, J. P., and Parker, C. W. (1979). *J. Immunol.* **122,** 1556–1562.
Lee, C. W., Lewis, R. A., Austen, K. F., and Corey, E. J. (1982). *Fed. Proc., Fed. Am. Soc. Exp. Biol.* **41,** 487a.
Levine, L., Alam, I., Gjika, H., Carty, T. J., and Goetzl, E. J. (1980). *Prostaglandins* **20,** 923–933.
Lewis, R. A., and Austen, K. F. (1981). *Nature (London)* **293,** 103–108.
Lewis, R. A., Austen, K. F., Drazen, J. M., Clark, D. A., Marfat, A. M., and Corey, E. J. (1979). *Proc. Natl. Acad. Sci. U.S.A.* **77,** 3710–3714.
Lewis, R. A., Holgate, S. T., Roberts, L. J., Oates, J. A., and Austen, K. F. (1981). *Kroc Found. Ser.* **14,** 239–254.
Lindgren, J. A., Hammarström, S., and Goetzl, E. J. (1983). *FEBS Lett.* **152,** 83–88.
Lundberg, U., Rådmark, O., Malmsten, C., and Samuelsson, B. (1981). *FEBS Lett.* **126,** 127–132.
Maas, R. L., Brash, A. R., and Oates, J. A. (1981). *Proc. Natl. Acad. Sci. U.S.A.* **78,** 5523–5527.
Naccache, P. H., Sha'afi, R. I., Borgeat, P., and Goetzl, E. J. (1981). *J. Clin. Invest.* **67,** 1584–1587.
Nagy, L., Lee, T. H., Goetzl, E. J., Pickett, W. C., and Kay, A. B. (1982). *J. Clin. Exp. Immunol.* **47,** 541–547.
Örning, L., and Hammarström, S. (1980). *J. Biol. Chem.* **255,** 8023–8026.

Palmer, R. M. J., Steprey, R. J., Higgs, G. A., and Eakins, K. E. (1980). *Prostaglandins* **20,** 411–418.
Paterson, N. A. M., Wasserman, S. I., Said, J. W., and Austen, K. F. (1976). *J. Immunol.* **117,** 1356–1362.
Payan, D. G., and Goetzl, E. J. (1981). *J. Clin. Immunol.* **1,** 266–270.
Payan, D. G., and Goetzl, E. J. (1983). *J. Immunol.* **131,** 551–553.
Payan, D. G., Trentham, D. E., and Goetzl, E. J. (1982). *J. Exp. Med.* **156,** 756–765.
Pickett, W. C., Goldman, D. W., and Goetzl, E. J. (1983). *Life Sci.,* (in press).
Piper, P. J., and Vane, J. R. (1971). *Ann. N.Y. Acad. Sci.* **180,** 363–385.
Salmon, J. A., Simmons, P. M., and Palmer, R. M. J. (1982). *Prostaglandins* **24,** 225–235.
Samuelsson, B. (1980). *Trends Pharmacol. Sci.* **1,** 227–230.
Samuelsson, B. (1981). *Kroc Found. Ser.* **14,** 1–12.
Samuelsson, B. (1982). *In* "Leukotrienes and Other Lipoxygenase Products" (B. Samuelsson and R. Paoletti, eds.), pp. 1–17. Raven Press, New York.
Schulman, E. S., Newball, H. H., Demers, L. M., Fitzpatrick, F. A., and Adkinson, N. F. (1981). *Am. Rev. Respir. Dis.* **124,** 402–406.
Siegel, M. I., McConnell, R. T., Porter, N. A., and Cuatrecasas, P. (1980a). *Proc. Natl. Acad. Sci. U.S.A.* **77,** 308–312.
Siegel, M. I., McConnell, R. T., Porter, N. A., Selph, J. L., Turax, J. F., Vinegar, R., and Cuatrecasas, P. (1980b). *Biochem. Biophys. Res. Commun.* **92,** 688–695.
Snyderman, R., and Goetzl, E. J. (1981). *Science* **213,** 830–837.
Spagnulo, P. J., Ellner, J. J., Hassid, A., and Dunn, M. J. (1980). *J. Clin. Invest.* **66,** 406–414.
Stenson, W. F., and Parker, C. W. (1979). *J. Clin. Invest.* **64,** 1457–1465.
Tappel, A. L., Lundberg, W. O., and Boyer, P. D. (1953). *Arch. Biochem. Biophys.* **42,** 293–299.
Turk, J., Maas, R. L., Brash, A. R., Roberts, L. J., and Oates, J. A. (1982). *J. Biol. Chem.* **257,** 7068–7077.
Turk, J., Rand, T. H., Maas, R. L., Lawson, J. L., Brash, A. R., Roberts, L. J., Colley, E. J., and Oates, J. A. (1983). *Biochim. Biophys. Acta* **750,** 78–90.
Vanderhoek, J. Y., and Lands, W. E. M. (1973). *Biochim. Biophys. Acta* **296,** 374–381.
Vanderhoek, J. Y., Bryant, R. W., and Bailey, J. M. (1980a). *J. Biol. Chem.* **255,** 5996–5998.
Vanderhoek, J. Y., Bryant, R. W., and Bailey, J. M. (1980b). *J. Biol. Chem.* **255,** 10064–10065.
Walker, J. R., and Dawson, W. (1979). *J. Pharm. Pharmacol.* **31,** 778–780.
Weissman, G., Smolen, J. E., and Korchak, H. (1980). *Adv. Prostaglandin Thromboxane Res.* **8,** 1637–1646.

10

Pulmonary Pharmacology of the Leukotrienes

A. G. LEITCH

Department of Rheumatology and Immunology
Brigham and Women's Hospital, Harvard Medical School
Boston, Massachusetts

J. M. DRAZEN

Department of Medicine
Brigham and Women's Hospital
Harvard Medical School and
Department of Physiology
Harvard School of Public Health
Boston, Massachusetts

THE LEUKOTRIENES

I. SLOW-REACTING SUBSTANCE OF ANAPHYLAXIS (SRS-A)

A. Background

Slow-reacting substance of anaphylaxis (SRS-A) is now known to be composed of a number of leukotriene constituents. However, before this identification was made, a substantial amount of investigation was conducted on the pharmacological properties of SRS-A generated biologically and purified to various degrees. In order to view leukotriene pharmacology in the proper perspective, it is instructive to review what is known of SRS-A pharmacology.

Feldberg and Kellaway (1938) initially demonstrated the formation and release from envenomed dog and monkey lungs of a substance that caused a delayed and slow contraction of the guinea pig jejunum; subsequently Kellaway and Trethewie (1940) described release of a slow-reacting substance (SRS) during acute anaphylaxis of the guinea pig lung. Brocklehurst (1953, 1960) later reported the formation of an SRS, which he called slow-reacting substance of anaphylaxis (SRS-A), during anaphylaxis of guinea pig, rabbit, monkey, and human lungs. This substance had similar activity to SRS on guinea pig ileum, and its activity was unaffected by the newly developed antihistamine, mepyramine. Release of SRS-A was demonstrated during antigen-induced constriction of bronchioles isolated from subjects with asthma, consistent with a role for SRS-A in antigen-induced bronchoconstriction (Schild *et al.*, 1951) and suggesting that SRS-A might be of major importance in the pathogenesis of human asthma (Orange and Austen, 1969).

Subsequent development of techniques for the generation and partial purification of SRS-A from the rat peritoneal cavity (Orange *et al.*, 1973) from intact guinea pig lung (Engineer *et al.*, 1978a) and from isolated human (Lewis *et al.*, 1974) and pig (Paterson *et al.*, 1981) lung cells allowed investigation of the pulmonary pharmacology of partially purified SRS-A both *in vivo* and *in vitro* (Orange and Austen, 1975).

B. Effects of SRS-A *in Vivo*

Berry and Collier (1964), using histamine-free charcoal-purified material, showed that intravenous (iv) administration of SRS-A to the guinea pig increased the impedance to inflation of guinea pig lungs (Konzett-Rossler preparation) *in vivo*. This action was unaffected by pretreatment with mepyramine, atropine, or bromolysergic acid diethylamide (a serotonin antagonist) but was abolished at low doses of SRS-A by pretreatment with sodium acetylsalicylate. However, bronchoconstriction was observed after higher doses of SRS-A even in the presence of sodium acetylsalicylate, suggesting both a direct effect at high doses and one mediated through cyclooxygenase products at low doses.

In 1974, Drazen and Austen reported that iv administration of SRS-A (purified by the technique of Orange *et al.,* 1973) to the unanesthetized guinea pig caused dose-dependent decrements in pulmonary dynamic compliance (C_{dyn}) but only minor effects on pulmonary resistance. The pulmonary consequences of SRS-A infusion differed in two important respects from the effects of infusion of histamine, bradykinin, and prostaglandin $F_{2\alpha}$ in the same preparation: first, SRS-A had a preferential effect on C_{dyn} when compared with the other agonists, a profile of response suggesting a predominant action in the pulmonary periphery; second, its action was prolonged in duration in comparison with the other three agonists.

Administration of similarly purified SRS-A by aerosol (Patterson *et al.,* 1978) or by intratracheal instillation (Michoud *et al.,* 1979) to anesthetized *Ascaris*-sensitive rhesus monkeys results in changes in pulmonary resistance and C_{dyn} that were slower in onset and more prolonged than the responses to aerosol antigen challenge, histamine, or prostaglandin $F_{2\alpha}$ in the same animals. In the former study, changes in pulmonary resistance and C_{dyn} of similar magnitude occurred, whereas in the latter study, SRS-A–induced decrements in C_{dyn} predominated. It seems likely that these differences could be attributed to the different methods of administration of SRS-A. These studies confirmed the prolonged duration of action of SRS-A–induced airway constriction, the issue of the predominant site of action in the lung being less well defined. Clearly, SRS-A was a peripheral airway agonist; however, the selectivity of this effect was reasonably well but not completely established.

C. Effects of SRS-A *in Vitro*

The contractile effects of SRS-A on a variety of *in vitro* preparations of pulmonary tissues are recorded in Table I. Quantitative comparisons between these observations are complicated by the use of different sources of SRS-A, different degrees of purification of SRS-A, and different approaches to standardization of SRS-A units. Nevertheless, it is apparent that SRS-A constricts airway smooth muscle from a variety of species including the guinea pig, rabbit, cow, and human, and that in the species where lung parenchymal strip responses were studied, the guinea pig and the human, contraction was also observed.

In the guinea pig, the lung parenchymal strip (GPLS) is more sensitive to SRS-A than the trachea when compared with histamine responses (Drazen *et al.,* 1979), in keeping with the *in vivo* observation in this species of a

TABLE I

Effects of SRS-A *in Vitro*[a]

Tissue	SRS	Response	Reference
Human bronchi	SRS[gp]	More sensitive than gp trachea	Berry and Collier (1964)
Guinea pig trachea	SRS[gp]	Contraction	Berry and Collier (1964)
Rabbit trachea	SRS[gp]	Contraction (contractions antagonized by NSAID)	Berry and Collier (1964)
Human bronchi		Contraction	Mathe and Strandberg (1971)
Bovine bronchi and trachea	SRS[bov]	Bronchi more sensitive than trachea; inhibited by NSAID	Burka and Eyre (1977)
Guinea pig trachea and lung parenchymal strip	SRS[rat]	Lung parenchyma more sensitive than trachea; FPL55712 inhibition	Drazen et al. (1979)
Human bronchi and lung parenchymal strip	SRS[gp]	Equipotent on both tissues	Ghelani et al. (1980)

[a] Abbreviations: gp, guinea pig; bov, bovine; NSAID, nonsteroidal antiinflammatory drugs.

selective peripheral airway response to iv infusion of SRS-A (Drazen and Austen, 1974). Selective peripheral airway responses to SRS-A were not observed in the one study of isolated human tissues where such a comparison was possible, but this study employed tissues that had been stored overnight, a treatment that may have had differential effects on tissue response (Ghelani et al., 1980).

A number of studies (Berry and Collier, 1964; Burka and Eyre, 1977) describe inhibition of the contractile effects of SRS-A on the airways of a number of species, including guinea pig, cow, and human, by drugs that inhibit the activity of the cyclooxygenase enzyme system. Similar effects have been observed with nonanaphylactically produced SRS-A (Strandberg, 1973). Further, it has been shown that injection of SRS-A into the pulmonary artery of isolated perfused guinea pig lungs results in the release of thromboxanes and prostaglandins (Engineer et al., 1978b). These observations suggest that some of the contractile effects of SRS-A may be due to bronchoconstrictor cyclooxygenase products synthesized in response to SRS-A.

In guinea pig (Drazen et al., 1979) and human (Ghelani et al., 1980) pulmonary tissues, the contractile response to SRS-A is partially inhibited by FPL55712 (Augstein et al., 1973), a relatively specific antagonist of SRS-A. That FPL55712 also inhibited the release of bronchoconstrictor cyclooxygenase products from the isolated perfused guinea pig lung challenged with

SRS-A (Engineer *et al.*, 1978b) raises the possibility that its antagonist action on pulmonary tissue contractile responses to SRS-A might partly reflect inhibition of cyclooxygenase product release.

D. Summary

In vivo and *in vitro* studies with SRS-A performed before the determination of its chemical structure demonstrated prolonged contractile activity compared to histamine on pulmonary tissues from a number of species. A selective effect on peripheral airways was suggested by a number of *in vivo* and *in vitro* studies. In all species where the effect of cyclooxygenase inhibition had been examined, an inhibitory effect of these agents on SRS-A–induced contraction could be shown, suggesting that thromboxanes and prostaglandins might be important secondary mediators of this response. Finally, FPL55712, a presumed selective SRS-A antagonist, could inhibit and reverse SRS-A–induced contractile responses in most species studied, consistent with the presence of (a) specific SRS-A receptor(s).

II. THE STRUCTURE AND BIOSYNTHESIS OF LEUKOTRIENES

This subject is considered in detail elsewhere in this book (Chapter 2); a brief summary is given only for convenience here. Metabolism of arachidonic acid by the lipoxygenase pathway results in the formation of 5-hydroperoxyeicosatetraenoic acid, which is converted to 5,6-oxido-7,9-*trans*-11,14-*cis*-eicosatetraenoic acid or LTA_4 (Borgeat and Samuelsson, 1979b), the proposed structure being confirmed by chemical synthesis with elucidation of the stereochemistry (Rådmark *et al.*, 1980). This unstable intermediate may be converted enzymatically to 5,12-dihydroxy-6,8,10,14-eicosatetraenoic acid (LTB_4) (Borgeat and Samuelsson, 1979a; Rådmark *et al.*, 1980) or to (5*S*)-hydroxy-(6*R*)-*S*-glutathionyl-7,9-*trans*-11,14-*cis*-eicosatetraenoic acid (LTC_4) (Hammarström *et al.*, 1979, 1980; Murphy *et al.*, 1979). The latter compound (LTC_4) may be converted by γ-glutamyl transferase to LTD_4 (Örning and Hammarström, 1980), which may, in turn, be converted to LTE_4 by a dipeptidase (Bernstrom and Hammarström, 1981).

The major leukotriene product of polymorphonuclear leukocytes, LTB_4 (Borgeat and Samuelsson, 1979a), is a potent chemotactic factor for polymorphonuclear leukocytes (PMN) as well as having some smooth muscle-contractile activity (Bray *et al.*, 1981; Lewis *et al.*, 1981b). Workers have succeeded in generating LTC_4, LTD_4, and LTE_4 *in vitro* from rat peritoneal (Bach *et al.*, 1980a,b; Lewis *et al.*, 1980a,b) and human pulmonary (Lewis *et al.*, 1980a; Leitch *et al.*, 1982e) cells, and the SRS-A of guinea pig lung has been shown to contain LTD_4 (Morris *et al.*, 1980a,b). The C_4, D_4, and E_4 leukotrienes have potent contractile effects on smooth muscle. The availability of synthetic leukotrienes (Corey *et al.*, 1980a,b,c; Lewis *et al.*, 1980b; Rokach *et al.*, 1980) has allowed the investigations of the pulmonary pharmacology of the leukotrienes that are outlined below.

III. LEUKOTRIENES AND THE LUNG

A. Activity of Leukotrienes *in Vivo*

1. *Intravenous Administration*

GUINEA PIGS. Intravenous administration of LTC_4, LTD_4, or LTE_4 causes dose-dependent bronchoconstriction in unanesthetized (Drazen *et al.*, 1980, 1982) and anesthetized mechanically ventilated guinea pigs (Drazen *et al.*, 1980, 1982; Hedqvist *et al.*, 1980; Welton *et al.*, 1981; Folco *et al.*, 1982; Schiantarelli *et al.*, 1981; Vargaftig *et al.*, 1981) (Fig. 1). In the mechanically ventilated anesthetized guinea pig studied in the body plethysmograph (Amdur and Mead, 1958), the pulmonary response to intravenous LTC_4 (1

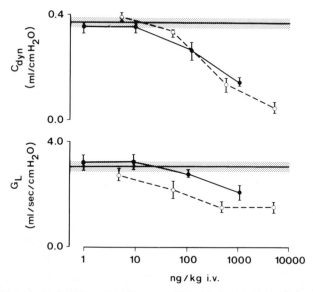

Fig. 1. Dose-dependent responses of pulmonary conductance (G_L) and dynamic compliance (C_{dyn}) to intravenous infusions of LTC_4 (●—●) and LTD_4 (○---○) to anesthetized guinea pigs. (From Drazen *et al.*, 1980).

μg/kg) or LTD$_4$ (0.5 μg/kg) is characterized by maximal falls in lung conductance (G_L) and C_{dyn} 30 sec after the iv infusion with subsequent return of G_L to baseline at 15 to 20 min, while C_{dyn} remains below baseline for at least 30 min. The ratio of percentage change of G_L to percentage change of C_{dyn} ($G_L/C_{dyn}\%$ ratio) is persistently less than one suggesting a predominant effect on the peripheral airways (Drazen *et al.*, 1980; Leitch *et al.*, 1982c). However, following iv infusion of LTE$_4$ (3 μg/kg) to mechanically ventilated anesthetized guinea pigs, the early effect on pulmonary mechanics is less apparent (Drazen *et al.*, 1982), and the $G_L/C_{dyn}\%$ ratio approaches unity, suggesting that the effect of LTE$_4$ is more uniformly distributed to both small and large airways.

2. Aerosol Administration

A. GUINEA PIGS. Administration of 30 tidal breaths of an aerosol generated by Collison nebulizer from solutions of LTC$_4$ (1 μg/ml) or LTD$_4$ (0.5 μg/ml) to mechanically ventilated anesthetized guinea pigs results in decrements in G_L and C_{dyn}. These effects develop slowly, peaking in magnitude between 3 and 5 min with a return to prechallenge values at 15 min following LTD$_4$, significant changes persisting for 30 min following LTC$_4$. The $G_L/C_{dyn}\%$ ratio is less than one following administration of both LTC$_4$ and LTD$_4$ (Leitch *et al.*, 1982b).

B. MONKEYS. Intratracheal instillation of LTC$_4$ and LTD$_4$ followed by inhalation of aerosolized saline produced dose-dependent decrements in G_L and C_{dyn} in anesthetized *Ascaris*-sensitized rhesus monkeys (Bach *et al.*, 1981). The effects on G_L and C_{dyn} were approximately equal with $G_L/C_{dyn}\%$ ratios of about 1. Maximal responses developed 15 to 35 min after administration, with persistent effects for 60 to 180 min.

C. HUMAN. The effects of inhalation of an aerosol of LTC$_4$ or LTD$_4$ by two normal human volunteers were first described by Holroyde *et al.* (1981). In both subjects, leukotriene inhalation resulted in a decrease in maximal expiratory flow rates low in the vital capacity. The time course was prolonged, with significant effects persisting for more than 30 min after aerosol inhalation. It was found that LTC$_4$ and LTD$_4$ were equipotent, with a nebulizer concentration of 5 μg/ml of either material required for a 30% reduction in flow rates. Both subjects developed cough after the 90-sec aerosol administration of LTs, leading the authors to suggest that there was a significant large-airway or irritant component associated with the bronchoconstriction.

Weiss and co-workers (1982a) also studied the effects of inhalation of aerosols of LTC_4 (10 inspirations to 60% vital capacity) in normal human volunteers. They found a dose-dependent decrease in maximal expiratory flow, measured as a percentage change in flow at 30% of vital capacity ($\Delta \dot{V}_{30}$) using partial expiratory flow volume (PEFV) curves. The onset of response was slow, with a peak effect at 12 min after inhalation; the effect persisted on the average for 30 min (Fig. 2). The exquisite sensitivity of the human lung to aerosol administration of LTC_4 is indicated in Table II, which shows that 600–9500 times higher concentrations of aerosolized histamine are needed to produce identical changes in $\Delta \dot{V}_{30}$.

Weiss and co-workers (1982b) also found that LTD_4 was a bronchoconstrictor of similar potency to LTC_4, but that LTD_4 had a more rapid onset and briefer duration of action than LTC_4. The prolonged effect of LTC_4 compared to LTD_4 could be due to action at different receptors, different degrees of lipid solubility, metabolism of LTC_4 to LTD_4 to achieve an effect, or other as yet unknown factors. Differential effects on the cyclooxygenase system seem unlikely, as ingestion of acetylsalicylic acid had no significant effect on the LTD_4 response (Weiss *et al.*, 1982b). Furthermore, these investigators found neither LTC_4 nor LTD_4 induced cough or upper airway irritation. This finding differed distinctly from that reported by Holroyde *et al.* (1981), the reason for the difference being at present unknown.

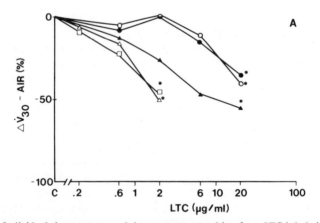

Fig. 2. Individual time courses and dose response resulting from LTC inhalation. (A) Percentage change from control of maximum expiratory flow rate at 30% vital capacity of ($\dot{V}_{30}$) while the subject was breathing air. Asterisks indicate the effect of repeated challenge with the highest concentration in each subject. Statistically significant changes ($p < .05$) are those greater than 20% for each subject. Symbols represent subjects: ●, R.L.; ○, P.W.; ▲, J.D.; △, W.W.; □, N.C. (B) Time course of response to inhalation of highest dose [shown in (A)] of LTC in each subject. Control values ($\pm$ SEM) are shown on the ordinate at zero time. Moving average (○—○); individual data points (●). (From Weiss *et al.*, 1982a.)

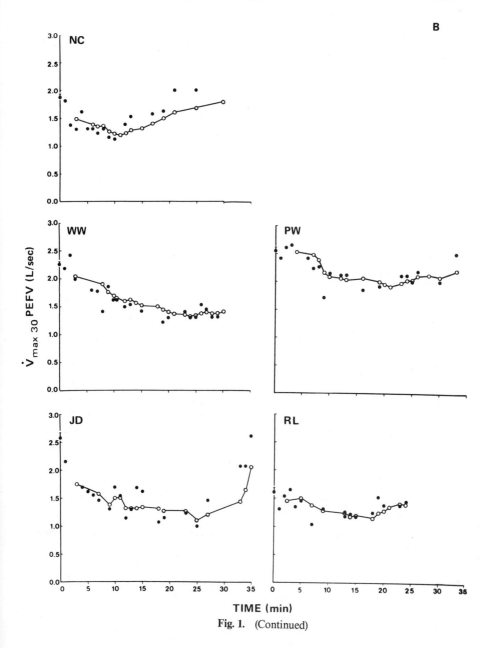

Fig. 1. (Continued)

TABLE II

TABLE II

Comparison of Bronchial Sensitivity to LTC_4 and to Histamine in Five Normal Subjects[a]

Subject no.	Concentration for EC_{30}		Ratio histamine: LTC_4
	LTC_4 (μM)	Histamine (mM)	
1	33.0	90.0	2800
2	4.3	34.0	7900
3	1.4	9.0	6400
4	27.0	16.2	600
5	19.0	18.0	9500

[a] From Weiss et al. (1982a).

B. Effect of Antagonists on *in Vivo* Responses to Leukotrienes

Intravenous Leukotriene Administration

A. CYCLOOXYGENASE INHIBITORS. Vargaftig et al. (1981) reported that aspirin pretreatment almost totally inhibited the increase in pulmonary impedance to inflation in mechanically ventilated anesthetized guinea pigs receiving iv infusions of LTC_4 or LTD_4 (0.1–0.9 μg/kg). Schiantarelli et al. (1981) also showed in the guinea pig Konzett-Rossler preparation that indomethacin pretreatment (0.2–1.0 mg/kg iv) inhibited 70–90% of the pulmonary mechanical response to iv infusion of LTC_4 (0.8 μg/kg). Leitch et al. (1982c) examined the time-dependent changes in G_L and C_{dyn} in indomethacin-pretreated (30 mg/kg ip) and nonpretreated mechanically ventilated anesthetized guinea pigs receiving iv infusions of LTC_4 (1 μg/kg) or LTD_4 (0.5 μg/kg). They showed that indomethacin pretreatment had the following effects:

1. It totally inhibited the decrement in G_L and C_{dyn} in the first minute following iv LT infusion. The residual response was slow-reacting in nature, with maximal decrements occurring 5–7.5 min after infusion (Fig. 3).
2. It potentiated the G_L response to iv infusion of both LTs (Fig. 3).
3. It resulted in $G_L/C_{dyn}\%$ ratios approaching unity, compared to 0.3 without indomethacin pretreatment (Fig. 3).

B. FPL55712. The SRS-A antagonist FPL55712 (1 mg/kg iv), when administered 2 min before leukotriene infusion, resulted in 60% inhibition of the guinea pig pulmonary response to iv LTC_4 (0.8 mol/kg) (Schiantarelli et al., 1981). FPL55712 also inhibited the bronchoconstrictor response of anesthe-

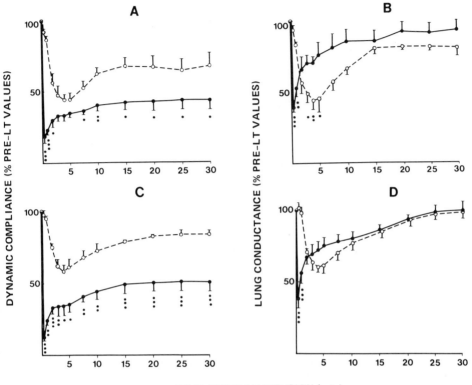

TIME AFTER LT INFUSION (min)

Fig. 3. Pulmonary mechanical response, measured as dynamic compliance and lung conductance and expressed as a percentage of preinfusion values, to intravenous infusion of (A and B) LTC_4 (1 μg/kg, $n = 4$) or (C and D) LTD_4 (0.5 μg/kg, $n = 5$) to control (●—●) and indomethacin-pretreated (○---○) anesthetized guinea pigs (n, number of animals). Values shown are means ± SEM. The significance of difference between means is shown by asterisks: *$p < .05$; **$p < .01$; ***$p < .001$.

tized guinea pigs to iv LTE_4 in a dose-related fashion (Welton *et al.*, 1981). Similarly, FPL55712 administered by aerosol has been reported to inhibit the guinea pig pulmonary response to iv LTD_4 and LTE_4 in a dose-related manner (O'Donnell and Welton, 1982). In humans, FPL55712 and FPL59257 (a related SRS-A antagonist) completely blocked the cough and partially blocked the bronchoconstrictor responses to aerosolized LTs (Holroyde *et al.*, 1981).

C. ANTICHOLINERGIC AGENTS. Folco *et al.* (1982) have shown that both the bronchoconstriction and the increase in circulating thromboxanes (Omini *et al.*, 1981) induced by intravenous infusion of LTC_4 to the guinea pig can be inhibited in a dose-response fashion by anticholinergic agents such as atropine and ipratropium bromide. These authors also demonstrated that the anticholinergic agents had similar activity on the thromboxane release and bronchoconstriction induced by iv infusion of histamine and bradykinin.

D. β-ADRENERGIC AGENTS. Aerosolized isoprenaline protects against the bronchoconstriction produced by iv infusion of LTE_4 (25 μg/kg) in the guinea pig (O'Donnell and Welton, 1982).

E. β-ADRENERGIC BLOCKING AGENTS. Welton *et al.* (1981) reported that pretreatment with propranolol (0.1 mg/kg iv) potentiated the dose-dependent bronchoconstrictor response of the guinea pig to iv LTE_4 approximately 10-fold. Since propranolol also enhances the response to other bronchoconstrictor agents, this may well be a nonspecific effect.

C. Summary

These *in vivo* studies with synthetic leukotrienes have amply confirmed and extended many of the earlier observations made with SRS-A. In all species studied, whether administered intravenously or by aerosol the leukotrienes at low concentrations have profound dose-dependent effects on pulmonary function. When administered by aerosol, the onset of action is slow and the duration of activity prolonged in comparison with other known agonists such as histamine or prostaglandin $F_{2\alpha}$. This time course more closely resembles the time course of pulmonary effects observed following antigen challenge in allergic individuals (Rosenthal *et al.*, 1976) than that of any other agonist, suggesting a primary role for the leukotrienes in the asthmatic response.

The rapid onset of pulmonary mechanical effect observed following iv infusion of LTs to the guinea pig (maximal activity at 30 sec) differs from the slow-reacting responses seen following aerosol administration. The studies with cyclooxygenase inhibitors have confirmed previous observations with SRS-A that cyclooxygenase products may indeed be involved in the pulmonary responses to the leukotrienes and suggest that these products contribute to the response in two opposing ways. The findings in the indomethacin-treated guinea pigs suggest that following iv infusion of LTs at least two cyclooxygenase activities are generated and released: one acts within the first minute after infusion to produce a bronchoconstriction preferentially in the pulmonary periphery; the other, a bronchodilator activity, acts later to inhibit the G_L response to LT infusion. When both activities are inhibited by indomethacin, the preferential small-airway response, previously described for SRS-A (Drazen and Austen, 1974) and confirmed with the synthetic LTs

(Leitch *et al.*, 1982c), is no longer evident; that is, the $G_L/C_{dyn}\%$ ratios resulting from LT infusion approach unity.

Thromboxanes are the most likely candidates for this secondarily mediated bronchoconstrictor effect seen in the first minutes following LT infusion. Evidence supporting this hypothesis is that thromboxanes (*a*) are present in plasma following iv infusion of LTs in the guinea pig (Omini *et al.*, 1981; Schiantarelli *et al.*, 1981), (*b*) may be generated from guinea pig pulmonary parenchyma (Gryglewski *et al.*, 1976) or platelets (Hamberg *et al.*, 1975a), (*c*) have a short biological half-life (Hamberg *et al.*, 1975a,b), and (*d*) have preferential activity on small airways (Schneider and Drazen, 1980). Furthermore, such a contribution from thromboxanes is supported by the observation that OKY 1581, a selective thromboxane synthetase inhibitor, also partially inhibits LT-induced airway constriction (Ueno *et al.*, 1982).

The potentiation by indomethacin of the G_L response to LTC_4 and LTD_4 infusion—from the second minute after infusion (Fig. 3)—resembles the potentiation by indomethacin of the tracheal contractile response to histamine, acetylcholine, and LTs that has been reported (Orehek *et al.*, 1973; Adcock and Garland, 1980; Brink *et al.*, 1981; Krell *et al.*, 1981). This potentiation has been attributed to inhibition of local formation of PGE_2 (Burka *et al.*, 1981; Grodzinska *et al.*, 1975), which plays a regulatory role (Orehek *et al.*, 1973), its bronchodilator effect operating to restrict responses to contractile agonists. In contrast, the activity attributed to thromboxanes seen in the first minute following iv infusion is absent when the LTs are administered by aerosol, raising the possibility that thromboxanes are not generated locally in the lungs but may derive from platelets (Hamberg *et al.*, 1975a), mononuclear cells (Gordon *et al.*, 1981), other blood components, or even the vascular endothelium.

The bronchoconstriction produced by LTs *in vivo* can be partially inhibited by FPL55712, possibly implicating a specific leukotriene receptor. In addition, anticholinergic and β-adrenergic agents also inhibit LT-induced bronchoconstriction, probably not only by a direct action on smooth muscle but also, at least in the case of the anticholinergics, by inhibiting the release of bronchoconstrictor thromboxanes. It remains to be determined whether β-adrenergic agents and FPL55712 also inhibit LT-induced thromboxane release *in vivo*.

D. Activity of Leukotrienes *in Vitro*

1. Lung Parenchymal Strip Preparations

A. *GUINEA PIG.* Contraction of the guinea pig lung parenchymal strip (GPLS) is believed to represent constriction of parenchymal contractile elements rather than vascular elements (Drazen and Schneider, 1978), a view that is supported by the observation that pulmonary arteries from the guinea pig are much less sensitive to leukotrienes than the GPLS itself (Hand et al., 1981).

Dose-dependent contraction of the GPLS is produced by LTB_4 (Sirois et al., 1980, 1981a,b; Lewis et al., 1981b; Leitch et al., 1982a) with an EC_{25} of 10^{-7} M, the contractile response being critically dependent on the stereochemistry of the 6-, 8-, and 10-olefinic bonds (Sirois et al., 1981a; Lewis et al., 1981b), the naturally occurring isomers having the most contractile activity.

Of the sulfidopeptide leukotrienes, LTD_4 is the most potent agonist on GPLS (Drazen et al., 1980; Piper and Samhoun, 1981), with an EC_{50} of 8×10^{-10} M. The C_4 (Drazen et al., 1980; Hedqvist et al., 1980; Piper and Samhoun, 1981; Sirois et al., 1981b) and E_4 (Lewis et al., 1980a,b; Leitch et al., 1982a; Piper and Samhoun, 1982) LTs are approximately equipotent on the GPLS, with EC_{50} values of 2×10^{-8} M. All four leukotrienes are more potent than histamine (EC_{50} 3×10^{-6} M) as contractile agonists for GPLS.

B. HUMAN. The human lung parenchymal strip has been reported to be almost as sensitive as the GPLS to leukotrienes B_4, C_4, and D_4 (Hanna et al., 1981; Sirois et al., 1981b).

C. OTHERS. Rat and rabbit lung parenchymal strips are much less responsive than guinea pig or human tissues to LTB_4, LTC_4, and LTD_4, with only weak contractions present at bath concentrations of 10^{-9} M (Piper and Samhoun, 1981; Sirois et al., 1981b).

2. Tracheobronchial Preparations

A. GUINEA PIG. The guinea pig tracheal spiral preparation is much less responsive to LTs than the GPLS, LTC_4 and LTD_4 being approximately equipotent and 30–100 times more active than histamine (Drazen et al., 1980; Holme et al., 1980; Krell et al., 1981; Sirois et al., 1981b). Leukotriene B_4 is almost totally inactive in this preparation (Sirois et al., 1981b).

B. HUMAN. Human bronchial strips contract in a dose-dependent fashion in the presence of LTC_4 and LTD_4, which are approximately 1000 times more potent than histamine and 500 times more potent than $PGF_{2\alpha}$ in causing contraction of this preparation (Dahlen et al., 1980; Hanna et al., 1981; Sirois et al., 1981b). Human bronchial smooth muscle appears to be more sensitive to LTC_4 than tracheal smooth muscle (Davis et al., 1982). Leukotriene B_4 may be as potent as LTD_4 on human bronchial strips (Sirois et al., 1981b).

E. Effect of Antagonists on *in Vitro* Responses to Leukotrienes

1. Cyclooxygenase Inhibitors

The contractile effect of LTB_4 on GPLS is substantially decreased by indomethacin pretreatment (1 μg/ml) (Sirois *et al.*, 1980; Leitch *et al.*, 1982a) (Fig. 4), suggesting that its contractile activity is dependent on the generation and release of thromboxanes and prostaglandins. Such an effect has been demonstrated in both isolated perfused lungs (Sirois *et al.*, 1980) and GPLS *in vitro* (Dahlen *et al.*, 1982) in response to LTB_4.

Indomethacin over the concentration range 0.1–10 μg/ml is without effect on the GPLS contractile response to LTC_4, LTD_4, and LTE_4, except for an

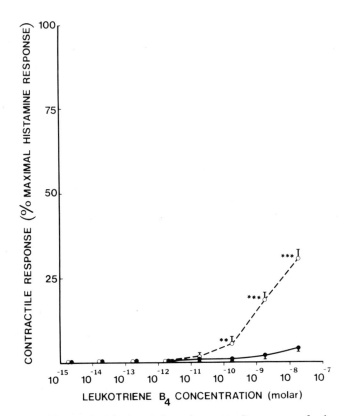

Fig. 4. Effect of indomethacin (1 μg/ml) on the contractile response of guinea pig lung parenchymal strips to LTB_4 (**$p < .01$; ***$p < .001$) ($n = 10$). LTB_4(○---○); LTB_4 + Indomethacin (●—●). (From Leitch *et al.*, 1982a.)

approximately 25% inhibition of the contractile response to high concentrations $(10^{-10} - 10^{-8}\ M)$ of LTD_4 by indomethacin 1 μg/ml (Leitch *et al.*, 1982a). The findings with LTC_4 have been confirmed by Dahlen *et al.* (1982), who showed that indomethacin (2 μg/ml) totally inhibited thromboxane release from the GPLS but had no effect on the contractile response to LTC_4. These findings differ from reports where aspirin (Vargaftig *et al.*, 1981) and indomethacin (Piper and Samhoun, 1981; Zijlstra *et al.*, 1982) inhibited 60% or more of the GPLS contractile response to *low* concentrations (less than $10^{-10}\ M$) of LTC_4 and LTD_4.

Indomethacin (2 μg/ml) had no effect on the guinea pig tracheal spiral contractile response at concentrations of LTC_4 less than $10^{-7}\ M$. At concentrations above $10^{-7}\ M$, indomethacin enhanced the contractile response to LTC_4 (Krell *et al.*, 1981).

2. Thromboxane Synthetase Inhibitors

Clotrimazole $(10^{-5}\ M)$, a thromboxane-synthetase inhibitor (Gordon *et al.* 1981), had no effect on LTC_4-induced contraction of GPLS but did partially inhibit the contraction caused by higher concentrations of LTD_4 $(10^{-11} - 10^{-8}\ M)$, a finding similar to the effects of indomethacin (Austen *et al.*, 1983).

3. FPL55712

FPL55712 (1 μg/ml) has no effect on the LTB_4-induced contraction of GPLS (Sirois *et al.*, 1981b).

Two groups (Drazen *et al.*, 1980; Krell *et al.*, 1981) have described failure of FPL55712 to inhibit LTC_4-induced contraction of GPLS, whereas dose-related inhibition of LTD_4-induced contraction was found. Others (Hedqvist *et al.*, 1980; Piper and Samhoun, 1981; Vargaftig *et al.*, 1981; Piper and Samhoun, 1982) report that FPL55712 antagonizes contractions induced by LTC_4, LTD_4, and LTE_4, but K_B or pA_2 values have not been determined in these studies.

Both LTC_4 and LTD_4 contractions of guinea pig trachea are antagonized by FPL55712 (Holme *et al.*, 1980; Krell *et al.*, 1981). Contractions of human bronchial tissue induced by LTC_4 and LTD_4 are reversed in a dose-related manner by the addition of FPL55712 (Dahlen *et al.*, 1980; Hanna *et al.*, 1981).

4. β-Adrenergic Agents

Zijlstra *et al.* (1981) have reported that not only does isoprenaline inhibit LTC_4-induced contraction of GPLS, but the inhibition is also associated with a parallel reduction in thromboxane A_2 release from the tissue. Davis *et al.* (1982) have also described relaxation of LTC_4- and LTD_4-induced contraction in human bronchus and trachea by β-adrenergic agents.

5. *Calcium Channel Blockers*

Cerrina *et al.* (1982) found that verapamil, diltiazem, and nicardipine are capable, in high concentrations (EC_{50} 5×10^{-5} M), of completely inhibiting LTD_4-induced contractions of guinea pig trachea.

6. *Other Agents*

Mepyramine (10^{-5} M), propranolol (10^{-5} M), atropine (10^{-5} M), methysergide (10^{-7} M), disodium cromoglycate (10^{-5} M), and phenoxybenzamine (10^{-7} M) have no effect on LTC_4- and LTD_4-induced contractions of GPLS over an LT concentration range of 10^{-14}–10^{-8} M (A. G. Leitch *et al.,* unpublished observations).

F. Summary

These *in vitro* observations show that LTB_4 has no primary contractile effect on pulmonary tissue. Instead, its contractile activity, which is much less than that of the sulfidopeptide leukotrienes, results from the generation and release of cyclooxygenase products, possibly as a function of its established ionophore effect (Serhan *et al.,* 1982). In keeping with these findings is the absence of any inhibitory effect of FPL55712 on LTB_4-induced contractions.

The sulfidopeptide leukotrienes LTC_4, LTD_4, and LTE_4 produce sustained contractions of guinea pig and human pulmonary preparations at concentrations 100–7500 times less than histamine. The time course and duration of these sulfidopeptide LT-mediated contractile responses is similar to the FPL55712-inhibitable prolonged phase of the contractions seen on antigen challenge of sensitized guinea pig and human lung (Adams and Lichtenstein, 1979), which may suggest a pathophysiological role for LTs in the antigen response. The prolonged nature of the contractile response *in vitro* presumably reflects absent or extremely slow metabolism to inactive products. Metabolism of LTC_4 to LTD_4 and subsequently LTE_4 would not be associated with any great loss of contractile activity. Although inactivation is slow *in vitro,* it clearly occurs *in vivo,* where the pulmonary responses have a duration in keeping with the rapid metabolism of LTC_3, which has been described in the monkey *in vivo* (Hammarström *et al.,* 1981).

The sulfidopeptide LT contractile responses, unlike the LTB_4 responses, are primary, since indomethacin blocks none or only a fraction of GPLS contraction, suggesting that a contribution from cyclooxygenase products generation and release may only be present in some preparations. A possible methodological explanation for the different percentage contribution of cyclooxygenase products to the LT contractile response recorded by different groups of workers may be in the use of the superfusion cascade system by Zijlstra *et al.* (1982) and Piper and Samhoun (1981), whereas a conventional organ bath was used by Leitch *et al.* (1982a) and Dahlen *et al.*, (1982). Superfusion could produce agitation of the tissues resulting in release of cyclooxygenase products (Orehek *et al.*, 1973). Where a contribution from cyclooxygenase products is present, the principal active product appears to be thromboxane rather than PGD_2 or $PGF_{2\alpha}$, as shown by the effect of thromboxane synthetase inhibition (Austen *et al.*, 1983). The limited nature of the contribution from cyclooxygenase products to the contractile response of GPLS to LT *in vitro* possibly suggests an extrapulmonary source for the thromboxanes, that are released following iv infusion of LTs.

Cyclooxygenase products do not contribute to the guinea pig tracheal spiral contractile response to sulfidopeptide LTs, and, indeed, at higher agonist concentrations the contractile response is enhanced, presumably as a result of inhibition of PGE_2 generation (Burka *et al.*, 1981), a finding that is in keeping with the enhancement of the G_L response to iv LT by indomethacin *in vivo* (Leitch *et al.*, 1982c) and suggests local rather than systemic generation of PGE_2 in that response.

The inhibitory effect of β-adrenergic agents in asthma is reflected in the observations that isoprenaline can inhibit LT-induced contraction in guinea pig and human pulmonary tissue presumably by its activity on smooth muscle β receptors. That thromboxane generation and release are also inhibited by this drug suggests both another possible site of action and a beneficial effect.

The ability of FPL55712 to prevent sulfidopeptide leukotriene-induced constriction in most tissues in a dose-dependent fashion is in keeping with blockade of a leukotriene receptor that would appear to be common to all three leukotrienes except, possibly, in GPLS. The inability to block LTC_4 activity on the GPLS in a dose-dependent fashion with FPL55712 suggests the possibility that in this preparation there may be a separate receptor for LTC_4.

IV. LEUKOTRIENE ANALOGS

A. Leukotrienes Derived from Eicosapentaenoic and Eicosatrienoic Acid

Arachidonic acid is the usual cell membrane-derived precursor for both the cyclooxygenase and lipoxygenase pathways. When it is substituted by eicosatrienoic or eicosapentaenoic acids in tissue culture of mouse mastocytoma cells (Hammarström, 1980a,b), triene and pentaene leukotrienes can be generated. Pentaene leukotrienes have also been generated by mouse mastocytoma cells implanted in the peritoneal cavity of mice eating a menhaden diet (Murphy *et al.*, 1981) and from the peritoneal cavity of rats eating a menhaden diet (Leitch *et al.*, 1982d).

Fish-eating communities such as the Eskimos (Dyerberg and Bang, 1978) and some Japanese (Hirai *et al.*, 1982) have a prolonged bleeding time related to the production of 3-series prostaglandins and thromboxanes secondary to their high eicosapentaenoic acid intake. Thromboxane A_3 is relatively inactive in platelet aggregation (Dyerbert *et al.*, 1978; Needleman *et al.*, 1979), thus explaining the prolonged bleeding time. With evidence that such a minor structural alteration in thromboxane can alter function, it was obviously of importance to explore the activities of the triene and pentaene leukotrienes.

Early studies on guinea pig ileum suggested that LTC_3 and LTD_3 had similar activities to LTC_4 and LTD_4 (Hammarström, 1980a), but that LTC_5 might be less active than LTC_4 on this preparation (Hammarström, 1980b). Dahlen *et al.* (1982) have reported that LTC_3, LTC_4, and LTC_5 are equiactive on the GPLS, indicating that the pulmonary mechanical effects of the leukotrienes are not affected by this minor structural alteration. Drazen *et al.* (1981) have confirmed this result for LTC_3 and LTD_3.

B. Synthetic Leukotriene Analogs

The activity of a number of leukotriene analogs synthesized in E. J. Corey's laboratory has been assessed on the GPLS and ileum with a view to determining the structural features of the leukotriene molecules necessary for contractile activity on the lung (Drazen *et al.*, 1981; Lewis *et al.*, 1981a). These analogs have also been examined for antagonist activity on the GPLS. The chemical names, structural modification, and EC_{50} ratios of the 39 compounds studied are cited in the quoted references.

C. Summary

The analog studies demonstrate distinct structural requirements for LT activity on airway tissues. The ω portion of the molecule must remain hydrophobic, although the precise structural details of this hydrophobic portion are not critical. The sulfidopeptide chain is required for activity, but its configuration may be varied substantially without major effect. The sulfur of the thioether link probably does not participate in the contractile response, as altering its valence state is without effect. The C-5 and C-6 chiral centers are probably of major importance, as alteration of the stereochemistry at these loci has a substantial effect on contractile response.

V. CONCLUSIONS

The sulfidopeptide leukotrienes LTC_4, LTD_4, and LTE_4 are known to be released following IgE-dependent immunological challenge of human lung cells *in vitro* (Leitch *et al.*, 1982e) and can be demonstrated in the blood of sensitive dogs in association with the bronchoconstriction that follows aerosol challenge with either specific antigen or citric acid, a nonspecific irritant (Hirschman *et al.*, 1982). These observations, coupled with the profound and sustained effects that low concentrations of leukotrienes have on guinea pig and human pulmonary tissues *in vivo* and *in vitro*, as described in this chapter, suggest a major role for leukotrienes not only in the bronchoconstriction of allergic asthma but possibly also in nonallergic airway obstruction. Confirmation of these possibilities must await the development of either lipoxygenase inhibitors or competitive inhibitors of the leukotrienes that can be safely administered *in vivo* in appropriate dosage.

REFERENCES

Adams, G. K., and Lichtenstein, L. M. (1979). *J. Immunol.* **122**, 555–562.
Adcock, J. J., and Garland, L. G. (1980). *Br. J. Pharmacol.* **69**, 167–169.
Amdur, M. D., and Mead, J. (1958). *Am. J. Physiol.* **192**, 364–368.
Augstein, J., Farmer, J. B., Lee, T. B., Sheard, P., and Tattersall, M. L. (1973). *Nature (London) New Biol.* **245**, 215–217.
Austen, K. F., Corey, E. J., Drazen, J. M., and Leitch, A. G. (1983). *Br. J. Pharmacol.* **80**, 47–53.
Bach, M. K., Brashler, J. R., Hammarström, S., and Samuelsson, B. (1980a). *J. Immunol.* **125**, 115–117.
Bach, M. K., Brashler, J. R., Hammarström, S., and Samuelsson, B. (1980b). *Biochem. Biophys. Res. Commun.* **93**, 1121–1126.
Bach, M. K., Brashler, J. R., Johnson, H. G., and McNee, M. L. (1981). *In* "SRS-A and Leukotrienes" (P. J. Piper, ed.), pp. 161–189. Wiley.
Bernström, K., and Hammarström, S. (1981). *J. Biol. Chem.* **256**, 9579–9582.
Berry, P. A., and Collier, H. O. J. (1964). *Br. J. Pharmacol. Chemother.* **23**, 201–216.
Borgeat, P., and Samuelsson, B. (1979a). *J. Biol. Chem.* **254**, 2643–2646.
Borgeat, P., and Samuelsson, B. (1979b). *J. Biol. Chem.* **254**, 7865–7869.
Bray, M. A., Ford-Hutchinson, A. W., and Smith, M. J. H. (1981). *Br. J. Pharmacol.* **74**, 788P.
Brink, C., Duncan, P. G., and Douglas, J. S. (1981). *Prostaglandins* **22**, 729–738.
Brocklehurst, W. E. (1953). *J. Physiol. (London)* **120**, 16P.
Brocklehurst, W. E. (1960). *J. Physiol. (London)* **151**, 416–435.
Burka, J. F., and Eyre, P. (1977). *Eur. J. Pharmacol.* **44**, 169–177.
Burka, J. F., Ali, M., McDonald, J. W. D., and Paterson, N. A. M. (1981). *Prostaglandins* **22**, 683–691.
Cerrina, J., Renier, A., Floch, A., Durous, P., and Advenier, R. (1982). *Am. Rev. Respir. Dis.* **125**(2), 226.
Corey, E. J., Clark, D. A., Goto, G., Marfat, A., Mioskowski, C., Samuelsson, B., and Hammarström, S. (1980a). *J. Am. Chem. Soc.* **102**, 1436–1439.
Corey, E. J., Clark, D. A., Marfat, A., and Goto, G. (1980b). *Tetrahedron Lett.* **21**, 3143–3146.

Corey, E. J., Marfat, A., Goto, G., and Brion, F. (1980c). *J. Am. Chem. Soc.* **102**, 7984–7985.
Dahlen, S.-E., Hedqvist, P., Hammarström, S., and Samuelsson, B. (1980). *Nature (London)* **288**, 484–486.
Dahlen, S.-E., Hedqvist, P., Granström, E., Lindgren, J. A., and Petroni, A. (1982). *Proc. Int. Conf. Prostaglandins, 5th,* p. 320.
Davis, C., Jones, T. R., and Daniel, E. E. (1982). *Am. Rev. Respir. Dis.* **125**,(2), 65.
Drazen, J. M., and Austen, K. F. (1974). *J. Clin. Invest.* **53**, 1679–1685.
Drazen, J. M., and Schneider, M. W. (1978). *J. Clin. Invest.* **61**, 1441–1447.
Drazen, J. M., Lewis, R. A., Wasserman, S. I., Orange, R. P., and Austen, K. F. (1979). *J. Clin. Invest.* **63**, 1–5.
Drazen, J. M., Austen, K. F., Lewis, R. A., Clark, D. A., Goto, G., Marfat, A., and Corey, E. J. (1980). *Proc. Natl. Acad. Sci. U.S.A.* **77**, 4354–4358.
Drazen, J. M., Lewis, R. A., Austen, K. F., Toda, M., Brion, F., Marfat, A., and Corey, E. J. (1981). *Proc. Natl. Acad. Sci. U.S.A.* **78**, 3195–3198.
Drazen, J. M., Venugopalan, C. S., Austen, K. F., Brion, F., and Corey, E. J. (1982). *Am. Rev. Respir. Dis.* **125**, 290–294.
Dyerberg, J., and Bang, H. O. (1978). *Lancet* **1**, 152.
Dyerberg, J., Bang, H. O., Stofferson, E., Moncada, S., and Vane, J. R. (1978). *Lancet* **2**, 117–119.
Engineer, D. M., Niederhauser, U., Piper, P. J., and Sirois, P. (1978a). *Br. J. Pharmacol.* **62**, 61–66.
Engineer, D. M., Morris, H. R., Piper, P. J., and Sirois, P. (1978b). *Br. J. Pharmacol.* **64**, 211–218.
Feldberg, W., and Kellaway, C. H. (1938). *J. Physiol. (London)* **94**, 187–226.
Folco, G., Omini, C., Rossoni, G., Vigano, T., and Berti, F. (1982). *Eur. J. Pharmacol.* **78**, 159–166.
Ghelani, A. M., Holroyde, M. C., and Sheard, P. (1980). *Br. J. Pharmacol.* **71**, 107–112.
Gordon, D., Nouri, A. M. E., and Thomas, R. U. (1981). *Br. J. Pharmacol.* **74**, 469–475.
Grodzinska, L., Panczenko, B., and Gryglewski, R. J. (1975). *J. Pharm. Pharmacol.* **27**, 88–91.
Gryglewski, R. J., Dembinska-Kiec, A., Grodzinska, L., and Panczenko, B. (1976). *In* "Lungs Cells in Disease" (A. Bouhuys, ed.), p. 196. North-Holland Publ., Amsterdam.
Hamberg, M., Svensson, J., and Samuelsson, B. (1975a). *Pros. Natl. Acad. Sci. U.S.A.* **72**, 2294–2298.
Hamberg, M., Hedqvist, P., Standberg, J., Svensson, J., and Samuelsson, B. (1975b). *Life Sci.* **16**, 451–462.
Hammarström, S. (1980a). *J. Biol. Chem.* **225**, 7093–7094.
Hammarström, S. (1980b). *J. Biol. Chem.* **256**, 2275–2279.
Hammarström, S., Murphy, R. C., Samuelsson, B., Clark, D. A., Mioskowski, C., and Corey, E. J. (1979). *Biochem. Biophys. Res. Commun.* **91**, 1266–1272.
Hammarström, S., Samuelsson, B., Clark, D. A., Goto, G., Marfat, A., Mioskowski, C., and Corey, E. J. (1980). *Biochem. Biophys. Res. Cummun.* **92**, 946–953.
Hammarström, S., Bernström, K., Orning, L., Dahlen, S.-E., and Hedqvist, P. (1981). *Biochem. Biophys. Res. Commun.* **101**, 1109–1115.
Hand, J. M., Will, J. A., and Buckner, C. K. (1981). *Eur. J. Pharmacol.* **76**, 439–442.
Hanna, C. J., Bach, M. K., Pare, P. D., and Schellenberg, R. R. (1981). *Nature (London)* **290**, 343–344.
Hedqvist, P., Dahlen, S.-E., Gustaffson, L., Hammarström, S., and Samuelsson, B. (1980). *Acta Physiol. Scand.* **110**, 331–333.
Hirai, A., Terano, J., Hamazaki, T., Sajiki, J., Tamura, Y., and Kumagai, A. (1982). *Proc. Int. Conf. Prostaglandins, 5th, 1982* p. 694.
Hirschman, C. A., Peters, T. E., Butler, J., Hanifin, J., Downs, H., and Lynn, R. K. (1982). *Am. Rev. Respir. Dis.* **125**,(2), 65.
Holme, G., Burnet, G., Piechuta, H., Masson, P., Girard, Y., and Rokach, J. (1980). *Prostaglandins* **20**, 717–728.

Holroyde, M. A., Altounyan, R. E. C., Cole, M., Dixon, M., and Elliott, E. V. (1981). *Lancet* **2**, 17–18.

Kellaway, C. H., and Trethewie, E. R. (1940). *Q. J. Exp. Physiol. Cogn. Med. Sci.* **30**, 121–145.

Krell, R. D., Osborn, R., Vickery, L., Falcone, K., O'Donnell, M., Gleason, J., Kinzig, C., and Bryan, D. (1981). *Prostaglandins* **22**, 387–407.

Leitch, A. G., Austen, K. F., Corey, E. J., and Drazen, J. M. (1982a). *Fed. Proc., Fed. Am. Soc. Exp. Biol.* **41**, 1047.

Leitch, A. G., Corey, E. J., Austen, K. F., and Drazen, J. M. (1982c). *Am. Rev. Respir. Dis.* **125**(2), 66.

Leitch, A. G., Prickett, J., Robinson, D., Lewis, R. A., Corey, E. J., and K. F. Austen (1982d). Submitted for publication.

Leitch, A. G., Lewis, R. A., Corey, E. J., and Austen, K. F. (1982e). *Chest* (in press).

Leitch, A. G., Corey, E. J., Austen, K. F., and Drazen, J. M. (1983). Submitted for publication. **128**, 639–643.

Lewis, R. A., Wasserman, S. I., Goetzl, E. J., and Austen, K. F. (1974). *J. Exp. Med.* **140**, 1133–1146.

Lewis, R. A., Austen, K. F., Drazen, J. M., Clark, D. A., Marfat, A., and Corey, E. J. (1980a). *Proc. Natl. Acad. Sci. U.S.A.* **77**, 3710–3714.

Lewis, R. A., Drazen, J. M., Austen, K. F., Clark, D. A., and Corey, E. J. (1980b). *Biochem. Biophys. Res. Commun.* **96**, 271–277.

Lewis, R. A., Drazen, J. M., Austen, K. F., Toda, M., Brion, F., Marfat, A., and Corey, E. J. (1981a). *Proc. Natl. Acad. Sci. U.S.A.* **78**, 4579–4583.

Lewis, R. A., Goetzl, E. J., Drazen, J. M., Soter, N. A., Austen, K. F., and Corey, E. J. (1981b). *J. Exp. Med.* **154**, 1243–1248.

Mathé, A. A., and Strandberg, K. (1971). *Acta Physiol. Scand.* **82**, 460.

Michoud, M.-C., Pare, P. D., Orange, R. P., and Hogg, J. D. (1979). *Am. Rev. Respir. Dis.* **119**, 419–424.

Morris, H. R., Taylor, G. W., Piper, P. J., and Tippins, J. R. (1980a). *Nature (London)* **285**, 104–108.

Morris, H. R., Taylor, G. W., Rokach, J., Girard, Y., Piper, P. J., Tippins, J. R., and Samhoun, M. N. (1980b). *Prostaglandins* **20**, 601–607.

Murphy, R. C., Hammarström, S., and Samuelsson, B. (1979). *Proc. Natl. Acad. Sci. U.S.A.* **76**, 4275–4279.

Murphy, R. C., Pickett, W. C., Culp, B. R., and Lands, W. E. M. (1981). *Prostaglandins* **22**, 613–622.

Needleman, P., Raz, A., Minkes, M. S., Ferrendelli, J. A., and Sprechel, H. (1979). *Proc. Natl. Acad. Sci. U.S.A.* **76**, 944–948.

O'Donnell, M., and Welton, A. F. (1982). *Fed. Proc., Fed. Am. Soc. Exp. Biol.* **41**, 821.

Omini, C., Folco, T., Vigano, T., Rossoni, G., Brunelli, G., and Berti, F. (1981). *Pharmacol. Res. Commun.* **13**, 633–640.

Orange, R. P., and Austen, K. F. (1969). *Adv. Immunol.* **10**, 105–144.

Orange, R. P., and Austen, K. F. (1975). *Am. Rev. Respir. Dis.* **112**, 423–436.

Orange, R. P., Murphy, R. C., Karnovsky, M. L., and Austen, K. F. (1973). *J. Immunol.* **110**, 760–770.

Orehek, J., Douglas, J. S., Lewis, A. J., and Bouhuys, A. (1973). *Nature (London)* **245**, 84–85.

Örning, L., and Hammarström, S. (1980). *J. Biol. Chem.* **255**, 8023–8026.

Paterson, N. A. M., Burka, J. F., and Craig, I. D. (1981). *J. Allergy Clin. Immunol.* **67**, 426–434.

Patterson, R., Orange, R. P., and Harris, K. E. (1978). *J. Allerg. Clin. Immunol.* **62**, 371–377.

Piper, P. J., and Samhoun, M. N. (1981). *Prostaglandins* **21**, 793–803.

Piper, P. J., and Samhoun, M. N. (1982). *Pros. Int. Conf. Prostaglandins, 5th, 1982* p. 481.

Rådmark, O., Malmsten, C., Samuelsson, B., Clark, D. A., Goto, G., Marfat, A., and Corey, E. J. (1980). *Biochem. Biophys. Res. Commun.* **92**, 954–961.

Rokach, J., Girard, Y., Guindon, Y., Atkinson, J. G., Larue, M., Young, R. N., Masson, P., and Holme, G. (1980). *Tetrahedron Lett.* **21**, 1485–1488.

Rosenthal, R. R., Fish, J. E., Permutt, S., Menkes, H., and Norman, P. S. (1976). *J. Allergy Clin. Immunol.* **57**, 220.

Schiantarelli, P., Borgrani, S., and Folco, G. (1981). *Eur. J. Pharmacol.* **73**, 363–366.

Schild, H. O., Hawkins, D. F., Mongar, J. L., and Herxheimer, H. (1951). *Lancet* **2**, 376–382.

Schneider, M. W., and Drazen, J. M. (1980). *Am. Rev. Respir. Dis.* **121**, 835–842.

Serhan, C. N., Fridovich, J., Goetzl, E. J., Dunham, P. B., and Weissman, G. (1982). *J. Biol. Chem.* **257**, 4746–4752.

Sirois, P., Borgeat, P., Jeanson, A., Roy, S., and Girard, G. (1980). *Prostaglandins Med.* **5**, 429–444.

Sirois, P., Roy, S., Borgeat, P., Picard, S., and Corey, E. J. (1981a). *Biochem. Biophys. Res. Commun.* **99**, 385–390.

Sirois, P., Roy, S., Tetrault, J. P., Borgeat, P., Picard, S., and Corey, E. J. (1981b). *Prostaglandins Med.* **7**, 327–340.

Strandberg, K. (1973). *Acta Pharmacol. Toxicol.* **32**, 33–45.

Ueno, A., Tanaka, K., Hirose, R., Shishido, M., and Katori, M. (1982). *Proc. Int. Conf. Prostaglandins, 5th, 1982* p. 483.

Vargaftig, B. B., Lefort, J., and Murphy, R. C. (1981). *Eur. J. Pharmacol.* **72**, 417–418.

Weiss, J. W., Drazen, J. M., Coles, N., McFadden, E. R., Weller, P. F., Corey, E. J., Lewis, R. A., and Austen, K. F. (1982a). *Science* **216**, 190–197.

Weiss, J. W., Drazen, J. M., McFadden, E. R., Lewis, R. A., Weller, P., Corey, E. J., and Austen, K. F. (1982b). *Clin. Res.* **30**, 571A.

Welton, A. F., Crowley, H. J., Miller, D. A., and Yaremko, B. (1981). *Prostaglandins* **21**, 287–296.

Zijlstra, F. J., Bonta, I. L., Adolfs, M. J. P., and Vincent, J. E. (1981). *Eur. J. Pharmacol.* **76**, 297–298.

Zijlstra, F. J., Adolfs, M. J. P., Vincent, J. E., and Bonta, I. L. (1982). *Proc. Int. Conf. Prostaglandins, 5th, 1982* p. 342.

11

Pharmacologic Antagonism of
the Leukotrienes

ROBERT D. KRELL, FREDERICK J. BROWN,
ALVIN K. WILLARD, AND RALPH E. GILES

Stuart Pharmaceuticals
Division of ICI Americas, Inc.
Biomedical Research Department
Wilmington, Delaware

I. INTRODUCTION

Leukotrienes are products of the lipoxygenase pathway of arachidonic acid metabolism (Samuelsson, 1982). The peptidoleukotrienes C$_4$, D$_4$, and E$_4$ (LTC, D, and E) comprise the biologic activity of the crude material referred to for over 40 years as slow-reacting substance of anaphylaxis (SRS-A). It is generally presumed that these leukotrienes are the mediators of much of the symptomatology accompanying allergic asthmatic episodes.

271

The evidence for this hypothesis, however, is circumstantial and may be summarized as follows:

1. SRS-A is released from sensitized human lung tissue and sensitized peripheral basophils following exposure to specific antigen as well as non-immunologic stimuli (Sheard *et al.*, 1967; Orange *et al.*, 1971; Grant and Lichtenstein, 1974).

2. An SRS-A – like material is present in human plasma following allergic asthmatic episodes (Orange and Langer, 1974).

3. Leukotrienes have been demonstrated to possess extraordinarily potent contractile activity on human airway smooth muscle both *in vitro* (Dahlén *et al.*, 1980; Hanna *et al.*, 1981) and *in vivo* (Weiss *et al.*, 1982).

4. These materials also have the ability to increase vascular permeability, resulting in edema, which often accompanies allergic asthmatic episodes (Dahlén *et al.*, 1981; Sugio *et al.*, 1981).

5. Mucus hypersecretion frequently accompanies asthmatic episodes, and the leukotrienes have been demonstrated to possess potent secretogogic activity in human airway explants (Marom *et al.*, 1982).

6. In Schultz-Dale type reactions in sensitized human bronchial smooth muscle, the leukotrienes appear to contribute to the antigen-evoked contraction (Adams and Lichtenstein, 1979). This observation is based solely on the ability of the "selective" leukotriene antagonist FPL55712 (Augstein *et al.*, 1973) to reverse antigen-induced contractile responses.

7. Drugs capable of inhibiting the synthesis and/or release of the leukotrienes, such as disodium cromoglycate and steroids, have found a place in the therapeutic armamentarium.

8. FPL55712 inhibits antigen-induced decreases in FEV_1 in human allergic asthmatics (Lee *et al.*, 1981).

9. Drugs capable of inhibiting either the synthesis and/or release or blocking the end organ effects of other putative mediators such as histamine, prostaglandins, and thromboxane have not proved clinically useful. Leukotrienes presently occupy center stage as the principal putative mediators of the pathophysiology of allergic asthma.

Accepting this hypothesis, it follows that agents capable of inhibiting either (1) the biosynthesis and/or release of the peptidoleukotrienes or (2) their effects at the target tissue (e.g., airways and vascular smooth muscle, mucus glands) may prove to have desirable therapeutic properties in the treatment of allergic asthma and perhaps other allergic disorders as well.

With regard to antagonists to the leukotrienes, the design of such agents could be enhanced by increasing our knowledge of leukotriene receptors. The purpose here is to review the current status of information on leukotriene receptors.

II. PHARMACOLOGIC APPROACHES TO STUDYING RECEPTORS

A. Classification of Receptors

Over the past quarter of a century, several experimental approaches to characterizing, classifying, and subclassifying receptors have been devised.

Ahlquist (1948) studied the relative order of potency of a series of substituted 3,4-dihydroxyphenylethanolamines in various tissues to classify adrenergic receptors into two types, α and β. He observed that the relative order of activity was dependent on whether a β or an α receptor dominated in the tissue.

A second approach has been to utilize the optical isomers of agonists (Patil *et al.*, 1971) or antagonists (Buckner and Patil, 1971) to classify receptors. With this method, the isomeric activity ratios for agonists or antagonists from various tissues are studied under rigidly controlled experimental conditions. Theoretically, the isomeric activity ratios should be similar in tissues where receptors are of a single type, whereas significant differences in ratios are suggestive of differences in receptor populations.

A third more commonly utilized technique is to conduct a Schild analysis (Arunlakshana and Schild, 1959) of a selective receptor antagonist in different tissue preparations. This method permits the calculation of dissociation constants for the receptor–antagonist complex according to strict criteria. Comparing dissociation constants for a single receptor–antagonist combination can reveal the similarity or dissimilarity of receptors among various tissues. Furthermore, it can be used to determine whether two agonists are acting on the same or dissimilar types of receptors in a single preparation. This technique can also determine the mechanism of action (e.g., competitive or noncompetitive) of antagonists.

The last technique to be described, and by far the most popular today, is ligand receptor-binding studies. This approach employs radioactive ligands (agonists or antagonists) of high specific activity that bind selectively to various types of receptors. The ability of various unlabeled ligands to compete with labeled ligands from tissues or, more frequently, tissue homogenates reveals the similarity or dissimilarity of receptors (Snyder, 1978).

B. Characterization of Receptors

The ability of an agonist to interact with a receptor requires a certain degree of complementary molecular structure between the two. Indeed, such complementarity provides the basis of specificity of action of an agonist. For an agonist to induce a response it must possess an ability to combine with the receptor (i.e., affinity), as well as an ability to produce the appropriate conformational change in the receptor (i.e., intrinsic activity or efficacy). Ligands that possess only affinity are antagonists for those agents that possess both affinity and efficacy.

Molecular modifications of agonists can be helpful in determining which portions of the molecule impart affinity and efficacy. This type of analysis ultimately permits one to map indirectly the molecular topography of the receptor. Initial results from this type of approach have been obtained for the leukotrienes and are discussed in the following section.

III. LEUKOTRIENE RECEPTORS

A. Peptidoleukotriene Receptors

1. Distribution and Evidence for Their Existence

The peptidoleukotrienes C, D, and E contract a variety of isolated smooth muscle preparations including airways (Drazen *et al.*, 1980; Krell *et al.*, 1981a; Dahlén *et al.*, 1980), gastrointestinal (Hedqvist *et al.*, 1980; Feniuk *et al.*, 1982), vascular (Hand *et al.*, 1981; Dahlén *et al.*, 1981; Kito *et al.*, 1981), and uterine smooth muscle (Hedqvist *et al.*, 1980; Weichman and Tucker, 1982). Furthermore, LTD_4 has been demonstrated to produce an excitation of Purkinje cells in the central nervous system (Palmer *et al.*, 1981). In most instances these various activities of the leukotrienes have been demonstrated to be susceptible, at least in part, to the LT antagonist FPL55712 (Augstein *et al.*, 1973). The selective effect of FPL55712 on leukotriene responses is most easily explained via competitive interaction with a cellular recognition site (i.e., receptor). In addition, several other "selective" LT antagonists have been described (see Section III,A,2,b,ii), indicating that FPL55712 is not an anomaly.

Equally interesting are those tissues or organs that have been demonstrated not to elicit responses to the leukotrienes. A partial listing includes rabbit (Hedqvist *et al.*, 1980), rat (Krell *et al.*, 1981a), hamster, and dog trachea (R. D. Krell, unpublished observations), as well as guinea pig and rabbit aortic strips (Berkowitz *et al.*, 1981), rat uterus (Hedqvist *et al.*, 1980), human gastrointestinal smooth muscle (Ghelani and Holroyde, 1981), and rabbit duodenum (Hedqvist *et al.*, 1980). Thus the leukotrienes, unlike the prostaglandins, exhibit rather remarkable tissue and species specificity. The simplest explanation for the absence of tissue responsiveness to peptidoleukotrienes would be that these tissues *lack* a cellular recognition site (receptor) for the leukotrienes.

2. Characteristics of Leukotriene Receptors

The search for a leukotriene antagonist is greatly hampered by the fact that little is known about the postulated leukotriene receptor(s). Critical information about the geometric and electronic characteristics of the active site of such receptors is presently unavailable. Consequently, the two main leads guiding the design of receptor blockers are the structures of the few known, but clinically nonviable, leukotriene antagonists such as FPL55712 and the structures of the leukotrienes themselves.

In this section, a detailed compilation of all the reported spasmogenic activities of LTD structural analogs will be presented, followed by a review of what is known concerning active derivatives and antagonists of LTB.

A. ANALOGS OF PEPTIDOLEUKOTRIENES. If the key structural features of the leukotrienes that are recognized and accommodated by the receptor can be identified, indirect knowledge is gained about the requirements of the receptor and what chemical moieties may be required for a potential antagonist. The delineation of the critical functionalities present in the leukotrienes, the structures of which are provided in Fig. 1, has been greatly aided by the efforts of synthetic chemists. Among others, groups at Harvard (Corey *et al.,* 1980a), Merck-Frosst (Rokach *et al.,* 1980), and Hoffmann LaRoche (Rosenberger and Neukom, 1980) have pioneered synthetic routes to the leukotrienes that have made available a number of isomers and analogs.

In vitro biologic testing of these synthetic modified leukotrienes has provided some indications as to the portions of the molecule critical to activity. Much of the work has focused on analogs of LTD. The contractile activities of these derivatives, relative to the parent LTD, are summarized in Table I. In no case have any of these analogs been reported to exhibit leukotriene antagonism. Similar trends are usually observed when the corresponding structural modifications are made in the LTC and LTE series, although much less data are available. The relative activities of given derivatives are also generally comparable when derived from *in vitro* testing on guinea pig tissues other than parenchyma, such as ileum or trachea. However, since the data have been generated in different laboratories using different tissue preparations and agonists of varying purity, discrepancies do occur in specific cases. It is nonetheless possible to discern some general structure – activity relationships.

The leukotrienes possess in common several functional groups whose importance for activity can be assessed. The data indicate that only one of the two carboxylic acid moieties in LTD is required for spasmogenic activity, and that the glycine carboxyl is the more important of the two. The observa-

TABLE I

Comparative Contractile Activities of LTD$_4$ Analogs on Guinea Pig Parenchyma

Entry	Compound	Activity	Reference
	$(5S,6R)$-$\Delta^{7,9}$-E-$\Delta^{11,14}$-Z- [LTD$_4$; Fig. 1 (**1b**)]	1.0	
	Carboxyl Modifications		
1	C-1 Monoamide	1.0	Lewis *et al.* (1981b)
2	Gly monoamide	0.10	Lewis *et al.* (1981b)
3	Bisamide	<0.001	Lewis *et al.* (1981b); Okuyama *et al.* (1982)
4	Gly dimethylmonoamide	0.006	Lewis *et al.* (1981b)
	Sulfur Oxidation State		
5	Less polar sulfoxide	0.10	Corey *et al.* (1982)
6	More polar sulfoxide	<0.001	Corey *et al.* (1982)
7	Sulfone	0.32[a]	Girard *et al.* (1982); Jones *et al.* (1982a)
8	LTE$_4$-sulfone[b]	0.63[a]	Jones *et al.* (1982a)
	Amine Modifications		
9	N-acetyl	0.03	Lewis *et al.* (1982)
10	Desamino	1.0; 0.05	Okuyama *et al.* (1982); Lewis *et al.* (1982)
11	Desamino, bisamide	<0.001	Lewis *et al.* (1982)
12	Desamino, bisdimethylamide	<0.001	Okuyama *et al.* (1982)
	C-5, C-6 Substituents and Chirality		
13	$(5R,6R)$	0.004; 0.007[a]	Lewis *et al.* (1982); Tsai *et al.* (1982)
14	$(5S,6S)$	0.004; <0.001[a]	Lewis *et al.* (1982); Tsai *et al.* (1982)
15	$(5R,6S)$	0.004; 0.001[a]	Baker *et al.* (1981); Tsai *et al.* (1982)
16	5-Desoxy either $(6R)$ or $(6S)$	<0.01	Corey and Hoover (1982)
17	5-Desoxy-7E-hexahydro	<0.001	Lewis *et al.* (1981b)
18	$(5S)$-OMe LTC$_4$[c]	0.01	Okuyama *et al.* (1982)
	Amino Acid Modifications		
19	L-Cys, Gly → Glutathione [LTC$_4$; Fig. 1 (**1a**)]	1.26; 0.08; 0.20; 0.28[d]	Jones *et al.* (1982a); Lewis *et al.* (1980); Okuyama *et al.* (1982); Lewis *et al.* (1980)
20	→ L-Cys [LTE$_4$; Fig. 1(**1c**)]	0.38; 0.32[a]; 0.20[d]	Lewis *et al.* (1980); Jones *et al.* (1982a); Lewis *et al.* (1980)
21	→ L-Cys, L-Glu [LTF$_4$; Fig. 1 (**1d**)]	0.1; 0.004[d,e]	Okuyama *et al.* (1982); Ellis *et al.* (1982)
22	→ L-Cys, D-Ala	0.11	Lewis *et al.* (1981b)
23	→ L-Cys, L-Ala	0.09	Lewis *et al.* (1981b)

TABLE I *(Continued)*

Entry	Compound	Activity	Reference
24	→ L-Cys, <u>Pro</u>	0.03	Lewis *et al.* (1981b)
25	→ L-Cys, <u>Val</u>	0.008	Lewis *et al.* (1981b)
26	→ <u>D-Cys</u>, Gly	0.11	Lewis *et al.* (1981b)
27	→ <u>D-Homocysteine</u>, Gly	0.26	Lewis *et al.* (1981b)
28	→ <u>D-Penicillamine</u>, Gly	<0.001	Lewis *et al.* (1981b)
29	→ $-S(CH_2)_3NHCH_2CO_2H$	0.01	Okuyama *et al.* (1982)
30	→ $-S(CH_2)_3N(CH_3)_2$	0.001	Okuyama *et al.* (1982)
Modifications of Tetraene			
31	14,15-Dihydro (LTD$_3$)	1.0[d]; 0.66	Hammerström (1981); Drazen *et al.* (1981)
32	11-*E*	0.30; 0.10; 0.27[a]; 0.10[a]	Lewis *et al.* (1980); Baker *et al.* (1982); Tsai *et al.* (1982); Baker *et al.* (1982)
33	11-*E*-(5*R*,6*S*)	0.002[a]	Tsai *et al.* (1982)
34	9-*Z*	0.10; 0.22[a]	Baker *et al.* (1982)
35	9-*Z*-11-*E*	0.45; 0.33[a]	Baker *et al.* (1982)
36	9-*Z*-11,12-dihydro-LTC$_4$[c]	0.50	Okuyama *et al.* (1982)
37	7-*Z*	0.10[d]	Ernest *et al.* (1982)
38	7-*Z*-9,10-dihydro-LTC$_4$[c]	0.01	Okuyama *et al.* (1982)
39	7-*E*-hexahydro	0.019	Drazen *et al.* (1981)
40	5-Desoxy-7-*E*-hexahydro	<0.001	Lewis *et al.* (1981)
41	7-*Z*-hexahydro	0.03	Drazen *et al.* (1981)
42	Octahydro	<0.001	Okuyama *et al.* (1982)
43	8,10-*Z*-12-*E*-14-*Z*	0.002[a]	Baker *et al.* (1982)
44	13-*E*-15-OH	<0.001	Drazen *et al.* (1981)

[a] Relative contractile activity on guinea pig trachea.
[b] Relative contractile activity compared to LTE$_4$.
[c] Relative contractile activity compared to LTC$_4$.
[d] Relative contractile activity on guinea pig ileum.
[e] Compound was a mixture of 5,6-diastereomers.

tion that the glycine dimethylamide (Table I, entry 4) is considerably less active than the corresponding primary amide (Table I, entry 2) suggests hydrogen bonding at the carboxyl-accommodating site of the receptor is an important binding interaction. The presence of a divalent, nucleophilic sulfur atom is not a requirement for activity, since derivatives with oxidized sulfur, especially the sulfones, retain considerable activity.

There is conflicting evidence regarding the importance of the free-amine functionality in LTD. Lewis *et al.* (1982) reported that desamino-LTD is 20

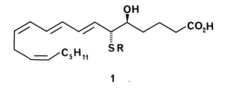

COMPOUND	-SR	
1a	·S CH₂CH NHCOCH₂CH₂ CH CO₂H CONHCH₂CO₂H NH₂	LTC₄
1b	·S CH₂CHNH₂ CONHCH₂CO₂H	LTD₄
1c	·S CH₂ CHNH₂ CO₂H	LTE₄
1d	·S CH₂ CHNHCOCH₂CH₂CHCO₂H CO₂H NH₂	LTF₄

Fig. 1. Structures of the peptidoleukotrienes.

times less potent than LTD, but Okuyama *et al.* (1982) found the two compounds to be equally active. However, further data for both amine-modified LTC and LTE imply, to the extent that the same or similar receptors to those for LTD are involved, that the free amine is not critical. Thus desamino-LTC (Okuyama *et al.,* 1982) and the *N*-acetyl derivative of LTE (Lewis *et al.,* 1981b) retain 50 and 31% of the contractile activity of their respective parents on guinea pig parenchyma. Furthermore, desamino-LTD is only five times less active than LTD on guinea pig ileum (Lewis *et al.,* 1981b).

The hydroxyl group at C-5 appears to play an important role, perhaps by hydrogen bonding with the receptor or by enforcing a particular preferred conformation on the molecule via intramolecular hydrogen bonding. Deshydroxy-LTD and O-methylated LTC are 100 times less potent than the parent compounds. A further indication that carbons 5 and 6 comprise a key region is the strong chirality requirement for recognition of an agonist by the leukotriene receptor. Any change in the natural (5*S*,6*R*)-configuration results in a precipitous decrease in activity. The only exception to this generalization is the report that (5R,6S)-LTE remains 50% as potent as the natural stereoisomer on guinea pig ileum (Rosenberger and Neukom, 1980). It is pertinent to mention that detailed ^{1}H-NMR studies of LTD have demonstrated the existence of a preferred solution conformation about the critical 5,6 and 6,7 carbon–carbon bonds (Loftus and Bernstein, 1982). The methine protons at C-6 and C-7 were shown to be anti. Furthermore, the sulfidopeptide and the C-5 to C-1 carboxylic acid chain prefer a trans orientation.

A common structural feature of the leukotrienes is the presence of a sulfido peptide. Several modifications can be tolerated in this portion of the molecule. If it is assumed that all the leukotrienes act on similar receptors, the substantial activities of LTC and LTE relative to LTD would indicate that quite a large variation is permitted in the peptide-receiving region of the receptor. The LTD analog containing an unnatural D-cysteine residue (Table I, entry 26) possesses 11% of the spasmogenicity of the natural isomer, providing additional evidence that a free amino group is not a key element for recognition of the agonist by the receptor. The length of the carbon chain between the sulfur atom and the amide bond can be increased by one carbon (D-homocysteine replacing L-cysteine) with only a four-fold decrease in potency. The addition of a methyl group (Table I, entries 22 and 23), but not an isopropyl group (Table I, entry 25), α to the peptidyl carboxylic acid of LTD is tolerated fairly well. In contrast, the presence of geminal methyl substituents α to the sulfur atom (Table I, entry 28) causes a decrease in potency of three orders of magnitude. This loss of activity may well reflect the introduction of too much steric bulk near the critical C-5,C-6 region of the molecule. Formal reductive elimination of the amide carbonyl from a desamino-LTD analog (Table I, entry 29) causes a 100-fold drop in spasmogenicity. With LTC, removal of the glycine residue lowers the potency by a factor of two (Okuyama et al., 1982).

The final major structural unit of the leukotrienes is the lipophilic tetraene chain. A large degree of flexibility is tolerated in this portion of the molecule. There are, however, definite receptor recognition elements present in the tetraene chain, since perhydro-LTD is inactive. Saturation of the nonconjugated Δ^{14}-double bond causes only a 1.5-fold drop in potency. Similar results have been reported for LTC (Lewis et al., 1982; Okuyama et al., 1982). The introduction of an additional double bond at C-17 in LTC results in a lowering of the potency (Hammarström, 1980). The Δ^{11}-cis-double bond can be formally isomerized to the trans geometry without precipitating much loss in activity. The analogous change in LTC and LTE gave isomers having 70 and 8% of their respective parents' contractile activity on guinea pig parenchyma (Lewis et al., 1980). A biologically generated Δ^{11}-trans-LTE is reported to be equipotent to LTE on guinea pig ileum (Bernström and Hammarström, 1981). The geometry of the Δ^9- or Δ^7-double bonds can be altered without causing more than one order of magnitude loss in potency. The Δ^9-*cis*-, Δ^{11}-*trans*-, or Δ^9-*cis*-, Δ^{11}-dihydro analogs remain quite active. A graphic depiction of the relative spatial orientations of some of these more active LTD olefin isomers is provided in Fig. 2. The assumption has been made that the tetraene chain will in each case prefer the most extended conformation, as has been found for LTD (Loftus and Bernstein, 1982). Such a superpositioning of the active isomers may help define the steric variations acceptable to the tetraene-accommodating region of the leukotriene receptor.

If the conjugation of the Δ^7-double bond is interrupted, more serious losses in contractile activity occur. Both the Δ^7-*cis*- or Δ^7-*trans*-hexahydro-LTD analogs and Δ^7-*cis*, Δ^9-dihydro-LTC show close to 100-fold decreases in potency. However, it has been reported that Δ^7-*trans*-hexahydro-LTC retains 19% of the spasmogenicity of LTC on guinea pig parenchyma (Lewis *et al.*,

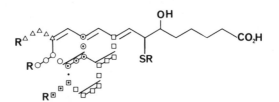

CODE	ISOMER	ACTIVITY
——	7-E, 9-E, 11-Z (LTD₄)	1
· · ·	7-E, 9-Z, 11-E	0.33
Δ Δ Δ	7-E, 9-E, 11-E	0.27
○ ○ ○	7-E, 9-Z, 11-Z	0.22
□ □ □	7-Z, 9-E, 11-Z	0.10[a]

Fig. 2. Relative spatial orientations and contractile activities of geometric olefin isomers of LTD on guinea pig trachea. (*a* Relative activity on guinea pig ileum.)

1982). The importance of the presence of a double bond at C-7 is demonstrated by the large loss in activity observed for the conjugated $\Delta^{8,10,12,14}$-tetraene (Table I, entry 43).

The maintenance of lipophilicity in the tetraene tail of the leukotrienes is very important. If a hydroxyl group is introduced at C-15 (Table I, entry 44), the activity drops by more than three orders of magnitude. Either diastereomer resulting from moving the peptide group of LTC to C-12 with concomitant rearrangement of the conjugated triene to Δ^6-*cis, $\Delta^{8,10}$-trans* is inactive (Lewis *et al.,* 1982). Likewise isomers of LTC or LTD with the peptide at C-15 and the hydroxyl group at C-14 are also inactive (Lewis *et al.,* 1982). The corresponding 12-hydroxyl, 11-peptidyl analogs of both LTC and LTD were more than 1000 times less active than the natural leukotrienes (Lewis *et al.,* 1982).

In summary, several conclusions may be made concerning the molecular features characterizing a good leukotriene agonist and hence what factors constitute the critical recognition elements for the leukotriene receptor. The most important functional moieties of the leukotrienes are the peptidyl carboxyl group, the C-5 hydroxyl group, and a conjugated olefin at C-7. It is likely that neither the free amine of LTD nor the sulfur atom at C-6 plays a significant role. The stereochemistry in the C-5 to C-6 portion of the molecules is extremely important, suggesting that a particular orientation of the three "tails" emanating from this central region is important for receptor binding. The peptide-receiving portion of the receptor can tolerate some variation in both stereochemistry and the chain length between the sulfur atom and the peptidyl carboxyl terminus. The receptor site accommodating the tetraene requires a lipophilic moiety with some conjugated, olefinic character, but considerable geometric latitude is tolerated.

B. ANTAGONISTS OF THE PEPTIDOLEUKOTRIENES.   i. Historical.   During the 40 years between the discovery of SRS-A (Kellaway and Trethewie, 1940) and its structural elucidation (for review, see Samuelsson, 1982), several reports have appeared in the literature regarding the ability of various types of compounds to antagonize the smooth muscle-contractile activity of this crude material. Berry and Collier (1964) clearly demonstrated the ability of acetylsalicylic acid, as well as other nonsteroidal antiinflammatory agents, to inhibit *in vivo* pulmonary responses in the guinea pig induced by exogenous guinea pig lung-derived crude SRS-A. In later studies, a "selective" antagonism of SRS-A–induced contractions of isolated human bronchial smooth muscle by both meclofenamate and flufenamate (Collier and Sweatman, 1969) was demonstrated.

The observations of Collier that nonsteroidal antiinflammatory agents antagonize the bronchoconstrictive activity of SRS-A in the *in vivo* guinea pig has been repeatedly confirmed with synthetic leukotrienes (Seale and Piper, 1978; Piper and Samhoun, 1982; Vargaftig *et al.,* 1981; Folco *et al.,* 1981; Zijlstra *et al.,* 1981; Schiantarelli *et al.,* 1981; Mathé *et al.,* 1977; Weichman *et al.,* 1982b). The underlying mechanism appears related to the ability of the leukotrienes to induce the release of thromboxane A_2 (TxA_2) from guinea pig lung, which contributes to the leukotriene-induced contraction. Inhibition of cyclooxygenase by nonsteroidal antiinflammatory agents reduces TxA_2 production and consequently antagonizes the contractile response to the leukotrienes.

In contrast, the nonsteroidal antiinflammatory agent indomethacin does not alter the contractile activity of LTC or LTD on isolated human bronchial smooth muscle (Jones *et al.,* 1982b), suggesting that cyclooxygenase products do not contribute to the contractile response in this species. Superficially, it would appear that these recent observations conflict with the earlier studies by Collier and Sweatman (1969) with meclofenamate and flufenamate. However, identical studies with leukotrienes and the fenamates must be conducted before such a conclusion is warranted.

Mathé and Strandberg (1971) reported that polyphloretin phosphate antagonized the contractile activity of SRS-A on isolated human bronchi and the guinea pig ileum. Although they concluded that the material was a competitive antagonist in this tissue, the data appear more suggestive of noncompetitive antagonism.

ii. Recent Discoveries of Leukotriene Antagonists. Having mapped the geometric requirements of the leukotriene receptor(s) from the viewpoint of the various modified leukotrienes, and having revisited historical aspects of leukotriene antagonists, it is appropriate to consider the structures of contemporary antagonists. Study of these receptor blockers presumably offers an opportunity for additional exploration of the molecular properties required for recognition by the leukotriene receptor and thus contributes to the rational design of better antagonists.

A discussion of chemical structures that have been reported to antagonize the action of leukotrienes or SRS-A properly emanates from the classic antagonist FPL55712 [Fig. 3(2); for review, see Chand, 1979]. Although the compound has a variety of pharmacologic effects and suffers from a fleeting biologic half-life, FPL55712 has played a critical role in the isolation and characterization of SRS-A. Augstein *et al.* (1973) first reported its structure and suggested its value as a pharmacologic tool to help define the role of SRS-A in immediate hypersensitivity reactions. A universal criterion during the isolation and purification of SRS-A was that the isolated contractile activity be antagonized by FPL55712.

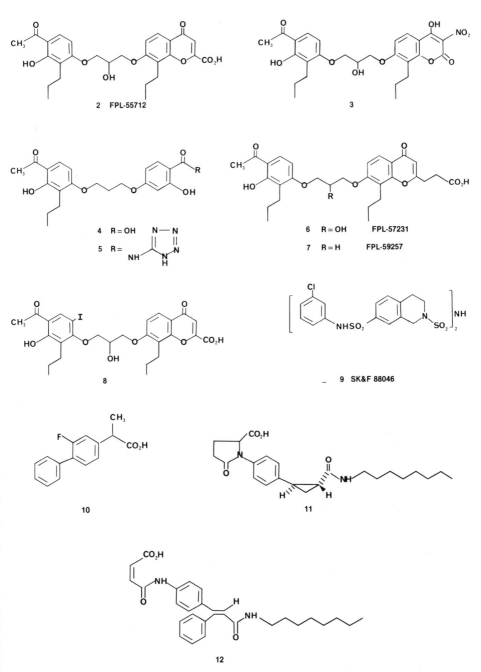

Fig. 3. Structures of compounds reported to be leukotriene antagonists.

Analogs of FPL55712 were broadly explored (Appleton *et al.*, 1977) before the structure of SRS-A was known. This effort examined the chromone ring, the hydroxyacetophenone ring, and the polymethylenedioxy chain connecting the two. Only removal of the hydroxyl group from the polymethylenedioxy chain produced any increase in potency. This did not translate to an advantage *in vivo.*

Others soon joined the effort to discover a better FPL55712. Buckle *et al.* (1979) developed a broad series of structure–activity relationships centered on nitrocoumarins. One of the best compounds in this series was the analog **3** (Fig. 3), closely related to FPL55712. Many of these compounds included modifications of the hydroxyacetophenone ring. Notably, the same substitution pattern reported as optimal by Appleton *et al.* (1977) produced the highest potency in their series. Another related series of compounds has been patented by Oxford and Ellis (1981). Although claim is made to a broad range of compounds, only the salicylic acid (**4**) (Fig. 3) and its derivative (**5**) (Fig. 3) are specifically mentioned in the claims. No biologic data are reported.

Much attention has focused on the short biologic half-life of FPL55712. Sheard *et al.* (1982) reported the two propionic acid analogs [Fig. 3(**6** and **7**)] of FPL55712. Analog FPL59257 [Fig. 3(**7**)] was less potent than FPL55712 but gave a longer, more consistent response *in vivo* in both guinea pigs and humans (Holroyde *et al.*, 1982). This activity *in vivo* was accompanied by an *in vitro* profile different from FPL55712. It was difficult to wash FPL59257 out of preparations of guinea pig ileum; frequently, control responses could not be reestablished. The authors suggest that this *in vitro* profile and the longer duration *in vivo* can be explained by FPL59257 binding tightly to the leukotriene receptor.

Other evidence of the attention given to the short half-life of FPL55712 comes in the form of another patent (Rokach *et al.*, 1981). This patent covers a single derivative [Fig. 3(**8**)] of FPL55712 and claims, among other advantages, that this iodo derivative is longer-acting than the known antagonists. No specific reports of the biologic activity have appeared.

Several series of compounds whose structures are not closely related to FPL55712 have been reported to antagonize the leukotrienes or SRS-A. Ali *et al.* (1982a,b) have described a series of imidodisulfamides that were reported to be antagonists of SRS-A. One of these, SK&F88046 [Fig. 3(**9**)] has been highlighted (Gleason *et al.*, 1982). The compound is equipotent with FPL55712 against contraction of the guinea pig ileum by partially purified SRS-A and against contraction of guinea pig lung parenchymal strips by LTD. It appeared that SK&F88046 was less rapidly metabolized than FPL55712. More recent data, however, suggest that it is an antagonist of TxA_2, rather than LTD (Mong *et al.*, 1983).

Greig and Griffin (1975) have reported that hydratropic acids including flurbiprofen (Fig. 3; **10**) antagonized the contraction of the guinea pig tracheal chain by rat SRS-A. This *in vitro* activity was correlated with protection of sensitized guinea pigs against anaphylactic shock when challenged at 3 to 4 weeks after sensitization (but not after 5 to 8 weeks). The compounds antagonized contraction of tracheal chains by arachidonic acid, prostaglandin $F_{2\alpha}$, and bradykinin at somewhat higher doses.

A series of patents have been issued from Pfizer Laboratories claiming compounds represented by structures **11** and **12** (Fig. 3) and related analogs as antagonists of SRS (Kadin, 1981, 1982). The compounds were tested against SRS-induced contractions of guinea pig ileum. No details of biologic data were presented.

Structural relationships between these reported antagonists and the leukotriene derivatives discussed earlier are not obvious, although the antagonist activities of several of the compounds have been reported to be competitive. One striking observation is that in *in vitro* smooth muscle preparations, the leukotrienes are active in the range of 10^{-9} to 10^{-12} M, but the reported antagonists are only active at concentrations down to 10^{-6} or 10^{-7} M. It should be possible to take advantage of better receptor recognition in order to obtain stronger binding.

There is no evidence that promising therapeutic candidates lie in these various series of leukotriene antagonists. Oral activity has yet to be reported, and increases in duration of activity beyond FPL55712 have not been dramatic. The availability of synthetic leukotrienes and synthetic routes that provide analogs and derivatives such as those discussed, along with the identification of several series of molecules with leukotriene antagonist activity, give medicinal chemists an excellent basis for the design of novel, potent antagonists. As well, these agonists and antagonists provide pharmacologists with the necessary tools to characterize the *in vitro* pharmacology of new antagonists and to develop relevant models for the *in vivo* evaluation of the compounds.

B. Analogs and Antagonists of Leukotriene B₄

Leukotriene B_4 (LTB_4) exerts a variety of pharmacologic actions including neutrophil chemotaxis and chemokinesis (Ford-Hutchinson *et al.,* 1981b; Malmsten *et al.,* 1980), enhanced vascular permeability (Bray *et al.,* 1981), and a bronchoconstrictor activity probably mediated through products of the cyclooxygenase pathway in the guinea pig (Sirois *et al.,* 1980). According to current understanding of drug action, LTB must combine with some macromolecular component of tissues (i.e., the receptor). While dose–response relationships have been generated in certain studies (Malmsten *et al.,* 1980), direct evidence for the existence of specific LTB receptors is lacking. For example, classical studies using selective inhibitors of LTB in a variety of tissues to evaluate the receptor and to calculate pA_2 values in order to discern the similarity or differences of receptor type in a variety of effector organs are missing. However, as will be discussed, certain evidence is available to suggest indirectly that specific receptors do exist.

Because of the minute quantities of material available from biologic sources, the complete identification of the structure of LTB depended on comparison of natural LTB with material prepared by synthetic chemists. In this effort a series of isomers of LTB was made available for comparison with the natural material. These isomers begin to provide an idea of the specificity of LTB for its putative receptor(s). Leukotriene B [Fig. 4(**13**)] has now been rigorously identified as (5*S*,12*R*)-dihydroxy-6,14-*cis*-8,10-*trans*-eicosatetraenoic acid (Corey *et al.*, 1980b). Any change in the configuration of the triene unit results in a loss of at least two orders of magnitude in chemotactic activity (Lewis *et al.*, 1981a; Goetzl and Pickett, 1981; Ford-Hutchinson *et al.*, 1981b). The two diastereoisomers with the correct double-bond geometry, but with a different configuration of the hydroxyl group at either C-5 or C-12, have not been reported.

Several derivatives of LTB have been prepared or isolated from natural sources. The chemotactic activity of LTB-methyl ester [Fig. 4(**14**)] is equal to that of the parent acid, but the stability of the methyl ester to the assay conditions was not established. The diacetate of LTB [Fig. 4(**15**)] had 10–35% of the chemotactic activity of LTB itself (Goetzl and Pickett, 1981; Lewis *et al.*, 1982). Products of metabolic modifications of LTB, 20-hydroxy LTB, and 20-carboxy LTB, are one to two orders of magnitude less active than LTB as stimulators of neutrophil migration (Palmblad *et al.*, 1982) or degranulation (Feinmark *et al.*, 1981) but are somewhat more potent stimulators of the contraction of guinea pig lung strips (Hansson *et al.*, 1981).

Three derivatives or analogs of LTB have been reported to antagonize the activity of LTB in various assays. The diacetate [Fig. 4(**15**)] competitively inhibits the chemotactic response of equimolar concentrations of LTB. Similar concentrations had no effect on the chemotactic responses to fragments of C-5 or to f-Met-Leu-Phe (Goetzl and Pickett, 1981). The dimethylamide of LTB [Fig. 4(**16**)] inhibits neutrophil degranulation induced by LTB with an apparent $K_D = 2 \times 10^{-7}$ M. At the concentrations used, the dimethylamide had negligible agonist activity (Showell *et al.*, 1982) The antagonist activity has a slow onset and may manifest itself through a desensitization mechanism. The dimethylamide does not show agonist activity at higher concentrations. Two groups have reported that (5*S*,12*S*)-dihydroxy-6,10-*trans*-8,14-*cis*-eicosatetraenoic acid (5,12-diHETE) [Fig. 4(**17**)] antagonizes

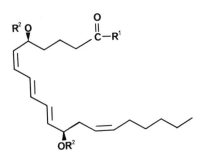

13	R¹ = OH ,	R² = H	LTB₄
14	R¹ = OCH₃,	R² = H	
15	R¹ = OH ,	R² = CH₃CO	
16	R¹ = NMe₂ ,	R² = H	

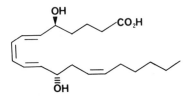

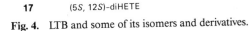

17   (5*S*, 12*S*)–diHETE

Fig. 4. LTB and some of its isomers and derivatives.

LTB-induced degranulation by a similar mechanism (Feinmark *et al.,* 1981; Showell *et al.,* 1982).

Because of the mechanistic complexity of the *in vitro* assays for LTB, the antagonist activity reported cannot yet be assigned to a receptor-mediated event. Again, the availability of both agonists and putative antagonists allow both pharmacologists and chemists to proceed with the task of designing and identifying LTB antgonists.

C. Classification of Leukotriene Receptors

Although these are early days in the biology of the leukotrienes, several reports have appeared purporting evidence for the existence of different populations of peptidoleukotriene receptors. Heterogeneity of receptor populations is highly precedented in pharmacologic literature. Examples include histamine H_1 and H_2 receptors originally postulated by Ash and Schild (1966), for which convincing evidence was finally obtained in 1972 by Black *et al.* with the discovery of the selective histamine H_2-receptor antagonist burimamide. Subclassification of β-adrenergic receptors into β_1 and β_2 was accomplished in 1967 by Lands *et al.* and eventually led to the development of β_2-selective agonists for the treatment of bronchial asthma.

For present purposes it seems appropriate to separate current evidence for heterogeneity of leukotriene receptors into two categories: (1) circumstantial and (2) direct pharmacologic evidence.

1. Circumstantial Evidence for Diversity of Leukotriene Receptors

A. PULMONARY SMOOTH MUSCLE. The first evidence regarding the possible heterogeneity of leukotriene receptors was obtained by Drazen *et al.* (1980) on isolated guinea pig lung parenchymal strips. These investigators demonstrated that FPL55712 antagonized the contractile activity of low concentrations of LTD but was without apparent effect on the upper portion of the LTD dose–response curve. Moreover, FPL55712 completely lacked activity against LTC in this tissue.

Similar observations were obtained by Krell *et al.* (1981a) on guinea pig parenchyma except that FPL55712, at most concentrations, did appear to produce a concentration-dependent rightward shift of the entire LTD dose–response curve. However, the dissociation constant (K_B value) for the FPL55712-receptor complex was found not to be independent of antagonist concentration, a criterion that must be satisfied to conclude that FPL55712 is a competitive antagonist of LTD.

As expected, a Schild analysis (Arunlakshana and Schild, 1959) for FPL55712 versus LTD yielded a line slope of 1.29 instead of the theoretical value of 1.0 that should be obtained for a competitive antagonist. Both studies tentatively concluded that the qualitatively different effects obtained with FPL55712 versus LTC and D were suggestive of differences in the receptor populations.

Weichman *et al.* (1982b) have reported that in the presence of the cyclooxygenase inhibitor indomethacin, FPL55712 did not antagonize the contractile activity of LTD on guinea pig lung parenchymal strips. Thus results obtained thus far from different laboratories provide evidence for partial, complete, or no antagonism of LTD by FPL55712 in this preparation.

These discordant results may be fashioned into a more cohesive picture when other pharmacologic effects of both LTD and FPL55712 are taken into account. As referenced in a preceding section (III,A,2,b,i), LTD-induced contraction of the guinea pig lung parenchymal strip appears to be mediated both indirectly through the release of thromboxane A_2, which contracts airways, and directly. In addition, FPL55712 has been shown to possess the ability to inhibit the synthesis of thromboxanes via inhibition of thromboxane synthetase. Consequently, the apparent antagonism of LTD by FPL55712 may be mediated through inhibition of the indirect effects rather than via a direct antagonism of LTD receptors in this tissue. This hypothesis would account for the apparent lack of antagonism of LTD by FPL55712 when thromboxane synthesis has been inhibited by cyclooxygenase inhibitors (Weichman *et al.*, 1982b), as well as the absence of an appropriate Schild analysis.

A further area of apparent disagreement are the reports of Piper and Samhoun (1981, 1982) regarding the ability of FPL55712 to antagonize the contractile activity of LTC in guinea pig parenchymal lung strip, which contasts with the observations of Drazen *et al.* (1980) and Krell *et al.* (1981a). As with LTD, the discrepancy may be more apparent than real, since (like LTD) LTC induces release of thromboxanes from the parenchyma (see preceding Section III,A,2,b,i). A modest, apparently concentration-related shift of the extreme lower portion of the LTC dose–response curve was obtained with FPL55712 (Krell *et al.*, 1981a). The studies of Piper and Samhoun (1981, 1982) demonstrated a similar antagonism of low concentrations of LTC by FPL55712; however, these investigators did not construct full dose–response curves (probably because they lacked an adequate leukotriene supply). Consequently, the lack of effect of FPL55712 over the middle and upper portion of the curve would not have been observed. Thus it is possible that FPL55712 inhibits the indirect but not the direct component of the LTC contraction.

Piper and Samhoun (1981) have also observed that both rabbit and rat parenchymal lung strips contract to both LTC and LTD, but that neither cyclooxygenase inhibitors nor FPL55712 antagonize the contraction. It appears that leukotriene contraction of lung parenchymal strips from several species is not susceptible to blockade by FPL55712.

In marked contrast to parenchyma, FPL55712 does antagonize the contractile activity of LTC, D, and E on normal isolated guinea pig trachea and bronchial smooth muscle (Krell *et al.*, 1981a, 1983a; Fleisch *et al.*, 1982; Weichman *et al.*, 1982b; Armour *et al.*, 1982).

In summary, qualitative differences in the susceptibility of the contractile activity of peptidoleukotrienes in peripheral and conducting airways is suggestive of heterogeneity of receptors. To provide a proper perspective for these observations, it should be noted that the contractile activity of the leukotrienes on human conducting and peripheral airways is susceptible to antagonism by FPL55712 (Hanna *et al.*, 1981; Jones *et al.*, 1982b).

B. MUCUS SECRETION. Using human airway explants incubated with [^{3}H]glucosamine to label mucin macromolecules, Marom *et al.* (1982) demonstrated the ability of both biosynthetic and synthetic LTC and D to stimulate, in a concentration-dependent manner, the release of mucus. Low concentrations of FPL55712 abrogated the stimulatory effect of biosynthetic LTC and D.

In isolated cat trachea, Peatfield *et al.* (1982) failed to stimulate mucus release with LTC. However, when similar experiments were conducted *in vivo*, LTC at very high concentrations enhanced mucus secretion, and this effect was partially inhibited by FPL55712.

In an elegant series of studies, Johnson *et al.* (1983a–d) demonstrated the ability of LTC and D to enhance canine basal respiratory mucus secretion *in vivo*. A detailed pharmacologic analysis indicated that atropine, FPL55712, and hexamethonium, but not interruption of the preganglionic nerve supply, inhibited the secretogogic effect of LTC. One interpretation for these findings is that the FPL55712-sensitive LTC receptor is located on the preganglionic cholinergic nerve and serves to enhance or stimulate the release of acetylcholine, which, in turn, stimulates the postganglionic fiber. If this is correct, then the lack of effect with LTC *in vitro* in the cat (Peatfield *et al.*, 1982), which contrasted with the positive *in vivo* findings, may be explainable via a similar mechanism.

In any event, it appears that mucus secretion in human and canine airways induced by the leukotrienes is susceptible to blockade by FPL55712, whereas in the cat an effect is less prominent. One explanation for these differences is that heterogeneity in the receptor types may account for the variable effect of FPL55712.

C. VASCULAR SMOOTH MUSCLE. Hand *et al.* (1981) have demonstrated that both LTC and LTD exert potent contractile activity on the guinea pig pulmonary artery. Only the effect of LTC was antagonized by FPL55712, however, suggesting possible differences in the nature of the C and D receptors in this tissue.

D. CARDIAC. Letts and Piper (1982) have demonstrated the ability of both LTC and LTD to reduce coronary flow and, to a more modest extent, contractility of the Langendorff perfused guinea pig heart. Both indomethacin and FPL55712 inhibited the effects of LTC on both parameters. Both compounds were less efficacious against LTD than LTC.

Similar physiologic results have been obtained by Burke *et al.* (1982) in the isolated perfused guinea pig heart. However, rather substantial qualitative and quantitative pharmacologic differences were observed compared with Letts and Piper. These investigators did not find that indomethacin antagonized either decreased contractility or coronary flow caused by either LTC or D. Furthermore, FPL55712 shifted LTC dose–response curves by about 10-fold on both parameters, whereas the same concentration shifted LTD by about 100-fold—observations that are in direct contrast to the studies of Letts and Piper (1982). It is at present impossible to reconcile the rather remarkable differences in results obtained by the two groups utilizing the same species and basically an identical experimental design. Nevertheless, the quantitative differences between LTC and D with regards to antagonism by FPL55712 provides further circumstantial evidence for heterogeneity of leukotriene receptors.

Burke *et al.* (1982) also observed that LTC and D induced a dose-dependent *relaxation* of spirally cut canine coronary arteries. Neither indomethacin nor FPL55712 blocked the response. This represents the first report demonstrating a relaxant effect for the peptidoleukotrienes and provides additional suggestive evidence for heterogeneity in leukotriene receptors.

E. SUMMARY. Although the studies just cited provide considerable circumstantial evidence for heterogeneity of leukotriene receptors in various tissues and species, much more detailed pharmacologic evidence will be required before definitive conclusions can be reached. For example, several possible indirect mechanisms exist that could account for the activity of the leukotrienes in tissues. Included among these are (1) histamine release from mast cells or nonmast cell stores within the tissue and (2) release of endogenous neurotransmitters from nerves. Indeed, the ability of the peptidoleukotrienes to cause the release of pharmacologically active quantities of cyclooxygenase products has been repeatedly documented (see Section III,A,2,b,i). It is equally possible that many of the observed activities of the leukotrienes may be mediated via other indirect mechanisms.

2. Direct Evidence for Heterogeneity in Peptidoleukotriene Receptors

Fleisch *et al.* (1982) were the first to provide direct pharmacologic evidence for the existence of multiple populations of peptidoleukotriene receptors. Using the method of Arunlakshana and Schild (1959) to obtain dissociation constants for the antagonist FPL55712 against LTD in guinea pig ileum, trachea, and parenchyma, it was clearly established that leukotriene D receptors in the ileum possessed a significantly higher affinity for FPL55712 than did trachea and parenchyma, which demonstrated approximately equal affinity. Thus leukotriene receptors in ileum appear to differ from trachea and parenchyma.

Subsequent to the studies of Fleisch *et al.* (1982) it was demonstrated that LTD receptors in guinea pig trachea could be further subdivided into two distinct subpopulations (Krell *et al.,* 1983a). Based on Schild analysis of the interaction of FPL55712 with LTD in trachea, two significantly different dissociation constants for the antagonist were obtained (i.e., $pA_2 = 6.5$ and 5.99), suggesting high- and low-affinity receptors, respectively. It appears that LTE interacts preferentially with the high-affinity site.

Feniuk *et al.* (1982) have obtained evidence for differences in LTD receptors between guinea pig ileum and rat fundic strip. As with the previous studies, conclusions were based on a Schild analysis of FPL55712 against partially purified rat peritoneal SRS.

Table II summarizes pA_2 values obtained for FPL55712 in a variety of tissues and species against LTC, D, or E.

One generalization obvious from Table II is that guinea pig ileal leukotriene receptors have higher affinity for FPL55712 than any other tissue investigated thus far. It should also be cautioned that the pA_2 values may be more apparent than real, as antagonism of LTD by FPL55712 may represent inhibition of thromboxane synthetase rather than direct antagonism of LTD

TABLE II

Dissociation Constants for FPL55712 Antagonism of Peptidoleukotrienes in Various Tissues

Tissue	Agonist	pA_2	Reference
Guinea pig ileum	LTC	7.1	Sheard *et al.* (1982)
	LTD	7.59	
	LTC	6.4	Holme, as quoted by Sheard *et*
	LTD	7.1	*al.* (1982)
	LTD	7.25	Fleisch *et al.* (1982)
	SRS	7.4	Feniuk *et al.* (1982)
Guinea pig lung parenchymal strip	LTD	6.93	Krell *et al.* (1981a)
	LTD	6.03	Fleisch *et al.* (1982)
Guinea pig trachea	LTD	6.51	Fleisch *et al.* (1982)
	LTD	6.53[a] 5.99[b]	Krell *et al.* (1983a)
	LTE	6.51	
Rat fundic strip	SRS	6.90	Feniuk *et al.* (1982)

[a] High-affinity site.
[b] Low-affinity site.

at its receptor. It is also worthy of note that, where direct comparisons of the potency of FPL55712 have been made against both LTC and D, the dissociation constant is lower against the former; this again is suggestive that LTC and D may interact with distinct receptors.

Recently, direct pharmacologic evidence for the existence of a distinct LTC receptor has been obtained in guinea-pig trachea (Snyder *et al.,* 1983). It was demonstrated that when the metabolic conversion of LTC to LTD, *via* the enzyme γ-glutamyl transpeptidase, was inhibited with L-serine borate, FPL55712 failed to significantly antagonize the contractile activity of LTC. It was concluded that the apparent ability of FPL55712 to antagonize responses to LTC in normal guinea-pig trachea was probably due to the conversion of LTC to the FPL55712-sensitive LTD and LTE. Additional credenance for this hypothesis came from studies providing direct evidence for the metabolic conversion of LTC to LTD and LTE by trachea (Aharony *et al.,* 1983).

Pong *et al.* (1983) have recently described the stereo-selective binding of [³H]LTC to a membrane preparation obtained from rat lung. LTD demonstrated a 100-fold lower affinity for the site than did LTC, leading the authors to suggest that the physiologic effects of LTC and D may be mediated through separate receptors in this tissue.

Thus, preliminary pharmacologic and biochemical studies have provided direct evidence for a multiplicity of LT receptors in tissues from several species.

3. Required Experimental Conditions and Difficulties in Studying Peptidoleukotriene Receptors

It has long been recognized that strict experimental conditions must be observed to study receptors accurately (Furchgott, 1972). For example, sites of loss such as metabolism or tissue uptake should, if possible, be controlled, as should receptors mediating opposing physiologic responses with which the agonist is known or suspected to be capable of interacting. Some such conditions have been and undoubtedly will continue to be established for leukotrienes.

Peptidoleukotrienes are capable of activating the cyclooxygenase pathway of arachidonic acid metabolism, which culminates in the release of physiologically active quantities of prostacyclin, thromboxanes, and/or prostaglandins (See Section III,A,2,b,i; Krell *et al.,* 1981a; Letts and Piper, 1982; Terashita *et al.,* 1981). Consequently, inhibition of the enzyme cyclooxygenase by a nonsteroidal antiinflammatory agent is obligatory for studying leukotriene receptors unless clear evidence for a lack of cyclooxygenase product release has been determined.

Second, evidence has been obtained that LTC and D are metabolized to

LTE by the conducting airways of the guinea pig (Krell *et al.*, 1983b; Aharony *et al.*, 1983). Undoubtedly, other as yet unidentified metabolic pathways exist that may confound interpretation of data.

And finally, FPL55712 is the only compound generally available for study as a leukotriene antagonist. This agent possesses a variety of pharmacologic effects that must be taken into account when investigating receptors. These include the following:

1. Inhibition of antigen-induced mediator release from fragmented lung of several species (Krell *et al.*, 1980; Welton *et al.*, 1981) and inhibition of passive cutaneous anaphylactic reactions in rats (Sheard, 1981) and passive peritoneal anaphylaxis in rats (Buckle *et al.*, 1979). This antiallergic activity may well complicate the interpretation of Schultz-Dale type experiments in which the compound is administered before antigen provocation. However, the simple expediency of reversing the order of FPL and antigen should overcome this potential problem.

2. Inhibition of thromboxane synthetase activity with an IC_{50} of 6.5 μM (Welton *et al.*, 1981), is an activity that may be extremely important, as the leukotrienes have been demonstrated to release cyclooxygenase products, including thromboxane A_2, from a variety of tissues (Vargaftig *et al.*, 1981; Folco *et al.*, 1981; Zijlstra *et al.*, 1981; Piper and Samhoun, 1981, 1982; Terashita *et al.*, 1981; Weichman and Tucker, 1982).

3. It has been shown that FPL55712 enhances, in a non-concentration-related manner, the contractile activity of muscarinic and histamine H_1-receptor agonists on guinea pig airway smooth muscle (Krell *et al.*, 1981b).

4. Finally, FPL55712 is a potent inhibitor of both cyclic AMP and cyclic GMP phosphodiesterases, with IC_{50} values of 3.0 and 13.0 μM, respectively (Chasin and Scott, 1978). This latter activity may bear a relationship to the antiallergic effects of the compound. These additional pharmacologic activities should be borne in mind and, if possible, controlled for when using this compound for experimental purposes.

IV. ANTAGONISM OF PEPTIDOLEUKOTRIENES AS AN APPROACH TO THE TREATMENT OF ALLERGIC DISEASES

If indeed peptidoleukotrienes are involved substantially with the various pathophysiologic changes that frequently or consistently accompany allergic asthmatic episodes, antagonists should prove useful therapeutic entities. Retrospectively, expectations such as these undoubtedly accompanied the discovery and development of histamine H_1-receptor antagonists over a quarter of a century ago. At that time it was widely held that histamine played a role in the pathophysiology of allergic asthma. As of this writing, H_1 antihistamines are labeled as contraindicated for use in asthmatic patients as required by the Food and Drug Administration. One can only hope that the same fate does not befall leukotriene antagonists and lipoxygenase inhibitors.

Assuming the positive, antagonists should be useful prophylactic as well as therapeutic entities. This is perhaps a major advantage over other approaches to the manipulation of leukotrienes such as synthesis inhibitors. While synthesis inhibitors should be prophylactically useful, they would be expected to offer limited therapeutic potential, since they are incapable of reversing the effects of synthesized leukotrienes. An agent capable of antagonism as well as inhibition of leukotriene synthesis may be viewed as optimal.

Potential pitfalls associated with leukotriene antagonism are numerous. A partial listing includes the following:

1. It is possible that peptidoleukotrienes may play a role in normal physiologic as well as pathophysiologic processes. Antagonism of the former would be expected to produce untoward side effects.

2. Preliminary evidence suggests that leukotrienes "feed back" to inhibit their own synthesis and/or release (Weichman *et al.*, 1982a). If this effect is receptor-mediated, antagonists may be expected to inhibit this process and abrogate, at least partially, their therapeutic utility.

3. The potential for receptor heterogeneity looms large at present. Consequently, it appears possible that some but not all effects of the leukotrienes may be blocked by selective compounds.

These caveats notwithstanding, leukotriene receptor antagonism remains a viable but theoretical approach to the treatment of allergic diseases.

ACKNOWLEDGMENTS

The authors wish to express their appreciation to Mrs. Becky Krell for her assistance in the preparation of this manuscript.

REFERENCES

Adams, G. K., III, and Lichtenstein, L. (1979). *J. Immunol.* **122**, 555–562.
Aharony, D., Dobson, P. and Krell, R. D. (1983). *Pharmacologist* **25**, 205.
Ahlquist, R. P. (1948). *Am. J. Physiol.* **153**, 586–600.
Ali, F. E., Dandridge, P. A., Gleason, J. G., Krell, R. D., Kruse, C. H., Lavanchy, P. G., and Snader, K. M. (1982a). *J. Med. Chem.* **25**, 947–952.

Ali, F. E., Gleason, J. G., Hill, D. T., Krell, R. D., Kruse, C. H., Lavanchy, P. G., and Volpe, B. W. (1982b). *J. Med. Chem.* **25**, 1235–1240.

Appleton, R. A., Bantick, J. R., Chamberlain, T. R., Hardern, D. N., Lee, T. B., and Pratt, A. D. (1977). *J. Med. Chem.* **20**, 371–379.

Armour, C. L., Nicholls, I. J., and Schellenberg, R. R. (1982). *Eur. J. Pharmacol.* **82**, 229–232.

Arunlakshana, O., and Schild, H. O. (1959). *Br. J. Pharmacol. Chemother.* **14**, 45–58.

Ash, A. S. F., and Schild, H. O. (1966). *Br. J. Pharmacol. Chemother.* **27**, 427–439.

Augstein, J., Farmer, J. B., Lee, T. B., Sheard, P., and Tattersall, M. L. (1973). *Nature (London) New Biol.* **245**, 215–217.

Baker, S. R., Boot, J. R., Jamieson, W. B., Osborne, D. J., and Sweatman, W. J. F. (1981). *Biochem Biophys. Res. Commun.* **103**, 1258–1264.

Baker, S. R., Boot, J. R., Dawson, W., Jamieson, W. B., Osborne, D. J., and Sweatman, W. J. F. (1982). *Adv. Prostaglandin, Thromboxane Leukotriene Res.* **9**, 223–227.

Berkowitz, B., Zabko-Potapovich, B., and Gleason, J. (1981). *Fed. Proc., Fed. Am. Soc. Exp. Biol.* **40**, 690.

Bernström, K., and Hammarström, S. (1981). *J. Biol. Chem.* **256**, 9579–9582.

Berry, P. A., and Collier, H. O. J. (1964). *Br. J. Pharmacol. Chemother.* **23**, 201–216.

Black, J. W., Duncan, W. A. M., Durrant, C. J., Ganellin, C. R., and Parsons, M. E. (1972). *Nature (London)* **236**, 385–390.

Bray, M. A., Cunningham, F. M., Ford-Hutchinson, A. W., and Smith, M. J. H. (1981). *Br. J. Pharmacol.* **72**, 483–486.

Buckle, D. R., Outred, D. J., Ross, J. W., Smith, H., Smith, R. J., Spicer, B. A., and Gasson, B. C. (1979). *J. Med. Chem.* **22**, 158–168.

Buckner, C. K., and Patil, P. N. (1971). *J. Pharmacol. Exp. Ther.* **176**, 634–649.

Burke, J. A., Levi, R., Guo, Z.-G., and Corey, E. J. (1982). *J. Pharmacol. Exp. Ther.* **221**, 235–241.

Chand, N. (1979). *Agents Actions* **9**, 133–140.

Chasin, M., and Scott, C. (1978). *Biochem. Pharmacol.* **27**, 2065–2067.

Collier, H. O. J., and Sweatman, W. J. F. (1969). *Nature (London)* **219**, 664–665.

Corey, E. J., and Hoover, D. J. (1982). *Tetrahedron Lett.* pp. 3463–3466.

Corey, E. J., Clark, D. A., Goto, G., Marfat, A., Miokowski, C., Samuelsson, B., and Hammarström, S. (1980a). *J. Am. Chem. Soc.* **102**, 1436–1439.

Corey, E. J., Marfat, A., Goto, G., and Brion, F. (1980b). *J. Am. Chem. Soc.* **102**, 7984–7985.

Corey, E. J., Oh, H., and Barton, A. E. (1982). *Tetrahedron Lett.* pp. 3467–3470.

Dahlén, S.-E., Hedqvist, P., Hammarström, S., and Samuelsson, B. (1980). *Nature (London)* **288**, 484–485.

Dahlén, S.-E., Björk, J., Hedqvist, P., Arfors, K.-E., Hammarström, S., Lindgren, J.-Å., and Samuelsson, B. (1981). *Proc. Natl. Acad. Sci. U.S.A.* **78**, 3887–3891.

Drazen, J. M., Austen, K. F., Lewis, R. A., Clark, D. A., Goto, G., Marfat, A., and Corey, E. J. (1980). *Proc. Natl. Acad. Sci. U.S.A.* **77**, 4354–4358.

Drazen, J. M., Lewis, R. A., Austen, K. F., Toda, M., Brion, F., Marfat, A., and Corey, E. J. (1981). *Proc. Natl. Acad. Sci. U.S.A.* **78**, 3195–3198.

Ellis, F., Mills, L. S., and North, P. C. (1982). *Tetrahedron Lett.* **23**, 3735–3736.

Ernest, I., Main, A. J., and Menasse, R. (1982). *Tetrahedron Lett.* **23**, 167–170.

Feinmark, J., Lindgren, J. A., Claesson, H.-E., Malmsten, C., and Samuelsson, B. (1981). *FEBS Lett.* **136**, 141–144.

Feniuk, L., Kennedy, I., and Whelan, C. J. (1982). *J. Pharm. Pharmacol.* **34**, 586–588.

Fleisch, J. H., Rinkema, L. E., and Baker, S. R. (1982). *Life Sci.* **31**, 577–581.

Folco, G., Hansson, G., and Granström, E. (1981). *Biochem. Pharmacol.* **30**, 2491–2493.

Ford-Hutchinson, A. W., Bray, M. A., Cunningham, F. M., Davidson, E. M., and Smith, M. J. H. (1981a). *Prostaglandins* **21**, 143–152.

Ford-Hutchinson, A. W., Smith, M. J. H., and Bray, M. A. (1981b). *J. Pharm. Pharmacol.* 33, 32.

Furchgott, R. F. (1972). *In* "Catecholamines" (H. Blaschko and E. Muscholl, eds.), pp. 283–335. Springer-Verlag, Berlin and New York.

Ghelani, A., and Holroyde, M. C. (1981). *Methods Find. Exp. Clin. Pharmacol.* 3, 385–386.

Girard, Y., Larue, M., Jones, T. R., and Rokach, J. (1982). *Tetrahedron Lett.* 23, 1023–1026.

Gleason, J. G., Krell, R. D., Weichman, B. M., Ali, F. E., and Berkowitz, B. (1982). *In* "Leukotrienes and Other Lipoxygenase Products (B. Samuelsson and R. Paoletti, eds.), pp. 243–250. Raven Press, New York.

Goetzel, E. J., and Pickett, W. C. (1981). *J. Exp. Med.* 153, 482–487.

Grant, J. A., and Lichtenstein, L. M. (1974). *J. Immunol.* 112, 897–904.

Greig, M. E., and Griffin, R. L. (1975). *J. Med. Chem.* 18, 112–115.

Hammarström, S. (1980). *J. Biol. Chem.* 255, 7093–7094.

Hammarström, S. (1981). *J. Biol. Chem.* 256, 2275–2279.

Hand, J. H., Will, J. A., and Buckner, C. K. (1981). *Eur. J. Pharmacol.* 76, 439–442.

Hanna, C. J., Bach, M. K., Pare, P. D., and Schellenberg, R. R. (1981). *Nature (London)* 290, 343–344.

Hansson, G., Lindgren, J. A., Dahlén, S.-E., Hedqvist, P., and Samuelsson, B. (1981). *FEBS Lett.* 130, 107–112.

Hedqvist, P., Dahlén, S.-E., Gustafsson, L., Hammarström, S., and Samuelsson, B. (1980). *Acta Physiol. Scand.* 110, 331–333.

Holyroyde, M. C., Altounyan, R. E. C., Cole, M., Dixon, M., and Elliot, E. V. (1982). *In* "Leukotrienes and Other Lipoxygenase Products" (B. Samuelsson and R. Paoletti eds.), pp. 237–242. Raven Press, New York.

Johnson, H. G., and McNee, M. L. (1983). *Prostaglandins* 25, 237–243.

Johnson, H. G., Chinn, R. A., Chow, A. W., Bach, M. K., and Nadel, J. A. (1983a). *Int. J. Immunopharmacol.* 5, 391–396.

Johnson, H. G., Chinn, R. A., Morton, D. R., McNee, M. L., Miller, M. D., and Nadel, J. A. (1983b). *Agents Actions* 13, 1–4.

Johnson, H. G., McNee, M. L., Johnson, M. A. and Miller, M. D. (1983c). *Int. Arch. Allergy Appl. Immunol.* 71, 214–218.

Jones, T., Masson, P., Hamel, R., Brunet, G., Holme, G., Girard, Y., Larue, M., and Rokach, J. (1982a). *Prostaglandins* 24, 279–291.

Jones, T., Davis, C., and Daniel, E. E. (1982b). *Can. J. Physiol. Pharmacol.* 60, 638–643.

Kadin, S. B. (1981). U. S. Patents 4,296,120 and 4,296,129.

Kadin, S. B. (1982). U. S. Patents 4,331,683, 4,342,781, and 4,343,813.

Kellaway, C. H., and Trethewie, E. R. (1940). *Q. J. Exp. Physiol. Cogn. Med. Sci.* 30, 121–125.

Kito, G., Okuda, H., Ohkawa, S., Terao, S., and Kikuchi, K. (1981). *Life Sci.* 29, 1325–1332.

Krell, R. D., McCoy, J., Osborn, R., and Chakrin, L. W. (1980). *Int. J. Immunopharmacol.* 2, 55–63.

Krell, R. D., Osborn, R., Vickery, L., Falcone, K., O'Donnell, M., Gleason, J., Kinzig, C., and Bryan, D. (1981a). *Prostaglandins* 22, 387–409.

Krell, R. D., Osborn, R., Falcone, K., and Vickery, L. (1981b). *Prostaglandins* 22, 423–432.

Krell, R. D., Tsai, B.-S., Berdoulay, A., Barone, M., and Giles, R. A. (1983a). *Prostaglandins* 25, 171–178.

Krell, R. D., Tsai, B.-S., Macia, R. A., and Giles, R. G. (1983b). *Fed. Proc., Fed. Am. Soc. Exp. Biol.* 42, 443.

Lands, A. M., Arnold, A., McAuliff, J. P., Luduena, F. P., and Brown, T. G., Jr. (1967). *Nature (London)* 214, 597–598.

Lee, T. H., Walport, M. J., Wilkinson, A. H., Turner-Warwick, M., and Kay, A. B. (1981). *Lancet* 2, 304–305.

Letts, L. G., and Piper, P. J. (1982). *Br. J. Pharmacol.* **76,** 169–176.

Lewis, R. A., Drazen, J. M., Austen, K. F., Clark, D. A., and Corey, E. J. (1980). *Biochem. Biophys. Res. Commun.* **96,** 271–277.

Lewis, R. A., Goetzl, E. J., Drazen, J. M., Soter, N. A., Austen, K. F., and Corey, E. J. (1981a). *J. Exp. Med.* **154,** 1243–1248.

Lewis, R. A., Drazen, J. M., Austen, K. F., Toda, M., Brion, F., Marfat, A., and Corey, E. J. (1981b). *Proc. Natl. Acad. Sci. U.S.A.* **78,** 4579–4583.

Lewis, R. A., Austen, K. F., Drazen, J. M., Soter, N. A., Figueiredo, J. C., and Corey, E. J. (1982). *Adv. Prostaglandin, Thromboxane, Leukotriene Res.* **9,** 137–151.

Loftus, P., and Bernstein, P. R. (1982). *J. Org. Chem.* **47,** 40–44.

Malmsten, C. L., Palmblad, J., Udén, A.-M., Rådmark, C., Engstedt, L., and Samuelsson, B. (1980). *Acta Physiol. Scand.* **110,** 449–451.

Marom, Z., Shelhamer, J. H., Bach, M. K., Morton, D. R., and Kaliner, M. (1982). *Am. Rev. Respir. Dis.* **126,** 449–451.

Mathé, A. A., and Strandberg, K. (1971). *Acta Physiol. Scand.* **82,** 460–465.

Mathé, A. A., Strandberg, K., and Yen, S.-S. (1977). *Prostaglandins* **14,** 1105–1115.

Mong, S., Hogaboom, G. K., Wu, H-L., Clark, M. and Crooke, S. T. (1983) *Pharmacologist* **25,** 201.

Okuyama, S., Miyamoto, S., Shimoji, K., Kionishi, Y., Fukushima, D., Nuva, H., Arai, Y., Toda, M., and Hayashi, M. (1982). *Chem. Pharm. Bull.* **30,** 2453–2462.

Orange, R. P., and Langer, H. (1974). *In* "Allergology" (Y. Yamamura, O. L. Frick, Y. Horiuchi, S. Kishimoto, T. Miyamoto, P. Naranjo, and A. deWeck, eds.), pp. 325–333. Excerpta Medica, New York.

Orange, R. P., Austen, W. G., and Austen, K. F. (1971). *J. Exp. Med.* **134,** 136s–148s.

Oxford, A. W., and Ellis, F. (1981). U. K. Patent Application GB 2,058,785.

Palmblad, J., Uden, A.-M., Lindgren, J.-A., Rådmark, O., Hansson, G., and Malmsten, C. L. (1982). *FEBS Lett.* **144,** 81–84.

Palmer, M. R., Matthews, W. R., Hoffer, B. J., and Murphy, R. C. (1981). *J. Pharmacol. Exp. Ther.* **219,** 91–96.

Patil, P. N., Patel, D. G., and Krell, R. D. (1971). *J. Pharmacol. Exp. Ther.* **176,** 622–633.

Peatfield, A. C., Piper, P. J., and Richardson, P. S. (1982). *Br. J. Pharmacol.* **77,** 391–393.

Piper, P. J., and Samhoun, M. N. (1981). *Prostaglandins* **21,** 793–803.

Piper, P. J., and Samhoun, M. N. (1982). *Br. J. Pharmacol.* **77,** 267–275.

Pong, S.-S., DeHaven, R. N., Kuehl, F. A., Jr. and Egan, R. W. (1983). *J. Biol. Chem.* **256,** 9616–9619.

Rokach, J., Girard, Y., Guindon, Y., Atkinson, J. G., Larue, M., Young, R. N., Masson, P., and Holme, G. (1980). *Tetrahedron Lett.* **21,** 1485–1488.

Rokach, J., Hamel, P. A., and Hirschman, R. F. (1981). U. S. Patent 4,252,818.

Rosenberger, M., and Neukom, C. (1980). *J. Am. Chem. Soc.* **102,** 5426–5427.

Samuelsson, B. (1982). *In* "Leukotrienes and Other Lipoxygenase Products" (B. Samuelsson and R. Paoletti, eds.), pp. 1–17. Raven Press, New York.

Schiantarelli, P., Bongrani, S., and Folco, G. (1981). *Eur. J. Pharmacol.* **73,** 363–366.

Seale, P. J., and Piper, P. J. (1978). *Eur. J. Pharmacol.* **52,** 125–128.

Sheard, P. (1981). *In* "SRS-A and Leukotrienes (P. J. Piper, ed.), pp. 209–218. Wiley, New York.

Sheard, P., Killingback, P. G., and Blair, A. M. J. N. (1967). *Nature (London)* **216,** 283–284.

Sheard, P., Holroyde, M. C., Ghelani, A. M., Bantick, J. R., and Lee, T. B. (1982). *Adv. Prostaglandin, Thromboxane, Leukotriene Res.* **9,** 229–235.

Showell, H. J., Oherness, I. G., Marfat, A., and Corey, E. J. (1982). *Biochem. Biophy. Res. Commun.* **106,** 741–747.

Sirois, P., Borgeat, P., Jeanson, A., Roy, S., and Girard, G. (1980). *Prostaglandins Med.* **5,** 429–444.

Snyder, S. H. (1978). *In* "Neurotransmitter Receptor Binding" (H. I. Yamamura, S. J. Enna, and M. J. Kuhar, eds.), pp. 1–11. Raven Press, New York.

Snyder, D. W., Barone, M., Morrissette, M. P., Bernstein, P. R. and Krell, R. D. (1983). *Pharmacologist* **25**, 205.

Sugio, K., Ohuchi, K., Sugata, M., and Tsurufuji, S. (1981). *Prostaglandins* **21**, 649–653.

Terashita, Z.-I., Fukui, H., Hirata, M., Terao, S., Ohkawa, S., Nishikawa, K., and Kikuchi, S. (1981). *Eur. J. Pharmacol.* **73**, 357–361.

Tsai, B. S., Bernstein, P., Macia, R. A., Conaty, J., and Krell, R. D. (1982). *Prostaglandins* **23**, 489–506.

Vargaftig, B. B., Lefort, J., and Murphy, R. C. (1981). *Eur. J. Pharmacol.* **72**, 417–418.

Weichman, B. M., and Tucker, S. S. (1982). *Prostaglandins* **24**, 245–253.

Weichman, B. M., Hostelley, L. S., Bostick, S. P., Muccitelli, R. M., Krell, R. D., and Gleason, J. G. (1982a). *J. Pharmacol. Exp. Ther.* **221**, 295–302.

Weichman, B. M., Muccitelli, R. M., Osborn, R. R., Holden, D. A., Gleason, J. G., and Wasserman, M. A. (1982b). *J. Pharmacol. Exp. Ther.* **222**, 202–208.

Weiss, J. W., Drazen, J. M., Coles, N., McFadden, E. R., Jr., Weller, P. F., Corey, E. J., Lewis, R. A., and Austen, K. F. (1982). *Science* **216**, 196–198.

Welton, A. F., Hope, W. C., Tobias, L. D., and Hamilton, J. G. (1981). *Biochem. Pharmacol.* **30**, 1378–1382.

Zijlstra, F. J., Bonta, I. L., Adolfs, M. J. P., and Vincent, J. E. (1981). *Eur. J. Pharmacol.* **76**, 297–298.

INDEX

A

Acetone phenylhydrazone, 118
Δ^4-Acetylenic acids, 157–158
Δ^5-Acetylenic acids, 156
Δ^6-Acetylenic acids, 159
Δ^7-Acetylenic acids, 159–161
Δ^8-Acetylenic acids, 158–159
Acetylenic fatty acids, 156–160, 174–176,
    206, 236
Acetylsalicylic acid, 248–249
Acivicin, 181
Airways
    response to leukotrienes, 6–7, 217–221
    response to slow-reacting substance of
        anaphylaxis, 249–251
Alveolar macrophages, lipoxygenases, 234
Aminopeptidase, 146–147
5-Aminosalicylic acid, 171
Anaphylactic reaction, 186–187
Angina, 228
Anticholinergic agents, 257–258
Antiinflammatory compounds, nonsteroid,
    166, 205, 281–282
Antioxidants, 119, 167
Aprotic solvents, 179
Arachidonate:oxygen oxidoreductase, *see*
    Lipoxygenase
Arachidonic acid
    metabolism, 196–200
    mobilization from phospholipids, 104, 164,
        195
        inhibitors, 168–174

Arthritis, 205
    rheumatoid, 227
Arylsulfatases, 3–4, 23
Aspirin, 116, 205, 236, 256
Asthma, 9–10, 221, 227–228, 248, 258, 264
    allergic, 271–273, 294–295
Atropine, 258, 263, 290

B

Basophil, 242–243
Benoxaprofen, 166, 207, 236
Benzoyl chloride phenylhydrazone, 118
Beta-adrenergic agents, 258, 262
Beta-adrenergic blocking agents, 258
Bile acids, 179
Bilirubin, 171, 179
p-Bromophenacyl bromide, 174
Bromosulfophthaleins, 179
Bronchi, 249–250
Buthionine sulfoximine, 171, 180
BW755C, 119, 166, 206–209

C

Calcium
    activation of 5-lipoxygenase, 130–133,
        140–143
    in leukocyte activation, 238
Calcium channel blockers, 263
Calcium ionophore, 4–6
Calmodulin, 133
o-Carboxyphenyl-γ-D-glutamyl hydrazine, 181

Peroxidases, 116, 235
Peroxides
  activation of lipoxygenases, 115–116
  inactivation of 5-lipoxygenase, 155
Phenidone, 166, 206
Phenoxybenzamine, 263
Phenylhydrazines, 168
Phenylhydrazones, 118–119
1-Phenyl-3-pyrazolidin, *see* Phenidone
Phorbol myristate ester, 131
Phospholipase(s), platelet, 104
Phospholipase A$_2$, 173–174, 217, 220
Phospholipase C, 173
Phospholipids, activation of 5-lipoxygenase,
  132–134
Plasma exudation, 155–156, 222
Plasma membrane, 146–147
Platelet-activating factor, 134
Platelets
  aggregation, 120–121
  cyclooxygenase, 104–105
  in hemostasis, 104
  5-lipoxygenase, 140
  lipoxygenases, 103–121, 128, 204–205
  phospholipases, 104
  prostaglandins, 104–105
  thromboxanes, 105
Polymorphonuclear leukocytes (PMN), 3
  chemokinesis, 201–204
  chemotaxis, 201–204, 236–237
  effect
    of leukotrienes, 236–240
    of prostaglandins, 239–240
    of thromboxanes, 239–240
  leukotriene receptors, 237–238
  5-lipoxygenase, 130–131
  lipoxygenases, 128, 134, 197–198, 204–205
Polyphloretin phosphate, 282
Propranolol, 258, 263
Prostacyclin, 14–16, 105
  biological action, 196
  biosynthesis, 196–197
Prostaglandins, 14–16
  activation of lipoxygenases, 116
  biological action
    in chemotaxis, 203–204
    in inflammatory response, 195–196, 209
    in lung, 249, 259, 261
    in microvasculature, 222
    in polymorphonuclear leukocytes,
      239–240

  in vascular permeability, 200–201
  biosynthesis, 196–197
  platelet, 104–105
Protease, 23
Psoriatic skin, 205, 227

Q

Quercetin, 167, 170

R

RBL-1 cells, 131
  glutathione *S*-transferase, 179–180
  5-lipoxygenase, 132–134, 140–160
Receptors, C3B, 237
Receptors, leukotriene, 165, 264
  in cardiovascular system, 290–291
  characterization, 273–285
  classification, 273, 288
  experimental conditions for study, 293–294
  in gastrointestinal smooth muscle, 219
  heterogeneity, 8, 288–293
  in lung, 288–290
  for peptidoleukotrienes, 274–285
  in polymorphonuclear leukocytes, 237–238
  in smooth muscle, 8
  species specificity, 275
  specificity, 238
  tissue specificity, 274
Reticulocytes, lipoxygenases, 128
Rotenone, 181–182

S

Salicyclic acid, 284
Schild analysis, 273
Serine borate, 7, 146–147, 181, 293
Silychristin, 167
SK&F88046, 284
  structure, 283
Skin
  effect of leukotrienes, 222–223
  lipoxygenases, 128, 205
Slow-reacting substance of anaphylaxis
  (SRS-A), 232
  in allergic asthma, 271–273
  biological action, 216
  characterization, 2–4, 216, 248
  chemical synthesis, 23–29
  component identification, 3–6
  diethylcarbamazine inhibition, 6

SYNTHETIC CHEMISTRY